Grammar Links 3

A Theme-Based Course for Reference and Practice

SECOND EDITION

Janis van Zante

Debra Daise
University of Colorado,
International English Center

Charl Norloff
University of Colorado,
International English Center

Randee Falk

M. Kathleen Mahnke
Series Editor
Saint Michael's College

HEINLE
CENGAGE Learning

Australia • Brazil • Japan • Korea • Mexico • Singapore • Spain • United Kingdom • United States

HEINLE
CENGAGE Learning

Publisher: Patricia A. Coryell
Director of ESL: Susan Maguire
Senior Development Editor: Kathleen Sands Boehmer
Editorial Assistant: Evangeline Bermas
Senior Project Editor: Margaret Park Bridges
Senior Manufacturing Coordinator: Marie Barnes
Marketing Manager: Annamarie Rice
Marketing Associate: Laura Hemrika

Cover image: Stock Illustration Source ©
2003 David Ridley, *Multicultural Figures*

Photo Credits: p. 1: AP/Wide World Photos/Michael Dwyer; p. 2: Digital Vision/Getty Images; p. 33: California State Railroad Museum Foundation; p. 40: World Perspectives/Getty Images; p. 43: Ron Chapple/Getty Images; p. 44 left: Russell Lee/Getty Images; p. 44 right: Thinkstock/Getty Images; p. 57 top: © Clark James Mishler/IPN/Aurora; p. 57 bottom: Sylvain Grandadem/ Getty Images; p. 60 left: FPG/Getty Images; p. 60 right: AP/Wide World Photos/Damian Dovarganes; p. 79: Colin Anderson/Getty Images; p. 85: Randy Wells/Getty Images; p. 90 top and middle: © Gail Mooney/Corbis; p. 90 bottom: © Francis G. Mayer/Corbis; p. 93: Image © 2004 Board of Trustees, National Gallery of Art, Washington DC; p. 105: © James Leynse/Corbis; p. 108: National Aeronautics and Space Administration; p. 118: © Hulton Deutsch Collection/Corbis; p. 120: Alamy; pp. 128: © Bettman/Corbis; p. 139: Ian Mckinnell/Getty Images; p. 184: Sandro Miller/Getty Images; p. 189: Holos/Getty Images; p. 205 top and bottom left and bottom middle: James Darrel/Getty Images; p. 205 top and bottom right: Lori Adamski Peek/Getty Images; p. 205 top middle: Dale Durfee/Getty Images; pp. 214 left, 215: Getty Images; p. 214 middle: ASAP Ltd./Index Stock Imagery;p. 214 right: Index Stock Imagery; p. 221: © Bettman/Corbis; p. 222 top left: Andrew Wakeford/Getty Images; p. 222 middle left: Jacobs Stock Photography/Getty Images; p. 222 bottom left: Teri Dixon/Getty Images;p. 222 top right: Elke Selzle/Getty Images; p. 222 middle right: SW Productions/Getty Images; p. 222 bottom right: Ryan McVay/Getty Images; p. 229: Stock Montage Inc.; p. 250: Courtesy of Lucasfilm Ltd. Raiders of the Lost Ark © 1981 Lucasfilm Ltd. & TM. All rights reserved. Used under authorization. Unauthorized duplication is a violation of applicable law.; p. 254: © Raymond Gehman/Corbis; p. 257: Stewart Cohen/Getty Images; p. 291: © Robbie Jack/Corbis; p. 295: Lambert/Getty Images; p. 297 left: © Shepard Sherbell/ Corbis Saba; p. 297 middle: Amy Neunsinger/Getty Images; p. 297 right: Lisette Le Bon/SuperStock; p. 309:Phil Stevens Photography; p. 318 left: © 2003 Rich Clarkson and Associates; p. 318 right: John Edwards/Getty Images; p. 330 top: AP/Wide World Photos/Scott Audette; p. 330 middle: AP/Wide World Photos/Charlie Bennett; p. 330 bottom: AP/Wide World Photos/ Uwe Lein; p. 343: Rob Atkins/Getty Images; p. 344 top left: Don Farrall/Getty Images; pp. 344 bottom left and top right, 364, 371: AP/Wide World Photos; p. 344 bottom right: AP/Wide World Photos/Anchorage Times/Joe Rychetnik; p. 356: National Oceanic and Atmospheric Administration/Department of Commerce; p. 367: AP/Wide World Photos/David Zalubowski; p. 377:© Warren Faidley/Weatherstock; p. 385: © Attar Maher/ Corbis Sygma; p. 425: Laurent Delhourme/Getty Images; p. 434: Life Stock Photos; p. 447: BananaStock/SuperStock; p. 452: © Michael S. Yamashita/Corbis

For permission to use material from this text or product, submit all requests online at **cengage.com/permissions** Further permissions questions can be emailed to **permissionrequest@cengage.com**

Library of Congress Control Number: 2003115026

ISBN 13: 978-0-618-27414-7
ISBN 10: 0-618-27414-6

Heinle
25 Thomson Place
Boston, MA 02110.

Cengage Learning is a leading provider of customized learning solutions with office locations around the globe, including Singapore, the United Kingdom, Australia, Mexico, Brazil and Japan. Locate your local office at: international.cengage.com/region

Cengage Learning products are represented in Canada by Nelson Education, Ltd.

Visit Heinle online at elt.heinle.com
Visit our corporate website at cengage.com

Printed in Canada.
6789-HES-12 11 10 09 08

Contents

Introduction

WELCOME TO *GRAMMAR LINKS*!

Grammar Links is a comprehensive five-level grammar reference and practice series for students of English as a second or foreign language. The series meets the needs of students from the beginning through advanced levels:

- *Grammar Links Basic*: beginning
- *Grammar Links, Book 1*: high beginning
- *Grammar Links, Book 2*: intermediate
- *Grammar Links, Book 3*: high intermediate
- *Grammar Links, Book 4*: advanced

Available with each *Grammar Links* student text are an audio program and printable Web-based teacher's notes; the teacher's notes are accompanied by the answer key and tapescripts for each book. Tests and other materials are also available on the Website and are described below. In addition, *Grammar Links 1–4* feature workbooks for further practice of all grammar points introduced in the student books.

NEW IN THIS EDITION

- A fresh, new design with eye-catching art, realia, and a focus on ease of use
- Streamlined, easy-to-read grammar charts showing structures at a glance
- Succinct explanations of grammar points for easy understanding
- Simplified content coverage accompanied by vocabulary glosses to let students focus on grammar while learning about topics of interest
- An even greater number and variety of activities than before, now signaled with icons for easy reference:

 Listening activities for receptive practice of grammar structures in oral English

 Communicative activities that lead to fluent use of grammar in everyday speaking

 Writing activities for productive practice of targeted structures in extended written discourse

Links to the World Wide Web for:
  - Model paragraphs for writing assignments
  - Practice tests, both self-check tests for student use and achievement tests for teacher use
  - Links to interesting sites related to unit themes for further reading and discussion
  - Vocabulary flashcards for review of the content-related vocabulary that is used in text readings and exercises
  - Much more! See for yourself at elt.heinle.com/grammarlinks.

TO THE TEACHER

Series Approach

Recent research in applied linguistics tells us that when a well-designed communicative approach is coupled with a systematic treatment of grammatical form, the combination is a powerful pedagogical tool.

Grammar Links is such a tool. The grammar explanations in *Grammar Links* are clear, accurate, and carefully sequenced. All points that are introduced are practiced in exercises, and coverage is comprehensive and systematic. In addition, each grammar point is carefully recycled in a variety of contexts.

The communicative framework of *Grammar Links* is that of the theme-based approach to language learning. Unlike other approaches, theme-based models promote the development of both communicative and linguistic abilities through in-depth contextualization of language in extended discourse. The importance of this type of contextualization to grammar acquisition is now well documented. In *Grammar Links*, content serves as a backdrop for communication; high-interest topics are presented and developed along with the grammar of each chapter. As a result, *Grammar Links* exercises and activities are content-driven as well as grammar-driven. While learning about adjective clauses in Book 3, for example, students explore various aspects of the discipline of psychology. While they are practicing gerunds and infinitives in Book 2, they read about successful American entrepreneurs. And while practicing the simple present tense in Book 1, students learn about and discuss North American festivals and other celebrations. Throughout the series, students communicate about meaningful content, transferring their grammatical training to the English they need in their daily lives.

Complementing the communicative theme-based approach of the *Grammar Links* series is the inclusion of a range of successful methodological options for exercises and activities. In addition to more traditional, explicit rule presentation and practice, we have incorporated a number of less explicit, more inductive techniques. Foremost among these are our discovery exercises and activities, in which students are asked to notice general and specific grammatical features and think about them on their own, sometimes formulating their own hypotheses about how these features work and why they work the way they do. Discovery exercises are included in each unit opener. They are frequently used in chapter openers as well and are interspersed throughout the *Grammar Practice* sections, particularly at the higher levels.

In short, the *Grammar Links* approach provides students with the best of all possible language learning environments—a comprehensive, systematic treatment of grammar that employs a variety of methods for grammar learning within a communicative theme-based framework.

About the Books

Each book in the *Grammar Links* series is divided into approximately 10 units. Each unit looks at a well-defined area of grammar, and each unit has an overall theme. The chapters within a unit each focus on some part of the targeted unit grammar, and each chapter develops some specific aspect of the unit theme. In this way, chapters in a unit are linked in terms of both grammar coverage and theme, providing a highly contextualized base on which students can build and refine their grammatical skills.

Grammar coverage has been carefully designed to spiral across levels. Structures that are introduced in one book are recycled and built upon in the next. Students not only learn increasingly sophisticated information about the structures but also practice these structures in increasingly challenging contexts. Themes show a similar progression across levels, from less academic in Books 1 and 2 to more academic in Books 3 and 4.

Grammar Links is flexible in many ways and can be easily adapted to the particular needs of users. Although its careful spiraling makes it ideal as a series, the comprehensive grammar coverage at each level means that the individual books can also stand alone. The comprehensiveness and careful organization also make it possible for students to use their text as a reference after they have completed a course. The units in a book can be used in the order given or can be rearranged to fit the teacher's curriculum. Books can be used in their entirety or in part. In addition, the inclusion of ample practice allows teachers to be selective when choosing exercises and activities. All exercises are labeled for grammatical content, so structures can be practiced more or less extensively, depending on class and individual needs.

Unit and Chapter Components

- **Unit Objectives.** Each unit begins with a list of unit objectives so that teachers and students can preview the major grammar points covered in the unit. Objectives are accompanied by example sentences, which highlight the relevant structures.

- **Unit Introduction.** To illustrate grammar use in extended discourse, a reading and listening selection introduces both the unit grammar and the unit theme in a unit opener section entitled *Grammar in Action*. This material is followed by a grammar consciousness-raising or "noticing" task, *Think About Grammar*. In *Think About Grammar* tasks, students figure out some aspect of grammar by looking at words and sentences from the *Grammar in Action* selection, often working together to answer questions about them. Students induce grammatical rules themselves before having those rules given to them. *Think About Grammar* thus helps students to become independent grammar learners by promoting critical thinking and discussion about grammar.

- **Chapter Introduction.** Each chapter opens with a task. This task involves students in working receptively with the structures that are treated in the chapter and gives them the opportunity to begin thinking about the chapter theme.

- ***Grammar Briefings.*** The grammar is presented in *Grammar Briefings*. Chapters generally have three or four *Grammar Briefings* so that information is given in manageable chunks. The core of each *Grammar Briefing* is its **form** and **function** charts. In these charts, the form (the *what* of grammar) and the function (the *how, when,* and *why*) are presented in logical segments. These segments are manageable but large enough that students can see connections between related grammar points. Form and function are presented in separate charts when appropriate but together when the two are essentially inseparable. All grammatical descriptions in the form and function charts are comprehensive, concise, and clear. Sample sentences illustrate each point.

- ***Grammar Hotspots.*** *Grammar Hotspots* are a special feature of *Grammar Links*. They occur at one or more strategic points in each chapter. *Grammar Hotspots* focus on aspects of grammar that students are likely to find particularly troublesome. Some hotspots contain reminders about material that has already been presented in the form and function charts; others go beyond the charts.

- ***Talking the Talk.*** *Talking the Talk* is another special feature of the *Grammar Links* series. Our choice of grammar is often determined by our audience, whether we are writing or speaking, the situations in which we find ourselves, and other sociocultural factors. *Talking the Talk* treats these factors. Students become aware of differences between formal and informal English, between written and spoken English.

- ▨ *Grammar Practice.* Each *Grammar Briefing* is followed by comprehensive and systematic practice of all grammar points introduced. The general progression within each *Grammar Practice* is from more controlled to less controlled, from easier to more difficult, and often from more receptive to more productive and/or more structured to more communicative. A wide variety of innovative exercise types is included in each of the four skill areas: listening, speaking, reading, and writing. The exercise types that are used are appropriate to the particular grammar points being practiced. For example, more drill-like exercises are often used for practice with form. More open-ended exercises often focus on function.

  In many cases, drill-like practice of a particular grammar point is followed by open-ended communicative practice of the same point, often as pair or group work. Thus, a number of exercises have two parts.

  The majority of exercises within each *Grammar Practice* section are related to the theme of the unit. However, some exercises depart from the theme to ensure that each grammar point is practiced in the most effective way.

- ▨ **Unit Wrap-Ups.** Each unit ends with a series of activities that pull the unit grammar together and enable students to test, further practice, and apply what they have learned. These activities include an error correction task, which covers the errors students most commonly make in using the structures presented in the unit, as well as a series of innovative open-ended communicative tasks, which build on and go beyond the individual chapters.

- ▨ **Appendixes.** Extensive appendixes supplement the grammar presented in the *Grammar Briefings.* They provide students with word lists, spelling and pronunciation rules, and other supplemental rules related to the structures that have been taught. The appendixes are a rich resource for students as they work through exercises and activities.

- ▨ **Grammar Glossary.** A grammar glossary provides students and teachers with definitions of the grammar terms used in *Grammar Links* as well as example sentences to aid in understanding the meaning of each term.

Other Components

- ▨ **Audio Program.** All *Grammar Links* listening exercises and all unit introductions are recorded on audio CDs and cassettes. The symbol 🎧 appears next to the title of each recorded segment.

- ▨ **Workbook.** *Grammar Links 1–4* student texts are each accompanied by a workbook. The four workbooks contain a wide variety of exercise types, including paragraph and essay writing, and they provide extensive supplemental self-study practice of each grammar point presented in the student texts. Student self-tests with TOEFL® practice questions are also included in the workbooks.

- ▨ **Teacher's Notes.** The *Grammar Links* teacher's notes for each student text can be downloaded from elt.heinle.com/grammarlinks. Each contains an introduction to the series and some general and specific teaching guidelines.

- ▨ **Tapescript and Answer Keys.** The tapescript and the answer key for the student text and the answer key for the workbook are also available at the *Grammar Links* Website.

- ▨ **Links to the World Wide Web.** As was discussed above, the *Grammar Links* Website elt.heinle.com/grammarlinks has been expanded for the second edition to include student and teacher tests, teacher notes, model writing assignments, content Web links and activities, and other material. Links are updated frequently to ensure that students and teachers can access the best information available on the Web.

TO THE STUDENT

Grammar Links is a five-level series that gives you all the rules and practice you need to learn and use English grammar. Each unit in this book focuses on an area of grammar. Each unit also develops a theme—for example, business or travel. Units are divided into two or three chapters.

Grammar Links has many special features that will help you to learn the grammar and to use it in speaking, listening, reading, and writing.

FEATURE	BENEFIT
Interesting Themes	Help you link grammar to the real world—the world of everyday English
Introductory Reading and Listening Selections	Introduce you to the theme and the grammar of the unit
Think About Grammar Activities	Help you to become an independent grammar learner
Chapter Opener Tasks	Get you started using the grammar
Grammar Briefings	Give you clear grammar rules in easy-to-read charts, with helpful example sentences
Grammar Hotspots	Focus on especially difficult grammar points for learners of English—points on which you might want to spend extra time
Talking the Talk	Helps you to understand the differences between formal and informal English and between written and spoken English
Grammar Practice	Gives you lots of practice, through listening, speaking, reading, and writing exercises and activities
Unit Wrap-Up Tasks	Provide you with interesting communicative activities that cover everything you have learned in the unit
Vocabulary Glosses	Define key words in readings and exercises so that you can concentrate on your grammar practice while still learning about interesting content
Grammar Glossary	Gives you definitions and example sentences for the most common words used to talk about English grammar—a handy reference for now and for later
Websites	Guide you to more information about topics of interest
	Provide you with self-tests with immediate correction and feedback, vocabulary flashcards for extra practice with words that might be new to you, models for writing assignments, and extra practice exercises

All of these features combine to make *Grammar Links* interesting and rewarding—and, I hope, FUN!

M. Kathleen Mahnke, Series Editor
Saint Michael's College
Colchester, VT USA

ACKNOWLEDGMENTS

▨ Series Editor Acknowledgments

This edition of *Grammar Links* would not have been possible without the thoughtful and enthusiastic feedback of teachers and students. Many thanks to you all!

I would also like to thank all of the *Grammar Links* authors, from whom I continue to learn so much every day. Many thanks as well to the dedicated staff: Joann Kozyrev, Evangeline Bermas, and Annamarie Rice.

A very special thanks to Kathy Sands Boehmer and to Susan Maguire for their vision, their sense of humor, their faith in all of us, their flexibility, their undying tenacity, and their willingness to take risks in order to move from the mundane to the truly inspirational.

M. Kathleen Mahnke, Series Editor

▨ Author Acknowledgments

Many people made valuable contributions to this book. We would like to acknowledge and thank the following:

The staff for their constant patience and encouragement

Each other and the other *Grammar Links* authors, for inspiration, advice, and continued friendship throughout the writing and production process

Our students, for their willingness to test the material

Linda Butler, author of *Grammar Links Basic* and *Grammar Links 1*, for her many valuable insights based on her classroom experience with the first edition of this book

Michael Masyn, of the International English Center at the University of Colorado, for his experience and suggestions

Bob Jasperson, Director of the International English Center, for his support

Len Neufeld, for ensuring that the *Grammar Briefings* were presented in the clearest and best possible way.

In addition, we thank the following reviewers:

Brian McClung, North Lake College

Janet Selitto, Valencia Community College

Finally, we are immensely grateful for the support, encouragement, and patience of our close friends and families, especially Lakhdar Benkobi, Len Neufeld, Richard, Jonathan, and Joshua Norloff, and Peter van Zante.

Debra Daise, Randee Falk, Charl Norloff, and Janis van Zante

Present and Past: Simple and Progressive

TOPIC FOCUS
Natural Time and Clock Time

UNIT OBJECTIVES

■ **the simple present and present progressive**
(The earth *revolves* around the sun. We *are studying* the solar system this year.)

■ **verbs with stative meanings**
(We *own* four clocks and several watches.)

■ **the simple past and past progressive**
(I *called* a friend last night. He *was eating* dinner.)

■ **time clauses**
(*Before she went to school,* she drank a cup of coffee.)

■ ***used to* and *would***
(People *used to tell* time by the sun. They *would follow* the sun's shadow on a dial.)

Grammar in Action

Read and listen to this article.

When Did Time Begin?

Did time **have** a beginning? If it did, how **did** it **begin**? When **did** it **begin**? Scientists (think) that our universe **began** from a very small point of space-time. About 14 billion years ago, this point suddenly **exploded**

An Explosion

outward. We **call** this gigantic explosion the big bang. **Did** time **exist** before the big bang? No one **knows**. But the big bang **was** the beginning of time as humans **are** able to understand it now.

At the moment of the big bang, the universe **began** to expand and change. It **is** still **expanding** and **is** still **changing**. Nowadays, scientists **are observing** distant parts of the universe, and they **are learning** more about its early history. About 10 billion years ago, galaxies **were forming** from clouds of stars, dust, and gas. While our galaxy, the Milky Way, **was moving** through space, our solar system

formed within it. Our solar system **includes** the sun and the planets that **revolve** around it. The motions of our planet, Earth, **give** us natural time cycles—days, nights, and seasons of the year. These cycles **repeat** themselves regularly, over and over again.

Natural time cycles **had** an important influence in the development of life on earth. From the beginning, the activities of living things **followed** earth's patterns of daylight and darkness and the seasons of the year. As a result, all living things, including human bodies, **follow** these natural time cycles. Our daily pattern of sleeping and waking is one of our natural cycles.

Long ago, people everywhere **lived** in a way that was closely connected to the cycles of nature. They **depended** on natural time, measured by changes in the sun, moon, and

A Galaxy

stars. But now we **have** a mechanical measure of time, clock time, and people often **schedule** their lives according to it.

Are you feeling sleepy or hungry now, even though the clock **says** it**'s** not time to sleep or eat? What **is** your body **telling** you? Perhaps it**'s trying** to follow nature instead of the clock.

Our Solar System

> *gigantic* = very, very big. *expand* = grow bigger. *observe* = look at. *revolve* = move around. *have an influence* = cause an effect. *mechanical* = operated by a machine.

Think About Grammar

A. Work with a partner. Look at the boldfaced verbs in the article. Underline the verbs that describe an action or state that finished in the past or that was in progress at a time in the past. Circle the verbs that describe an action or state that includes the present or that is in progress in the present.

B. Some of the verbs that you underlined or circled describe an action in progress in the present or in the past. These verbs are in the present progressive or past progressive tense. Write *past progressive* or *present progressive* next to each of the verbs.

1. is expanding _____

2. is changing _____

3. are observing _____

4. are learning _____

5. were forming _____

6. was moving _____

7. is telling _____

8. is trying _____

C. Answer the questions.

1. Progressive verbs all end in the same three letters. What are they? _____

2. Progressive verbs all have the same auxiliary (helping) verb. What is it? _____

D. The other verbs are in the simple present or the simple past tense. Write *simple present* or *simple past* next to each of the verbs.

1. think _____

2. exploded _____

3. says _____

4. had _____

5. began _____

6. were _____

7. followed _____

8. revolve _____

Chapter 1

Simple Present and Present Progressive

Introductory Task: True or False?

A. Work with a partner. Read the statements about a group of students. Then answer the questions.

  a. Most people in the group **use** an alarm clock to wake up on weekdays.
  b. Only two people **are wearing** contact lenses at the moment.
  c. Everyone **sleeps** more than six hours every night.
  d. Three people **are feeling** sleepy now.
  e. Most people **wear** a watch every day.
  f. Right now, fewer than half of the students **are thinking** about food.

1. Habits are things that people do regularly or routinely. Which statements describe

   people's habits? _a_____   _____   _____

   Are the boldfaced verbs in these statements in the simple present or the present

   progressive? _____

2. Which statements describe things people are doing at this moment in time?

   _____   _____   _____

   Are these boldfaced verbs in the simple present or the present progressive?

   _____

B. Follow these steps to find out if the statements in Part A are true or false for your class:

1. Work together as a class to write a question for each statement. The questions should be ones that can be answered *yes* or *no*. Follow these examples: *Do you use an alarm clock to wake up on weekdays? Are you wearing contact lenses?*

2. Each student goes around the class asking the other students the questions. Keep track of the number of *yes* and *no* answers.

3. What are your results? Are the statements true or false for your class?

Simple Present and Present Progressive I

FORM

A. Affirmative Statements

SIMPLE PRESENT		
SUBJECT	BASE FORM OF VERB (+ -S/-ES)	
I	**play**	every day.
Joe	**plays**	every day.
They	**play**	every day.

(See Appendix 1 for spelling rules for the -s/-es form of the verb. See Appendix 2 for pronunciation rules for the third person singular form of the simple present tense.)

PRESENT PROGRESSIVE		
SUBJECT	*BE* + BASE FORM OF VERB + *-ING**	
I	**am playing**	now.
He	**is playing**	now.
We	**are playing**	now.

(See Appendix 3 for spelling rules for the -*ing* form of the verb.)

B. Negative Statements

SIMPLE PRESENT		
SUBJECT	*DO* + *NOT* + BASE FORM OF VERB*	
I	**do not work**	every day.
She	**does not work**	every day.
You	**do not work**	every day.

PRESENT PROGRESSIVE		
SUBJECT	*DO* + *NOT* + BASE FORM OF VERB + *-ING**	
I	**am not working**	now.
She	**is not working**	now.
You	**are not working**	now.

C. *Yes/No* Questions and Short Answers

SIMPLE PRESENT	
QUESTIONS	SHORT ANSWERS
Do they **work** every semester?	Yes, they **do.**
	No, they **don't.**
Does he **work** every evening?	Yes, he **does.**
	No, he **doesn't.**
Do you **work** every semester?	Yes, I **do.**
	No, I **don't.**

PRESENT PROGRESSIVE	
QUESTIONS	SHORT ANSWERS
Am I **working** this semester?	Yes, you **are.**
	No, you **aren't.**
Is he **working** this evening?	Yes, he **is.**
	No, he **isn't.**
Are you **working** this evening?	Yes, I **am.**
	No, I'm **not.**

(continued on next page)

D. Wh- Questions

Wh- Questions About the Subject

SIMPLE PRESENT	PRESENT PROGRESSIVE
Who works with you?	**Who is working** with you?
What usually **happens**?	**What is happening**?

Other Wh- Questions

SIMPLE PRESENT	PRESENT PROGRESSIVE
Where do you **play**?	**When am** I **playing**?
How long does she **play**?	**Why is** Anna **playing**?
	Who are you **playing** with?

*CONTRACTIONS: SIMPLE PRESENT	*CONTRACTIONS: PRESENT PROGRESSIVE
do + not → don't does + not → doesn't	I + am → I'm he/she/it + is → he's/she's/it's we/you/they + are → we're/you're/they're is + not → isn't are + not → aren't he/she/it + is + not → he's/she's/it's not OR he/she/it isn't we/you/they + are + not → we're/you're/they're not OR we/you/they aren't

GRAMMAR **HOT**SPOT!

1. In conversation, these contractions are common:

   - *Do/be* + *not* (e.g., *don't*, *aren't*)

   - Subject pronoun + *be* (e.g., *he's, we're*)

   - *Wh-* word + *is* (e.g., *who's* and *what's*)

   In some formal writing, contractions are avoided.

Tina and Bob **don't** play baseball.
They're playing basketball.
Why's she playing?
Why is the climate changing?

2. Affirmative short answers are never contracted.

Yes, I am.   **NOT:** Yes, ~~I'm.~~

3. When two verbs with the same subject are connected with *and* or *but,* it isn't necessary to repeat the subject.

She **works** and **plays** every day.
She **works** but **doesn't play**.

4. When these verbs include a form of *be* (or of *have*; see Unit Two), it isn't necessary to repeat that form.

She is **working** and **playing**.
She is **working** but **not playing**.

Simple Present and Present Progressive I

1 Simple Present—Form: A Conversation About Time

A student and an astronomer are getting acquainted. Use the words in parentheses to complete the statements and questions in the simple present. Complete the short answers. Use contractions with subject pronouns and with *not*.

Q: <u>Do you work</u> at an observatory?
　　　1 (you, work)

A: Yes, <u>I do</u> .
　　　　　2

Q: I <u>don't know</u> much about astronomy. What <u>does your work involve</u> ?
　　　3 (not, know)　　　　　　　　　　　　　　　　　　4 (your work, involve)

A: Well, I _____ about measuring time, motion, and space.
　　　　　　　5 (think)

Q: What _____ between astronomy and the measurement of time?
　　　　　　6 (the connection, be)

A: We _____ our ability to measure time from observing the motions of
　　　　　7 (get)

the stars, the earth, and the moon. These motions _____ us natural time
　　　　　　　　　　　　　　　　　　　　　　　　　8 (give)

periods, that is, days and nights and the seasons of the year.

Q: If we have natural time, why _____ clock time, too?
　　　　　　　　　　　　　　　　　9 (we, use)

A: Natural time _____ us small or precise enough units of time.
　　　　　　　　　10 (not, give)

Q: _____ on both natural time and clock time?
　　　11 (I, live)

A: Yes, _____ . Your body and some of your activities
　　　　　　12

_____ regular natural time cycles, or patterns. However,
　　13 (follow)

in our culture, most people _____ the feeling that clock time
　　　　　　　　　　　　　　14 (have)

_____ their lives and routines. For example, they
　　15 (control)

_____ when their body tells them to. They
　　16 (not, eat)

_____ when the clock says it's lunch or dinner time.
　　17 (eat)

Q: Well, my English teacher _____ the clock, and it
　　　　　　　　　　　　　　　　18 (watch)

_____ time for me to go to class. Thanks for answering my questions!
　　19 (be)

> *astronomy* = the science that deals with the study of the sun, moon, planets, stars, etc.
> *observatory* = a building built for the purpose of looking at the sky through a
> telescope. *precise* = correct, accurate.

 For more information about astronomers and astronomy, go to the *Grammar Links* Website.

2 Simple Present—*Yes/No* and *Wh-* Questions: Where Does Natural Time Come From?

A. Use the cues to write questions about the information in each paragraph.

I. The earth and other planets move around the sun. It takes the earth about 365¼ days to orbit the sun. When we talk about the solar system, we call 365 days an "Earth year."

Yes/No Questions:

1. Does the earth move around the sun   ?
   (the earth / move / around the sun)

2. _____ ?
   (it / take / the earth / about 365¼ days / to orbit the sun)

Wh- Questions:

1. What do we call 365 days _____ ?
   (we / call / 365 days)

2. How long _____ ?
   (an "Earth year" / be)

3. How long _____ ?
   (it / take / the earth / to orbit / the sun)

II. The length of a planet's year depends on the planet's distance from the sun. So years on Venus aren't as long as Earth years, but years on Mars are longer than Earth years. It takes Venus 224½ Earth days to orbit the sun. It takes Mars 687 Earth days to orbit the sun.

Yes/No Questions:

1. _____ ?
   (years on Venus / be / as long as / Earth years)

2. _____ ?
   (years on Mars / be / longer than / years on Venus)

Wh- Questions:

1. What _____ ?
   (the length of a planet's year / depend on)

2. How long _____ ?
   (it / take / Venus / to orbit the sun)

3. How long _____ ?
   (it / take / Mars / to orbit the sun)

III. The planets rotate as they orbit the sun. The earth rotates on its axis once every 24 hours. This rotation makes day and night on Earth. When one side of the earth faces the sun, it is daytime on that side. When that side turns away from the sun, it is night.

Yes/No Questions:

1. _____ ?
   (the planets / rotate / as they orbit the sun)

2. _____ ?
   (the earth / rotate / on its axis / once every year)

Wh- Questions:

1. How often _____?
   (earth / rotate / on its axis)

2. What _____?
   (make / day and night / on earth)

3. When _____?
   (it / be / daytime / on one side of the earth)

B. Work with a partner. Take turns asking and answering the questions you wrote in Part A. Give short answers to *yes/no* questions.

Example: Student A: *Does the earth move around the sun?* Student B: *Yes, it does.*
Student B: *What do we call 365 days?* Student A: *An Earth year.*

 See the *Grammar Links* Website to find out more about our solar system and natural time.

3 Present Progressive—Form: Time Talk

A. Use the words in parentheses to complete the statements and questions in the present progressive. Complete the short answer. Use contractions with subject pronouns and with *not*.

I. A mother and son:

A: Peter, why _aren't you doing_ anything?
   1 (you, not, do)

B: I _'m doing_ something. I _____ here and
   2 (do)   3 (sit)

_____.
4 (think)

A: You _____. You _____ television!
   5 (not, think)   6 (watch)

B: I _____ a nature program. It _____
   7 (watch)   8 (help)

me think about serious environmental problems.

A: That nature program _____ you do your homework. You
   9 (not, help)

_____ time!
10 (waste)

II. Three young men:

A: Hey, guys! What's up? Why _____ here on the sidewalk with all this stuff?
   1 (you, sit)

B: We _____ to buy concert tickets. The line
   2 (wait)

_____ very fast.
3 (not, move)

C: We _____ to entertain ourselves while we wait. We
   4 (try)

_____ to the radio and _____ card games.
5 (listen)   6 (play)

A: I get it. You _____ time.
   7 (kill)

III. Three grandmothers:

A: How _____ nowadays, Mildred?
1 (your children, get along)

B: They _____ just fine. Jennie _____
2 (get along) 3 (work)

in Chicago, and Carl _____ to be a lawyer. And the
4 (study)

grandchildren _____ fast!
5 (grow)

C: Good morning! _____ anything important?
6 (I, interrupt)

B: No, _____. We _____ the time of day
7 8 (pass)

chatting about our families. Please join us.

 B. Work in pairs or small groups. In Part A, people are "wasting time," "killing time,"
and "passing the time of day." Discuss these idioms and think of other examples of
each. Then choose one and work together to write a dialogue that uses it. Use the
present progressive at least four times. Present your dialogue to the class.

 See the *Grammar Links* Website for a model dialogue for this assignment.

GRAMMAR BRIEFING 2

Simple Present and Present Progressive II
■ Simple Present

FUNCTION

A. Uses of the Simple Present

1. Use the simple present to talk about habitual and repeated actions in the present. These actions started in the past and will probably occur in the future.

   Farmers **get up** early every morning.
   They sometimes **go out** with friends.

2. Use the simple present to talk about things that are generally accepted as true, including scientific facts.

   Farmers **grow** crops.
   The earth **revolves** around the sun.

3. The simple present is also used with verbs with stative meaning.
   (See Grammar Briefing 3, page 17.)

   They **know** about the test.
   She **has** a new car.

(continued on next page)

B. Time Expressions and Adverbs of Frequency with the Simple Present

1. Time expressions used with the simple present include *every day* (*week, month, year,* etc.), *on Mondays* (*weekends, holidays,* etc.), *in the morning* (*the fall, the first semester,* etc.), and *at noon* (*3:00 p.m., the end of the day,* etc.).

    He works **every week.**
    I go **on weekends.**
    Classes begin **in the fall.**
    We finish **at 3:00 p.m.**

2. Adverbs of frequency ([*almost*] *always, usually, often, sometimes, seldom, rarely,* [*almost*] *never,* etc.) are also often used with the simple present.

    (See Appendix 4 for the position of adverbs of frequency in a sentence.)

    We **sometimes** work on the weekend.
    I **usually** drink tea.
    She is **almost never** at home in the evening.

■ Present Progressive

FUNCTION

A. Uses of the Present Progressive

1. Use the present progressive to talk about actions in progress at this moment.

    Right now, the sun **is shining.**
    We **are sitting** in the park now.

2. Use the present progressive to talk about actions in progress through a period of time including the present. The actions began before now and will probably continue after now, but they do not have to be happening at this moment.

    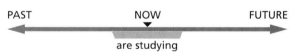

    Rosa **is taking** an astronomy course this semester.
    At present, scientists **are studying** new methods to measure time.

3. The present progressive can be used to emphasize that a situation is temporary. The simple present indicates a more permanent situation.

    They **are living** in Chicago this summer.
      (temporary situation)
    They **live** in New York.
      (more permanent situation)
    She's not **earning** much money now.
      (temporary situation)
    She **doesn't earn** much money.
      (more permanent situation)

(continued on next page)

B. Time Expressions with the Present Progressive

1. *Now, right now,* and *at the moment* can be used with the present progressive to talk about a point in time or a period of time.

> I'm working **right now**.
> He's studying **at the moment**.

2. *Nowadays, at this time, at present, these days,* and *this week* (*month,* etc.) are used to talk about a period of time.

> They're working at a lab **these days**.
> We're studying the solar system **this week**.

TALKING THE TALK

The present progressive can be used with *always* to express a complaint.

> Dudley **is** always **arriving** late. I'm tired of waiting for him.

GRAMMAR PRACTICE 2

Simple Present and Present Progressive II

4 Simple Present and Present Progressive—Uses: Watches

Why is the simple present or the present progressive used in these sentences? For each boldfaced verb, choose a reason.

Simple Present
Habitual or repeated action
Scientific fact, thing generally accepted as true

Present Progressive
Action in progress at this moment
Action in progress through a period of time including the present

Digital Watch

1. Tiny batteries **provide** the power for digital electronic watches.

   Scientific fact, thing generally accepted as true
   _____

2. Please don't interrupt me! I'**m trying** to set my watch.

   _____

3. Megan never **wears** a watch.

   _____

4. Rachel's watch has been running slow for a while. Its battery **is wearing out**.

   _____

5. How often **do** you **look** at your watch each day?

   _____

6. Why **are** you **looking** at your watch? Are we late?

   _____

7. Our watches have beepers, so we sometimes **use** them as alarms.

   _____

8. Keith's watch **is beeping**. It's lunch time.

   _____

9. Watches come in many different styles these days. Some people **are wearing** colorful ones.

   _____

10. A watch is one type of chronometer. Chronometers **measure** time.

   _____

5 Adverbs of Frequency and Time Expressions with Simple Present: Routines

A. Use the adverbs of frequency and time expressions to write true statements about your routines.

1. usually + in the evening   <u>I usually drink a cup of hot tea in the evening</u>_____.

2. often + in the morning _____.

3. seldom + at night _____.

4. always + once a day _____.

5. usually + once a week _____.

6. sometimes + on weekends _____.

7. always + every semester _____.

8. almost never + in the summer _____.

B. Now change one (any one) of the sentences so that it tells a lie. That is, the routine it states is not true for you.

                                        a glass of hot milk
Example: "I usually drink ~~a cup of hot tea~~ in the evening."

C. 1. Work with a partner. Use the cues in 2–8 of Part A to ask a question about each of your partner's routines. Student A uses "*What do you* + adverb of frequency + *do* + time expression?" in each question. Student B answers the questions, pretending that the lie is one of his or her routines.

Example:
Student A asks: *What do you usually do in the evening?*
Student B answers: *I usually drink a glass of hot milk in the evening.*

2. Which of your partner's routines is the lie? Find out by asking *yes/no* questions. Try to detect the lie with as few questions as possible.

Example:
Student A asks: *Is it true? Do you usually drink a glass of hot milk in the evening?*
If the routine is a true one, Student B answers, *Yes, I do.*
If the routine is the lie, Student B answers, *No, I don't. In fact, I usually drink a cup of hot tea in the evening.*

3. Now switch roles. Student B asks questions and Student A answers. Who is a better lie detector?

6   Simple Present Versus Present Progressive: Usually, but Not Today

A. Work in pairs. People sometimes change their routines temporarily. Use the cues to write questions in the simple present. Then answer each question, using your own ideas and following the pattern in the example. In each answer, include *usually* and the time expression given and use the simple present and the present progressive.

1. Q: _Where do Arthur and Nancy eat dinner_____?
   (where / Arthur and Nancy / eat dinner)

   A: _They usually eat dinner at home, but tonight they're eating dinner at a restaurant._
   (tonight)

2. Q: _____?
   (what kind of clothes / Flora / wear)

   A: _____
   (today)

3. Q: _____?
   (which language / Elena and Frank / speak)

   A: _____
   (right now)

4. Q: _____?
   (how / Theresa / get to school)

   A: _____
   (these days)

5. Q: _____?
   (when / the neighbors / go on vacation)

   A: _____
   (this year)

 B. Now work on your own. What about your own routines? Write three statements like those in Part A about temporary changes in your habits or situation. In each statement, include *usually* and a time expression such as *now, today, these days, this semester,* and *this year,* and use the simple present and the present progressive.

Example: *I usually live in Mexico, but this year I'm living in the United States.*

7 **Simple Present Versus Present Progressive; Present Progressive with *Always*:**
Dudley's Driving Me Crazy!

A. Complete the e-mail message with the simple present or the present progressive of the verbs in parentheses. Use contractions with subject pronouns and with *not*.

From: Chris
Sent: October 2   7:16 p.m.
To: Max
Subject: Dudley's Driving Me Crazy!

Hi, Max! College __is__ great! I __'m enjoying__ my classes this
　　　　　　　　　 1 (be)　　　　　　　　 2 (enjoy)

semester. Also, I _____ along well with all my housemates these days, except
　　　　　　　　　　3 (get)

for Dudley. Everyday life with Dudley _____ very well right now. Let me tell
　　　　　　　　　　　　　　　　　 4 (not, go)

you about his habits. First of all, Dudley often _____ other people's food and
　　　　　　　　　　　　　　　　　　　　　 5 (eat)

even _____ their cookies! Not only that, but he usually
　　　　6 (steal)

_____ his dirty dishes in the sink for someone else to wash. In fact, Greg
　　7 (put)

_____ Dudley's breakfast, lunch, and dinner dishes now.
　　8 (wash)

Dudley and his friends _____ parties here almost every night.
　　　　　　　　　　　　　　 9 (have)

At the moment, they _____ CDs very loudly and
　　　　　　　　　　　 10 (play)

_____ on the telephone, too.
　　11 (talk)

On top of that, Dudley often _____ our things without asking.
　　　　　　　　　　　　　　　 12 (borrow)

He _____ my favorite sweater today.
　　 13 (wear)

Finally, Dudley _____ our mail sometimes.
　　　　　　　　　 14 (read)

I _____ this message quickly, just in case he comes in.
　 15 (type)

Dudley won't change his bad habits. Slowly but surely, he _____
　　　　　　　　　　　　　　　　　　　　　　　　　　　　　 16 (drive)

me crazy!

Your buddy, Chris

B. Work with a partner. Imagine that you are Dudley's housemates. Dudley is driving you crazy, too. Use the information in Chris's message to complain to each other about Dudley's bad habits. Use the present progressive and *always*.

Example: *He's always eating my food!*

8 Simple Present Versus Present Progressive: Studying the Universe and Time

Matt just ran into an old friend from high school. Use the words in parentheses to complete the statements and questions in the simple present or the present progressive. Use contractions with subject pronouns and with *not.*

Matt: Hi, Ashley! It's good to see you again. What __are you doing__ back here?

1 (you, do)

_____ your parents?

2 (you, visit)

Ashley: I _____ at home with them this summer, and I

3 (live)

_____ as a waitress at night. But I _____

4 (work)   5 (look)

for a day job, too, because part-time waitresses _____

6 (not earn)

enough money.

Matt: Why _____ so hard this summer?

7 (you, work)

Ashley: I _____ to save money for my second year of college.

8 (try)

_____ to college these days?

9 (you, go)

Matt: Not yet. At this point, I _____ to figure out what subjects would

10 (try)

interest me.

Ashley: I _____ interested in astronomy and cosmology.

11 (get)

Matt: Let's see, astronomers _____ the planets and the stars. But what

12 (observe)

_____?

13 (cosmologists, do)

Ashley: They _____ the universe as a whole. These days cosmologists

14 (study)

_____ to understand the beginning of the universe and the nature

15 (try)

of time. They're my heroes.

Matt: Really? Maybe I should consider studying cosmology, too!

GRAMMAR BRIEFING 3

Verbs with Stative Meaning

FORM and FUNCTION

A. Overview

1. Verbs with stative meaning refer to states. They occur in the simple tenses, rather than the progressive, even for uses where other verbs occur in the progressive.

We **know** more about the moon these days.
  NOT: We ~~are knowing~~ more about the moon these days.

The sky **seems** dark now.
  NOT: The sky ~~is seeming~~ dark now.

2. Verbs with stative meaning often concern thoughts, attitudes, emotions, possession, the senses, or description. Common verbs with stative meaning include:

THOUGHTS	ATTITUDES	EMOTIONS	POSSESSION	SENSES	DESCRIPTION
believe	appreciate	fear	belong to	feel	appear
feel (= think)	(dis)agree	(dis)like	have	hear	be
forget	doubt	hate	owe	see	cost
know	hope	love	own	smell	look (like)
mean	mind		possess	taste	seem
realize	need				sound (like)
remember	prefer				tend
suppose	want				weigh
think	wish				
understand					

B. Verbs with Stative and Active Meanings

1. Some of the verbs above have both a stative meaning and an active meaning:

STATIVE MEANING	ACTIVE MEANING
People **think** astronomy is exciting. (opinion)	People **are thinking** about solutions to environmental problems. (mental action)
She **doesn't see** well at night. (sense)	He's **seeing** a client at the moment. (meeting with)
The air **smells** good. (sense)	They **are smelling** the roses. (action)
The soup **tastes** salty. (sense)	The chef **is tasting** the soup. (action)
The pillow **feels** soft. (sense)	She's **feeling** the bath water. (action of touching)
They **look** happy. (description)	They **are looking** for their mother. (action)
He **weighs** 180 pounds. (state)	He **is weighing** himself on the scale. (action)
I **have** a good watch. (possession)	I'm **having** a good time. (experience)
She **has** a lot of strength. (quality)	We're **having** dinner. (action)

2. In their active meaning, these verbs can occur in the progressive and simple tenses.

He **is thinking** about his future now.

He often **thinks** about his future.

In conversation, certain verbs with stative meaning are sometimes used in the progressive. The present progressive emphasizes emotion or a sense of a process or change.

> They **love** it here.
>
> They**'re loving** it here! (emphasis on the emotion)
>
> Digital watches **cost** less these days.
>
> Digital watches **are costing** less these days. (emphasis on change in cost)

1. The verb *be* can have an active meaning, and occur in the progressive, when followed by an adjective describing a behavior that can change. These adjectives include *bad, careful, foolish, good, impolite, kind, lazy, nice, patient, polite, rude,* and *silly*.

> Tom **is** rude. (Tom is generally rude.)
>
> Tom **is being** rude. (Tom is behaving in a rude way now.)

2. In addition to the uses shown above, *feel* can be followed by an adjective describing health or emotions (e.g., *fine, happy, lonely, sick, strange, tired, well*). In this use, *feel* can occur in the simple or progressive.

> Peter **is feeling** pretty lonely today. = Peter **feels** pretty lonely today.
>
> Andrew **is feeling** sick. = Andrew **feels** sick.

GRAMMAR PRACTICE 3

Verbs with Stative Meaning

9 **Identifying Verbs with Active Meaning and Verbs with Stative Meaning: Astronomy Class I**

Mark the boldfaced verbs that have active meaning with an *A* and the verbs that have stative meaning with an *S*.

>   A   S
> ¹Calvin**'s taking** an astronomy class this semester. ²He **hates** the class. ³He often **complains**
>
> about it. ⁴Calvin **needs** help. ⁵Patricia's **studying** astronomy this semester, too. ⁶She really
>
> **enjoys** the class. ⁷She **likes** the professor, too. ⁸Patricia often **tries** to help Calvin. ⁹She
>
> **explains** things to him. ¹⁰He **listens** to her carefully. ¹¹He **understands** her explanations.
>
> ¹²Calvin **appreciates** Patricia's help.

10 Verbs with Both Active and Stative Meanings: Astronomy Class II

In each pair of sentences, mark the boldfaced verb with active meaning with an *A* and the boldfaced verb with stative meaning with an *S*.

1. a. Calvin **is** shy.
           S

   b. He**'s being** foolish about his problems.
           A

2. a. Calvin doesn't need glasses. He **sees** well.

   b. Calvin**'s seeing** the professor in his office now.

3. a. We **think** about time and space in astronomy class.

   b. I **think** astronomy is fascinating.

4. a. The observatory **has** two telescopes.

   b. We **have** astronomy class in the observatory once a week.

5. a. We **look** for distant stars and planets with the telescopes.

   b. There's Venus! It **looks** beautiful.

11 Simple Present Versus Present Progressive; Stative Versus Active Meaning: Astronomy Class III

Use the words in parentheses to complete the statements and questions in the simple present and present progressive. Use contractions with subject pronouns and with *not*.

I. Teacher: I ___have___ something interesting to show you. I ___'m holding___ a
            1 (have)   2 (hold)

rock that came from the moon. It _____ to the university museum
                            3 (belong)

now. Sylvia, let me hand the rock to you.

Sylvia: Wow, I _____ this. I _____ a real moon
                   4 (not, believe)   5 (feel)

rock! Actually, it _____ much different from an Earth rock.
                   6 (not, feel)

Raymond: Hey, Sylvia. You _____ too much time with that rock. Let me hold it
                   7 (spend)

now. I _____ with Sylvia. I _____
           8 (not, agree)   9 (think)

that it _____ lighter than an Earth rock. It _____
          10 (feel)   11 (look)

different, too. It _____ to have a slightly different color.
                12 (appear)

II. Sylvia: Raymond, what _____ to that rock now?
                   1 (you, do)

Raymond: I _____ it. It _____ different from an Earth rock, too.
         2 (smell)   3 (smell)

Sylvia: I _____ that. Rocks _____.
            4 (doubt)   5 (not, smell)

            _____ about tasting it, too?
            6 (you, think)

Raymond: Of course. I _____ in using all my senses to experience
                        7 (believe)

            nature. I _____ this rock _____
                      8 (suppose)   9 (be)

            pretty old, so it probably _____ very good.
                                        10 (not, taste)

Sylvia: Raymond, you _____ silly today!
                          11 (be)

12 **Using Verbs with Stative Meaning and Verbs with Active Meaning:
Are You a Lark or an Owl?**

All humans naturally tend to be awake during the day and to
sleep at night. However, some people tend to be "day people"
(morning larks), while others tend to be "night people" (night owls).

A. A typical lark and a typical owl are speaking about themselves at two different
times of one day. Use the simple present or the present progressive of the words in
parentheses to complete the statements. Use contractions with subject pronouns
and with *not*.

Lark

Owl

"It's 7 a.m. I _'m enjoying_ the sunrise.
              1 (enjoy)

I _'m feeling/feel_ wide awake now, and I
   2 (feel)

_____ to talk to other
3 (want)

people. I _____ already
          4 (work)

because I _____ a lot of
          5 (have)

energy. In fact, I _____
                    6 (think)

about going jogging soon."

"It's 7 a.m. I _'m enjoying_ my bed.
              1 (enjoy)

I _'m feeling/feel_ really tired now, and I
   2 (feel)

_____ to talk to anyone.
3 (not, want)

I _____ yet because I
  4 (not, move)

_____ much energy.
5 (not, have)

I _____ about
  6 (not, think)

exercising at this hour."

"It's 10 p.m. At this moment, I _____ 7 (feel) exhausted and grumpy. In fact,

I _____ 8 (fall) asleep. I

_____ 9 (need) to get into my nice,

warm bed. I _____ 10 (not, want) to go

anywhere now."

"It's 10 p.m. I _____ 7 (not, feel)

sleepy at all now. I _____ 8 (start)

to feel alert, cheerful, and energetic!

I _____ 9 (study) hard now.

I _____ 10 (plan) to go out with

some friends soon."

B. 1. Work with a partner. Interview each other. Ask questions about your partner's tendencies.

Examples: *How do you usually feel at 7 a.m.? At what time of day do you have the most energy? Do you prefer to go to bed early or late?*

2. Compare your partner's tendencies to those of the lark and the owl in Part A. Is your partner a lark or an owl or in between?

Check out the *Grammar Links* Website to find out more about larks, owls, and the sleep-wake cycle.

C. 1. Now work with a partner whose tendencies are different from yours. Role-play a telephone conversation between a lark and an owl. Imagine that it is now 7 a.m. The lark tries to persuade the owl to go out and do something. Or imagine that it is now 10 p.m. The owl tries to persuade the lark to go out and do something.

Example: Lark: *Good morning!*
Owl: *Why are you calling so early? I'm still sleeping. I feel so tired.*
Lark: *I want to go out now. . . .*

2. Perform your role-play for the class.

Check your progress! Go to the Self-Test for Chapter 1 on the *Grammar Links* Website.

Chapter 2

Simple Past and Past Progressive

Introductory Task: What Were You Doing?

A. Work with a partner. Find out what your partner was doing at various times yesterday. Take turns using the cues to ask and answer questions. Use the past progressive (e.g., *was/were working, was/were eating*) in each question and answer.

Example: Student A: What were you doing yesterday at 6 a.m.?
Student B: I was sleeping. What were you doing yesterday at 6 a.m.?
Student A: I was studying.

1. 6 a.m.
2. 9 a.m.
3. noon

4. 3 p.m.
5. 6 p.m.
6. 9 p.m.

B. Report to the class about the different things you and your partner were doing at the same time. Use the past progressive and *while*.

Example: At 6 a.m., while I was sleeping, Natalie was studying.

C. Work on your own. Write short sentences about five things you did yesterday. Use the simple past (e.g., *worked, ate*).

Example: Yesterday, I studied English. I talked to a friend.

1. _____
2. _____
3. _____
4. _____
5. _____

Simple Past and Past Progressive I

FORM

A. Affirmative Statements

SIMPLE PAST				PAST PROGRESSIVE		

SUBJECT	BASE FORM OF VERB + -ED	
I	**played**	yesterday.
Joe	**played**	yesterday.
They	**played**	yesterday.

SUBJECT	BE + BASE FORM OF VERB + -ING	
I	**was playing**	then.
He	**was playing**	then.
We	**were playing**	then.

(See Appendix 5 for spelling rules for the -*ed* form of the verb. See Appendix 6 for pronunciation rules for the -*ed* form of the verb. Some verbs have irregular forms in the simple past; see Appendix 7 for these irregular verbs.)

(See Appendix 3 for spelling rules for the -*ing* form of the verb.)

B. Negative Statements

SUBJECT	DID + NOT + BASE FORM OF VERB*	
I	**did not work**	at night.
She	**did not work**	at all.
You	**did not work**	on Mondays.

SUBJECT	BE + NOT + BASE FORM OF VERB + -ING*	
I	**was not working**	then.
She	**was not working**	then.
You	**were not working**	then.

C. *Yes/No* Questions and Short Answers

SIMPLE PAST		PAST PROGRESSIVE	
QUESTIONS	SHORT ANSWERS	QUESTIONS	SHORT ANSWERS
Did they **work** every semester?	Yes, they **did.** / No, they **didn't.**	**Was** I **working** here then?	Yes, you **were.** / No, you **weren't.**
Did he **work** every evening?	Yes, he **did.** / No, he **didn't.**	**Was** he **working** that evening?	Yes, he **was.** / No, he **wasn't.**
Did you **work** every semester?	Yes, I **did.** / No, I **didn't.**	**Were** you **working** here then?	Yes, I **was.** / No, I **wasn't.**

(continued on next page)

D. *Wh-* Questions

Wh- Questions About the Subject

SIMPLE PAST	PAST PROGRESSIVE
Who worked with you?	**Who was working** with you?
What happened?	**What was happening** at that time?

Other *Wh-* Questions

SIMPLE PAST	PAST PROGRESSIVE
Where did you **work**?	**Who were** you **working** with?
How did Joan **work**?	**Why was** Joan **working**?

*CONTRACTIONS: SIMPLE PAST	*CONTRACTIONS: PAST PROGRESSIVE
did + not → didn't	was + not → wasn't were + not → weren't

GRAMMAR PRACTICE 1

Simple Past and Past Progressive I

1 **Simple Past—Form:** Natural Time

Use the words in parentheses to complete the statements and questions in the simple past. Complete the short answers. Use contractions with *not*.

Child: Tell me about the old days, Grandpa. How _did people live_ a long time ago?

1 (people, live)

Grandfather: Life _was_ very different then.

2 (be)

Child: How _____ their time?

3 (people, spend)

Grandfather: In those days, most people _____ farmers. A farmer

4 (be)

_____ hard from early morning until night.

5 (work)

Child: _____ alarm clocks?

6 (the farmers, have)

Grandfather: No, _____. They _____ them.

7   8 (not, need)

Their life _____ nature's cycles of day and night. People

9 (follow)

_____ at sunrise. They _____ late,

10 (wake up)   11 (not, stay up)

because they _____ electricity.

12 (not, have)

Child: _____ alive in those days, Grandpa?

13 (you, be)

Grandfather: No, _____.

14

Child: How _____ about life in the old days, Grandpa?
15 (you, learn)

Grandfather: I _____ about it from *my* grandpa.
16 (learn)

2 Simple Past—Irregular Verbs; Questions: Clock Time

A. Debbie's busy life is ruled by the clock. Yesterday her alarm clock rang at 5:45 a.m. and she raced through the day. Use the cues in the box to tell your version of what Debbie did at each time listed below. Use the simple past.

begin working	~~get out of bed~~	read business reports
fall asleep	have dinner with her sister	speak to her boss
drive to work	leave her office	take a shower
eat some french fries	make some phone calls	write some letters
drink a cup of instant coffee	put on her clothes and makeup	see a movie with her boyfriend

1. 5:55 a.m. *She got out of bed at 5:55.*   9. 12:35 p.m.
2. 6:10   10. 1:00
3. 6:30   11. 3:45
4. 6:40   12. 5:45
5. 7:05   13. 6:00
6. 8:00   14. 8:20
7. 9:15   15. 11:30
8. 11:20

B. Work with a partner. Compare your versions of Debbie's schedule by asking and answering *yes/no* and *wh-* questions.

Example: What time did Debbie get out of bed? She got out of bed at 5:55 a.m.
Did Debbie and her boyfriend see the movie at 3:45 p.m.? No, they didn't.
They saw the movie at 8:20.

3 Past Progressive—Form: Observing Mr. Doe

A. Two men who live in Washington, D.C., are getting acquainted. Use the words in parentheses to complete the statements and questions in the past progressive. Complete the short answers. Use contractions with *not*.

Q: It's nice to meet you. What kind of work do you do?

A: Well, mostly I observe people and write reports about them. For example, last week I

___was observing_____ a man, John Doe.
1 (observe)

Q: That sounds interesting. What <u>was Mr. Doe doing</u> last week?
2 (Mr. Doe, do)

A: Well, last Monday at noon, Mr. Doe _____. When I checked at
3 (sleep)

2 p.m., though, he _____ anymore.
4 (not, sleep)

Q: _____ at 2:00?
5 (Mr. Doe, work)

A: No, _____. But he _____ ready
6   7 (get)

to start working. He _____ off his beard. And by 4 p.m. he
8 (shave)

_____ with some other men.
9 (meet)

Q: What _____ about?
10 (they, talk)

A: I'm not sure. They _____ loudly enough for me to hear.
11 (not, speak)

I think they _____ something. Mr. Doe
12 (plan)

_____ much then. At midnight, though, Mr. Doe was very
13 (not, say)

alert, and he _____ a lot of phone calls from a hotel room.
14 (make)

Q: Making phone calls at midnight? That isn't normal! I'm suspicious. Are you a spy?

_____ Mr. Doe because he's a spy?
15 (you, watch)

A: No, _____. I'm a scientist. Last week I
16

_____ the effects of air travel across many time zones. Mr. Doe
17 (study)

is a businessman from Honolulu. He flew to Washington on Sunday night. While he

_____ here, he _____
18 (stay)   19 (experience)

jet lag. That's normal!

> *jet lag* = a tired and confused feeling resulting from high-speed air travel through
> several time zones.

 B. While Mr. Doe was staying in Washington, he was thinking about home. What was happening in Honolulu? What was his family doing? Write three sentences about what was happening at each time.

1. When it was noon in Washington, it was 7 a.m. in Honolulu.

   Example: *People were driving to work. Mrs. Doe was fixing breakfast....*

2. When it was 9 p.m. in Washington, it was 4 p.m. in Honolulu.

3. When it was 3 a.m. in Washington, it was 10 p.m. in Honolulu.

Simple Past and Past Progressive II
■ Simple Past

FUNCTION

A. Uses of the Simple Past

1. Use the simple past to talk about actions that began and ended in the past:

   - The actions can be single actions, or they can be repeated actions.

She **left** her office at 5:00. (single action)	
They **milked** the cows every day. (repeated action)	

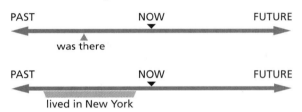

   - They can take place at a moment of time or over a period of time.

   I **was** there yesterday. (moment of time)

   He **lived** in New York for three years. (period of time)

2. The simple past is also used with verbs with stative meaning to talk about states in the past.
   (See Chapter 1, Grammar Briefing 3, page 17.)

   Galileo **was** a scientist.

B. Time Expressions and Adverbs of Frequency with the Simple Past

1. Time expressions used with the simple past include *yesterday, last Monday* (*week, year,* etc.), *a month* (*a year, a day,* etc.) *ago, in 1980* (*January, the fall,* etc.), *on Sunday* (*March 1, the weekend,* etc.), *at 8:00 a.m.* (*night, the end of the month,* etc.).

   I stayed home **last weekend**.

   I was there **two months ago**.

   Classes began **in the fall**.

2. Adverbs of frequency (*[almost] always, usually, often, sometimes, seldom, rarely, [almost] never,* etc.) are also used with simple past.
   (See Appendix 4 for the position of adverbs of frequency in a sentence.)

   We **sometimes** worked on the weekend.

   I **usually** drank tea.

   She was **almost never** on time.

(continued on next page)

■ Past Progressive

A. Uses of the Past Progressive

1. Use the past progressive to talk about actions in progress at a particular moment or over a period of time in the past. The past progressive emphasizes that the action was in progress.

At nine o'clock last night, I **was studying** for a math test. (particular moment)

During the 1990s, he **was working** at that company. (period of time)

2. In contrast to the simple past, the past progressive doesn't specify whether the action was completed. (The simple past emphasizes completion of the action.)

She **was writing** a paper last night. (She might or might not have finished writing the paper.) *Compare*: She **wrote** a paper last night. (She finished writing the paper.)

3. Use the past progressive in stories to give background information. This information sets the scene for the action which is in the simple past.

The wind **was blowing** fiercely and the rain **was beating** against the house. (background) Suddenly, the lights **went out**. (action)

B. Time Expressions with the Past Progressive

1. The past progressive is often used in time clauses with *when* and *while*.

    (See Grammar Briefing 3, page 31.)

He was doing the dishes **while** she was studying.

2. Time expressions used with the past progressive include *then, at that moment, at that time, during the fall (the past year, that period, etc.), last Monday (week, year, etc.)*.

He was studying **at that moment**.

We were living in the United States **last year**.

Simple Past and Past Progressive II

4 **Simple Past and Past Progressive—Meaning:** Spring Forward

Nell made the following statements. Read each statement and the sentence that follows it. If the sentence is true, mark it with a ✓. If there isn't enough information to decide whether or not it is true, mark it with a ?.

1. I **was explaining** something to a friend last week.

    Nell finished the explanation. ____?____

2. An event **happened** last April.

    The event ended in April. ____✓____

3. I **was teaching** English at that time.

    Nell began teaching before that time. _____

4. That Sunday, I didn't read the newspaper, watch television, or listen to the radio because I **was preparing** for my class.

    Nell finished preparing on Sunday. _____

5. I **wrote** several letters that evening.

    Nell finished writing the letters. _____

6. My students are sometimes a little late for class. But that Monday morning I came to class, and all of them **were sitting** in the classroom.

    All the students arrived before Nell. _____

7. They were tired of waiting and wanted to leave, so they **were writing** a note to me.

    The students finished the note. _____

8. They **explained** the reason. I felt really embarrassed about forgetting!

    They finished the explanation. _____

Nell was late because she forgot something that starts on the first Sunday of every April in

most of the United States. What is it? _____

5 Using Simple Past and Past Progressive in Stories: Setting the Scene and Telling the Story

A. Work in pairs. Write sentences in the past progressive to continue setting the scene for the action that follows.

I.

My friends and I were having a party. *People were laughing and singing.*
_____1_____

_____
2

_____
3

Suddenly, the music stopped. . . .

II.

Henry was sitting at his desk. _____
1

_____
2

_____
3

Then the door opened. . . .

B. Write sentences in the simple past to tell the actions in the story.

I.

It was getting dark, and snow was beginning to fall. I was hurrying home.

Then I heard footsteps behind me.
_____1_____

_____
2

_____ . . .
3

II.

Andrea was working in the art studio. She was painting and listening to the radio.

_____
1

_____
2

_____ . . .
3

C. Write a one-paragraph story of your own. Use the past progressive to set the scene and the simple past to tell the actions.

 See the Grammar Links Website for a model story for this assignment.

Simple Past and Past Progressive in Time Clauses

FORM

TIME CLAUSE	MAIN CLAUSE
When he woke up,	he took a shower.

1. A clause has a subject and a verb.

    S   V
John took a shower.

2. A time clause begins with a time word like *when,* *while, before,* or *after.* A time clause cannot stand alone; it must be used with a main clause.

   time clause   main clause
When he woke up, he took a shower.
NOT: ~~When he woke up.~~

3. The time clause can come before or after the main clause, with no difference in meaning. Use a comma between clauses when the time clause is first but not when the main clause is first.

When he woke up, he took a shower.
= He took a shower when he woke up.

FORM and FUNCTION

A. Simple Past + Simple Past in Sentences with Time Clauses

Use simple past for two completed actions. Use *before, after, when,* or *while* in the time clause. These actions can occur:

- One before the other.

  later action   earlier action
He **took** a bath **when/after** he **woke** up.

earlier action   later action
He **shaved before** he **ate** breakfast.

- At the same time.

              same time
When/While he had breakfast,

        same time
he **listened** to the radio.

(continued on next page)

B. Simple Past + Past Progressive in Sentences with Time Clauses

Use simple past + past progressive to talk about an action that began and ended while another action was in progress. Use the simple past for the completed action and the past progressive for the action that was in progress.

Use *while* or *when* in the time clause:

- Clauses with the past progressive can begin with *while* or *when*.

- Clauses with the simple past must begin with *when*.

action in progress
While/When he **was working**,
completed action
Charlie **spilled** his coffee.

action in progress   completed action
He **was working** when he **spilled** his coffee.

NOT: He was working ~~while~~ he spilled his coffee.

C. Past Progressive + Past Progressive in Sentences with Time Clauses

Use past progressive + past progressive to talk about two actions that were in progress at the same time. Use *when* or *while* in the time clause.

action in progress
While/When she **was eating**,
action in progress
she **was thinking** about her homework.

Simple Past and Past Progressive in Time Clauses

Time Zones

6 **The Simple Past and Time Clauses—Meaning:** Standard Time

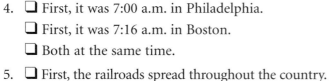 Which event happened first (that is, earlier in time)? Listen once for the main ideas. Then listen again and check (✓) the correct answer.

1. ❑ First, most people were farmers.
   ❑ First, it wasn't important for them to know the exact time.
   ☑ Both at the same time.

2. ❑ First, clock time became important.
   ❑ First, modern transportation and communications began to develop.
   ❑ Both at the same time.

3. ❑ First, the United States had standard time.
   ❑ First, each town or city had its own time.
   ❑ Both at the same time.

4. ❑ First, it was 7:00 a.m. in Philadelphia.
   ❑ First, it was 7:16 a.m. in Boston.
   ❑ Both at the same time.

5. ❑ First, the railroads spread throughout the country.
   ❑ First, the differences in times became a problem.
   ❑ Both at the same time.

6. ❑ First, the passengers traveled across the country.
   ❑ First, they changed their watches.
   ❑ Both at the same time.

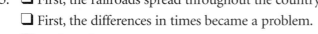

The railroads spread throughout the country in the 1880s.

7. ❑ First, train schedules were confusing.
   ❑ First, railroad officials decided to set their clocks to a standard time.
   ❑ Both at the same time.

8. ❑ First, standard time started.
   ❑ First, officials divided the United States into four time zones.
   ❑ Both at the same time.

9. ❑ First, it was 7:00 a.m. in Philadelphia.
   ❑ First, it was 7:00 a.m. in Boston.
   ❑ Both at the same time.

 See the *Grammar Links* Website for more information about standard time and time zones.

7 **The Simple Past and Past Progressive in Time Clauses; Combining Sentences:** Early Calendars

Use the time expressions to combine the sentences into a sentence with two clauses. You must use the time expression with the right clause. Use a comma when necessary.

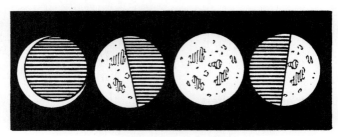

A Moon (Lunar) Cycle

1. Ancient peoples needed to be able to predict the seasons.

   Ancient peoples began to farm.

   + (after)

   After ancient peoples began to farm, they needed to be able to predict the seasons. OR Ancient peoples needed to be able to predict the seasons after they began to farm.

2. They learned to recognize the moon's patterns.

   They observed the moon's changes for a long time.

   + (before)

3. They recorded the moon's cycles.

   They were observing the moon.

   + (while)

4. They made a calendar based on lunar months.

   They understood the cycles of the moon.

   + (after)

5. They were using the lunar calendar.

   They found a problem with the lunar calendar.

   + (while)

6. A few years passed.

   The calendar and the seasons didn't match anymore.

   + (after)

7. The calendar became more accurate.

   They added days to the year.

   + (when)

A lunar month averages 29½ days. A year equals 365 days. Approximately how many days did they need to add to12 lunar months to make the calendar more accurate?

 To learn more about the history of calendars, go to the *Grammar Links* Website.

8 The Simple Past Versus Past Progressive in Time Clauses: A Night Person's Bad Day

A. Complete the sentences with the simple past or past progressive of the verbs in parentheses.

1. When Charlie's alarm clock __rang_____ , he

   __felt_____ sleepy and confused.
       (feel)

2. After Charlie _____ , he _____
       (wake up)   (remember)

   that he had an early appointment with the dentist.

3. Charlie _____ his watch into the tub while he
       (drop)

   _____ his bath.
       (take)

4. When Charlie _____ the bus, he
       (ride)

   _____ asleep and _____
       (fall)   (miss)

   his stop.

5. While Charlie _____ back to the dentist's office, he
       (run)

   _____ and _____ his knee.
       (trip)   (hurt)

6. While Charlie _____ lunch, he
       (have)

   _____ coffee on his new shirt.
       (spill)

7. Charlie finally _____ to feel more alert before he
       (start)

   _____ to go to work at the observatory.
       (leave)

8. After it _____ dark, Charlie
       (get)

   _____ to observe the stars.
       (begin)

9. While he _____ through the telescope, an idea
       (look)

   _____ him: He was definitely a night person.
       (hit)

10. Before the sun _____ , Charlie
        (come up)

    _____ a decision: He would always be an astronomer.
        (make)

B. Think of times when things went wrong for you. Write three kinds of sentences about those times.

1. Write two sentences using *when*, *before*, or *after* and the simple past for two completed actions.

   Example: After I got to class, I realized that my homework was at home. OR
                 I remembered the answer when the test was over.

2. Write two sentences using *when* or *while* and the simple past and past progressive for action that occurred when another action was in progress.

   Example: When I was traveling to the United States, the airline lost my luggage. OR I cut myself while I was shaving.

3. Write two sentences using *when* or *while* and the past progressive for two actions in progress at the same time. Then add sentences that tell what happened.

   Example: I was studying while I was eating lunch. I spilled my soup on my book. OR When I was driving to class, I was putting on my makeup. I almost had an accident.

9 Simple Past, Past Progressive, and Time Clauses: A Legend of Discovery

Complete the paragraph with the simple past or the past progressive of the words in parentheses. In some cases, either tense is possible.

Galileo Galilei __was_____
                        1 (be)

an Italian scientist. He _____
                              2 (live)

from 1564 to 1642. Galileo _____
                                  3 (make)

one of his first discoveries while he

_____ a service at
4 (attend)

the cathedral in Pisa. During the service, he

_____ a hanging
5 (notice)

lamp. Air currents _____
                        6 (blow)

gently through the cathedral at the time, and the

lamp _____ back and
        7 (swing)

forth. While Galileo _____
                          8 (watch)

the lamp, he _____
                  9 (realize)

that each swing took an equal amount of time,

no matter how wide it was. After he

_____ home, he
10 (go)

_____ experiments, using weights and strings. In this way, he
11 (make)

_____ the principle of the pendulum (from a Latin word meaning
12 (discover)

"hanging" or "swinging"). In 1656, a Dutch astronomer, Christiaan Huygens,

_____ Galileo's discovery to build the first pendulum clock.
13 (use)

Used To

FORM

A. Affirmative Statements

We **used to believe** in the man in the moon.

B. Negative Statements

They **didn't use to have** clocks.

C. *Yes/No* Questions

Did you **use to play** every day?

D. *Wh-* Questions

Where **did** you **use to play**?

Who **used to play** with you?

FUNCTION

Talking About Past Actions and States: *Used To* Versus *Would*

1. Use *used to* to talk about actions and states that existed in the past but don't exist anymore. *Used to* emphasizes a contrast between the past and present.

   People **used to tell** time by the sun (but they don't anymore).

   People **didn't use to have** digital watches (but now they do).

2. *Would*, like *used to*, can be used to talk about repeated actions in the past. *Would* can't be used to talk about states.

   When I was young, I **would go/used to go** swimming every chance I got.

   I **used to be** a good swimmer.
   NOT: I ~~would be~~ a good swimmer.

   I **used to like** going to the beach.
   NOT: I ~~would like~~ going to the beach.

GRAMMAR **HOT**SPOT!

Use *used to* except in sentences with *did* (negatives, *yes/no* questions, and *wh-* questions with *did*). In those sentences, use *use to*.

What **did** you **use to do**?
NOT: What did you ~~used to~~ do?

Used To

10 Used To—Form: Long, Long Ago

An Hourglass

A Water Clock

A Sundial

Rewrite the following sentences. Use *used to*.

1. People didn't know as much about the solar system and the universe as we do now.

   People didn't use to know as much about the solar system and the universe as we do now.

2. What did people believe about the earth?

   _____

3. People believed the earth was the center of the universe.

   _____

4. They didn't know that the universe has no center.

   _____

5. How did people measure time?

   _____

6. People didn't have mechanical clocks or watches.

   _____

7. They used the natural motion of the sun to measure time with sundials.

   _____

8. The Greeks had water clocks for measuring time.

   _____

9. What other kinds of clocks did people use?

   _____

10. Some of them kept time with sand clocks, or hourglasses.

    _____

11 *Used To* Versus *Would*: When We Were Children

A. Replace *used to* with *would* in the sentences where it can be used. If *would* can't be used, write NC (no change).

1. My older brother used to want to be a firefighter.
   (NC above "used to")

2. He used to play with his toy fire trucks for hours at a time.
   (would written above, "used to" crossed out)

3. In the summer time, my brother used to pretend that the plants in our garden were on fire.

4. He used to spray water on the plants to put out the pretend fire.

5. I used to like to watch him spray water all over the place.

6. Our neighbors used to complain whenever he sprayed water into their garden.

7. We didn't use to understand why they minded getting wet.

8. We used to think that grownups didn't know how to have fun.

B. Write three pairs of sentences about things that you did in your childhood but don't do any longer. In each pair of sentences, use *used to* in the first sentence. Then use *would*, if possible, or *used to* in the next sentence.

Example: I used to spend a lot of time with my grandmother in the summers. She would tell me about life in the old days.

12 *Used To; Wh-* and *Yes/No* Questions: Did You Use To . . . ?

Work with a partner. Using the verbs in the box, write three *yes/no* and three *wh-* questions to ask your partner about his or her past. Take turns asking and answering the questions.

drink	go	have	play	use	want
eat	hate	like	study	visit	wear

Example: What did you use to want to be? OR
Did you use to want to be an astronomer?

Now tell the class one thing about your partner's past.

Example: Anna used to want to be a race car driver.

Check your progress! Go to the Self-Test for Chapter 2 on the *Grammar Links* Website.

Wrap-up Activities

1 **A Telescope in Space:** EDITING

Correct the 13 errors in the article. There are errors in verb forms and tenses. Some errors can be corrected in more than one way. The first error is corrected for you.

A Telescope in Space

Astronomers didn't ~~used~~ **use** to have powerful telescopes to look into space and observe distant parts of the universe. Most scientists use to believe that the universe was static. (In this case, the word "static" is meaning "not becoming larger or smaller.") Then, in the 1920s, an American astronomer, Edwin Hubble, was having the opportunity to use a big new telescope in California to observe nearby galaxies. In 1929, he made a discovery. The galaxies were moving

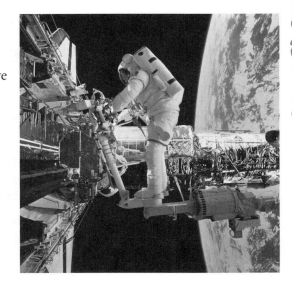

away from each other. The universe were expanding. This meant that it once was very, very small. Hubble's discovery helped cosmologists to develop the theory of the big bang.

But in order to learn more about the beginning of the universe, scientists were needing a telescope outside Earth's atmosphere to provide a clear view of distant galaxies. After years of planning, a team of scientists and engineers at the National Aeronautics and Space Administration (NASA) sended a large telescope into space in 1990. They were naming it the Hubble Space Telescope (HST) after Edwin Hubble. After they were putting HST into orbit, they got an unpleasant surprise. HST didn't worked correctly. Why was this? They were building HST, while they made an error. In 1993, astronauts correct the error. In simple terms, NASA corrected the telescope's vision by fitting it with contact lenses. These days, HST sending clear, beautiful images to Earth. So now we are learning more about the expansion of the universe, the big bang, and the beginning of time.

2 What Was the Question? WRITING/SPEAKING

The following are the answers that a student gave to questions asked in an interview.

Step 1 Work with a partner. Write questions that fit the answers.

1. Q: _How old are you?_____

   A: Twenty, almost twenty-one.

2. Q: _____

   A: One brother and two sisters.

3. Q: _____

   A: Two. My native language and English.

4. Q: _____

   A: Swim, play the guitar, and go to movies.

5. Q: _____

   A: Yes, this semester I'm doing that.

6. Q: _____

   A: Three years ago.

7. Q: _____

   A: A year ago today, I was working and thinking about going back to school.

8. Q: _____

   A: Yes, I used to, but not now.

Step 2 Now work with a different partner. Use the questions you wrote in Step 1 to interview each other. Then report to the class. Tell the most interesting thing you learned about your partner.

3 Origin Story: WRITING

The big bang is the scientific explanation of the origin of the universe and the beginning of time. Read the beginning of an origin story from some of the first people who lived in Australia:

> In the beginning, the earth was an endless cloudy plain. It was separated from both the sky and the sea and covered by shadowy twilight. Above the earth, there were no stars or sun or moon. On the surface of the earth, there were no plants or animals. But underneath the surface, the stars were twinkling, the sun was shining, and the moon was becoming larger and smaller while all the forms of life were sleeping and waiting to come to life. Then, on the morning of the first day, the sun burst through the earth's surface and covered the land with its light....

Adapted from: Chatwin, Bruce. *The Songlines.* London: Jonathan Cape Ltd., 1987, p. 72.

Write a one-paragraph origin story. You can write a story that you know or make one up. Use the simple past and past progressive. Include at least two sentences with time clauses.

 See the *Grammar Links* Website for a model story for this assignment.

4 Terratoo: SPEAKING

Step 1 Work in small groups. Imagine that you and your partners now live on Terratoo, an Earth-like planet in a distant galaxy. Discuss what your imaginary planet is like and what is going on there. Decide on the answers to these questions about it:

1. *Time*: How long are the days, nights, seasons, and years? What other measures of time do you use?
2. *The planet*: How does it look? What is the weather like? What kinds of plants and animals live there?
3. *Daily life*: What kind of language do you speak? What kind of food do you eat? What do you like to do for fun?
4. *Activities*: What time is it on your part of the planet right now? What's happening? What are the people around you doing?

Step 2 Describe your version of Terratoo to the class.

Step 3 Now imagine that you must all go to live on one planet together. As a class, discuss the different versions of Terratoo and decide which one you want to live on.

Present and Past: Perfect and Perfect Progressive

TOPIC FOCUS
The Pace of Life

UNIT OBJECTIVES

■ **the present perfect and the present perfect progressive**
(Many people *have learned* to use computers. We *have been working* with them for years.)

■ **the present perfect versus the simple past**
(I *have been* to Egypt. I *went* there several years ago.)

■ **the past perfect and the past perfect progressive**
(Before he came to the United States, he *had studied* English. He *had been taking* classes for several months before he decided to study abroad.)

Grammar in Action

🎧 Reading and Listening: The Pace of Life

Read and listen to this passage from a textbook.

The pace, or speed, of life **hasn't** always **been** as fast as it is now. In the last 200 years, there **have been** important changes in technology. The first changes led to the industrial age, which lasted from the early 1800s to the mid-1900s. More recent changes **have led** to the information age, which continues today. In the industrial age, the pace of life became much faster. That trend **has continued** in the information age.

Transportation in the Industrial Age

Before the industrial age began, people **had followed** the cycles of nature. They lived as their parents and grandparents **had lived**. People and information **had** never **moved** faster than the speed of a fast horse or sailing ship. The pace of life **had stayed** much the same for thousands of years. But during the 1800s, new technology, such as trains and the telegraph, changed everything. By the late 1800s, the speed of transportation and communications **had increased** greatly. And because the new technology **had made** it possible for people to do more in less time, the pace of life started to speed up, too.

Since the middle of the 1900s, we **have been experiencing** an important and rapid change in information technology. Before the 1960s, very few people **had** ever **worked** with a computer. Since then, millions of people **have become** computer users. The computer **has given** us the ability to store, send, and receive very large amounts of information instantly. In the information age, the speed of change **has** also **speeded up**—lately, things **have been changing** faster than ever before. And it seems that time and life **have been moving** faster, too.

Communication in the Information Age

How **have** people **reacted** to the new technology and new speeds? Some people believe that the new technology **has brought** us many benefits and **made** our lives more convenient and exciting. Others believe that our lives **haven't improved** because the fast pace isn't natural and it **has caused** us too much stress.

How **have** you **been feeling** about the pace of your life recently? **Has** it **been** too fast, just right, or too slow?

---

technology = the use of scientific knowledge for practical purposes. *age* = a period of time in history. *trend* = a general direction or tendency. *telegraph* = a system for sending messages electrically over a wire.

Think About Grammar

A. Read each pair of sentences. Circle the boldfaced verbs that talk about actions that occurred before a time in the past. Underline the boldfaced verbs that talk about actions that began in the past but continue to the present.

1. a. Since the information age began, people <u>**have experienced**</u> many changes.

   b. Before the industrial age began, people ⟨**had experienced**⟩ few changes.

2. a. By the late 1800s, the speed of communications **had gotten** much faster.

   b. Since the beginning of the information age, the speed of communications **has gotten** much faster.

3. a. In recent times, many people **have worked** with computers.

   b. Before the 1960s, only a few people **had worked** with computers.

4. a. The speed of technological change **has increased** since computers were introduced.

   b. The speed of technological change **had increased** by the 1990s.

5. a. Until the early 1800s, the pace of life **had stayed** slow.

   b. Lately, the pace of life **has stayed** fast.

B. Work with a partner. Compare and discuss your answers to Part A. The circled verbs are in the past perfect. The underlined verbs are in the present perfect. How are the forms for these tenses similar? How are they different?

 To learn more about the industrial age and the information age, go to the *Grammar Links* Website.

Present Perfect and Present Perfect Progressive

Introductory Task: Quiz: What Is Your Time Type?

A. Write sentences with a verb in the present perfect (e.g., *have become*) to answer the following questions. In each sentence, include the adverb of frequency that is most appropriate for you: *often*, *sometimes*, or *rarely*.

Example: I have sometimes become irritated when I had to wait in line. OR I have rarely gotten angry when traffic was moving slowly.

Your Time Type Quiz

1. How frequently have you become irritated when you had to wait in line?

   _____

2. How frequently have you gotten angry when traffic was moving slowly?

   _____

3. How frequently have you worried about being late for a party?

   _____

4. How frequently have you felt anxious when you didn't have anything to do?

   _____

5. How frequently have you wanted to make every moment of your life count?

   _____

6. How frequently have you wished that you had more time in a day?

   _____

B. Work with a partner. Find out your partner's time type. Read your partner's answers and give 3 points for each answer with *often*, 2 points for each *sometimes*, and 1 point for each *rarely*. Then add up the points and look at page A-1 to learn what the score means.

C. Report to the class. What have you learned about your partner? Is your partner a "fast" or "slow" person?

Present Perfect and Present Perfect Progressive I

FORM

A. Affirmative Statements

PRESENT PERFECT			PRESENT PERFECT PROGRESSIVE		
SUBJECT	*HAVE/HAS* + PAST PARTICIPLE*		SUBJECT	*HAVE/HAS + BEEN +* PRESENT PARTICIPLE*	
I	**have done**	that.	I	**have been doing**	that.
She	**has done**	that.	She	**has been doing**	that.

(See Appendix 7 for the past participles of irregular verbs.)

(See Appendix 3 for spelling rules for the *-ing* form of the verb.)

B. Negative Statements

PRESENT PERFECT			PRESENT PERFECT PROGRESSIVE		
SUBJECT	*HAVE/HAS + NOT +* PAST PARTICIPLE*		SUBJECT	*HAVE/HAS + NOT + BEEN* + PRESENT PARTICIPLE*	
Bob	**has not done**	that.	Bob	**has not been doing**	that.
We	**have not done**	that.	We	**have not been doing**	that.

C. *Yes/No* Questions and Short Answers

PRESENT PERFECT		PRESENT PERFECT PROGRESSIVE	
QUESTIONS	SHORT ANSWERS	QUESTIONS	SHORT ANSWERS
Have you **done** that?	Yes, I **have**.	**Have** you **been doing** that?	Yes, I **have (been)**.
	No, I **haven't**.		No, I **haven't (been)**.
Has he **done** that?	Yes, he **has**.	**Has** he **been doing** that?	Yes, he **has (been)**.
	No, he **hasn't**.		No, he **hasn't (been)**.

(continued on next page)

D. *Wh-* Questions

Wh- Questions About the Subject

PRESENT PERFECT*	PRESENT PERFECT PROGRESSIVE*
Who has done that?	**Who has been doing** that?
What has happened?	**What has been happening**?

Other *Wh-* Questions

PRESENT PERFECT*	PRESENT PERFECT PROGRESSIVE*
What have they **done**?	**What have** they **been doing**?
Where has it **gone**?	**Why has** she **been doing** that?

*CONTRACTIONS

I + have → I've
he/she/it + has → he's/she's/it's
we/you/they + have → we've/you've/they've
wh- word + has → who's, what's, where's, etc.

have + not → haven't
has + not → hasn't

GRAMMAR **HOT**SPOT!

The contraction *'s* can be *is* or *has*:

- *'s* + present participle = *is*.

  She**'s climbing** Mount Everest. (present progressive, *'s* = *is*; *climbing* is the present participle of *climb*)

- *'s* + past participle = *has*.

  She**'s climbed** Mount McKinley. (present perfect, *'s* = *has*; *climbed* is the past participle of *climb*)

  She**'s been climbing** mountains for a long time. (present perfect progressive, *'s* = *has*; *been* is the past participle of *be*)

Present Perfect and Present Perfect Progressive I

1 Present Perfect—Form: A Conference on the Pace of Life

Use the words in parentheses to complete the statements and questions in the present perfect. Complete the short answers. Use contractions with subject pronouns and with *not*.

Moderator: People used to live according to natural time, but they don't anymore. What

<u>has happened</u> as a result? _____ their
1 (happen)   2 (people, lose)

sense of natural time?

Participant 1: Yes, _____. Natural time _____.
3   4 (not, change)

However, people's ideas and feelings about time _____.
5 (change)

Moderator: Why _____?
6 (this, happen)

Participant 2: Modern technology _____ many changes.
7 (cause)

Moderator: Time _____, but it seems to go faster.
8 (not, speed up)

_____?
9 (life, speed up)

Participant 3: Yes, _____. And some people
10

_____ well to the fast pace of life.
11 (not, react)

They _____ a lot of stress.
12 (feel)

Participant 1: I agree. Lately, we Americans _____ the feeling that we don't
13 (have)

have enough time.

Moderator: But new technology _____ to many products to help us save
14 (lead)

time: microwave ovens, personal computers, cell phones, and so on.

Participant 2: That's true. But it _____ that way. In the end,
15 (not, work out)

the new technology _____ more time than
16 (take)

it _____ us.
17 (give)

> *conference* = a meeting to discuss a subject. *moderator* = the person who directs a discussion.

 Go to the *Grammar Links* Website to find out more about technology and the pace of life.

2 Present Perfect Progressive—Form: What Have People Been Doing? I

Use the words in parentheses to write statements and questions. Use present perfect progressive. Complete the short answers. Use contractions with subject pronouns and with *not*.

Lauren, who is from a small town, has been visiting the big city where her friend Shelly lives. They planned to meet in the park at noon. It's now 12:30.

Lauren: Hi, Shelly. You look tired. <u>Have you been running</u> ?
1 (you / run)

Shelly: Yes, _____. I'm sorry I'm late.
2

Lauren: That's okay. _____.
3 (I / have / a good time)

Shelly: Really? _____?
4 (what / you / do)

Lauren: _____. It's been interesting.
5 (I / watch / all the people)

Shelly: Interesting? _____?
6 (what / the people / do)

_____?
7 (they / relax / in the park)

Lauren: No, _____. Everyone has been really busy. Do you
8

see that guy sitting on the bench over there?

Shelly: The one with the laptop computer? _____?
9 (he / work)

Lauren: Yes, _____.
10

_____.
11 (he / eat / lunch / at the same time)

_____.
12 (that woman / make / calls on her cell phone)

_____.
13 (everything / move / fast)

Except for the traffic. _____.
14 (the traffic / not / move / at all)

3 Contractions with Present Progressive, Present Perfect, and Present Perfect Progressive: Answering Questions

Listen and complete the answer to each question. Use *is* or *has*. Then listen again to check your answers.

1. Lisa <u>has</u>.
2. The stress <u>is</u>.
3. Someone else _____.
4. I think her father _____.
5. His job _____.
6. I'm not sure, but something _____.
7. The computer _____.
8. Something _____.
9. Another person _____.
10. Her job _____.
11. I don't know, but something _____.
12. The boredom _____.
13. I think his mother _____.
14. Jason _____.
15. The printer _____.
16. Everything _____.

Present Perfect and Present Perfect Progressive II
■ Present Perfect

FUNCTION

A. Actions and States at an Unspecified Time in the Past

1. Use the present perfect to talk about actions and states that occurred at an unspecified time in the past. The actions and states can be single or repeated:

We **have read** the paper.

I **have rewritten** the paper three times.

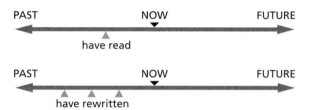

2. The present perfect indicates that the past action or state is connected to the present in some way. For example:

- It occurred recently.

  I**'ve** just **graduated** from college.

- The speaker thinks it could happen again.

  I**'ve played** tennis a few times.

- It is relevant to the present situation.

  I can do the job because I**'ve had** experience with those machines.

Time Expressions and Adverbs of Frequency

1. When used to talk about actions and states at an unspecified time in the past, the present perfect can occur with time expressions including:

- *Already*, *yet* (in questions and negatives), *so far*, and *still*.

  She has **already** graduated from college.

  I haven't finished **yet**.

- *Just*, *recently*, and *lately*, if the action or state was recent.

  We have **just** eaten in that restaurant.

2. The present perfect can also occur with adverbs of frequency, including *ever* (in questions and negatives); *never*, *sometimes*, *always*, etc.; and *once* (*three times*, etc.).

  Have you **ever** been to Spain?

  He has **never** eaten in that restaurant.

  I've been there **twice**.

(continued on next page)

B. Actions and States Continuing to the Present

Use the present perfect with a time expression of duration (see below) to talk about actions and states that began in the past and continue to the present.

They **have lived** here **for 10 years**.

PAST   NOW   FUTURE

10 years
lived here

Time Expressions of Duration

Time expressions of duration begin with *for*, *since*, or *all*. They tell how long an action or state has been occurring:

- *For* and *all* tell the length of time. (*For* can sometimes be omitted.)

I have taught **(for) five years**.

They've lived here **all their lives**.

PAST   NOW   FUTURE

5 years
taught

- *Since* tells the beginning of the time period.

He's been sick **since Monday**.

PAST   NOW   FUTURE

Monday
got sick

■ Present Perfect Progressive

FUNCTION

Actions Continuing to the Present

Use the present perfect progressive to talk about actions that began in the past and continue to the present. It often emphasizes that the action is ongoing.

She**'s been working**.

We**'ve been taking** the kids to school.

PAST   NOW   FUTURE

's been working

The present perfect progressive can occur with *for*, *since*, or *all* and with the other time expressions used with the present perfect (*recently*, *lately*, etc.). It is **not** used with adverbs of frequency.

I've been snowboarding **for three years**.

We've been singing in a band **since 1996**.

Joe**'s** been practicing a lot **lately**.
   NOT: Joe's been practicing ~~often/three times~~.

Present Perfect and Present Perfect Progressive II

4 **Present Perfect—Actions at Unspecified Past Times:** Free Time

A. Work in pairs. Student A uses the cues in List A to ask Student B questions. Then Student B uses the cues in List B to ask Student A questions. Use the present perfect and *ever* in each question.

Example: Student A: Have you ever been to Disneyland?
Student B: No, I haven't. I've never been to Disneyland. OR No, I haven't been there yet.
OR Yes, I have. I've been to Disneyland once (twice/many times).

List A	List B
1. be to Disneyland	9. go on a vacation in India
2. build a campfire	10. get lost in a forest
3. drive a sports car	11. ride a camel
4. eat Korean food	12. drink carrot juice
5. read a novel in English	13. write a poem
6. swim across a lake	14. sleep on a beach
7. meet a movie star	15. see a comet
8. take a photo of a sunrise	16. draw a picture of your own face

B. Now ask your partner questions again. Use the verbs in the cues, but change what follows the verbs.

Example: Student A: Have you ever been to Las Vegas?
Student B: No, I haven't. I've never been to Las Vegas. OR Yes, I have.
I've been to Las Vegas once (twice/many times).

5 **Present Perfect—Actions and States Continuing to the Present:** Tell Me About Yourself

A. Work in pairs. Ask each other these questions. When your partner answers *yes* to a question, ask a second question, using the present perfect, to find out *how long* the fact has been true about him or her. Your partner answers using the present perfect and *since, for,* or *all.*

Example: A: Do you live in Rockville? B: Yes, I do. A: How long have you lived here?
B: I've lived here since 2001/for three months/all my life.

1. Do you live in _____?
   (name of city or town)

2. Are you a student at _____?
   (name of your school)

3. Are you married?

4. Are you a parent?

5. Do you have a job?

6. Do you know _____?
   (name of another student)

7. Do you drive?

8. Do you own a car?

9. Do you play _____?
   (a game or sport)

10. Do you like _____?
    (a kind of music, a certain food, etc.)

B. Tell the class two things about your partner. Use the present perfect and time expressions of duration.

Example: *Leticia has lived in Rockville for three months.*

6 Using Present Perfect Progressive: What Have People Been Doing? II

For Student A.

Café

 A. Work in pairs to role-play two cell-phone conversations. First, Student A looks at the picture on this page. Then Student B looks at the picture on page A-1. Imagine that you have spent thirty minutes in the place shown in your picture. Your partner calls you and wants to know what's been happening. Tell your partner what all the people have been doing. You can use your imagination to add details. Use the present perfect progressive. Use time expressions in some of your sentences.

Example: Student A: Hello.
Student B: *Hi. Where are you? What have you been doing?*
Student A: *I'm in a café. I've been watching all the people here.*
Student B: *Who's there? What have they been doing?*
Student A: *Well, there are two women here. They've been eating. They've also been talking about their husbands for the last 10 minutes. And there's . . .*

B. Write five sentences about what the people in one of the pictures have been doing. Use a time expression in each sentence.

Example: *The women have been talking about their husbands for 10 minutes.*

Present Perfect Versus Present Perfect Progressive

FUNCTION

A. Talking About Completed Actions and States

To talk about completed actions and states, use the present perfect. Do not use the present perfect progressive.	She **has graduated** from college. **NOT**: She ~~has been graduating~~ from college. **I've studied** French several times. **NOT**: I've ~~been studying~~ French several times.

B. Talking About Actions and States Continuing to the Present

1. For **actions** continuing to the present:	
• Use the **present perfect** with a time expression of duration (*for, since, all*).	They**'ve watched** TV **since this morning**.
• Use the **present perfect progressive** alone or with a time expression of duration.	They**'ve been watching** TV. They**'ve been watching** TV **since this morning**.
With time expressions of duration, there is little difference in meaning between the present perfect and present perfect progressive.	We**'ve worked all day**. = We**'ve been working all day**.
2. For **states** continuing to the present, use only the **present perfect**. Progressives are not usually used with verbs that have stative meaning.	This summer **has seemed** hotter than usual. **NOT USUALLY**: This summer ~~has been seeming~~ hotter than usual.

GRAMMAR **HOT**SPOT!

1. With some verbs, verb + object indicates progress toward a result (*write a paper, read a book, build a house*). In these cases, use the present perfect progressive to talk about actions continuing to the present. The present perfect **cannot** be used.	She**'s been writing** a novel for five years. (end result = a written novel) **NOT**: She's ~~written~~ a novel for five years.
2. In sentences without time expressions of duration, the present perfect and present perfect progressive have different meanings: The present perfect talks about completed events; the present perfect progressive talks about events continuing to the present.	**I've studied** chemistry. (I studied it at some time in the past.) **I've been studying** chemistry. (I'm still studying it.)

Present Perfect Versus Present Perfect Progressive

7 Present Perfect and Present Perfect Progressive—Meaning: People, Places, and Paces

Work with a partner. Decide whether **a** or **b** is the correct explanation of the meaning of the first sentence. Circle the letter.

1. Bruce **has been working** on a report about the pace of life in big cities.

   a. He finished the report at some time in the past.

   b. He's still working on the report.

2. Greta **has worked** in a big city.

   a. She worked in a big city at some time in the past, but she doesn't work there now.

   b. She's still working in a big city.

3. Andy **has worked** all week on his paper about the pace of life in small towns.

   a. He finished his paper at some time in the past.

   b. He's still working on his paper.

4. Gail and Brad **have lived** in the country since they finished school.

   a. They lived in the country at some time in the past, but they don't live there now.

   b. They're still living in the country.

5. James **has been living** in a small town for two years.

   a. He lived in a small town at some time in the past, but he doesn't live there now.

   b. He's still living in a small town.

6. Lesley and I **have lived** on a farm.

   a. We lived on a farm at some time in the past, but we don't live there now.

   b. We're still living on a farm.

8 Present Perfect Versus Present Perfect Progressive: Living in the Past in the Present

The Amish people immigrated to North America in the 1700s. Since then, their way of life has changed very little. Read about an Amish couple on a typical day in their lives. Use the words in parentheses to complete the sentences. Use the present perfect progressive where possible. Use the present perfect elsewhere. Use contractions with *not*.

10 a.m.: Jacob is working in a field on his farm. He <u>has been working</u> since 8 a.m., but he
                                                 1 (work)

<u>hasn't finished</u> plowing the field yet. As usual, he is using horses to pull the plow.
                2 (not, finish)

Because Amish farmers don't often use modern technology, Jacob _____
                                               3 (not, ever, use)

a tractor. His twelve-year-old son, Amos, is with him in the field.

He _____ his father this morning. Over the years, Amos
         4 (help)

_____ his father many times. Amos _____
         5 (help)   6 (always, know)

that someday he, too, will be a farmer and farm in the traditional way.

Noon: Rebecca is working in the house. She _____ by hand all
                                                    7 (sew)

morning. She _____ a quilt
                  8 (make)

for the past few weeks, and so far she

_____ half of it. Rebecca's
         9 (finish)

young daughter Rachel _____
                              10 (be)

at her side all morning. For the past six months,

Rebecca _____ Rachel how
              11 (teach)

to sew. Although Rachel isn't ready to make a quilt yet,

she _____ three dresses, and she wears them often.
        12 (already, make)

8 p.m.:   The Fishers are returning home from a visit to friends. Jacob is driving them in a buggy pulled by a

horse. He _____ for half an hour. Jacob _____
                13 (drive)   14 (ride)

in a car several times in his life, but he _____ a car even once. He
                                              15 (not, drive)

_____ to own a car. He believes that cars and other forms of modern
    16 (not, ever, want)

technology make it too easy for family members to spend time away from one another. The Fishers

_____ to live their lives at a slow pace and keep their family close.
    17 (always, prefer)

 See the *Grammar Links* Website to learn more about the Amish and their way of life.

Present Perfect Versus Simple Past

FUNCTION

A. Talking About Actions and States Continuing to the Present

To talk about a past action or state that continues to the present, use the **present perfect**. (The simple past is used only for completed actions.)	I **have taught** for 10 years (I still teach.) *Compare*: I **taught** for 10 years. (I don't teach anymore.)

B. Talking About Completed Actions and States

1. **If you mention when** a completed past action or state occurred, you must use the **simple past**.

   I **went** to France **in 1999/a few years ago**. NOT: I **ve gone** to France in 1999/a few years ago.

2. **If you don't mention when** a completed past action or state occurred:

   - You can use either the simple past or present perfect if the action or state **can** occur again.

     I've **lived** in France. OR I **lived** in France.

     I've **skied** several times. OR I **skied** several times.

   - You must use the simple past if the action or state **cannot** occur again.

     My son really **enjoyed** his high school graduation. (The graduation can't occur again.)

     Marilyn Monroe **made** many movies. (She's dead—she can't make more movies.) *Compare*: Jennifer Lopez **has made** many movies. (She can make more movies.)

GRAMMAR **HOT**SPOT!

1. In talking about completed actions or states, the present perfect expresses a connection to the present. The simple past does not.

   I **have seen** the Picasso exhibit. (implies that the exhibit is still there) *Compare*: I **saw** the Picasso exhibit. (implies that the exhibit is finished)

2. The simple past can be used instead of the present perfect with many time expressions, including *just*, *already*, and *yet*.

   Did you **eat yet**? = **Have** you **eaten yet**?

   I **already ate**, but Carolyn **didn't**. = I've **already eaten**, but Carolyn **hasn't**.

Present Perfect Versus Simple Past

9 **Present Perfect Versus Simple Past:** Timelines

Use the words in parentheses and the information from the timelines to complete the sentences. Use present perfect or simple past.

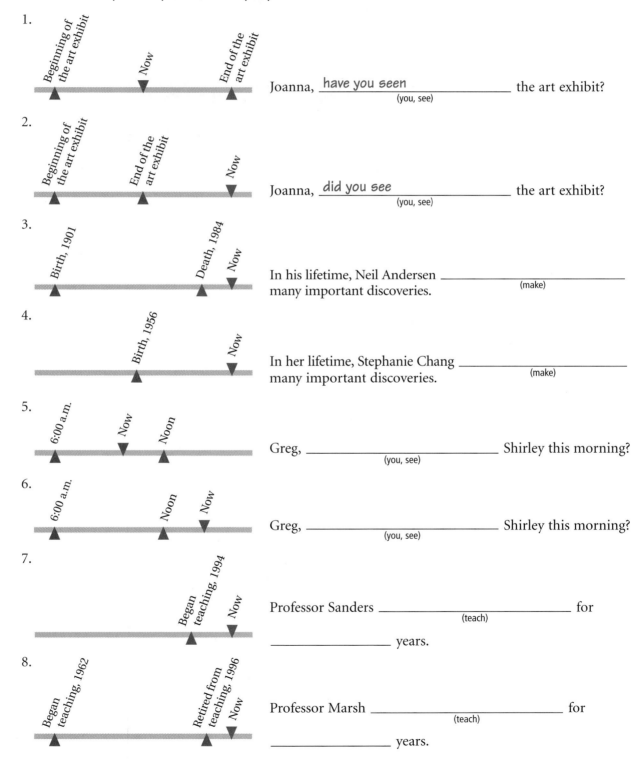

1. Joanna, <u>have you seen</u> the art exhibit?
   (you, see)

2. Joanna, <u>did you see</u> the art exhibit?
   (you, see)

3. In his lifetime, Neil Andersen _____ many important discoveries.
   (make)

4. In her lifetime, Stephanie Chang _____ many important discoveries.
   (make)

5. Greg, _____ Shirley this morning?
   (you, see)

6. Greg, _____ Shirley this morning?
   (you, see)

7. Professor Sanders _____ for
   (teach)
   _____ years.

8. Professor Marsh _____ for
   (teach)
   _____ years.

10 Present Perfect Versus Simple Past: Have You Ever . . . ?

Use the words in parentheses to complete the statements and questions. Use the present perfect where possible. Use the simple past elsewhere. Use contractions with subject pronouns and with *not*.

Born 1564   Born 1974
Died 1616

Tyler: <u>Have you ever been</u> to a Shakespeare play?
        1 (you, ever, be)

Annie: Yes, _____.
                        2

        I _____ several plays by Shakespeare.
            3 (see)

Tyler: How many plays _____?
                          4 (he, write)

Annie: I don't know exactly how many, but he _____ a lot of them.
                                                        5 (write)

Tyler: I _____ *Romeo and Juliet* in August.
            6 (saw)

        _____ it?
        7 (you, ever, see)

Annie: I _____ the play yet, but I _____
            8 (not, see)   9 (see)

        the movie.

Tyler: When?

Annie: I _____ it in a theater a few years ago. Actually, I
            10 (see)

        _____ it on video several times since then, too. Leonardo DiCaprio
        11 (watch)

        _____ the part of Romeo in the movie. I
        12 (play)

        _____ in love with him since I first saw it.
        13 (be)

Tyler: _____ many movies?
        14 (Leonardo DiCaprio, make)

Annie: He _____ enough for me. I hope he makes another one soon!
            15 (not, make)

11 Present Perfect and Simple Past: Telling About Your Experiences

A. Write a paragraph about four exciting, interesting, or unusual experiences you have had. Use the first sentence in the example. Then write two sentences about each experience. In the first, use the present perfect to tell what experience you have had. In the second, use the simple past to tell when it happened.

Example:

Several of the experiences in my life have been exciting, interesting, or unusual. For example, I have been to New York City. I went there when I was sixteen years old. Also, I have seen a World Cup soccer game. It was in Japan in 2002. . . .

See the *Grammar Links* Website for a complete model paragraph for this assignment.

B. Work in small groups. Read your paragraph to your group. Have the students in the group had very similar or very different experiences?

> Check your progress! Go to the Self-Test for
> Chapter 3 on the *Grammar Links* Website.

Chapter 4

Past Perfect and Past Perfect Progressive

Introductory Task: New Experiences

A. Sam left his country to come to the United States last year. Since then, he has had many new experiences. For each of his new experiences, write a follow-up sentence in the past perfect (*had* + past participle of the verb—e.g., *had been*). Use *never* and *before*.

1. Last year, Sam was away from his family. _He had never been away from his family before._

2. In August, he flew in an airplane. _He had never flown in an airplane before._

3. In September, he drank cranberry juice. _____

4. In December, he saw snow. _____

5. Last winter, he wore a heavy coat. _____

6. In February, he went skiing. _____

7. In March, he ate granola. _____

8. In May, he rode a horse. _____

B. Now write pairs of sentences about three new experiences of your own. Follow the pattern in Part A.

Example: _Last year, I tasted caviar. I had never tasted caviar before._

1. _____

2. _____

3. _____

Report to the class about your most interesting new experience.

> *granola* = a mixture of oats with dried fruits and nuts, often used as a breakfast cereal. *caviar* = the eggs of fish prepared with salt.

Past Perfect and Past Perfect Progressive

FORM

A. Affirmative Statements

PAST PERFECT			PAST PERFECT PROGRESSIVE		
SUBJECT	*HAD* + PAST PARTICIPLE*		SUBJECT	*HAD* + *BEEN* + PRESENT PARTICIPLE*	
I	**had eaten**	before she arrived.	I	**had been eating**	before she arrived.
Emily	**had eaten**	before she arrived.	He	**had been eating**	before she arrived.

(See Appendix 7 for the past participles of irregular verbs.)

(See Appendix 3 for spelling rules for the *-ing* form of the verb.)

B. Negative Statements

PAST PERFECT			PAST PERFECT PROGRESSIVE		
SUBJECT	*HAD* + *NOT* + PAST PARTICIPLE*		SUBJECT	*HAD* + *NOT* + *BEEN* + PRESENT PARTICIPLE*	
He	**had not studied**	that yet.	I	**had not been studying**	before dinner.
We	**had not studied**	that yet.	He	**had not been studying**	before dinner.

C. *Yes/No* Questions and Short Answers

PAST PERFECT		PAST PERFECT PROGRESSIVE	
QUESTIONS	SHORT ANSWERS	QUESTIONS	SHORT ANSWERS
Had they **done** that before she arrived?	Yes, they **had**. No, they **hadn't**.	**Had** you **been doing** that before she arrived?	Yes, I **had** (**been**). No, I **hadn't** (**been**).

D. *Wh-* Questions

Wh- Questions About the Subject

PAST PERFECT	PRESENT PERFECT PROGRESSIVE
Who had done that?	**Who had been doing** that?
Which student had done that?	**Which students had been doing** that?

Other Wh- Questions

PAST PERFECT	PAST PERFECT PROGRESSIVE
What had Joe **done** before she arrived?	**What had** Joe **been doing** before she arrived?
Where had they **gone**?	**Where had** they **been going**?

*CONTRACTIONS

I/he/she/you/we/they + had → I'd/he'd/she'd/you'd/we'd/they'd
had + not → hadn't

Past Perfect and Past Perfect Progressive

1 Past Perfect—Form: An Exchange Student—A Different Place

Use the words in parentheses to complete the statements and questions in the past perfect. Complete the short answers. Use contractions with subject pronouns and with *not*.

Jim: Hey, Dan. I heard that you spent last year as an exchange student. Tell me about your

experiences. __Had you studied_____ the language before you left?
           1 (you, study)

Dan: Yes, _____. I _____ it pretty well. And all
        2   3 (learn)

the students in my group _____ a lot of books about our host
                  4 (read)

country. But most of us _____ in any country with a really different
              5 (not, live)

culture before. We experienced some differences there that we _____
                      6 (not, be)

aware of before we left the United States.

Jim: What do you mean?

Dan: Well, until I went away, I _____ the importance of cultural differences
            7 (not, understand)

in how people think about time. By the time I left, I _____ lots of
                  8 (have)

experiences that taught me a different way of thinking about time.

Jim: Really? What kind of experiences?

Dan: Well, for example, one night I was really worried about being late. Earlier that day some students

_____ me and another American to a party at eight o'clock. The two
        9 (invite)

of us _____ lost on the way to the party, and when we got there it
      10 (got)

was almost nine.

Jim: _____ by then?
    11 (the other guests, already, arrive)

Dan: No, _____. The host _____ getting ready
      12   13 (not, finish)

for the party yet. He was really surprised that we _____ so early.
                    14 (come)

By the end of the year, he _____ me a lot about his culture's time
              15 (teach)

customs. And now that I'm back home, I'm experiencing culture shock here. I'm always late!

> *exchange student* = a person who studies in another country.

2 **Past Perfect Progressive—Form:** Two Views on the Pace of Life

Use the words in parentheses to complete the statements and questions. Use the past perfect progressive. Complete the short answer. Use contractions with subject pronouns and with *not*.

Frank: Last summer, I went with Paul to visit his family in the country. Before that, Paul

     <u>had been staying</u> in the city with me.
              1 (stay)

     We <u>'d been rushing</u> around day and night.
              2 (rush)

     We _____ a great time.
            3 (have)

Paul: Well, Frank _____ a great time, but I
                 4 (have)

     _____ it that much. The pace of life in the city was
           5 (not, enjoy)

     too fast for me.

Frank: Anyway, we took a bus to the country and back. Going there was okay, but the trip back

     was terrible because the bus was late.

Nuria: How long _____ by the time the bus came?
              6 (you, wait)

Frank: We _____ forever—two whole hours!
             7 (wait)

Paul: That's not true! We _____ long at all—only two hours.
               8 (not, wait)

     But Frank _____ the whole time about being late.
              9 (worry)

Nuria: What about you, Paul? _____?
                       10 (you, worry)

Paul: No, _____. My cousins _____
            11   12 (sit)

     with us and _____ to us. It was a great, relaxing afternoon!
              13 (talk)

Past Perfect

FUNCTION

A. Overview

Use the past perfect to talk about a past action or state that occurred before another past action or state or before a specified time in the past. (Note that the action or state can be repeated.)

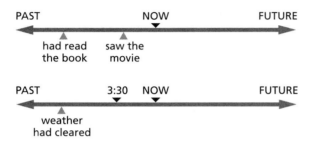

- The later past action or state is expressed with a simple past verb, often in a sentence with a time clause.

  (For information on time clauses, see Chapter 2, Grammar Briefing 3, page 31.)

- The two past actions or states don't have to be in the same sentence.

She **had read** the book (several times) before she saw the movie.

By 3:30, the weather **had cleared**.

                     time clause
She **had been** there three times <u>before he **went**</u>.

He **didn't recognize** her. She **had changed**.

B. Past Perfect in Sentences with Time Clauses

1. When the time clause begins with *before* or *until*, the verb in the main clause expresses the earlier action and is in the past perfect.

      earlier action   later action
   <u>We'**d lived** there</u> **before/until** <u>it **became** too expensive</u>.

2. When the time clause begins with *after*, the verb in the time clause expresses the earlier action and is in the past perfect.

             later action   earlier action
   <u>We **got** to the theater</u> **after** <u>the movie **had started**</u>.

3. When the time clause begins with *when*, either verb may express the earlier action and be in the past perfect.

             later action   earlier action
   When <u>we **got** there</u>, <u>he **had eaten**</u>.

           earlier action   later action
   When <u>he **had eaten**</u>, <u>he left</u>.

(continued on next page)

B. Past Perfect in Sentences with Time Clauses (continued)

4. With *before*, *until*, and *after*, the simple past is often used in place of the past perfect, because these time expressions make the order of the actions clear.

He **studied** the language before he left. =
He **had studied** the language before he left.

With *when*, the past perfect is needed, to make the order of the actions clear.

When they went to Rome, they **had gone** to Paris.
(first Paris, then Rome)

When they **had gone** to Rome, they went to Paris.
(first Rome, then Paris)

C. Time Expressions and Adverbs of Frequency

1. Time expressions such as *by/up to/before/until then* (*that time*, *three o'clock*, *the next day*, *2004*, etc.) are used in sentences with the past perfect to specify the later time.

We had eaten **by eight o'clock**.

Had you been there **before then**?

2. The past perfect is also used with:

    • Other time expressions including *already*, *just*, *yet* (in questions and negatives), and *still*.

We had **already** eaten by that time.

    • Adverbs of frequency including *ever* (in questions and negatives); *never*, *sometimes*, *always*, etc.; and *three times* (*many times*, etc.).

Had Jon **ever** driven there alone?

GRAMMAR **HOT**SPOT!

Use the past perfect only when an action or state occurred before another action, state, or time in the past. When there is no second action, state, or time, do **not** use the past perfect.

I **had given** him the key **before he left**.

I **had given** him the key **by then**.

Last night I **gave** him the key.
   NOT: Last night I ~~had given~~ him the key.

Past Perfect

3 **Past Perfect and Simple Past: "Rip Van Winkle"—A Different Time**

A. Use the words in parentheses to complete the sentences in the simple past and past perfect. Use contractions with *not*.

"Rip Van Winkle" is a well-known American story set in the late 1700s. While Rip Van Winkle was out hunting one day, he drank a strange liquor and fell asleep. When he woke up, he thought that he had slept for one night. But when he looked around, he discovered that things had changed. . . .

1. Rip's gun <u>had gotten</u> old and rusty, so it <u>didn't work</u>
                    (get)   (not, work)

   anymore.

2. His faithful dog _____ no longer beside him.
                               (be)

   It _____.
      (run away)

3. He _____ at his beard. It _____
         (look)   (grow)

   long and gray.

4. The clothes worn by the people in his village _____ strange
                                              (seem)

   to him because fashions _____.
                               (change)

5. He _____ surprised at the terrible condition of his house.
                (be)

   It _____.
      (fall apart)

6. His children _____, so he _____ them.
                (grow up)   (not, recognize)

7. His daughter _____ a child in her arms. Rip
                     (have)

   _____ a grandfather.
         (become)

8. His wife _____ there any longer.
              (not, be)

   She _____.
      (die)

9. His friends and neighbors

   _____ him,
      (forget)

   so they _____
            (think)

   he was a stranger.

10. The United States _____ its independence.
      (win)

    It _____ no longer a British colony.
      (be)

11. Finally, Rip _____ that he _____
      (discover)   (be)

    asleep for 20 years.

Check out the *Grammar Links* Website to learn more about the story of Rip Van Winkle.

B. Write a one-paragraph story about the experiences of someone like Rip who awoke after sleeping for a long time. You can write a story that you know or make one up. Use the past perfect and the simple past.

See the *Grammar Links* Website for a model story for this assignment.

4 **Past Perfect and Simple Past; Combining Sentences:** A New Experience

For each pair of sentences in this story, decide the order of events. Then combine the pair into one sentence using the time word shown, the simple past, and the past perfect. The order of events determines which verb is past perfect.

1. after: Sandra decided to study abroad. ___1___

             She applied to the university. ___2___

   After Sandra had decided to study abroad, she applied to the university.
   OR Sandra applied to the university after she had decided to study abroad.

2. before: She didn't fly in an airplane. _____

            She traveled to her host country. _____

3. until: She didn't experience another culture. _____

            She went to her host country. _____

4. before: She adapted to the customs of the new culture. _____

            She made a few embarrassing mistakes. _____

5. after: She learned the language well. _____

            She studied hard and practiced often. _____

6. when: She lived in the country for a while. _____

            She became more flexible. _____

7. after: She understood her own culture much better. _____

            She stayed in her host country for a few months. _____

---

adapt = change oneself so as to be right for a situation. *flexible* = being able or willing to change.

---

5 **Past Perfect and Simple Past—Order of Actions:** Place and Time

 A. Listen to the sentences once for the main ideas. Then listen again and circle the letter of the state or action that occurred earlier.

1. (a.) Robert Levine taught at a university in the United States.

   b. He went to Brazil to teach as a visiting professor.

2. a. Professor Levine went to Brazil.

   b. He was aware of differences in time customs between the North American and Brazilian cultures.

3. a. The professor didn't realize that the cultural differences were so confusing.

   b. He arrived at the Brazilian university.

4. a. Many of the students came to class.

   b. He began to lecture at 10 a.m.

5. a. Professor Levine's students got ready to leave.

   b. The class ended.

6. a. Quite a few of the students asked questions and listened to him.

   b. The class ended.

7. a. Professor Levine was in Brazil for a while.

   b. He became interested in studying cultural differences in people's sense of time and in the pace of life.

8. a. He began to study differences in the pace of life.

   b. He compared North American and Brazilian ideas about what it means to be on time or to be late.

9. a. Professor Levine thought a lot about how to measure the pace of life.

   b. He and his students began making observations in cities all over the world.

10. a. They measured the walking and working speeds of people in many cities.

    b. Professor Levine analyzed the differences.

11. a. He evaluated the data.

    b. He found that there were differences in the pace of life on every level.

 See the *Grammar Links* Website for more information about cultural differences in the pace of life and people's sense of time.

B. In his book *A Geography of Time*, Professor Levine has described cultural differences in the pace of life and in the way that people think about time. We often don't realize that people in another culture might not think about time in the same way that we do. Have you ever been confused by a different culture's sense of time? What happened? What had you thought before? What hadn't you realized until that happened? What did you learn about yourself and your own culture? Write a paragraph. Use the past perfect three or more times.

Example: *People in different cultures have different ideas about the best ways to use their time. I hadn't realized this until I came to the United States. I had been here for only a few days when I . . .*

6 Past Perfect Versus Simple Past: Speed

Use the words in parentheses to complete the sentences. Use the simple past or the past perfect. In cases in which both tenses are possible, use the past perfect.

1800   1860

It was around the year 1800 that Rip Van Winkle woke up and discovered that he had been asleep for 20 years.

After Rip ___had woken up___ , he ___noticed___
　　　　　1 (wake up)　　　　　　　　　　2 (notice)

some kinds of changes, but he probably ___didn't notice___ any
　　　　　　　　　　　　　　　　　3 (not, notice)

technological changes. Not much technological change _____
　　　　　　　　　　　　　　　　　　　　　　　　　4 (happen)

by that time in history. Before the beginning of the 1800s, nothing

_____ faster than the speed of a sailing ship or a horse.
5 (move)

After 1800, many changes _____ in the United States.
6 (happen)

By the mid-1800s, steamboats and trains _____ operating in
7 (begin)

many parts of the country. By 1860, the speed of transportation _____
8 (increase)

by twenty times. As a result, Americans of the 1860s _____ much
9 (travel)

more rapidly to distant places.

Communications _____ much faster by 1860, too.
10 (get)

In 1800, it _____ six weeks for a message from St. Louis,
11 (take)

Missouri, to reach Washington, D.C. However, by the 1850s, the telegraph

_____ an important means of communication. So, in the 1860s,
12 (become)

a message from St. Louis _____ Washington in a few seconds.
13 (reach)

To learn more about these changes, go to the *Grammar Links* Website.

7 Using Simple Past and Past Perfect: Milestones

Childhood is often measured by important accomplishments or "milestones": starting
school, learning how to read and write, learning how to ride a bike and play sports,
getting a first job, traveling alone for the first time, graduating, and so on.

1. Think about important milestones in your childhood and teenage years and the
ages at which you reached them. Mark three of these milestones, including the ages,
on the timeline.

BIRTH   NOW

2. Work with a partner. Tell your partner about the milestones you marked. Use the
simple past and the past perfect. Answer questions that your partner has about your
milestones. Then reverse roles.

Example: I started first grade when I was six. Before then, I had already learned how
to count and write my name. I hadn't learned to read yet. When I was
eight years old, I began playing soccer. By the time I was 10, I had become
a very good soccer player. . . .

3. Report to the class about what you learned about your partner.

Past Perfect Progressive; Past Perfect Progressive Versus Past Perfect

FUNCTION

A. Past Perfect Progressive

1. Use the past perfect progressive to talk about past actions that began before and continued to another past action or state or a specified time in the past. Use the simple past for the second action or state.

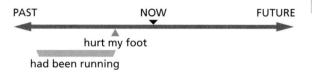

PAST	NOW	FUTURE

hurt my foot

had been running

I **had been running** a lot until I **hurt** my foot.

I **had been sleeping** late every day. But then I got a new work schedule.

At 3:00, she **had been talking** on the phone for five hours!

2. Sentences with the past perfect progressive often include a time clause. The time clause can start with *before*, *when*, or *until*. The main clause verb is in the past perfect progressive; the time clause verb is in the simple past.

   (For information on time clauses, see Chapter 2, Grammar Briefing 3, page 31.)

                                                    time clause

She **had been sleeping when** he arrived.

                                                    time clause

He **hadn't been studying until** he failed that test.

Time Expressions

Time expressions used with the past perfect (see Grammar Briefing 2, page 66) can also be used with the past perfect progressive.

Had you been planning your vacation **yet**?

I'd **already** been having problems with the car.

B. Past Perfect Progressive Versus Past Perfect

1. The past perfect progressive is used to talk about past actions that were **in progress** up to another past action, state, or time.

   Remember! For past states (i.e., with verbs that have stative meaning), do not use the progressive. Use the past perfect.

He'**d been doing** his homework when they arrived. (homework was in progress up to the time they arrived)

The summer **had seemed** hot before August. **NOT**: The summer ~~had been seeming~~ hot before August.

2. The past perfect is used to talk about past actions or states that were **completed** before another past action, state, or time.

He'**d done** his homework when they arrived. (homework was completed before they arrived)

Past Perfect Progressive; Past Perfect Versus Past Perfect Progressive

8 Past Perfect Progressive and Time Clauses: Once Upon a Time: Sleeping Beauty

Use the words in parentheses to complete the story. Use the simple past and the past perfect progressive. If the past perfect progressive is not possible, use the past perfect. Use contractions with subject pronouns and with *not*.

A beautiful baby girl was born to a king and queen.

Soon after her birth, an evil fairy put a curse on the

little princess. The princess <u>had been living</u>
_____1 (live)

happily in a big castle with her parents until they

<u>went</u>_____ away for a day.
    2 (go)

Then she was free to do as she wished.

She _____ the castle
            3 (explore)

for hours when she _____ to go into the tower.
                          4 (decide)

Until she _____ to the top of the tower,
              5 (climb)

she _____ about the little room there. She found an old
        6 (not, know)

woman in the room. The woman _____ thread when the
                                      7 (spin)

princess _____ in. The moment the princess pricked her
              8 (come)

finger on the old woman's spindle, the curse came true: The princess and everyone else in

the castle fell into a deep sleep. Handsome princes _____
                                                          9 (try)

to rescue Sleeping Beauty for a long time before the curse finally

_____. She _____ asleep
        10 (end)   11 (be)

for a hundred years before a brave and charming prince _____
                                                              12 (ride)

into the castle and _____ her. He kissed her, and she and
                        13 (find)

everyone else woke up.

---

curse = a promise that something bad will happen. *spindle* = a sharp tool for winding thread.

---

9 **Past Perfect Versus Past Perfect Progressive:** At the Stroke of Midnight

Use the verbs in parentheses to complete the story. Use past perfect progressive where possible. Use past perfect elsewhere.

1. When Cinderella's cruel stepmother came home, she saw Cinderella on the floor on her

   hands and knees. Part of the floor was clean and wet. When her stepmother came home,

   Cinderella __had been scrubbing__ the floor.

(scrub)

2. Cinderella's mean stepsisters were very happy because the prince __had invited__

(invite)

   them to a ball at his castle.

3. Soon after the stepsisters had left for the ball, Cinderella's fairy godmother appeared and looked

   closely at her. Cinderella's eyes had tears in them. Cinderella _____.

(cry)

4. After the fairy godmother _____ her a beautiful dress, Cinderella

(give)

   was able to go to the ball, too.

5. Cinderella was shocked when the clock struck midnight.

   Long before, she _____ the time.

(forget about)

6. Cinderella rushed home, but then she

   realized that she had only one shoe. She

   _____ the other one.

(lose)

7. Finally, the prince found Cinderella. He

   _____ her since he met her at the ball.

(search for)

8. After they were married, Cinderella lived in the castle. On his birthday, the prince

   went into the kitchen, where he saw Cinderella stirring flour, butter, sugar, and eggs.

   She _____ a cake for him.

(make)

9. Cinderella looked into the prince's library. He was holding a pen and looking thoughtfully at a

   piece of paper with a few words on it. The prince _____ a poem for her.

(write)

10. When the fairy godmother visited Cinderella and the prince recently, they thanked her and told

    her that they _____ very happily since their marriage.

(live)

Check your progress! Go to the Self-Test for Chapter 4 on the *Grammar Links* Website.

Wrap-up Activities

1 Time for Life: EDITING

Correct the 13 errors in the article. There are errors in verb forms and tenses. Some errors can be corrected in more than one way. The first error is corrected for you.

For many years, John Robinson ~~had~~ has been interested in how people use their time. He is now the director of the Americans' Use of Time Project. Robinson has first asked Americans to take part in a use-of-time survey in 1965. He has been repeating the surveys three times since then. Robinson has used the results of his surveys to answer two questions: How has Americans been spending their time recently? How they've been feeling about it?

Ten thousand people had taken part in the 1995 use-of-time survey. In 1995, the study participants have wrote down their activities in a "time diary" every day. In addition, they reported on their feelings about their amount of free time.

After the participants had completed the 1995 survey, Robinson had analyzed the results and compared them to previous survey results. He found some interesting changes in people's use of time. Americans actually spent less time working in 1995 than in 1985. By 1995, they have gotten more free time. However, many people believed that they had less time, and they felt more rushed and stressed. In 1997, Robinson has published a book, *Time for Life*, about the results of his surveys.

Why does it seem that we have so little time for life nowadays? According to Robinson, there are two reasons for this. First, since 1965, we spend more and more of our free time watching television. Most of us usually say that television is unnecessary or a waste of time. But in recent years we had spent more time on it than any other free time activity. Second, since Robinson did his first survey, we have been having many more opportunities and choices. We have been feeling more rushed because we want to do everything.

2 A Question Challenge—WRITING

Work in teams of two. Write questions for each of the answers below. The questions must be logical and grammatically correct. Each team must write at least three questions for each answer. The winning team is the one that writes the most correct questions within the time limit set by your teacher.

1. They've made new friends.

    What have the students done since the beginning of the semester?
    Why haven't Christina and Patrick been coming to our parties?
    Why are the visitors so happy?

2. Since I was a child.

3. Yes, they have many times.

4. For a very short time.

5. I've been setting my alarm clock.

6. Yes, she has been, but she hasn't been enjoying it.

7. We'd gotten lost.

8. Everything had changed.

9. Yes, he already had.

10. She'd been falling asleep.

11. No, when we arrived, they'd already finished.

3 Things Have Changed Since I Was a Child—SPEAKING

Step 1 Working in small groups, choose three areas that interest you. For example, you might choose from science, technology, communications, transportation, business, politics, art, movies, music, fashion, and sports.

Step 2 For each area, think of changes that have happened in your lifetimes. Talk about changes that occurred before some time in the past and changes that started in the past.

Example: *Most people hadn't used the Internet before the 1990s. The Internet has gotten much bigger and more important.*

Be sure to mention changes that are continuing now.

Example: *People have been finding new ways to use the Internet.*

Step 3 Make notes on the changes—past and ongoing—in each area that you discuss.

Step 4 Report to the class about the changes in those areas. Refer to your notes as necessary. Use sentences with the past perfect, past perfect progressive, present perfect, and present perfect progressive.

> When you sit with a nice girl for two hours, it seems like two minutes; when you sit on a hot stove for two minutes, it seems like two hours. That's relativity. —ALBERT EINSTEIN
>
> *Sad hours seem long.* —*William Shakespeare, Romeo and Juliet*

Have you ever had the feeling that time was racing by, dragging very slowly, moving in slow motion, or standing still? What caused this? Were you happy, sad, bored, busy, waiting, cold, hot, sick, nervous, frightened, or in love? Or have you ever had the feeling that you had experienced an event before it happened, even though you knew it wasn't possible? (This kind of experience is called *déjà vu.*)

Write a paragraph about a situation in which you experienced a changed feeling about the passage of time. Include the present perfect, past perfect, and past perfect progressive in your paragraph. Then read your paragraph to the class.

Example:

I'd been out on a date with a girl I really liked. We'd been having a very nice time, but the evening was passing much too quickly for me. It had been snowing all night, and I was driving home on a snowy street. Suddenly, a tree appeared right in front the car. I stamped on the brake, but the car kept moving forward. Time seemed to stretch out in slow motion while the car slid into the tree. With a big jolt, the car hit the tree, I broke the steering wheel with my chin, and time jumped back to normal. I've never forgotten that experience.

 See the *Grammar Links* Website for another model for this paragraph.

Future; Phrasal Verbs; Tag Questions

TOPIC FOCUS
Travel

UNIT OBJECTIVES

■ **expressing future time with *will* and *be going to***
(Your tour *will* be interesting. The guide *is going to* show you the museum.)

■ **expressing future time with the present progressive, the simple present, and *be about to***
(Lisa *is touring* the Capitol on Tuesday afternoon. Her tour *starts* at 1:00. It's 1:00 now, and the tour *is about to* start.)

■ **the future progressive with *will* and *be going to***
(The plane *will be taking off* soon. It *is going to be leaving* on time.)

■ **the future perfect with *will* and *be going to***
(The spacecraft *will have reached* Mars by the end of this month. You *are going to have seen* new photos of the planet before the end of the year.)

■ **the future perfect progressive with *will* and *be going to***
They *will have been preparing* for their trip. They *are going to have been traveling* for a long time by then.)

■ **phrasal verbs and verb–preposition combinations**
(An explorer *set off* for the South Pole. He *was looking for* adventure.)

■ **tag questions**
(Columbus was an explorer, *wasn't he?*)

Grammar in Action

🎧 Reading and Listening: Travel Bulletin Board

Read and listen to the advertisements and announcements.

TRAVEL BULLETIN BOARD

1 Outdoor Adventures Unlimited:

How **are** you **going to spend** your next summer vacation? We specialize in planning trips to national parks. You **will take** the outdoor vacation of your dreams at Mesa Verde or Yellowstone. Call us at 1-800-OUT-DOOR.

2 Tri-City Recreation Department:

We've planned the ultimate shopping escape for you. A bus **is taking** a group to the Mall of America next Saturday. When you **see** the mall, you**'re going to be** amazed. It's big enough to hold seven baseball stadiums or 32 Boeing 747s! The bus **leaves** at 7:00 on Saturday morning and **returns** at midnight.

3 CULTURAL TRAVEL, INC:

You **will experience** the best in New York or Washington, D.C., when you **take** a city museum vacation with us.

Tours **are departing** on June 18th and July 7th.

For further details, call 222-694-3000.

4 Travel Lecture—Exploration: On April 24th a noted space-science researcher **will talk** about a plan for the exploration of Mars. He believes that we **are going to send** successful human missions to Mars soon by using the strategies of past explorers like the explorers of the Americas and Antarctica. The lecture **begins** at 8:00 p.m. in Olin Hall.

5 Destination Mars:
The earth seems pretty crowded these days, doesn't it? In the years to come, it **is going to be getting** even more crowded. What does this mean for the 21st century? **Will** we **have found** a solution to our population problems before the end of the century? Don't worry: The answer is yes, thanks to Mars! By the end of the 21st century we **will have built** colonies on Mars, and in the 22nd century many people **will be living** there. Check out this website: www.marssociety.org.

> *mission* = an assignment that a person or group is sent to complete. *strategy* = a plan of action. *colony* = a group of people who settle in a distant place.

Think About Grammar

The boldfaced verbs in the advertisements and announcements express a future time meaning.

A. Work with a partner. Look at the boldfaced verbs in 1, 2, 3, and 4.

1. In 1–4, four different forms are used to express the future. Give an example of a verb in each form. *are going to spend*

    _____

    _____

    _____

2. a. Which two of the examples also can express another time?

    _____

    _____

    b. What other time do they express? _____

B. Look at the boldfaced verbs in 5.

1. Which two verbs express actions that will be ongoing at some time in the future?

    _____

    _____

2. Which two verbs express actions that will have happened before a time in the future?

    _____

    _____

Chapter 5

Future Time

Introductory Task: Vacation Plans and Predictions

A. Listen to the first part of the conversation. The speakers are talking about their future vacation **plans**. Then listen again and fill in the blanks with the verbs you hear.

A: This summer I ___'m taking___ an outdoor vacation with my family.
1

We ___'re going to go___ to a national park in Colorado.
2

B: That sounds great! When _____ you _____?
3

A: We _____ there on June 15th. What are your plans?
4

B: I _____ to Washington, D.C., in July. I _____
5   6

the National Gallery of Art and other museums there.

A: _____ your brother _____ to Washington with you?
7

B: Oh, no! He hates museums. He _____ his vacation at a shopping mall.
8

B. Listen to the second part of the conversation. The speakers are making **predictions** about their vacations. Then listen again and fill in the blanks with the verbs you hear.

A: A vacation in a shopping mall? Do you think he ___'ll have___ a good time?
1

B: It's not just any mall. It's the Mall of America. It has lots of things to do for fun, so I think

he ___'s going to enjoy___ it. And he _____ cool, too,
2   3

because the mall _____ air-conditioned. In Washington, the weather
4

_____ probably _____ hot and humid in July.
5

A: Yeah, but Washington is interesting. You _____ have a great trip!
6

Forms used to talk about the future include *will*, *be going to*, and the present progressive.

Which two of these forms are used to talk about future plans?

_____   _____

Which two are used to make predictions?

_____   _____

Will and *Be Going To* I

FORM

A. Affirmative Statements

WILL				BE GOING TO		
SUBJECT	WILL + BASE FORM OF VERB*			SUBJECT	BE + GOING TO + BASE FORM OF VERB*	
I	**will leave**	tomorrow.		I	**am going to leave**	tomorrow.

B. Negative Statements

WILL				BE GOING TO		
SUBJECT	WILL + NOT + BASE FORM OF VERB*			SUBJECT	BE + NOT + GOING TO + BASE FORM OF VERB*	
We	**will not leave**	in July.		We	**are not going to leave**	in July.

C. *Yes/No* Questions and Short Answers

WILL			BE GOING TO	
QUESTIONS	SHORT ANSWERS		QUESTIONS	SHORT ANSWERS
Will Jill **leave** this summer?	Yes, she **will**.		**Is** Jill **going to leave** this summer?	Yes, she **is**.
	No, she **won't**.			No, she **isn't**.

D. *Wh-* Questions

Wh- Questions About the Subject

WILL	BE GOING TO*
Who will leave next year?	**Who is going to leave** next year?

Other *Wh-* Questions

WILL	BE GOING TO*
When will they **leave**?	**When are** they **going to leave**?

---

*CONTRACTIONS: *WILL*

I/he/she/it/we/you/they + will →
  I'll/he'll/she'll/it'll/we'll/you'll/they'll
will + not → won't

*CONTRACTIONS: *BE GOING TO*

I + am + going to → I'm going to
he/she/it + is + going to → he's/she's/it's going to
we/you/they + are + going to → we're/you're/they're going to
is + not + going to → isn't going to
are + not + going to → aren't going to
he/she/it + is + not + going to → he's/she's/it's not going to
  OR he/she/it isn't going to
we/you/they + are + not + going to → we're/you're/they're not going to
  OR we/you/they aren't going to
wh- word + be going to → who's going to, etc.

Will and *Be Going To* I

1   *Will*—Form: An Outdoor Vacation—Mesa Verde National Park

Use *will* and the words in parentheses to complete the statements and questions.
Complete the short answer. Use contractions with subject pronouns and with *not*.

Four Corners Heritage Tours

Durango, CO 81301

Utah   Colorado

Mesa Verde ? • *Durango*

Arizona   New Mexico

Thank you for making a reservation to tour the ancient Native American

village, or "pueblo," at Mesa Verde National Park. We promise that you

__won't be_____ disappointed. Your tour __will be_____
         1 (not, be)   2 (be)

an educational and enjoyable experience—one that you _____!
                                                               3 (not, forget)

This information sheet answers the questions that our guests frequently ask.

Q: At what time _____?
                                       4 (the tour, begin)

A: The tour _____ at 8 a.m. The driver
                           5 (begin)

_____ for you, so please be ready. The trip from Durango
                           6 (not, wait)

to Mesa Verde _____ more than an hour.
                                7 (not, take)

Q: _____ small?
                               8 (my tour group, be)

A: Yes, _____. There _____ more
                        9   10 (not, be)

than eight people in your group.

Q: How long _____?
                               11 (the tour, last)

A: About four hours. You _____ plenty of time to
                               12 (have)

explore Mesa Verde's "cliff dwellings"—homes built high on the sides of steep,

flat-topped mountains.

Native Americans = people who were living in the Americas before the arrival of Europeans.

 To learn more about Mesa Verde and other national parks, go to the *Grammar Links* Website.

2 *Be Going To*—Form: A Shopping Vacation—The Mall of America

Use *be going to* and the words in parentheses to complete the statements and questions. Complete the short answer. Use contractions with subject pronouns.

Roger: Hey, Nick. I __'m going to go__ on a one-day vacation
　　　　　　　　　　　　　　1 (go)

next Saturday. Do you want to come along?

Nick: Where __are you going to go__?
　　　　　　　　　　　2 (you, go)

Roger: Believe it or not, I _____ the day at the
　　　　　　　　　　　　　　　3 (spend)

Mall of America, near Minneapolis. You should come.

It _____ a lot of fun.
　　　4 (be)

Nick: I don't believe it. Why _____ so far just to go
　　　　　　　　　　　　　　　5 (you, travel)

to a mall? _____ there?
　　　　　　　　6 (you, shop)

Roger: Yes, _____. Of course. The Mall of America is
　　　　　　7

the biggest indoor mall in the United States—it has over 500 stores.

Nick: Over 500 stores? No, no way. I hate shopping.

I _____ with you.
　　8 (not, come)

Roger: That's OK. I _____ lonely. My nephew Jeremy
　　　　　　　　　9 (not, feel)

and his friend Tyrone _____.
　　　　　　　　　　　10 (come)

We _____ Camp Snoopy, a huge amusement park
　　　11 (visit)

in the mall. Tyrone _____ at the golf course there.
　　　　　　　　12 (play)

Nick: Golf! I _____ coming after all!
　　　　　13 (think about)

Will and *Be Going To* II; Future Time Clauses

FUNCTION

A. Uses of Both *Will* and *Be Going To*

Use *will* or *be going to* to:

• Talk about future events that are (almost) certain.	The sun **will rise/is going to rise** at six o'clock tomorrow.
• Make predictions and state expectations.	He'**ll be/'s going to be** famous someday.
	The mail **will** probably **get/is** probably **going to get** here around three o'clock.

(See Chapter 14, Grammar Briefing 4, page 274, for other modals used to express predictions and expectations.)

B. Other Uses of *Will*

1. *Will* is usually used to express willingness (the idea that you are ready and able to do something). It is used to:

• Make offers.	If you want, I'**ll mail** those letters.
• Make promises.	We'**ll be** there promptly at 8:00 a.m.
• Make requests (ask about willingness).	**Will** you **take** these packages to the post office?
• Refuse to do something (express lack of willingness).	She **won't tell** me what's bothering her.

2. *Will* is often used in formal situations if both *will* and *be going to* could be used. For example, *will* is almost always used in written notices.

> The train **will depart** at ten o'clock (formal announcement)
> *Compare*: The train'**s going to leave** at ten o'clock. (less formal)

C. Other Uses of *Be Going To*

1. *Be going to* is usually used to talk about an intention or plan.

> She'**s going to discuss** the problem with the travel agent. (intention)
> They'**re going to go** on vacation next month. (plan)

2. *Be going to* is usually used to make a prediction about what will happen in the immediate future. Often the prediction is based on evidence in the present situation.

> That boy'**s going to spill** his drink. Grab it! (He's not paying attention and is moving his arm toward the glass.)

(continued on next page)

D. Time Expressions

Time expressions used in talking about future time include *tomorrow, tonight, next week* (*spring, Monday,* etc.), and *in two hours* (*a few days,* etc.).

He will help us **tomorrow**.

I'm going to go **next fall**.

We're going to leave **in two hours**.

FORM and FUNCTION

Expressing Future Time in Sentences with Time Clauses

In sentences about the future with time clauses:

- The time clause begins with expressions including *before, after, when, as soon as, until,* and *by the time.*
- Use a **present** form in the time clause.
- Use a future form in the main clause.

(See Chapter 2, Grammar Briefing 3, page 31, for more about time clauses.)

       time clause   main clause
Before he **comes**, we**'ll eat** dinner.
    NOT: Before he ~~will come~~, we'll eat dinner.

      time clause   main clause
When they**'re traveling**, they**'ll stay** in a hotel.
    NOT: When they~~'ll travel~~, they'll stay in a hotel.

TALKING THE TALK

In speech, *going to* is usually pronounced "gonna." "Gonna" is not used in writing.

Joe: Where are you gonna go on your vacation?
Hal: We're gonna go to Tahiti.

GRAMMAR PRACTICE 2

Will and *Be Going To* II; Future Time Clauses

3 | ***Will* and *Be Going To*—Predictions:** What Next?

A. Work with a partner. Discuss what you think will happen next in each of the following situations. Write two predictions for each situation. Use *will* for one prediction and *be going to* for the other one.

1. Len and Miranda have spent their vacation at Mesa Verde. Now they're on a plane, trying to get home. The plane is sitting on the runway. It was ready to take off an hour ago, but snow has been falling steadily since then.

   The passengers will get very nervous about the weather and ask to get off the plane.

   Len and Miranda aren't going to make it home tonight.

2. Mr. and Mrs. Miller and their six-year-old son, Ricky, are at the Mall of America. Mr. and Mrs. Miller have decided to separate for a few hours and meet later. Mr. Miller thinks that Ricky is with his mother. Mrs. Miller thinks that Ricky is with his father. Ricky is all alone in the biggest mall in the United States.

3. Vicky and Doug are driving to Yellowstone National Park in Wyoming. Doug decided to take a small road through the mountains to save time. He made a wrong turn, and they've been lost for hours. It's dark and late, and they haven't seen anyone else for a long time. Suddenly, their car sputters to a stop, out of gas.

4. Adrian and Marta have just arrived in New York City. They are planning to go to museums, the theater, and the opera. They're checking into their hotel now. Marta has just opened her purse and realized that she left all their cash, traveler's checks, and credit cards in the taxi that brought them from the airport.

B. Work in pairs or small groups to write two short paragraphs describing travel situations like the ones in Part A. Read your paragraphs to the class. The class should make predictions about each paragraph.

4   *Will* Versus *Be Going To*: Before an Outdoor Vacation

Decide whether each item expresses willingness (offers, refusals, etc.), a plan, or a prediction about the immediate future. Complete the items with the words in parentheses and *will/won't* or *be going to*. Use contractions with subject pronouns.

I.   Pam: Do you know where the newspaper is?

    Ryan: It's still on the porch. I __'ll get_____ it for you.
                                        1 (get)

II.   Ryan: Pam, why are you reading travel articles?

    Pam: I've been thinking about our summer vacation.

      I __'m going to find_____ something exciting for us to do.
                                   2 (find)

III.   Pam: How about taking a trip to New York City?

    Ryan: No, Pam. I refuse to spend my vacation in a city.

      I _____ there.
                          4 (go)

IV.   Ryan: I want to make a phone call, but I can't find the phone book.

      _____ me look for it?
                      4 (you, help)

    Pam: Sure. I _____ you.
                          5 (help)

      Who _____ ?
                        6 (you, call)

    Ryan: I _____ the travel agent to make reservations
                      7 (call)

      for our vacation.

V. Ryan: I'm making a tuna fish sandwich for myself for lunch. If you want,

I _____ one for you, too.

8 (make)

Pam: That sounds good. . . . Uh-oh, Ryan, the cat's in the kitchen.

It _____ onto the table. Quick!

9 (jump)

Catch it before it eats our tuna!

VI. Pam: Ryan made reservations for our vacation yesterday.

Diane: Where _____?

10 (you, go)

Pam: We _____ a trip to Yellowstone National Park.

11 (take)

_____ our cat for us while we're gone?

12 (you, look after)

5 *Will* and *Be Going To*: What Will They Say Next?

You're staying at a motel that has only one television, in the lobby. You want to watch the weather forecast, but a man has the remote control. He watches each show for a few seconds and then changes channels. Although these changes come in the middle of sentences, you have a good idea of how each sentence ends.

Listen once for the main ideas. Then listen again and circle *will* or *be going to* or both.

1. *Nature Program:* . . . the universe (will)/(is going to) end in a big crunch.

2. *Quiz Show:* . . . We ['ll / 're going to] get married next June.

3. *Soap Opera:* . . . I ['ll / 'm going to] change.

4. *News:* . . . prices [will / are going to] rise.

5. *Hospital Drama:* . . . Your son [is going to / will] be okay.

6. *Auto Racing:* . . . Renzo [will / is going to] win the race!

7. *Situation Comedy:* . . . [won't / 'm not going to] eat your food anymore.

8. *Prison Drama:* . . . Yeah, a shovel. [I'll / I'm going to] dig a tunnel.

9. *Weather Forecast:* . . . the sky [will / is going to] remain clear next week.

6 **Expressing the Future in Sentences with Time Clauses:**
A City Museum Vacation—The Cloisters

A. The Cloisters is a museum in New York City. Before a tour, the guide gives an introduction. Complete the introduction with the *will* future or simple present form of the words in parentheses. Use contractions with subject pronouns.

A Cloister

1. Before we __start__ the tour,
   (start)

   I __'ll describe__ the museum to you.
   (describe)

2. When we _____ the museum,
   (tour)

   you _____ three cloisters, or courtyards,
   (see)

   three chapels, and many tapestries and other works

   of art from the Middle Ages.

3. As soon as you _____ into the first cloister,
   (walk)

   you _____ some beautiful stone carvings.
   (see)

4. I _____ you into the first chapel after
   (take)

   everyone _____ at the carvings in the cloister.
   (look)

5. You _____ a recording of music from the
   (hear)

   Middle Ages as soon as we _____ the chapel.
   (enter)

Stone Carvings and Chapel

B. Combine the pairs of sentences into one sentence using the time word given, the simple present, and *be going to*. In each pair, the action in the first sentence happens earlier in time.

1. as soon as: We're going to leave the chapel.

   We're going to look at the unicorn tapestries.

   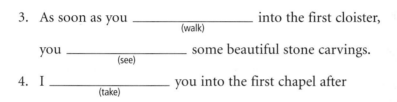

   As soon as we leave the chapel, we're going to look at the

   unicorn tapestries. OR We're going to look at the unicorn

   tapestries as soon as we leave the chapel.

Unicorn Tapestry

2. after: I'm going to point out flowers and plants that were grown during the Middle Ages.

   We're going to go into the second cloister.

   _____

3. when: You're going to enter the room called the Treasury.

   You're going to see many valuable religious objects.

   _____

4. until: You aren't going to be allowed to take photographs.

   We're going to go into the gardens outside the museum.

   _____

5. by the time: You're going to know much more about art in the Middle Ages.

   You're going to go home.

   _____

> *Middle Ages* = the period in European history from about 500 to about 1450.

 Go to the *Grammar Links* Website to learn more about the Cloisters.

7 Using *Will* and *Be Going To*: I'll Give You the Guided Tour

 A. Imagine that you are going to give a tour of a place that you know very well, for example, your school, your home, or your room. Write a one-paragraph introduction to tell the members of the tour group what they will see. Use *will*, and use at least three sentences with time clauses.

Example: Welcome to my house. After I tell you a little about it, I'll show you the living room. You'll see a couch and other furniture there. Before we go into the kitchen, I'll show you our new television. . . .

 See the *Grammar Links* Website for a complete model paragraph for this assignment.

 B. Work in small groups. The other students in your group are going to go on your tour. Tell them what they are going to see. You can base what you say on the paragraph that you wrote, but use *be going to* instead of *will*.

GRAMMAR BRIEFING 3

Expressing the Future with Present Progressive, Simple Present, and *Be About To*

FUNCTION

A. Present Progressive

The present progressive can be used to talk about planned future actions. A future time expression is stated or implied.	We're meeting her in Paris in a month. A: What are you doing tomorrow afternoon? B: I'm buying a bicycle.

(continued on next page)

B. Simple Present

1. The simple present can be used to talk about future actions or states that are scheduled. A future time expression is stated or implied.	The semester **ends** on December 17. Next week **I'm** on vacation. *A:* What time **does** our flight **leave** tomorrow? *B:* It **leaves** at 9:00 a.m.
2. The simple present is used in time clauses instead of the future. (See Grammar Briefing 2, page 86.)	<u>After he **comes**</u>, we'll visit many sites.

C. *Be About To*

Use *be about to* to talk about the immediate or very near future.	We're **about to leave** for the airport. Our bags are in the car. That glass **is about to** fall.
Time expressions are not usually used in sentences with *be about to*.	The plane **is about to** leave. **NOT:** The plane is about to leave ~~in five minutes~~.

GRAMMAR **HOT**SPOT!

1. Often, several forms can express the future. Here are the best forms to use:	
• Predictions, expectations: *will, be going to*.	Brazil **will win/is going to win** the World Cup this year.
If about the immediate future: *be going to, be about to*.	Be careful! You**'re going to knock over/'re about to knock over** that glass.
• Plans: *be going to*, present progressive.	He**'s going to start/'s starting** college in the fall.
If about the immediate future: *be about to*.	We**'re about to leave**.
• Scheduled events: simple present; also, *will, be going to*, present progressive.	School **starts/will start/is going to start/is starting** on September 3 this year.
2. Do **not** use the present progressive or simple present to talk about unplanned events in the future.	It **will rain/is going to rain** tomorrow. **NOT:** It ~~is raining/rains~~ tomorrow.

Expressing the Future with Present Progressive, Simple Present, and *Be About To*

8 **Present Progressive Versus *Will*:** In Washington, D.C.

Decide whether each item is expressing a planned future action or a prediction. Complete the items with the words in parentheses and the present progressive or *will*. Use contractions with subject pronouns and with *not*.

1. Lisa: I've decided to go to Washington, D.C., with Mike and Theo next week.

   Mariah: That sounds great! You __'ll have_____ a good time there.

(have)

2. Lisa: Did you listen to the weather forecast for Washington?

   Mike: Yes, I did. Bring your umbrella. It _____ tomorrow.

(probably, rain)

3. Airline Ticket Agent: Good morning, sir. Do you have your tickets?

   Theo: Yes, I do. We _____ to Washington, D.C.

(fly)

4. Theo: Has Lisa chosen a place for dinner tonight?

   Mike: Yes, she has. We _____ at an Indian restaurant near the White House.

(eat)

5. Lisa: There's a special exhibition at the National Gallery of Art. Let's go see it.

   Mike: That exhibition is really big. I want to see it, but it _____ a lot of time.

(take)

6. Mike: Let's go to the National Archives. I want to look at the Declaration of Independence.

   Theo: We don't have time to do everything. We _____ home tomorrow.

(go)

7. Lisa: It's almost time to go. Where's Mike?

   Theo: I'm not sure. I hope he gets here soon. He _____ the plane.

(miss)

8. Theo: Hey, Mike! We have to leave for the airport soon. Where's your bag?

   Mike: I _____ with you. I've decided to stay longer and see everything

(not, leave)
   in Washington.

 Go to the *Grammar Links* Website for information about the museums in Washington, D.C.

9 **Future Time with Present Progressive:** You're Going on Vacation Next Week!

 Imagine that next week you can spend a three-day vacation anywhere you want. Choose a place, and complete the chart with the activities you plan to do there. Then write a paragraph about your plans, using the present progressive.

Example: I'm going on vacation in San Francisco next week. On Thursday morning, I'm taking a tour of the city. In the afternoon, I'm visiting Golden Gate Park. Then I'm meeting a friend, and we're having dinner at a restaurant on Fisherman's Wharf in the evening. . . .

	Thursday	**Friday**	**Saturday**
Morning			
Afternoon			
Evening			

 See the *Grammar Links* Website for a complete model paragraph for this assignment.

10 **Future Time with Simple Present:** An Outdoor Vacation—
Yellowstone National Park

Work in pairs. Student A looks at the information on this page. Student B looks at
the information on page A-2. Ask *wh-* questions to get information to complete both
schedules. Use simple present and these verbs: *start*, *begin*, *end*, *finish*, *open*, *close*,
leave, and *return*.

Example: Student A: When does the summer season begin?
    Student B: It begins on April 15.

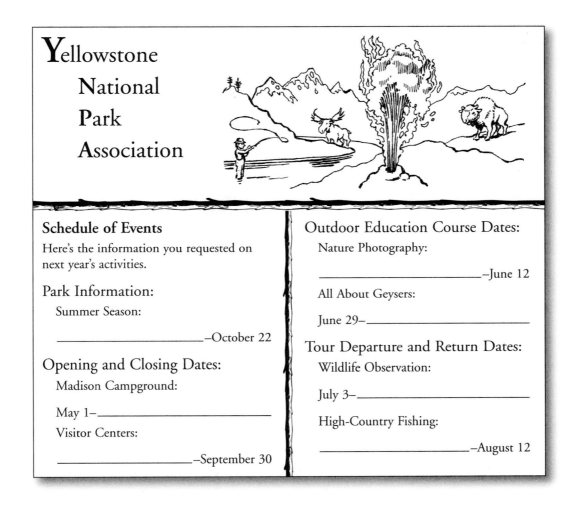

Yellowstone
    National
    Park
    Association

Schedule of Events

Here's the information you requested on
next year's activities.

Park Information:
    Summer Season:

    _____—October 22

Opening and Closing Dates:
    Madison Campground:

    May 1–_____
    Visitor Centers:

    _____—September 30

Outdoor Education Course Dates:
    Nature Photography:

    _____—June 12
    All About Geysers:

    June 29–_____

Tour Departure and Return Dates:
    Wildlife Observation:

    July 3–_____

    High-Country Fishing:

    _____—August 12

geyser = a natural hot spring that regularly erupts (sends a spray of steam and boiling water
up into the air). *wildlife* = animals living in nature. *high-country* = area in mountains.

11 Future Time with *Be About To*: Yellowstone Vacation

Work with a partner. Write a sentence about each of the pictures. Use *be about to*.

1. _They're about to go on a trip._
   _____

2. _____
   _____

3. _____
   _____

4. _____
   _____

5. _____
   _____

6. _____
   _____

12 Expressing Future Time: Vacation Finales

Work with a partner. Three forms for the future are given in each item in the conversations. Two of the forms are appropriate for expressing the future in the sentence and one is not. Cross out the form that is not appropriate.

I. Museum Vacation:

A: The museum <u>is closing / closes / ~~is about to close~~</u> in 15 minutes. I wish
1

we didn't have to leave.

B: I read about the museum's plans for a special exhibition next month.

Artists <u>give / are giving / are going to give</u> demonstrations.
2

A: That exhibition probably <u>is including / will include / is going to include</u> lots of
3

interesting art. Let's come back for it!

II. Shopping Vacation:

A: Hurry up! The bus <u>leaves / is leaving / is about to leave</u> in a few minutes.
4

You <u>miss / 're going to miss / 're about to miss</u> it. What have you been doing?
5

B: Did you know that the mall has a Fall Festival every year? I was buying a ticket because

I <u>'ll come back / 'm going to come back / 'm coming back</u> for it. Come back with me.
6

III. Outdoor Vacation:

A: Why are you setting the alarm clock?

B: I <u>'m getting up / 'm going to get up / 'll get up</u> in time to see the sun rise over the mountains
7

tomorrow. It's the last day of our vacation and our last chance to watch the sun rise.

A: I heard the weather forecast. The colors in the sky <u>are / will be / are going to be</u> beautiful
8

at sunrise tomorrow.

Early the next morning:

A: Look at the sky. It's really dark and cloudy. It<u>'ll rain / 's going to rain / 's raining</u> soon.
9

The weather forecast was wrong.

B: We <u>don't see / won't see / aren't going to see</u> the sun rise this morning, I'm afraid.
10

We'll have to come back to Mesa Verde again.

Check your progress! Go to the Self-Test for Chapter 5 on the *Grammar Links* Website.

Future Progressive, Future Perfect, and Future Perfect Progressive

Introductory Task: Predictions About Transportation and Travel in the Future

A. Work with a partner. Read the following statements. Some of the boldfaced verbs talk about actions that will be in progress at a time in the future. Circle them. Some of the boldfaced verbs talk about actions that will be completed at a time in the future. Underline them.

1. Twenty years from now, most international airlines **will be using** planes that fly faster than the speed of sound.

2. Twenty years from now, most students in the class **will have flown** faster than the speed of sound at least once.

3. Five years from now, most people **will be driving** cars that have computers connected to the Internet.

4. Ten years from now, at least one student in the class **is going to be driving** a car that steers itself.

5. By 2015, a spacecraft **will have brought** rocks from Mars back to Earth.

6. By 2015, scientists **are going to have proven** that life existed on Mars in the past.

B. 1. The circled verbs are in the future progressive. List them:

will be using, _____

2. The underlined verbs are in the future perfect. List them:

will have flown, _____

3. Compare the two forms. How are the future progressive and future perfect similar? How are they different?

C. Discuss the predictions in the sentences. Which ones do you think will prove to be accurate? Which ones do you think won't?

Future Progressive I

FORM

A. Affirmative Statements

WILL			BE GOING TO		
SUBJECT	WILL + BE + PRESENT PARTICIPLE*		SUBJECT	BE GOING TO + BE + PRESENT PARTICIPLE*	
I	**will be working**	tomorrow.	I	**am going to be working**	tomorrow.

(See Appendix 3 for spelling rules for the -ing form of the verb.)

B. Negative Statements

WILL			BE GOING TO		
SUBJECT	WILL + NOT + BE + PRESENT PARTICIPLE*		SUBJECT	BE + NOT + GOING TO + BE + PRESENT PARTICIPLE*	
We	**will not be working**	in July.	We	**are not going to be working**	in July.

C. Yes/No Questions and Short Answers

WILL		BE GOING TO	
QUESTIONS	SHORT ANSWERS	QUESTIONS	SHORT ANSWERS
Will Jill **be working** this summer?	Yes, she **will** (**be**).	**Is** Jake **going to be working** this summer?	Yes, he **is** (**going to be**).
	No, she **won't** (**be**).		No, he **isn't** (**going to be**).

D. Wh- Questions

Wh- Questions About the Subject

WILL	BE GOING TO*
Who will be traveling next year?	**Who is going to be traveling** next year?

Other Wh- Questions

WILL	BE GOING TO*
When will they **be traveling**?	**When are** they **going to be traveling**?

*For contractions with will and be going to (e.g., will + not → won't, you + are + going to → you're going to),
  see Chapter 5, Grammar Briefing 1, page 83.

Future Progressive I

1 Future Progressive with *Will*—Form: The Flight of the Future

It's possible that airlines will be using High-Speed Civil Transport (HSCT) planes in the future. What will the flights be like? Use the words in parentheses to complete the statements and questions in the future progressive with *will*. Complete the short answers. Use contractions with subject pronouns and with *not*.

Announcement: Flight 101 from Los Angeles to Tokyo <u>will be boarding</u> shortly.
                                                          1 (board)

A few minutes later:

Passenger: This is my first HCST flight, so I'm a little nervous. <u>Will the plane be taking off</u>
                                                  2 (the plane, take off)

                soon?

Flight Attendant: Yes, <u>it will/it will be</u>. Please fasten your seat belt, sir.
                                       3

Passenger: How fast _____? At what altitude
                                    4 (we, fly)

               _____?
                      5 (the plane, cruise)

Flight Attendant: The pilot _____ you that information soon.
                                  6 (give)

Pilot: Welcome aboard. We _____ in a few minutes.
                                     7 (take off)

          Then we _____ to an altitude of 60,000 feet.
                         8 (climb)

          The plane _____ the sound barrier until we
                         9 (not, break)

          are over the ocean. After that, we _____ at
                                      10 (cruise)

          1,800 miles per hour—almost two and a half times the speed of sound. Sit back and

          relax. The flight attendants _____ through the
                                  11 (come)

          cabin to make sure that you're comfortable.

Passenger: Excuse me. _____ dinner soon?
                           12 (you, serve)

Flight Attendant: No, _____. I _____
                         13   14 (not, bring)

          you dinner until the plane reaches its cruising altitude. Just relax until then.

Three and a half hours after takeoff:

Pilot: Please fasten your seatbelt. About ten minutes from now, we

          _____ at Tokyo's Narita Airport.
                    15 (arrive)

2 Future Progressive with *Be Going To*—Form: The Car of the Future

Use the words in parentheses to complete the statements and questions in the future progressive with *be going to*. Complete the short answers. Use contractions with subject pronouns and with *not*.

Reporter: What kind of cars <u>are people going to be driving</u> in the future?
1 (people, drive)

Engineer: In the future, people _____ much
2 (not, do)
of the driving. Cars _____ computer
3 (use)
technology to drive themselves.

Reporter: What new technology _____ me today?
4 (you, show)

Engineer: I _____ a computer-based system
5 (demonstrate)
called Ralph. Ralph is short for Rapidly Adapting Lateral Position Handler.

We _____ an automated car for a
6 (take)
test drive. Let's go. . . .

Reporter: _____ itself all the time?
7 (the car, drive)

Engineer: No, _____. I _____ it
8   9 (steer)
at first. But after I switch to the automated system, I _____
10 (not, control)
its steering or speed. Ralph _____ its tiny video
11 (use)
cameras and sensors to "see" the road. . . . Okay, Ralph is in control now.

In a few seconds, it _____ lanes to avoid that
12 (change)
car ahead of us.

Reporter: You seem very relaxed. _____ soon?
13 (you, fall asleep)

Engineer: No, _____. Don't worry. Ralph is good, but it isn't
14
perfect yet. Until it is, I _____ my eyes on the road.
15 (keep)

Future Progressive II; Future Progressive Versus Future with *Will* or *Be Going To*

FUNCTION

A. Future Progressive

Use the future progressive to talk about actions that will be in progress in the future. The action may be in progress:

- At a moment in time.

PAST   NOW   at this time tomorrow   FUTURE

'll be relaxing

At this time tomorrow, I**'ll be relaxing** on the beach.

- Over a period of time.

PAST   NOW   the next few years   FUTURE

's going to be working

She**'s going to be working** in Bangkok for the next few years.

Time Expressions

The time expressions used with the future progressive are the same as those used with *will* and *be going to* (see Chapter 5, Grammar Briefing 2, page 86). They include *tomorrow*, *next week* (*summer*, etc.), and *in a few months* (*a year*, etc.).

He will be working **tonight**.

We are going to be leaving **in three weeks**.

B. Future Progressive Versus Future with *Will* or *Be Going To*

1. To talk about actions over a **period of time** in the future, use the future progressive or the future with *will* or *be going to*. The sentences have the same basic meaning. The progressive emphasizes that the action will be ongoing.

We**'ll be living** in a new place. = We**'ll live** in a new place.

He**'s going to be studying** architecture. = He**'s going to study** architecture.

(continued on next page)

2. To talk about actions at a **moment of time** in the future:

    - Use the future progressive for actions in progress (i.e., actions that began before and continue through that moment).

    At ten o'clock tomorrow, I **will be flying** to Europe. (The plane will leave before ten o'clock.)

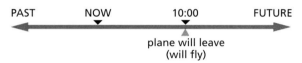

    - Use the future with *will* or *be going to* for actions that begin at that moment.

    At ten o'clock tomorrow, I **will fly** to Europe. (The plane will leave at ten o'clock.)

    PAST   NOW   10:00   FUTURE
    plane will leave
    (will fly)

3. Remember, progressives are not used to talk about states. With verbs that have stative meaning, use the future with *will* or *be going to*.

    After this course, you**'ll know** all about computers.
NOT: After this course, you'll be knowing all about computers.

> ### GRAMMAR **HOT**SPOT!

The future progressive is often used in the main clause of sentences that have time clauses. Remember that the verb in the time clause is in the present.

She**'ll be flying** to London <u>while we **are** at the meeting</u>.

<u>When we **arrive**</u>, he**'s going to be waiting**.

Future Progressive II; Future Progressive Versus Future with *Will* or *Be Going To*

3 **Future Versus Future Progressive:** Coming and Going

Work with a partner. Choose the form or forms—future, future progressive, or both—that can be used.

1. We plan to drive to Denver tomorrow. We <u>a, b</u> for eight hours.

   a. 're going to drive   b. 're going to be driving

2. My vacation starts tomorrow. At this time next week, I _____ a wonderful time in Hawaii.

   a. 'll have   b. 'll be having

3. I haven't gotten my itinerary from the travel agent yet. I _____ it tomorrow.

   a. 'll have   b. 'll be having

4. I don't want to go to the beach until you come. When you come, we _____ to the

   beach together.

   a. 'll go   b. 'll be going

5. Lily's making plans for her vacation. She _____ in a youth hostel for a week.

   a. 's going to stay   b. 's going to be staying

6. Casey is coming home late tonight, so we can't wait for him. When he comes,

   we _____.

   a. 're going to eat   b. 're going to be eating

7. Vincent is coming home late tonight, but we'll wait for him. When he comes, we _____.

   a. 're going to eat   b. 're going to be eating

8. My boyfriend promised to meet me at the airport. When I get there, he _____.

   a. 'll wait   b. 'll be waiting

4 **Using Future Progressive:** Making Predictions About Transportation of the Future

A. How are people going to be traveling in the future? What kinds of transportation will we be using? Write six sentences about your predictions for the transportation of the future. Use the future progressive with both *will* and *be going to*. Use *not* in at least two sentences. Include at least three of these time expressions: *in a few years, in 20 years, in 2050,* and *at the end of this century*.

Example: In 20 years, buses will be traveling at very high speeds and will be floating above the road. OR People won't be using transportation much in 2050. Instead, they're going to be using their computers to take virtual reality trips.

B. Work in small groups. Discuss your predictions and decide on four predictions that everyone likes best. Tell these predictions to the class.

5 **Future Progressive in Sentences with Time Clauses:** "Smart" Cars

A. A car salesman is trying to persuade a customer to buy a "smart" car. Use the words in parentheses to complete the sentences. Use the future progressive with *will* and the simple present. Use contractions with subject pronouns.

1. Before you <u>begin</u>_____ a trip, the car's computer
   (begin)
   <u>will be downloading</u>_____ useful information from the Internet.
   (download)

2. While the driver _____ the car, the computer
   (steer)
   _____ traffic conditions.
   (monitor)

3. The computer _____ to your voice commands
   (respond)
   while you _____ your eyes on the road.
   (keep)

4. When the car _____ in motion, a satellite
   (be)
   _____ track of its position.
   (keep)

5. The car's computer _____ a new route before
   (search for)
   the car _____ stuck in a traffic jam.
   (get)

6. The computer _____ your e-mail and faxes while
   (send)
   it _____ your favorite music.
   (play)

7. _____ one of our "smart" cars as soon as
   (you, drive)
   they _____ available?
   (be)

> *monitor* = keep track of something. *satellite* = a mechanical device in orbit around the earth. *route* = a road or way for traveling from one place to another.

 B. Think of some type of technology of the future, for example, a telephone or other communication device, a machine, a form of transportation, a computer program, or a robot. Write a paragraph that tries to persuade someone to buy it. Include at least four sentences with the future progressive and a time clause.

Example: Your Roboready will do everything you want it to do. Before you wake up, Roboready will be making your breakfast. Roboready will be cleaning the kitchen while you get ready for school. . . .

 See the *Grammar Links* Website for a complete model paragraph for this assignment.

Future Perfect and Future Perfect Progressive I

FORM

A. Affirmative Statements

FUTURE PERFECT			FUTURE PERFECT PROGRESSIVE		
SUBJECT	*WILL/BE GOING TO + HAVE + PAST PARTICIPLE**		SUBJECT	*WILL/BE GOING TO + HAVE + BEEN + PRESENT PARTICIPLE**	
I	**will have studied**	by then.	You	**will have been studying**	by then.
She	**is going to have eaten**	by then.	They	**are going to have been studying**	by then.

(See Appendix 7 for the past participles of irregular verbs.)

(See Appendix 3 for spelling rules for the *-ing* form of the verb.)

(continued on next page)

B. Negative Statements

FUTURE PERFECT

SUBJECT	WILL + NOT (OR BE + NOT + GOING TO) + HAVE + PAST PARTICIPLE*	
We	**will not have worked**	together yet.
They	**are not going to have worked**	together yet.

FUTURE PERFECT PROGRESSIVE

SUBJECT	WILL + NOT (OR BE + NOT + GOING TO) + HAVE + BEEN + PRESENT PARTICIPLE*	
You	**will not have been working**	together yet.
We	**are not going to have been working**	together yet.

C. *Yes/No* Questions and Short Answers

FUTURE PERFECT

QUESTIONS	SHORT ANSWERS
Will she **have studied** English by then?	Yes, she **will (have).**
Are you **going to have studied** English by then?	No, I'm **not (going to have).**

FUTURE PERFECT PROGRESSIVE

QUESTIONS	SHORT ANSWERS
Will he **have been studying** English by then?	Yes, he **will (have/have been).**
Are they **going to have been studying** English by then?	No, they **aren't (going to have/ going to have been).**

D. *Wh-* Questions

Wh- Questions About the Subject

FUTURE PERFECT*

Who will have visited Chicago by then?

What is going to have happened by then?

FUTURE PERFECT PROGRESSIVE*

What will have been happening by then?

Who is going to have been studying English by then?

Other *Wh-* Questions

FUTURE PERFECT*

Where will they **have traveled** by then?

What are they **going to have finished** before Tuesday?

FUTURE PERFECT PROGRESSIVE*

Where will they **have been living**?

How long are they **going to have been traveling** by then?

*For contractions with *will* and *be going to* (e.g., *will* + *not* → *won't*, *you* + *are* + *going to* → *you're going to*), see Chapter 5, Grammar Briefing 1, page 83.

Future Perfect and Future Perfect Progressive I

6 **Future Perfect with *Will* and *Be Going To*—Form:** The Mars Exploration Program

A. Use the words in parentheses to complete the statements and questions in the future perfect with *will*. Complete the short answer. Use contractions with subject pronouns and with *not*.

NASA's MARS EXPLORATION PROGRAM

Ask the Space Scientist:

Q: ___Will NASA have brought___ rocks back to Earth from Mars by 2010?
        1 (NASA, bring)

A: No, ___it won't/won't have___. But it's likely that by then NASA
              2

_____ a great deal of progress toward missions to bring
   3 (make)

rock samples back from Mars. For example, it _____ an
                                              4 (launch)

orbiter to photograph Mars.

Q: _____ landers to explore Mars before these missions begin?
   5 (NASA, send)

A: Yes, _____ . We _____
              6   7 (not, get)

enough information about Mars from orbiters alone. By the time the missions to bring back rocks

begin, scientists _____ a lot of knowledge about Mars's
                    8 (gain)

atmosphere and surface, and you _____ many interesting
                                   9 (see)

close-up photos of the planet.

Orbiter

Lander

B. Use the words in parentheses to complete the statements and questions in the future perfect with *be going to*. Complete the short answer. Use contractions with subject pronouns and with *not*.

Q: <u>Are humans going to have gone</u> to Mars by 2020?
        1 (humans, go)

A: No, <u>they aren't/aren't going to have</u>. Space scientists
               2

_____ a lot more about the history of Mars,
        3 (learn)

though. For example, it's possible that we _____ evidence
                                      4 (find)

that life existed on Mars in the past. But we _____
                                      5 (not, develop)

all the technology we need to send humans there by then.

Q: _____ a lot of progress toward a human
        6 (NASA, make)

mission to Mars by the time the Mars exploration program ends?

A: Yes, _____.
                 7

Q: How much progress _____?
                         8 (it, make)

A: The Mars exploration program _____
                                    9 (have)

successes and failures. I hope that it _____
                                      10 (not, have)

more failures than successes.

NASA = National Aeronautics and Space Administration (the U.S. government's agency for air and space science and technology).

 Check out the *Grammar Links* Website to get updates on the exploration of Mars and other planets.

7 Future Perfect Progressive with *Will* and *Be Going To*—Form: Terraforming Mars

A. Use the words in parentheses to complete the statements with the future perfect progressive with *will*. Use contractions with subject pronouns and with *not*.

Some people believe that it will be possible to "terraform" Mars, that is, to change it into an Earth-like environment that people can live in.

Terraforming Mars is a big challenge. But by the time we begin the project in the middle

of the twenty-first century, we <u>'ll have been preparing</u> _____
                                          1 (prepare)

for more than 50 years and will have plenty of information. Small crews of astronauts

_____ to Mars regularly by then.
                        2 (travel)

Scientists _____ for evidence of present or
                        3 (search)

past life. This search _____ everywhere on
                        4 (not, take place)

Mars—only where life is most likely. By the time people begin to colonize the planet,

astronauts and scientists _____ on
                        5 (stay)

Mars for long periods, and engineers _____
                        6 (build)

bases. We _____ many supplies from
                        7 (not, send)

Earth to these crews. Such supplies won't be necessary because the crews

_____ how to live on Mars with the
                        8 (learn)

resources that are available there.

B. Use the words in parentheses to complete the statements with the future perfect
progressive with *be going to*. Use contractions with subject pronouns and with *not*.

By the year 2150, the terraforming project _is going to have been going on_ for almost a
                                            1 (go on)

hundred years. Mars _____
                        2 (not, change)

rapidly, but some gradual changes _____.
                        3 (occur)

The colonists _____ the bases
                        4 (expand)

into towns. They _____ crops in
                        5 (raise)

greenhouses. Special equipment _____
                        6 (pump)

water to the surface of the planet. Other equipment _____
                        7 (add)

nitrogen, oxygen, and water vapor to the planet's atmosphere.

> *colonize* = create a new settlement in a distant place. *base* = a starting point or central
> place for supplies and activities. *resource* = something that can be used to support life.
> *greenhouse* = a building, usually made of glass, used for growing plants.

 Check out the *Grammar Links* Website to find out more about the possibility of
terraforming Mars.

Future Perfect and Future Perfect Progressive II

FUNCTION

A. Future Perfect

Use the future perfect to talk about an action or state that will occur before a future action, state, or time.

PAST   NOW   FUTURE

I will have cooked   you come home

I **will have cooked** dinner before you come home.

He**'ll have traveled** to Japan three times before the end of the month.

Often, the later action, state, or time is expressed:

- In a time clause, usually beginning with *before*, *when*, or *by the time*.

- With a time expression.

The movie is going to have started **by the time we get there.**

We will have finished **by next week.**

Time Expressions

1. Time expressions with *by* (*by then*, *by 2020*, etc.) or *before* (*before then*, *before next week*, etc.) often indicate the later time.

2. *Already*, *just*, and *yet* (in questions and negatives) are also used with the future perfect.

I'll have graduated from college **by then.**

By Monday, Eva will **already** have left Tokyo.

B. Future Perfect Progressive

Use the future perfect progressive to talk about an action that will continue to a future action, state, or time.

That action, state, or time is often expressed in a time clause or time expression with *by* (*by the time . . .* , *by then*, etc.).

PAST   NOW   FUTURE

driving   get to Chicago

By the time we get to Chicago, we**'ll have been driving** for eight hours.

By then, I**'m going to have been studying** Chinese.

Time Expressions

In addition to time expressions with *by*, *already* and *yet* are used, and *for* indicates duration.

By the time you get to the office, we'll **already** have been working **for several hours**.

(continued on next page)

C. Future Perfect Versus Future Perfect Progressive

1. The future perfect expresses actions and states that will be **completed** before some point in the future.

   By then, we **will have studied** chemistry.
   (The study of chemistry will be completed.)

2. The future perfect progressive expresses actions that will **continue up to** some point in the future.

   By then, we **will have been studying** chemistry.
   (The study of chemistry will be ongoing.)

3. Use the future perfect for states that continue. Progressives are not used with verbs with stative meaning.

   By then, we **will have been** here for a year.
   NOT: By then, we ~~will have been being~~ here for a year.

GRAMMAR **HOT**SPOT!

1. Sometimes the future perfect is used with *for*. In these sentences, the future perfect expresses continuing actions. The sentences have the same meaning as sentences with the future perfect progressive.

   By then, **I'll have studied** chemistry for a year.
   (= By then, I'll have been studying chemistry for a year.)

2. The action or state expressed by a verb in the future perfect or future perfect progressive doesn't have to **begin** in the future. It may even have begun in the past.

   We began driving on Monday. By the time we get to California, we'll have been driving three days.
   (The driving began in the past.)

3. Remember that in sentences about the future with a time clause, the verb in the time clause is in the simple present.

   Before I **leave** the United States, I **will have graduated** from the university.
   NOT: Before I ~~will have left~~ the United States, I will have graduated from the university.

Future Perfect and Future Perfect Progressive II

8 Using Future Perfect: Future Accomplishments

A. Work in pairs. Use the cues and the future perfect with *will* and *be going to* to ask and answer questions about what each of you expects to do in the future. First, Student A asks Student B all the questions. Then Student B asks Student A all the questions.

Example: Student A: What will you have done by ten o'clock tonight?
Student B: By ten o'clock tonight, I'll have finished my homework.
Student A: What are you going to have done by Saturday evening?
Student B: By Saturday evening, I'm going to have fixed my car.

will	be going to
1. ten o'clock tonight	2. Saturday evening
3. a week from today	4. the time this semester ends
5. a year from now	6. five years from now
7. 10 years from now	8. the time you are 60 years old

B. Which one of your partner's expectations seems to be the most ambitious, that is, like it will take the most effort to achieve? Report this expectation to the class.

Example: By five years from now, Mae is going to have gotten a Ph.D. in civil engineering.

9 Future Perfect Progressive in Sentences with Time Clauses: A Future Astronaut

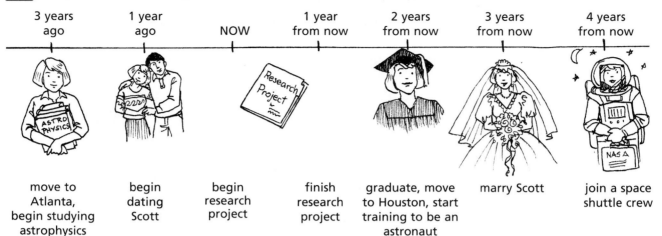

3 years ago	1 year ago	NOW	1 year from now	2 years from now	3 years from now	4 years from now
move to Atlanta, begin studying astrophysics	begin dating Scott	begin research project	finish research project	graduate, move to Houston, start training to be an astronaut	marry Scott	join a space shuttle crew

A. Courtney is a student and a future astronaut. Use the information given to complete sentences in the future perfect progressive. Use the future perfect progressive with *will*.

1. Courtney has been living in Atlanta for three years. She'll move to Houston two years from now. By the time she <u>moves to Houston</u>, she <u>'ll have been living in Atlanta</u> for five years.

2. She's been studying astrophysics for two years. She'll graduate two years from now. By the time she _____, she _____ for four years.

3. She and Scott have been dating for a year. They'll get married three years from now. By the time they _____, they _____ for four years.

4. She's working on her research project starting this year. She'll finish it a year from now. By the time she _____, she _____ for one year.

5. She'll train to be an astronaut starting two years from now. She'll join a space shuttle crew four years from now. By the time she _____, she _____ for two years.

 B. Draw a timeline like the one in Part A on a separate piece of paper. Fill it in with information and predictions about your life. Include activities beginning in the past, present, and future. Then write three groups of three sentences, using the items in Part A as a model. Use the future perfect progressive with *will* and a time clause in the third sentence of each group.

Example: I've been studying English for a year. I'll graduate from the English program in one year. By the time I graduate, I'll have been studying English for two years.

10 Future Perfect Versus Future Perfect Progressive: E-mail from an Astronaut

Circle the correct form or forms to complete the sentences.

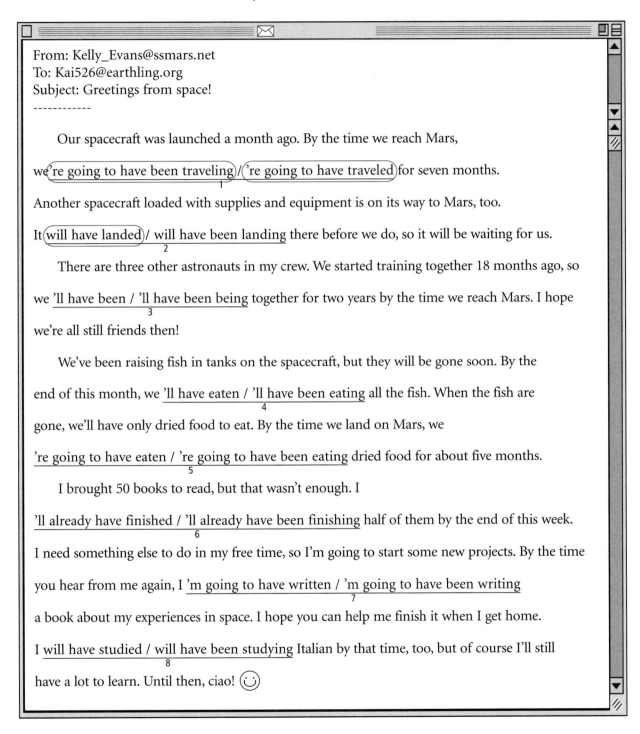

From: Kelly_Evans@ssmars.net
To: Kai526@earthling.org
Subject: Greetings from space!

Our spacecraft was launched a month ago. By the time we reach Mars,

we (**'re going to have been traveling**) / (**'re going to have traveled**) for seven months.
                                        1

Another spacecraft loaded with supplies and equipment is on its way to Mars, too.

It (**will have landed**) / will have been landing there before we do, so it will be waiting for us.
           2

There are three other astronauts in my crew. We started training together 18 months ago, so

we **'ll have been** / 'll have been being together for two years by the time we reach Mars. I hope
              3

we're all still friends then!

We've been raising fish in tanks on the spacecraft, but they will be gone soon. By the

end of this month, we **'ll have eaten** / 'll have been eating all the fish. When the fish are
                               4

gone, we'll have only dried food to eat. By the time we land on Mars, we

're going to have eaten / **'re going to have been eating** dried food for about five months.
                        5

I brought 50 books to read, but that wasn't enough. I

'll already have finished / 'll already have been finishing half of them by the end of this week.
                            6

I need something else to do in my free time, so I'm going to start some new projects. By the time

you hear from me again, I **'m going to have written** / 'm going to have been writing
                                              7

a book about my experiences in space. I hope you can help me finish it when I get home.

I **will have studied** / will have been studying Italian by that time, too, but of course I'll still
                    8

have a lot to learn. Until then, ciao! ☺

**Check your progress! Go to the Self-Test for
Chapter 6 on the *Grammar Links* Website.**

Chapter 7

Phrasal Verbs; Tag Questions

Introductory Task: Why Do Explorers Take On the Challenges?

A. Read these paragraphs.

Many people believe that it's necessary to **put off** a human mission to Mars until we have developed more advanced technology. But some space scientists think that better technology isn't necessary and that explorers will be able to **set off** soon on a mission to Mars.

Why will explorers **take on** the challenges of traveling to a cold, distant planet? They'll have the same motives that past explorers had: knowledge, fame, and profit. Profit might be the strongest motive. It will cost a lot to reach Mars, but explorers will **put up** the money to be the first to get there. Then they will have many possibilities for making even more money: They may be able to **take over** new territory; they'll **set up** bases and perhaps even colonies; they'll **bring back** valuable resources; and they'll **bring out** books, movies, and television programs for fascinated audiences on Earth.

B. Work with a partner. The boldfaced verbs in the paragraphs are phrasal verbs. Phrasal verbs have two words: a verb and a particle.

1. Look at the phrasal verbs in the paragraphs. Write the verbs next to their meanings.

    a. <u>bring back</u>_____: return with

    b. _____: produce or publish

    c. _____: delay

    d. _____: invest or pay in advance

    e. _____: accept responsibility for

    f. _____: get control or ownership of

    g. _____: start on a journey

    h. _____: build or establish

2. Are phrasal verbs with the same verb similar to each other in meaning? _____

3. What happens to the meaning of a verb when the verb combines with a particle to form a phrasal verb?

_____

4. Can you predict the meaning of a phrasal verb from the meanings of its two words? _____

---

motive = the cause for a person's doing something.

Phrasal Verbs I

FORM

A. Overview

1. Phrasal verbs consist of a verb + an adverb. (The adverb is called a particle; phrasal verbs are sometimes called two-word verbs.)

   The most common particles are *up, out, down, off, on,* and *over.* Others include *along, back, behind, in, through,* and *together.*

   > The receptionist **set up** the appointment.
   > He **found out** the truth.
   > Our car **broke down**.

2. Phrasal verbs can occur in any tense.

   > The plane **takes off** at 7:37 every day.
   > The plane **took off** on time.
   > The plane **will take off** at 6:10 tomorrow.

B. Phrasal Verbs Without Objects

Some phrasal verbs do not have objects.
(See Appendix 8 for a list of common phrasal verbs without objects.)

> **Watch out**!
> They **are coming over** soon.
> My friends **didn't show up**.

C. Phrasal Verbs with Objects

Some phrasal verbs have objects:

- If the object is a noun, it can come before or after the particle.

  > She **took** the book **back**. OR She **took back** the book.
  > **Turn** the light **off**. OR **Turn off** the light.

- If the object is a pronoun, it must come before the particle.

  > She **called** him **up**.
  >   NOT: She called up him.
  > I **will be picking** her **up** soon.
  >   NOT: I will be picking up her soon.

(See Appendix 8 for a list of common phrasal verbs with objects.)

Phrasal Verbs I

1 **Identifying Phrasal Verbs:** A Success I

Underline the phrasal verbs. If the verb has an object, circle the object. Including the examples, there are 10 phrasal verbs. Compare answers with a partner.

In the early twentieth century, the earth's polar regions seemed almost as far away and dangerous as Mars does today. The conditions were difficult, but a few polar explorers figured out (ways) to reach the poles and come back safely. One of these men was Roald Amundsen.

Amundsen was born in Norway in 1872. While he was growing up, he wanted to be a polar explorer. He therefore built up his strength in extremely cold and difficult conditions. He worked out by skiing long distances. As a result of this training, he got along well in very cold climates. Amundsen's strength and adaptability paid off later on. He understood the dangers of polar expeditions, especially freezing, hunger, and exhaustion. So before an expedition, he always prepared carefully.

In 1910, Amundsen decided to try to be the first to reach the South Pole. He planned an expedition and set off with a small crew. Then he found something out: A British expedition led by Robert Falcon Scott was also trying to reach the South Pole. Amundsen and Scott were in a race. How did this race turn out?

polar regions = areas around the North and South poles. *expedition* = a trip made by a group of people with a definite purpose. *adaptability* = ability to deal with changing conditions. *exhaustion* = the state of being extremely tired.

2 Phrasal Verbs: A Success II

Work with a partner. Use the appropriate form of the phrasal verbs in the box above each paragraph to complete the paragraph. (If necessary, look in Appendix 8 for help.)

let up	push on	~~set in~~	set up

Amundsen's ship landed in Antarctica in February 1911. Then he and his crew worked hard and fast before the dark, icy winter _set in_____. They stored supplies and
1
_____ trail markers along the first part
2
of their route. In October, after the Antarctic winter finally

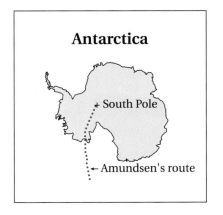
Antarctica

+ South Pole

← Amundsen's route

_____, Amundsen and four men started
3
south, traveling on skis and sleds pulled by dogs. There were some terrible snowstorms at first, but Amundsen and his men _____.
4

get through	head back	keep up	set back

The bad weather didn't _____ their progress _____ for
5
long, so they _____ their spirits _____. On December 14,
6
they reached the South Pole and realized that they had beaten the British! Amundsen placed Norwegian flags around the area. After three days, he and his crew _____
7
north. They returned on January 25, 1912, having traveled 1,860 miles in 99 days. Amundsen's adaptability, determination, and careful preparations had _____ them
8
_____.

---

store = put away for future use. *trail markers* = signs that show the way.
determination = unwillingness to quit.

3 Phrasal Verbs; Placement of Noun and Pronoun Objects: A Successful Failure

Use the words under the blanks to complete the sentences. Use appropriate verb forms. Place the objects after the particles where possible.

Ernest Shackleton, from England, failed to reach the South Pole in 1908 but then became a hero and became rich by telling stories about his experiences.

When Amundsen's expedition succeeded in 1911, Shackleton could no longer become the first to reach the South Pole, but this didn't

<u>keep him back</u>_____. He decided to
1 (keep back / him)

become the first explorer to travel across Antarctica. In 1915, he

<u>put together an expedition</u>_____. However, the
2 (put together / an expedition)

expedition's ship became trapped in thick ice. The pressure of the ice

_____. After their ship sank,
3 (break up / the ship)

Shackleton and the crew were left floating on a huge sheet of ice with very few

supplies. Shackleton _____
4 (think over / their situation)

and made a plan to reach safety. They still had a couple of small boats, and

they _____ as they walked
5 (pull along / them)

across the ice. After weeks of walking and sailing in the small boats, they reached

Elephant Island, a desolate ice-covered place. Many of the men were too weak to

go on. So Shackleton _____ and went to get help.
6 (leave behind / them)

He sailed 800 miles in a small open boat. After he got to the Falkland Islands, near South America,

he tried to rescue his men several times, but problems

_____
7 (drive back / him)

each time. Finally, 18 weeks later, he reached Elephant Island.

Miraculously the men were all still alive! After Shackleton

_____,
8 (pick up / the men)

he _____ to England.
9 (bring back / them)

And he _____, too.
10 (bring back / another exciting story)

Antarctica

South Georgia

Elephant Island

+ South Pole

Ross Sea

desolate = empty, without people or plants. *miraculously* = amazingly.

 To find out more about Shackleton, Amundsen, and other polar explorers, see the *Grammar Links* Website.

Phrasal Verbs II

FUNCTION

Meaning of Phrasal Verbs

1. The meaning of a phrasal verb is different from the meaning of the verb + the meaning of the particle. Phrasal verbs with the same verb but different particles are different in meaning.

   For example, *put* = place, set, or lay, but:

   - *Put up* = pay.
   - *Put off* = postpone.
   - *Put on* = host.
   - *Put down* = insult.

He **put up** the money for the tickets.
We **will put off** the trip until April.
They **are putting on** a great party.
He **was** constantly **putting** her **down**.

2. A phrasal verb may have more than one meaning. The phrasal verb may have an object in one meaning and not in another.

   For example:

   - *Set off* = start a journey.
   - *Set off* + object = make different from others.
   - *Set off* + object = cause to explode.
   - *Set off* + object = make angry.

We **will set off** tomorrow.
Her red hair **sets** her **off** from the rest of the family.
The town **has set off** fireworks on Independence Day for many years.
His lateness **set** her **off**.

1. The words used as particles in phrasal verbs can also occur in prepositional phrases. In this case, they are prepositions that indicate location or direction. The verb + preposition is not a phrasal verb; it has the meaning of the verb + the meaning of the preposition.

    prepositional phrase
    He climbed <u>up the tree</u>. (preposition *up* tells direction)

2. Sometimes the same words can be a phrasal verb + object or a verb followed by a prepositional phrase.* There are two ways to tell the difference:

    • The meaning of a phrasal verb is different from the meaning of its two words.

    phrasal verb + object
    They **looked up** a word. (*look up* = search for in a dictionary)

    verb + prepositional phrase
    They **looked up** the mountain. (*look up* = look in an upward direction)

    • A phrasal verb object can come before the particle, and if it's a pronoun, it must come before the particle.

    phrasal verb + object
    They **looked** a word **up**.

    They **looked** it **up**.
    NOT: They ~~looked up it~~.

    verb + prepositional phrase
    They **looked** up a mountain.
    NOT: They ~~looked a mountain up~~.

    They **looked** up it.
    NOT: They ~~looked it up~~.

*A verb + prepositional phrase is also different from a verb + preposition combination followed by an object (see Grammar Briefing 3, page 125).

Phrasal Verbs II

4 Phrasal Verbs—Meaning: Check This Out

A. Use the appropriate form of the phrasal verbs in the box to complete the sentences.

> bring down: cause something or somebody to lose power
> bring in: earn profits or income
> ~~bring on: cause something to appear~~
> bring out: produce of publish something
> bring up: take care of and educate

1. I have a terrible cold. I think that staying outside in cold, wet weather
   brought it _on_ .

2. My grandmother knows a lot about raising children. She _____

   eight of them.

3. He's written an adventure travel book. A publisher is going to _____

   it _____ later this year.

4. That movie was very popular. It _____ a lot of money.

5. The president of the country committed crimes. His actions _____

   his government _____.

B. Write the letter of the correct meaning before each sentence.

> Phrasal verb: *blow up*
> Meanings: a. ~~come into being, happen suddenly~~
> b. express anger suddenly and forcefully
> c. explode
> d. fill with air
> e. make (a photograph) larger

___a___ 1. When we were hiking in the mountains, a storm suddenly *blew up*, so we got cold
and wet.

_____ 2. My bicycle tire has lost all its air. Can I use your pump to *blow it up* again?

_____ 3. This photo is too small. Let's take it to Custom Camerawork. They'll *blow* it *up* for
us.

_____ 4. My sister has a tendency to get angry quickly. Whenever we get into an argument, she
just *blows up*.

_____ 5. Someone dropped a lighted match into the gas tank, and the car *blew up*.

5 **Particle Versus Preposition:** Look This Over

In one sentence of each pair, the underlined word is a particle (i.e., part of a phrasal verb); in the other, it is a preposition. Circle the letter of the sentence that contains the particle, and rewrite the sentence with the object before the particle.

1. (a.) When Carla and Bill left the house, they turned <u>off</u> the light.

   b. When Eugene got to the hotel, he turned <u>off</u> the road.

   <u>When Carla and Bill left the house, they turned the light off.</u>

2. a. When the car skidded on ice, it ran <u>off</u> the road.

   b. Everyone in the group needed a map, so Paula ran <u>off</u> some photocopies.

   _____

3. a. Judy checked <u>in</u> her purse to make sure that her plane ticket was still there.

   b. Ethan checked <u>in</u> his luggage at the airline counter.

   _____

4. a. When Mark and Terry talked long distance for hours, they ran <u>up</u> a huge bill.

   b. When the children got out of school, they ran <u>up</u> the street.

   _____

5. a. The committee passed <u>over</u> two other people and chose Tim for the job.

   b. You passed <u>over</u> the Hudson River when you drove across the bridge.

   _____

6. a. As soon as I looked <u>over</u> the top of the hill, I saw the valley below it.

   b. As soon as I looked <u>over</u> the exam, I saw that it wasn't difficult.

   _____

6 **Using Phrasal Verbs:** Turn This In

Write a one-paragraph story about a travel experience. The experience can be a real one or one that you make up. Include at least five phrasal verbs from the following list. You may include other phrasal verbs, too (see Appendix 8).

break down	go back	think over	put off
come along	find out	pick up	set off
come up	take off	point out	turn out

Example: Last year, my brother and I went back home for a vacation. The trip was a disaster. After we got to the airport, we found something out. The airline had put off our flight. It finally took off eight hours late. . . .

See the *Grammar Links* Website for a complete model story for this assignment.

Verb–Preposition Combinations; Phrasal Verbs with Prepositions

FORM and FUNCTION

A. Form of Verb–Preposition Combinations

1. Verbs and prepositions sometimes combine as a fixed unit. (Like phrasal verbs, these combinations are sometimes called two-word verbs.)

   Prepositions used in these combinations include *about, at, for, from, in, of, on, to,* and *with*.

   Verb–preposition combinations are always followed by an object.

   Think about your decision.

   They **confide in** us.

   We **lived on** pasta.

2. In some verb–preposition combinations, the verb can also have an object.

   (See Appendix 9 for a list of common verb–preposition combinations.)

   | | verb | obj | prep | obj |
   His coat **protected** him **from** the cold.

B. Meaning of Verb–Preposition Combinations

1. Verbs of attitude, sense, speech, and thought are common in verb–preposition combinations. The meaning of a combination can often be figured out from the meaning of the verb.

   I **agree with** you. (attitude)

   We **listened to** some music. (sense)

   Let's **talk to** him about it. (speech)

   I **didn't think of** the answer. (thought)

2. A verb–preposition combination + object is a verb + prepositional phrase, like those in the Grammar Hotspot on page 122. However, the combinations are fixed units, and, often, the preposition does not have its usual meaning.

   verb prep obj
   We **lived on** pasta. (survived by eating pasta— i.e., ate a lot of pasta)

   verb prep obj
   Compare: We **lived on** a hill. (lived in a location)

C. Phrasal Verbs with Prepositions

Phrasal verbs, too, can be combined with prepositions. (These combinations are sometimes called three-word verbs.)

(See Appendix 10 for a list of common phrasal verbs with prepositions.)

phrasal verb   prep
We**'re running out of** money this month.

He **hasn't caught up with** the group yet.

They **got back from** the hike.

Watch out for falling rocks!

GRAMMAR **HOT**SPOT!

Here are some ways to tell the difference between verb–preposition combinations and phrasal verbs: In verb–preposition combinations:

- The verb has its usual meaning.

- The object can't come between the two words.

- *Up*, *out*, *off*, and *down* are **not** used (they are common in phrasal verbs).

He **played with** the children. (*Play* has its usual meaning.)
NOT: He played the children with.
Compare the phrasal verb play down: He **played down** the problems. (*Play down* means "make seem less important.") OR He **played** the problems **down**.

GRAMMAR PRACTICE 3

Verb–Preposition Combinations; Phrasal Verbs with Prepositions

7 **Verb–Preposition Combinations:** Preparing for the Unexpected

A. Use the appropriate form of the verb–preposition combinations in the boxes to complete the sentences.

dream of	plan for

Both Roald Amundsen and Robert Falcon Scott were experienced explorers who

<u>dreamed of</u> _____ reaching the South Pole. But their personalities
₁

were very different, and they _____ their expeditions in
₂

different ways.

talk to	rely on	prepare for	concentrate on

Amundsen _____ practical experience and careful
₃

preparation. Before he explored an area, he _____
₄

experienced people and got useful information from them. In addition, Amundsen

_____ the details of an expedition. He always
₅

_____ the worst possible conditions, so he was ready for
₆

the unexpected.

worry about	believe in	agree with	prevent from

Scott was an officer in the British navy. He _____₇

tradition and determination, and he didn't _____₈ details.

Unfortunately, Scott's personal feelings often _____₉ him

_____ making wise decisions. For example, he felt that using dogs to

pull his sleds was cruel. He _____₁₀ people who believed that

the men should pull the sleds, although this was exhausting.

B. When you travel to a new place, how do you prepare for the trip? Write a paragraph describing your typical preparations. Use four verb–preposition combinations from Part A and Appendix 9.

Example: *Before I travel to a new place, I always read about it. I like to be well organized, so I worry about details. . . .*

See the *Grammar Links* Website for a complete model paragraph for this assignment.

8 **Verb–Preposition Combinations Versus Phrasal Verbs:** Do You Know About the Antarctic Region?

An explorer is questioning a person who wants to join an expedition. Complete the answers, changing the noun objects in the questions to pronouns. Be careful to put the pronoun in the correct position.

1. Q: I need someone who is knowledgeable. Do you know about the Antarctic region?
   A: Yes, I _know about it_____.

2. Q: My plans are summarized in these papers. Have you looked over these papers?
   A: Yes, I _'ve looked them over_____.

3. Q: These are the maps of the route I plan to follow. Have you looked at these maps?
   A: Yes, I _____.

4. Q: The members of the group must be adaptable. Do you learn from your mistakes?
   A: Yes, I _____.

5. Q: Our equipment must be tested in advance. Will you try out the equipment?
   A: Yes, I _____.

6. Q: The trip will be very dangerous. Have you thought about the dangers?
   A: Yes, I _____.

7. Q: You seem to be determined to come along. Have you thought over your decision?
   A: Yes, I _____.

9 Phrasal Verbs with Prepositions: Running Up Against Difficulties

Use the appropriate form of the phrasal verb–preposition combinations in the box above each paragraph to complete the paragraph. (If necessary, look in Appendix 10 for help.)

catch up + with	~~run up + against~~	stand up + to	start out + for

Scott's expedition __ran up against__ difficulties from the
1

beginning. Scott _____ the South Pole two weeks after
2

Amundsen because of problems with his equipment. He had planned to use motorized

sleds, but they didn't _____ Antarctic conditions. Scott
3

never _____ Amundsen.
4

close in + on	face up + to	keep on + at

Scott and his men began their journey south on November 1, 1911, but bad weather

soon _____ them. Although the conditions were terrible,
5

they _____ the tiring job of pulling their sleds to the
6

pole. They finally reached it on January 17, 1912—only to see the Norwegian flags that

Amundsen had left there. They _____ the fact that they
7

had been beaten.

cut down + on	gave up + on	run out + of

On the return journey, Scott's group _____ supplies
8

and luck. Because they _____ food, they became weak
9

and confused. They struggled on to a point only 11 miles from a place where they had

stored food. Each day they tried to start for it, but snowstorms drove them back. Finally,

they _____ their attempts. By the end of March, Scott
10

and his men had died from hunger, cold, and exhaustion.

10 Using Verb–Preposition Combinations and Phrasal Verbs with Prepositions: Your Expedition Diary

We know the story of Scott's expedition because he kept a diary, which was found later. In his final message, he wrote:

> *We took risks—we knew we took them; things have come out against us. . . . I do not think we can hope for any better things now. We shall stick it out to the end but we are getting weaker of course and the end cannot be far. . . . For God's sake, look after our people.*

Imagine that you are on an expedition in a distant and dangerous place, for example, Antarctica or a desert, jungle, or mountain. Write a two-paragraph diary entry. Use at least four verb–preposition combinations (see Appendix 9) and four phrasal verbs with prepositions (see Appendix 10). Here are some suggestions:

Verb–preposition combinations: *come from, depend on, happen to, hope for, learn from, live on, look for, prepare for, prevent (someone or something) from, recover from, search for, think about, wait for*

Phrasal verbs with prepositions: *catch up with, close in on, come up with, get back from, give up on, keep up with, put up with, run out of, run up against, start out for, watch out for*

Example:

Before we started out for the mountaintop, we had prepared for bad conditions. Then we ran up against difficulties. First, we met up with a bear. . . .

Now, we're living on crackers and juice. We haven't given up on getting to the top of the mountain. We've come up with a plan. . . .

See the *Grammar Links* Website for a complete model diary entry for this assignment.

Tag Questions I

FORM

A. Forming Tag Questions and Their Answers

TAG QUESTIONS			ANSWERS
STATEMENT	**TAG**		
	BE/DO/HAVE/ MODAL (+ *NOT*)	PRONOUN	
You're hungry now,	**aren't**	**you?**	Yes, I am./No, I'm not.
The bus didn't come,	**did**	**it?**	Yes, it did./No, it didn't.
They've already left,	**haven't**	**they?**	Yes, they have./No, they haven't.
Bob can drive us,	**can't**	**he?**	Yes, he can./No, he can't.

(continued on next page)

A. Forming Tag Questions and Their Answers (continued)

1. To form tag questions, add to a statement: *be/do/have*/modal (+ *not*) + pronoun.

   You haven't seen my pen, **have you?**

2. The tag can be affirmative or negative:

   - With an affirmative statement, use a negative tag, contracting the *not*.

     It**'s going to rain**, **isn't** it?

   - With a negative statement, use an affirmative tag.

     It **isn't going to rain**, **is** it?

3. The pronoun in the tag corresponds to the subject in the statement.

   Bob and John are leaving tomorrow, aren't **they?**

B. Verb Forms in Tags

1. If the statement has a modal auxiliary (*can*, *should*, etc.) or other auxiliary verb (*be, do, have*), use the auxiliary. If it has more than one auxiliary, use the first.

   We **can** get tickets, **can't** we?

   We **are** leaving now, **aren't** we?

   Pete **didn't** go, **did** he?

   He **hasn't been** practicing, **has** he?

   They **won't have** returned by June, **will** they?

2. If the statement doesn't have an auxiliary but has main verb *be*, use *be*.

   She **was** in the Bahamas last year, **wasn't** she?

3. It the statement doesn't have an auxiliary or main verb *be*, use *do*.

   You **go** to the beach every year, **don't** you?

   I **arrived** late, **didn't** I?

4. The verb usually agrees with the subject of the statement.

   It**'s** leaving at 8:00, **isn't** it?

   They**'re** leaving at 8:00, **aren't** they?

   Exceptions to this are:

   - With *I am*, the tag is *aren't I*.

     I**'m** leaving at 8:00, **aren't** I?

   - With indefinite pronouns that stand for people (*everyone, someone, nobody*, etc.), use plural verbs in the tag instead of singular verbs.

     Everyone is ready, **aren't** they?

     No one knows the answer, **do** they?

(continued on next page)

C. Other Subjects in Tags

1. If the subject in the statement is:

   - *This* or *that*, use *it* in the tag.

   | **This** isn't right, is **it**? |

   - *These* or *those*, use *they* in the tag.

   | **Those** aren't heavy, are **they**? |

2. If the subject is an indefinite pronoun:

   - With pronouns that stand for people (*everyone, someone, nobody,* etc.), use *they* in the tag.

   | **Everyone** is going to be here tomorrow, aren't **they**? |

   - With pronouns that stand for things (*everything, something, nothing,* etc.), use *it* in the tag.

   | **Something** is wrong, isn't **it**? |

3. If *there* is in subject position, use *there* in the tag.

   | **There**'s some pizza in the refrigerator, isn't **there**? |

GRAMMAR **HOT**SPOT!

1. When the statement includes *never* (= *not ever*), use an affirmative tag.

   | The bus **never comes** on time, **does** it? (= The bus doesn't ever come on time, does it?) |

2. When the subject of the statement is an indefinite pronoun with *no-* (*nobody, nothing*), use an affirmative tag.

   | **Nobody** is still hungry, **are** they? |
   | **Nothing** happened, **did** it? |

TALKING THE TALK

The tag of tag questions can be an expression such as *right, isn't that right, isn't that so,* or *correct.* These tags can be used with affirmative and negative statements and all tenses. The questions can be answered like other tag questions.

A: He won't be in today, **right**?
B: No, he won't.
A: She'll be back from her trip by then, **isn't that right**?
B: Yes, she will.

Tag Questions I

11 **Tag Questions—Form:** Test Anxiety—I'll Be Ready, Won't I?

A. For each statement, underline the subject and circle the first verb, auxiliary or main. Then complete the tag question.

1. Tests <u>cause</u> anxiety, _don't they_____?

2. Ms. Moore doesn't give difficult tests, _____?

3. The first test is going to cover Columbus's voyages to America, _____?

4. Christopher Columbus wasn't from Portugal, _____?

5. The other students already know a lot about the topic, _____?

6. You weren't absent from class, _____?

7. Kim and Oliver hadn't studied before this week, _____?

8. We can study together, _____?

B. Complete the tag questions.

1. Those weren't the right answers, _____?

2. There is a lot to learn, _____?

3. Someone will fail the test, _____?

4. Victoria was taking notes, _____?

5. That could be a question on the test, _____?

6. The library has all the information we need, _____?

7. Everything is going to be okay, _____?

8. This isn't taking too much time, _____?

9. You and I will have learned everything by tomorrow, _____?

10. I'm driving you crazy with all these questions, _____?

11. I've never failed an exam before, _____?

12. Nobody's perfect, _____?

Tag Questions II

FUNCTION

A. Uses of Tag Questions

1. Speakers use tag questions when they have some sense of the answer. (Otherwise, they use *yes/no* questions.)

Speaker thinks there might be a bus stop nearby: There's a bus stop nearby, isn't there?
Compare: speaker has no idea if a bus stop is nearby: Is there a bus stop nearby?

2. Speakers may use a tag question just to make conversation. (They know the answer.)

It's hot today, isn't it? (You're standing at a bus stop on a very hot day.)

Or they may use a tag question to confirm an answer. (They have a strong sense of the answer.)

This is Mr. Lee's class, isn't it? (You're quite sure it's his class.)

In these uses:

- The tag is spoken with falling intonation.

It's hot today, **isn't it**?

- The listener often just nods or responds with some expression of agreement.

Um. OR Uh-huh.

3. Speakers may use a tag question to get information. (They don't have a strong sense of the answer.)

It'll be hot today, won't it? (Yesterday was hot, but you haven't been out yet.)

This is Mr. Lee's class, isn't it? (You think it might be here or in some other room.)

In this use:

- The tag is spoken with rising intonation like a *yes/no* question.

It'll be hot today, **won't it**?

- The listener is likely to answer yes or no or otherwise give information.

Yes, it will. OR No, the forecast is for cooler weather today.

B. Speaker Expectations

The statement part of the tag question expresses the speaker's expectation about the answer:

- When speakers think the answer is yes, they usually use an affirmative statement.

We **have** a test tomorrow, don't we? (The speaker thinks there's a test.)

- When speakers think the answer is no, they usually use a negative statement.

We **don't have** a test tomorrow, do we? (The speaker thinks there isn't a test.)

(continued on next page)

C. Answering Tag Questions

1. Answer the question the same way regardless of whether the statement is affirmative or negative.

> A: You borrowed my book, didn't you?
> B: Yes, I did. (if B borrowed the book)
>
> A: You didn't borrow my book, did you?
> B: Yes, I did. (if B borrowed the book)
> **NOT**: ~~No~~, I did. OR ~~No~~, I borrowed your book.

2. Especially, if your answer doesn't agree with the speaker's expectations, you probably should give an explanation for your answer.

> A: We have a test on Friday, don't we?
> B: No, we don't. The teacher postponed it until next week.
>
> A: We don't have a test on Friday, do we?
> B: Yes, we do. The teacher told us about it yesterday at the end of class.

GRAMMAR PRACTICE 5

Tag Questions II

12 Listening to Tag Questions; Answering Tag Questions: Christopher Columbus

A. Listen to the questions once, paying attention to the speaker's intonation. Then listen again and decide whether the speaker wants confirmation or information. Check the correct choice.

	The speaker is sure and wants confirmation.	The speaker is not sure and wants information.
1.	☑	☐
2.	☐	☐
3.	☐	☐
4.	☐	☐
5.	☐	☐
6.	☐	☐
7.	☐	☐
8.	☐	☐
9.	☐	☐
10.	☐	☐
11.	☐	☐

B. Read the information about Columbus on page A-2. Listen to the questions again and answer each one orally as a class.

Example: "Columbus set out on his first voyage in 1492, didn't he?" *Yes, he did.*

 Visit the *Grammar Links* Website to learn more about Columbus and his voyages.

13 **Asking and Answering Tag Questions:** Test Anxiety Again

Work in pairs. Take turns asking and answering the questions in Exercise 11. Try to use falling intonation in asking the questions. Give the answer that agrees with the speaker's expectation.

Example: Student A: Tests cause anxiety, don't they?
Student B: Yes, they do.
Student B: Ms. Moore doesn't give difficult tests, does she?
Student A: No, she doesn't.

14 **Using Tag Questions:** You're from Spain, Aren't You?

A. How well do you know your classmates? Write five statements with information about your classmates that you're quite sure is true.

Example: Luis isn't from Spain.

Write five statements with information that you aren't so sure about.

Example: Amy has four sisters.

B. 1. Go around the classroom, checking the information in your statements by using tag questions. Use falling intonation for the information you're quite sure about:

Luis, you aren't from Spain, are you?

Use rising intonation for the information you aren't so sure about:

Amy, you have four sisters, don't you?

2. When answering your classmates' questions, give an explanation when your answer isn't the one your classmate expects or when you think an explanation is useful.

Example: A: Luis, you aren't from Spain, are you?
B: No, I'm not. (I'm from Argentina.) (expected answer) OR Yes, I am. I was born there, but I've lived in this country for five years.
A: Amy, you have four sisters, don't you?
B: Yes, I do. (expected answer) OR No, I don't. You're almost right, though, because I have three sisters.

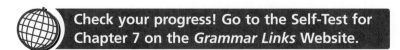

Check your progress! Go to the Self-Test for Chapter 7 on the *Grammar Links* Website.

Wrap-up Activities

1 Radio Talk Time: EDITING

Correct the 13 errors in the transcript of a radio show. There are errors in verb forms
and tenses and in tag questions. Some errors can be corrected in more than one way.
The first error is corrected for you.

Host: This is Radio Talk Time. If you have an interesting
         opinion, call ~~up me~~ *me up* and tell me.

Caller: What do you think about NASA's space program? I've
         thought it about. It's all a lie. Nothing is real,
         isn't it?

Host: You're joking, don't you?

Caller: No, I'm serious. NASA says that it's going to send a
         spacecraft to Mars next October. But they don't really
         send it to Mars in October. We'll believe that it's on
         Mars, but they'll be fooling us.

Host: How they'll do that? After the spacecraft reaches Mars,
         its cameras will take photos and send back them to
         Earth. We'll see those photos of Mars.

Caller: It's going to be seeming to us that a spacecraft is on
         Mars. Antarctica looks a lot like Mars, isn't it? By
         the time they'll launch the fake spacecraft next
         October, they'll have sent people to Antarctica with
         video cameras and a fake lander. After they set the
         cameras up there, they'll be able to send back pictures
         of the lander. While we're going to be watching the
         videos on television, we're going to be looking at
         Antarctica, not Mars. But we won't be knowing that,
         will we?

Host: I'm sorry, sir. We've run out of time. It's time for
         the weather forecast. It's snowing tomorrow.

Caller: Wait! Don't hang up on me! I'm right, aren't I?

2 **Your Island Vacation:** SPEAKING/WRITING

Work with a partner. Imagine that you are going to Getaway Island for a three-day vacation.

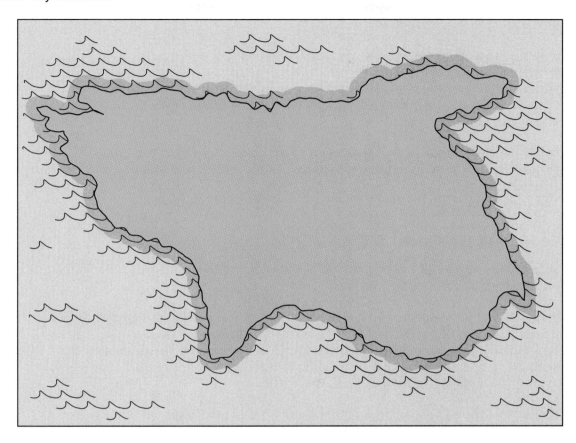

Getaway Island

Step 1 Use your imagination to fill in the map with the features of the island, for example, towns, beaches and other natural attractions, hotels and stores, amusement parks and other entertainment places—anything you want to include.

Step 2 Discuss what you are going to do when you visit the island, and make a plan for your vacation there.

Step 3 Write two paragraphs about your plans. In the first paragraph, describe what you'll be doing day by day. Use *will*, *be going to*, and the future progressive.

Example: On the first morning of our vacation, we're going to go to the beach. After we have lunch at an outdoor café, we'll rent motorbikes. We're going to be riding them to the waterfall in the center of the island in the afternoon. . . .

In the second paragraph, summarize what you'll have done by the end of the vacation. Use the future perfect.

Example: By the time our vacation ends, we're going to have had a lot of fun. We will have ridden our motorbikes all over the island. . . .

 See the *Grammar Links* Website for complete model paragraphs for this activity.

3 Your Outdoor Vacation: SPEAKING

Work in small groups to plan a trip to a national park in the United States.

Step 1 Find information about various national parks at a library or on the Internet. (If you look on the Internet, use "National Park Service" as the term for your search.)

Step 2 Discuss the possibilities and make plans: Which park are you going to visit? When will you go? How long will you stay? How are you going to get there? What activities are you going to do? What equipment and supplies will you need to take? What responsibilities will each member of the group have? Write notes about your plans.

Step 3 Give oral reports about your plans to the class, referring to your notes as needed. Which trip sounds the most adventurous? Which one sounds the most educational?

4 Game: Ask the Oracle: SPEAKING

Step 1 One member of the class should play the part of the oracle. He or she looks at page A-3 and follows the instructions there.

Step 2 The other members of the class each write three questions about their future travels to ask the oracle. Two of the questions should be *yes/no* questions; one should be a tag question. Use a different future form in each question. For example: *Am I going to go on a trip soon? Will I have gone to Mars by the time I'm 50? I'm going to spend my honeymoon in Hawaii, aren't I?*

Step 3 Take turns asking your questions for the oracle to answer.

> *oracle* = someone thought to have knowledge about the future.

5 Acting Out the Verbs: WRITING/SPEAKING

Work in small groups to write and then perform a skit.

Step 1 Each group chooses one of the lists of phrasal verbs on page A-3.

Step 2 Work together to write your skit. The story is up to you, but it should use all the phrasal verbs in your list and should include actions that will show the meanings of these verbs. Everyone in the group should have a role.

Step 3 Present your skit to the rest of the class.

 See the *Grammar Links* Website for a model skit for this activity.

Noun Phrases

TOPIC FOCUS
Food

UNIT OBJECTIVES

▨ **proper and common nouns**
(*Emily Custer* just opened a *restaurant*.)

▨ **count and noncount nouns**
(I can make some *suggestions* if you want *advice* about what to order.)

▨ **uses of definite and indefinite articles**
(*The* cake looks too sweet. I'll have *a* cookie instead.)

▨ **general quantifiers**
(I had *a lot of* coffee and *several* cookies.)

▨ **adjectives and other noun modifiers**
(I crave *delicious*, *fresh*, *home-grown* tomatoes.)

▨ **reflexive, reciprocal, and indefinite pronouns**
(Andrew made the cake *himself*. Liz and Val helped *each other* make the appetizers. *Everything* is ready now.)

▨ **possessives—determiners, nouns, pronouns, and phrases**
(This is *my* office. It isn't *Ms. Baca's* office. *Hers* is down the hall in the corner *of the building*.)

Grammar in Action

Read and listen to this passage from a guidebook for international visitors to the United States.

Food Choices

People from many countries have become familiar with one type of American food—fast food. So you may consider fast food to be the typical American food. And you'll find that **lots of Americans** do eat fast food, often because we want to save time. But as you travel through the country, you will also discover many interesting differences among places and people. Our regional, cultural, and individual differences influence our food choices and our eating habits. These choices and habits are always changing, and often the changes seem to go in different directions at the same time.

For example, recently Americans have been going out to eat at restaurants more than ever before. Does this mean that we don't have much interest in home cooking? Not at all. **Quite a few people** are taking up cooking as a hobby. They've been buying **lots of new cookbooks** and spending hours reading recipes on **the Internet**. Cooking programs on television have become popular; one TV channel has just cooking programs. In fact, **some professional chefs** have become **big celebrities**.

Some Americans don't worry much about **their diets**. But many of us are concerned about our diets and our health. We have questions about what's in **our food** and how safe it is. And we worry about eating too much fat. This doesn't mean that we can resist fatty foods, though. One person can't resist a chocolate bar; another can't resist an ice cream cone or **a delicious hot cheese pizza**.

At the end of your visit to **the United States**, you might not be able to make many general statements about our food except for this one: There's plenty of it!

---

celebrity = a famous person.

Think About Grammar

A phrase is a group of related words. One type of phrase is the noun phrase. Some of the noun phrases in the passage are boldfaced. Work with a partner. Look at the boldfaced noun phrases. Complete the sentences about the parts of noun phrases.

1. There are two types of nouns, proper nouns and common nouns. Proper nouns start with a capital letter. Examples of proper nouns are __Americans_____,

   _____, and _____.

2. Common nouns do not start with a capital letter unless they begin a sentence. Examples of common nouns are __countries_____, _____, and

   _____.

3. Quantifiers tell the amount or number of a noun. Examples of quantifiers are

   __lots of_____, _____, and

   _____.

4. Possessives indicate a noun as belonging to someone or something. Examples of possessives are

   __their_____ and _____.

5. Adjectives and other modifiers describe and give more information about nouns. Examples of modifiers are __new_____, _____, and

   _____.

Chapter 8

Nouns, Articles, and Quantifiers

Introductory Task: Survey on the Cooking and Eating Habits of Your Class

A. Work with a partner. Take turns asking each other the questions. Mark each of your partner's answers with a check (✔) in the appropriate box.

Survey Questionnaire

1. How much time do you spend cooking each day?

   ❏ 0 to 30 minutes   ❏ 30 to 60 minutes   ❏ 60 minutes or more

2. How many times do you go to fast-food restaurants each week?

   ❏ 0 times   ❏ one or two times   ❏ three to five times   ❏ six or more times

3. How much ice cream do you eat each week?

   ❏ no ice cream   ❏ not much ice cream   ❏ some ice cream   ❏ a lot of ice cream

4. How much fruit do you eat each day?

   ❏ no fruit   ❏ hardly any fruit   ❏ some fruit   ❏ a lot of fruit

5. How many vegetables do you eat each day?

   ❏ no vegetables ❏ not many vegetables ❏ some vegetables ❏ a lot of vegetables

6. How much coffee do you drink each day?

   ❏ no coffee   ❏ one or two cups of coffee   ❏ three or more cups of coffee

---

B. Find out about your class. Write the questions on the blackboard and add up the answers in each category. As a class discuss the results. What can you conclude about the group's habits?

Example: *We don't spend much time cooking.*

Nouns; Proper Nouns and Common Nouns

FORM and FUNCTION

A. Overview

1. Nouns name people, places, and things.

   teachers, children, Robert, city, Venezuela, school, food, trouble

2. There are various types of nouns:

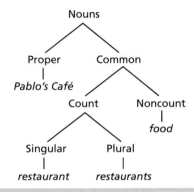

B. Proper Nouns

Proper nouns name particular people, places, and things.

They always start with a capital letter.

Names of people: **Mrs. Fields, Alex Dean**

Names of places: **South America, China, New Orleans, Lake Placid, Comfort Inn**

Titles: ***Good News Cookbook, Time, USA Today***

Days, months, holidays: **Friday, June, Thanksgiving**

Nationalities, languages, religions: **Mexican, Japanese, Islam**

(continued on next page)

Article Use with Proper Nouns

1. With most proper nouns, the articles *the* and *a/an* are not used.

   They climbed **Mount Everest**.
   NOT: They climbed ~~the Mount Everest~~.

2. With certain proper nouns, however, *the* must be used. These include some names of countries, regions, geographical features, buildings, and vehicles, as well as newspapers and magazines.

   (See Appendix 11 for more proper nouns with *the*.)

   The United States is in North America.

   The Middle East produces dates.

   We went to **the Rocky Mountains**.

   My favorite restaurant is **the New York Deli**.

   In 1620, some colonists sailed from England on **the *Mayflower***.

   I usually read **the *Washington Post***.

3. *The* is used with family names in the plural form.

   The Smiths are our neighbors. (the Smith family)

4. In some special uses, a proper noun does **not** refer to one particular person, place, or thing. When this happens, the proper noun can be used with an article or a number.

   Can I have an appointment on **a Saturday**? (not a particular Saturday)

   There are **three Jasons** in my class. (three students named Jason)

C. Common Nouns

Common nouns are not names of particular people, places, or things.

They do not start with a capital letter unless they begin a sentence.

(For more on common nouns, see Grammar Briefing 2, page 147.)

The **teacher** is talking to a **student** now. (people)

That **restaurant** is in the **city**. (places)

Computers are important in many **jobs**. (things)

Nouns; Proper Nouns and Common Nouns

1 **Identifying Proper and Common Nouns:** Celebrating with Food

Read the following passage. Capitalize the proper nouns. Underline the common nouns.

Celebrating with Food

When are you planning to be in the ~~united~~ ~~states~~? If you are here in
U   S

the <u>fall</u>, you might be here at the right time to have a special meal on

thanksgiving. This national holiday is on the fourth thursday in

november. In big cities, restaurants stay open and offer meals. In

chicago, the oak leaf restaurant at the westlake hotel is a good place

to go. The chef there is henry lee. Although mr. lee is vietnamese, he

speaks both french and english, and americans love his food,

especially the turkey. If you are in a small town, maybe you can cook

the special dinner. Look for recipes in newspapers like the *new york*

times. Or try a cookbook like *the thanksgiving table* by diane morgan.

Wherever you are, have a happy celebration!

2 Article Use with Proper Nouns: Regional Specialties I

Different regions of the United States have different food specialties. Work with a partner. Insert *the* where needed with proper nouns in the following sentences. (If necessary, look in Appendix 11 for help.)

1. When English colonists sailed across ^*the*^ Atlantic Ocean to North America on *Mayflower*, they landed in New England, an area that's known for its maple syrup, blueberries, lobster, and clams.

2. New Orleans, a city in Louisiana, where Mississippi River flows into Gulf of Mexico, has its own typical style of cooking, which shows influences from France and Africa.

3. After they settled in Midwest, immigrants from Germany, Sweden, Norway, and Netherlands continued to prepare the traditional foods of their native countries.

4. Cattle are raised on ranches in Rocky Mountains, so visitors often have steaks when they're staying at Brown Palace Hotel in Denver, the capital of Colorado.

5. The food of West Coast, like that of Hawaiian Islands in Pacific, has been influenced by Asia.

3 Articles and Numbers with Proper Nouns: Regional Specialties II

Use the article or number in parentheses or, if it is not appropriate, write *NA*.

A: Let's have a potluck dinner soon. We'll ask everyone to bring a special food from the region where they grew up.

B: That sounds like fun. We can have it on _a_____ Sunday next month.

1 (a, NA)

A: I think it would be better to have it on _____ Saturday next month.

2 (a, NA)

B: Okay. Let's invite _____ Callahans. They're from Boston, and they make great

3 (the, NA)
   clam chowder.

A: Let's invite _____ Tom, too. I talked to him on _____

4 (the, NA)   5 (a, NA)
   Tuesday, and I know he'd like to come.

B: I know _____ Toms. Which one do you mean?

6 (two, NA)

A: The one from Georgia. He makes delicious pecan pies!

Count Nouns and Noncount Nouns

FORM and FUNCTION

A. Overview

There are two types of common nouns:

- Count nouns—nouns that can be counted.

| idea: one idea, three ideas |

- Noncount nouns—nouns that cannot be counted.

| advice
NOT: ~~one advice, three advices~~ |

Be careful! Some nouns that are noncount nouns in English are count nouns in other languages.

B. Count Nouns

1. Count nouns generally have singular and plural forms.

| banana, bananas |

2. When the subject of a sentence is:
   - A singular count noun, the verb is singular.

| A **banana was** in the bowl. |

   - A plural count noun, the verb is plural.

| Two **bananas were** in the bowl. |

3. However, some count nouns have only a plural form. When they are the subject, the verb is plural.

| I need **glasses** for reading.
These **jeans are** too small for me. |

4. Regular plural count nouns add *-s/-es* to the singular form.

   (See Appendix 12 for spelling rules for regular plural count nouns and Appendix 13 for pronunciation rules.)

| school → **schools**
tomato → **tomatoes** |

   Irregular plural count nouns:

   - Differ from the singular form in some other way.

| man → **men**
mouse → **mice** |

   - Are the same as the singular form.

| sheep → **sheep**
deer → **deer** |

   - Come from another language and have kept their original plural form.

   (See Appendix 14 for more irregular plural count nouns.)

| bacterium → **bacteria**
analysis → **analyses** |

(continued on next page)

C. Noncount Nouns

1. Because noncount nouns are not countable, they cannot be plural. They always take a singular verb.

   Her **advice was** good.
   NOT: Her ~~advices were~~ good.

2. Many noncount nouns belong to certain categories:

NAMES OF GROUPS OF SIMILAR ITEMS	NATURAL PHENOMENA	ABSTRACT CONCEPTS
clothing, equipment, food, fruit, furniture, garbage, homework, jewelry, money, traffic	cold, electricity, fire, heat, humidity, rain, scenery, weather	advice, beauty, confidence, education, energy, freedom, fun, health, information, luck, progress, time

SOLIDS	LIQUIDS	GASES
glass, gold, ice, paper, silver, wood	coffee, milk, soup, tea, water	air, oxygen, smoke, steam

FOODS	ACTIVITIES	FIELDS OF STUDY
bread, butter, cheese, chicken, flour, rice, salt, spinach, sugar	chess, cooking, driving, soccer, traveling	business, chemistry, engineering, history

   (See Appendix 15 for more noncount nouns.)

3. Certain noncount nouns can be made "countable" with measure phrases, which put them into units (e.g., *a slice of*, *a box of*, *two pounds of*).

   I'd like **a cup of coffee**, please.

   We need **a quart of milk** and **two loaves of bread**.

D. Noncount Nouns Used as Count Nouns

1. Some noncount nouns that refer to solids, liquids, foods, and other substances can be used as count nouns. In this use they refer to a type or serving of the substance. (Examples: *aspirin, cake, cheese, chocolate, coffee, food, tea.*)

   I like many different **foods**. (types)
   Compare: All living things need food. (substance)

   I'd like **two coffees** to go, please. (servings)
   Compare: I like coffee in the morning. (substance)

2. Some noncount nouns that refer to abstract things can be used as count nouns. In this use they refer to individual examples of the abstract thing. (Examples: *art, business, crime, education, freedom, law, life, truth.*)

   He committed three **crimes**. (three individual examples of crime)
   Compare: Crime is a serious issue. (crime in general)

   My grandparents' **lives** were difficult. (the life of particular people)
   Compare: Life is sometimes difficult. (life in general)

1. Some noncount nouns end in *-s* (e.g., *news, physics*). These nouns are not plural. They take a singular verb.

    > Bad **news** travels quickly.

2. Collective nouns, which are usually count nouns, are nouns that refer to groups (e.g., *group, team, audience, committee*). Singular collective nouns are usually used with singular verbs and pronouns.

    > The **team** of experts **has** finished **its** work.

GRAMMAR PRACTICE 2

Count Nouns and Noncount Nouns

4 **Identifying Count and Noncount Nouns:** Food for Sightseeing

Read the following passage. Circle the count nouns. Underline the noncount nouns. Including the examples, there are 12 count nouns and 13 noncount nouns.

Food for Sightseeing

Will you be traveling through the United States in the warm(months)? If so, we have some <u>advice</u> for you: Have picnics often, especially when the weather is good. You'll be able to avoid crowded restaurants, save money, and have a lot of fun, too. You don't have to do any cooking—  just stop at a supermarket and pick up some food to take with you. You can get bread and cheese for sandwiches. Get some fruit, too, and fresh vegetables such as carrots or celery. You'll want to have a drink, so don't forget to buy bottled water or juice. Then put your purchases into your backpack and take off. When you find the perfect place, enjoy the beautiful scenery and your meal!

5 Count Nouns Versus Noncount Nouns; Plural Count Nouns: A Good Career Choice

Write the correct form of the noun in parentheses. Each noun is either a noncount noun or a plural count noun. (If necessary, look in Appendix 12, 14, or 15 for help.)

Allison: I wanted to get some __information__ about career choices, so I went to see
1 (information)

my advisor. It's always hard for me to make important __decisions__ .
2 (decision)

Magda: Did she have any _____ for you?
3 (advice)

Allison: She gave me a lot of helpful _____ . Now I'm thinking about
4 (suggestion)

becoming a professional cook.

Magda: That's an interesting possibility. Have you had any restaurant _____ ?
5 (experience)

Allison: I've had plenty of restaurant _____ . But so far I haven't had any
6 (job)

_____ . The advisor said that cooking has become an excellent
7 (training)

profession for _____ . They've made a lot of _____
8 (woman) _9 (progress)_

in the profession, and they're even getting jobs as executive chefs.

Magda: It will be exciting, but I think you can expect to do a lot of hard _____ ,
10 (work)

even when you become an executive chef. Before you go to cooking school, you'll need

to buy some really good _____ for peeling and chopping.
11 (knife)

Allison: Professional kitchens have lots of _____ to do things like that.
12 (machinery)

Magda: But really good restaurants don't use many _____ . The chefs
13 (machine)

prepare almost everything by hand, so they're on their _____ most
14 (foot)

of the day.

Allison: Yeah, but some of them are real _____ !
15 (celebrity)

> *executive chef* = the chef in charge of a restaurant kitchen.

 Go to the *Grammar Links* Website to find out more about cooking careers and celebrity chefs.

6 **Singular and Plural Count Nouns; Subject–Verb Agreement:**
Culinary Education

Circle the correct form of the verb or noun.

1. The news (is) / are good if you want to be a professional chef: There are lots of
   jobs available.

2. A committee choose / chooses the students to admit to cooking school.

3. Mathematics is / are important for chefs and restaurant managers.

4. Bacteria / Bacterias are becoming more dangerous, so it's important to keep
   kitchens clean.

5. Please be sure that your clothes is / are clean.

6. The professor's food-cost analysis / analyses have helped restaurants save money.

7. There were a lot of students in cooking school last year, and this year the group
   is / are even larger.

8. We've learned how to choose the freshest grocery / groceries.

9. "Venison" is meat from deer / deers, and "mutton" is meat from sheep / sheeps.

7 **Nouns Used as Count and Noncount Nouns:** Good Food and Good Fortune

A. Use the appropriate noun phrases from the boxes to complete each dialogue.

> food/foods

Dustin: I'm hungry. Let's get some _food___ . What do you like to eat?
                                    1

Joel: Well, I like many different ethnic _____ , but my favorite is Chinese.
                                          2

> tea/teas

Waitress: What would you like to drink?

Dustin: Do you have _____?
                     3

Waitress: Yes, of course we do.

Dustin: We'd like two _____ .
                      4

> business/a business

Joel: Naomi told me that you've gone back to school. What are you studying?

Dustin: I'm studying _____ . I'd like to own _____ in the future.
                     5   6

cake/a cake

Waitress: Are you ready for dessert? The chef made _____. It has almonds in it.
7

Joel: No, thanks. I don't really like _____. But I do want fortune cookies.
8

experience/experiences

Dustin: I like this fortune. It says, "You will have exciting _____."
9

Joel: Some of the fortunes aren't really fortunes. They're proverbs like "There's no better

teacher than _____."
10

life/lives

Joel: Here's another one: "Learn to treasure even the difficulties of _____."
11

Dustin: This one's better: "You and your loved ones will find more happiness than sadness in

your _____."
12

beauty/a beauty

Dustin: This is the last one: "You will find _____ everywhere you go."
13

Joel: I'd prefer one that says "You will meet _____, and she will love
14

you forever."

 B. Work with a partner. Write your own one-sentence fortunes or proverbs. Use each of these noncount/count pairs: *education/an education, friendship/a friendship, love/loves, opportunity/opportunities.* Read your sentences to the class.

 See the *Grammar Links* Website for model sentences for this assignment.

Articles

FORM and FUNCTION

A. Articles as Determiners

The articles (*the*, *a/an*, and [0]) are a type of determiner. Determiners come before common nouns. The other determiners are quantifiers (see Grammar Briefing 4, page 161), demonstratives (*this*, *that*, *these*, *those*), and possessive determiners (see Chapter 9, Grammar Briefing 4, page 182).

det   noun
The children went home. (article)

Some children went home. (quantifier)

Those children went home. (demonstrative)

My children went home. (possessive)

B. The Definite Article (*The*)

1. The definite article, *the*, is used with all common nouns—noncount, singular count, and plural count.

   The electricity is off. (noncount)

   I fed **the cat**. (singular count)

   The cookies were good. (plural count)

2. *The* is used when the noun refers to something specific and the speaker and listener know what it is. This can happen when:

   • The noun has already been mentioned.

   I made some cookies and a cake. **The cookies** were delicious, but **the cake** was horrible.

   • The noun is part of or clearly related to something that has already been mentioned.

   I baked a cake. **The frosting** was too sweet. (The frosting is part of the cake.)

   • The noun is made clear by other words in the sentence.

   The bread on the table is delicious. (*On the table* tells which bread.)

   • The noun is unique—there is only one.

   The sun is shining now.

   • The noun is part of everyday life for the speaker and the listener.

   Mom, I'll feed **the dog**. (The speaker and listener know this refers to their dog.)

   • The noun is part of the larger social context of the speaker and the listener.

   The president was on TV. (The speaker refers to the president of their country—part of their social context.)

   • The noun is part of the immediate situation—speaker and listener can see or hear it.

   Could you pass **the butter**? (The speaker and listener can see it.)

(continued on next page)

C. The Indefinite Article (*A/An*)

1. The indefinite article, *a/an*, is used only with singular count nouns.

   I need **a pen**.

   He ate **an apple**.

2. The indefinite article occurs as:

   - *A* before consonant sounds.

     a kitchen, **a** hospital, **a** uniform

   - *An* before vowel sounds.

     an orange, **an** honor, **an** umbrella

3. *A/an* is used when:

   - The noun doesn't refer to something specific.

     Jack needs to find **a job**. (any job, not a specific job)

     Can I take **an apple**? (any apple from a group, not a specific apple)

   - The noun refers to something specific but the speaker and listener don't **both** know what it is. That is, the noun hasn't been mentioned yet and the other reasons for using *the* don't apply (see section B, 2). *A/an* introduces the noun.

     A man is here to see you.

     I just started **a new job**.

4. *A/an* is also used in a subject complement (i.e., after *be* and similar verbs). *A/an* + noun describes the subject but doesn't refer to a specific person, place, or thing.

     My brother is **an electrician**. (*An electrician* is just a description of the brother; it doesn't refer to a particular person.)
     Compare: An electrician is here to fix the lights. (a particular person)

(continued on next page)

D. The [0] Article

1. The [0] article is used instead of *a/an* with plural count nouns and noncount nouns.

   | I put **[0] nuts** in the pie. (plural count noun) |
   | I put **[0] fruit** in the pie. (noncount noun) |
   | *Compare*: I put an egg in the pie. |

2. The [0] article + plural subject noun is often used in statements about categories of people, places, or things. The subject noun does **not** refer to specific members of the category.

   | **Oranges** are a good source of vitamin C. (*Oranges* doesn't refer to specific oranges; the sentence is about oranges in general.) |

3. Some words commonly occur with the [0] article, especially in certain phrases with prepositions; for example:

   - *Breakfast, lunch, dinner.*

     | We ate **[0] dinner** but didn't have a snack. |

   - *Go to/be in bed, school, class, college.*

     | The children haven't **gone to [0] bed** yet. |
     | He's **in [0] college** now. |

   - *Come by/go by train, bus,* etc.

     | She **came by [0] car.** |

   - *At night, before morning,* etc.

     | He eats a lot **at [0] night** but not in the morning. |

4. *Some* can be used instead of the [0] article to talk about an indefinite quantity of the noun.

   | After dinner, I'd like **[0]/some dessert**. (an indefinite quantity of dessert) |

   However, it **cannot** be used to talk about the noun in general.

   | I like **[0] dessert**. (*Some* can't be used; this is about dessert in general—not about a quantity of a dessert.) |

Articles

8   Definite and Indefinite Articles: The Eating Patterns of a North American Family

The conversations in Column I took place during a typical week in the life of Mona and Doug and their daughter, Erin. Listen once for the main ideas. Listen again and circle the correct choice. Then read the statements in Column II and circle the letter of the statement that fits the conversation.

Column I	Column II
1. Erin: Mom, I've got to hurry! The school bus is coming, and I can't find my lunch box. Mona: I haven't seen it. Did you leave it on (a) / the chair in the living room?	(1.) a. There's more than one chair in the family's living room. b. There's one chair in the family's living room.
2. Erin: Mom, I hope you had time to stop for groceries on your way home from work. Mona: They're in the car. You could help me by carrying in a / the bag.	2. a. There's more than one bag of groceries in the car. b. There's one bag of groceries in the car.
3. Doug: Erin, please don't turn on the television yet. You haven't finished your dinner. Erin: Do I have to? I don't really like [0] / the vegetables.	3. a. Erin doesn't like vegetables in general. b. Erin doesn't like tonight's vegetables.
4. Mona: Erin, if you want a snack, have a piece of fruit. Erin: I want a snack but fruit doesn't sound good. Could we go to a / the bakery?	4. a. Neither Mona nor Erin knows which bakery it is. b. Both Mona and Erin know which bakery it is.
5. Mona: I can't leave work until six tonight. Do you think you could cook dinner? Doug: Mona, you know I can't cook. Let's get fast food and then watch a / the movie.	5. a. This is the first time the movie has been mentioned. b. Doug and Mona have talked about the movie before.
6. Mona: Erin, try to eat more politely. You've got ketchup all over your face. Erin: I can't help it, Mom. I like [0] / the french fries a lot.	6. a. Erin likes french fries in general. b. Erin likes these particular french fries.
7. Erin: Are you and Mom going out to dinner alone tonight? Doug: Yes, we are. A / The babysitter is coming to take care of you.	7. a. Doug knows who the babysitter is, but Erin doesn't. b. Both Doug and Erin know who the babysitter is.
8. Doug: Can I have a taste of your dessert? It looks like it has a lot of good things in it. Mona: It does. I really like [0] / the chocolate.	8. a. Mona likes chocolate in general. b. Mona likes the chocolate in this dessert.

9 The Definite Article: The Story of Their Lives

Work with a partner. Read the dialogue between Stuart and his wife, Melissa. Above each boldfaced noun, write the letter of the reason why the speaker used *the*.

> A. The noun has already been mentioned.
>
> B. The noun is part of or is related to something that has already been mentioned.
>
> C. The noun is made definite by other words in the sentence.
>
> D. The noun is unique.
>
> E. The noun is part of Stuart and Melissa's everyday lives or larger social context.

Stuart: Melissa, I'm glad you're finally home. What's kept you so long?

Melissa: I had to work late, so I missed ¹**the bus** near my office. Then I took a different

          (C)

bus, but ²**the engine** broke down. By the time another bus came, it was already

dark and ³**the moon** had come up. Have you started cooking dinner?

Stuart: Not yet. I had a busy day, too. First, I went to a meeting. ⁴**The meeting** went on

for hours. Then I spent the whole afternoon learning how to use a new

computer. I had some trouble getting used to ⁵**the keyboard**. After I got home,

I wanted to read ⁶**the newspaper**. There's an interesting article about a new

scandal.

Melissa: What does ⁷**the article** say?

Stuart: ⁸**The mayor** might be involved in ⁹**the scandal**. She may have to resign.

Melissa: Let's not worry about that now. We need to think about dinner. We could

make sandwiches, but ¹⁰**the bread** in the cupboard is really old.

Stuart: That's because it's been days since either one of us has had time to go to

¹¹**the store**.

Melissa: This is ¹²**the story** of our lives, Stuart. Hand me ¹³**the phone**, please. I'm

going to order a pizza.

> *scandal* = something that shocks or offends the community. *mayor* = the highest
> official of a city or town.

10 Definite and Indefinite Articles: Food Here and There

A. Complete the conversations with *a*, *an*, *the*, or [0].

I. *In a university dormitory dining hall:*

Cindy: Good morning, Angela. Have you already had __[0]__ breakfast?
1

Angela: Yeah. I had __an__ omelet and __a__ doughnut. I hated
2 3

__the__ omelet because _____ filling tasted strange.
4 5

_____ F/food in this dormitory is disgusting.
6

Cindy: I think I'll have _____ doughnut.
7

Angela: I don't want to go to _____ school today. Look at _____ sky.
8 9

_____ W/weather is going to be terrible. I want to go back to
10

_____ bed.
11

Cindy: Stop complaining. We can go by _____ bus. Do you have plans
12

for tonight?

Angela: Yeah, I do. I'm going to _____ party. Do you want to come along?
13

Cindy: What time does _____ party start?
14

Angela: I'm not sure, but I'll look at _____ invitation.
15

II. *At the party:*

Cindy: Noah, I didn't expect to see you here. I heard that you went on _____
1

trip. I'd like to hear about it. We could have _____ lunch together
2

sometime.

Noah: What about tomorrow? We could meet at _____ restaurant, if you're free.
3

Cindy: Okay. Let's think of _____ interesting place to eat. Do you like
4

_____ salads?
5

Noah: Not really. But _____ salads are good for you, so I eat them sometimes.
6

Cindy: Let's go to Café Viva. You'll love _____ salads at Café Viva. My friend Liz
7

works there part-time. Do you know her? She's _____ great cook, and
8

she's _____ honor student, too.
9

Noah: I don't know Liz, but I've seen that café. It's close to _____ university, isn't it?
10

Cindy: Right. It's across from _____ library. I'm going to be in _____
11 12

class all morning. If _____ teacher lets us out on time, I can meet you at
13

_____ café at noon.
14

III. *At lunch the next day*:

Noah: When I was traveling, I found out that this isn't _____ only country with
1

lots of fast food. There are _____ American fast-food restaurants
2

everywhere now.

Cindy: Do they serve exactly _____ same things as they do here?
3

Noah: Sometimes they do. For example, I went into _____ fast-food restaurant
4

in Beijing. I ordered _____ hamburger. After I took off _____
5 6

wrapper, I lifted up _____ bun and looked at _____ meat.
7 8

It looked exactly like _____ hamburger from _____ fast-food
9 10

restaurant in Miami or Omaha. It tasted exactly like one, too.

Cindy: Was that _____ most interesting experience you had while you were
11

traveling?

Noah: I was interested in _____ hamburgers at that restaurant in Beijing because
12

I'm _____ international business major, and I'm interested in working
13

abroad. Someday I may be selling _____ hamburgers in China.
14

B. Listen to the conversations. Check your answers.

11 *The, A, Some,* [0]: Old and New Recipes

A. Use *a*, *the*, or *some* to complete the paragraphs.

I have my great-grandmother's recipes, but they're hard to use. For example, her

recipe for pancakes starts: "Make _a_____ thick batter by mixing
                                       1

_____ flour with _____ milk." _____
   2   3   4

recipe doesn't tell you how much flour or milk to use or how to cook

_____ batter.
    5

This is her recipe for soup: "Catch and kill _____ chicken, cut it
                                                      6

up, and put it into _____ boiling water. When _____
                        7   8

chicken is nearly done, add _____ chopped onions and
                                 9

_____ spices. If you have _____ fresh carrot, add it to
    10   11

_____ soup."
   12

B. For each pair, decide which sentence can be completed with *some* or [0] article and which should be completed with [0]. Write *some*/[0] or [0].

1. a. My hobby is finding _[0]_____ new recipes on the Internet.

    b. I've found _some/[0]_____ interesting recipes on the Internet.

2. a. One of the recipes was for _____ pancakes.

    b. I immediately used it to make _____ pancakes.

3. a. I thought about making _____ chicken soup for dinner.

    b. Everyone in my family likes _____ chicken soup.

4. a. I bought _____ fresh spinach at the farmers' market.

    b. I didn't know how to cook _____ spinach, so I found a recipe on the Internet.

C. Write a one-paragraph recipe like the ones in Part A. Pay attention to your use of *the*, *a(n)*, *some*, and [0].

Example: To make stewed apples, first peel and cut up some apples. Put the apples in a pan and add water. Put the pan on the stove and cook the apples. When they are very soft, stir in some sugar. Add lemon juice and cinnamon.

For links to thousands of recipes on the Internet, go to the *Grammar Links* Website.

12 Using *The*, *A*, *Some*, [0]: Two Memorable Meals

1. Work with a partner. Ask your partner to tell you about a very bad and a very good meal she or he has eaten. Your partner should tell you what dishes were included in the meals and describe each dish. Ask questions to get all the details. Both partners should pay attention to their use of the, a, some, and [0].

Example: Student A: Tell me about a very bad meal that you've had.
Student B: I had a terrible lunch at school once. The lunch was soup, some noodles, and a sweet dessert. Everything was awful.
Student A: What was the soup like?
Student B: It was just hot water with some meat in it. The meat was gray and slimy. The sauce on the noodles was gray, too. . . .

2. Tell the class about the worst and best parts of your partner's meals.

GRAMMAR BRIEFING 4

General Quantifiers

FORM and FUNCTION

A. Quantifiers

Like other determiners, quantifiers are used before nouns. Quantifiers include:

- Numbers and measure phrases, which indicate a specific amount.

- General quantifiers, which indicate a nonspecific amount.

Can I borrow **two eggs**?
Can I borrow **two cups of flour**?
Can I borrow **some eggs/some flour**?

B. General Quantifiers with Singular Count Nouns

Each and *every* are used with singular count nouns. Both mean "the total number."

I read **each paper** carefully.
I read **every paper**.

(continued on next page)

C. General Quantifiers with Plural Count Nouns and Noncount Nouns

Other quantifiers are used with plural count nouns, noncount nouns, or both.

> I need **a few quarters**.
>
> I have **a little money**.
>
> I have **some quarters/some money**.

	QUANTIFIERS USED		
	WITH PLURAL COUNT NOUNS	WITH NONCOUNT NOUNS	WITH BOTH
			all
			most
	a great many	a great deal of	a lot of/lots of
	many	much	plenty of
	a (large) number of	a/an (large) amount of	
	quite a few		
	several		some/any
			enough
	a few	a little	
	not many	not much	
	few	little	
			hardly any
			not any/no/none of

D. Notes on General Quantifiers Used with Plural Count Nouns and Noncount Nouns

Many and Much; A Lot

1. *Many* and *much* are used mainly:

   - To ask questions about quantity.

     > **How many** people were at the party?

   - In negative statements.

     > We **don't** have **much** milk left.

   - After *so* or *too* in affirmative statements.

     > The teacher gives **so/too much** homework.

2. In other affirmative statements, *a lot of* is more common. *Many* is considered formal. *Much* is even more formal and is usually avoided.

   > They had **a lot of** fun.

(continued on next page)

Some *and* Any

1. In affirmative statements, *some* is used.

   I'd like **some** dessert.

2. In questions, *any* is often used instead of *some*.

   Would you like **any/some** dessert?

3. In negatives, *any* is usually used.

   I **don't** want **any** dessert now.

A Few, A Little; Few, Little

1. *A few* and *a little* express the positive idea that there is some.

   Let's go to that restaurant. It has **a few** really healthy dishes.

   I have **a little** free time, because I finished my work.

2. *Few* and *little* express the negative idea that there is hardly any or not enough.

   Let's not go to that restaurant. It has **few** really healthy dishes.

   I have **little** free time, because I have so much work.

E. Notes on All General Quantifiers

1. *Of* is always part of certain general quantifiers (e.g., *a lot of*). It can also be part of all other general quantifiers (except for *no* and *every*) when the quantifier occurs with:

   • A pronoun.

   Each of them came.

   • *The*
     Demonstrative } + noun.
     Possessive

   Most of the students came.

   Most of those students came.

   Most of my students came.
   NOT: ~~Each/Most of students~~ came.

2. All of the quantifiers except *no* and *every* can be used without nouns if the meaning is clear.

   Each is good.

   I learned **a lot**.

GRAMMAR **HOT**SPOT!

In negative statements, do not use *no, none of*, or *hardly any*. This is often referred to as avoiding double negatives.

I don't want **any** dessert now.
   NOT: I don't want ~~no~~ dessert now.

He doesn't have **much** money.
   NOT: He doesn't have ~~hardly any~~ money.

General Quantifiers

13 **General Quantifiers:** A "Big" Trend

A. Complete the passage with the correct quantifiers.

There is a "big" trend in food in the United States—it seems that _____many_____

<u>1 (much / many)</u>

food portions and packages have become enormous. _____

<u>2 (Not much / Not many)</u>

Americans notice this trend anymore, but _____

<u>3 (quite a few / a large amount of)</u>

international visitors do. A first-time visitor from Europe commented, "They serve

_____ food in _____ restaurants here.

<u>4 (a great many / a lot of)</u>   <u>5 (every / most)</u>

_____ meal that I've had has been big." An Asian visitor added,

<u>6 (Each / All)</u>

"The meals are huge. How do you eat so _____ food?"

<u>7 (much / many)</u>

Marketing experts say that the "big" trend began in fast-food restaurants. It

takes only _____ money to "up-size" a fast-food meal, and

<u>8 (a little / a few)</u>

_____ customers pass up the chance to do it. After they

<u>9 (hardly any / not much)</u>

noticed the popularity of oversize portions in restaurants, food manufacturers began

to make _____ products in "grand," "jumbo," or

<u>10 (a large number of / a large amount of)</u>

"mammoth" sizes. They have had _____ success with

<u>11 (a great many / a great deal of)</u>

these packages. A new-products consultant says this success is natural.

"_____ years ago, health experts started warning us of the dangers of

<u>12 (Several / Little)</u>

eating such large portions. But _____ people seem to be able to resist

<u>13 (few / little)</u>

them. They just want to have _____ food."

<u>14 (plenty of / a large number of)</u>

---

marketing = the business activity that involves selling, advertising, and packaging
products. *consultant* = a person who gives expert or professional advice.

B. As a class, compare the portions discussed in Part A to portions in other
places you know about. What is your opinion of this trend toward big
packages and portions?

14 General Quantifiers: Market Research I

Circle the correct choice. Where both choices are correct, circle both.

Interviewer: Do you mind answering (a few) / a little questions about your purchases
1

today? It won't take (much) / (a lot of) time.
2

Shopper: I don't mind. I have some / any time.
3

Interviewer: Did you spend much / a lot of money shopping today?
4

Shopper: Yeah. I got much / lots of things. I bought ice cream because we don't have
5

some / any at home. I got three packages of hot dogs. I always like to have
6

plenty of / quite a few hot dogs.
7

Interviewer: It looks like you bought a great deal of / a lot of potato chips, too.
8

Shopper: Yes. We didn't have many / hardly any at home, and I wanted to be sure we
9

had any / enough.
10

Interviewer: Did you buy any / some fresh vegetables?
11

Shopper: No, as a matter of fact, I got none / no at all.
12

Interviewer: Did you buy many / some sweets?
13

Shopper: I don't usually buy any / no sweets, but I bought any / some today.
14   15

Interviewer: Do you have much / a lot of experience with shopping?
16

Shopper: I don't have much / a lot, but I know what I like.
17

15 *Few, A Few; Little, A Little*: Shopping Behavior

Complete each sentence with *few*, *a few*, *little*, or *a little*.

I. Marketing Expert: Let me give you _a little_ advice. Don't put important

items just inside the entrance of the store, because _few_

shoppers notice anything in that area. Also, shoppers, especially women

shoppers, don't like to be crowded. They don't like stores with

_____ space in the aisles.
3

Supermarket Manager: How many men do the food shopping for their families?

Marketing Expert: Not many. _____ men do the shopping because usually
4

women do the food shopping for their families.

II. Wife: I've got a lot to do today and _____ time to do it. Would you mind
5

going to the grocery store?

Husband: We don't need to go to the store yet. We have _____ cheese and
6

_____ pickles. We can make _____ sandwiches.
7   8

Wife: Never mind. I'll go. Do you have any money?

Husband: Sure, I have _____. How much do you need?
9

III. Marketing Expert: Women are usually more patient than men. Men seem to have

_____ patience for shopping. Also, children can talk their
10

fathers into buying almost anything. _____ fathers can refuse
11

their children's requests.

IV. Child: Look, Daddy, they have chocolate chip cookies in the bakery! Could we please get

some cookies?

Father: Okay, you can get _____, but let's not tell your mother.
12

16 Quantifiers with and Without *Of*: Focus Groups

Complete the sentences by writing *of* or 0 in the blanks.

1. Many _____0_____ companies want to know what products appeal to people.

2. A lot _____of_____ food manufacturers use focus groups to get information.

3. Each _____ the members of a focus group tries the new product.

4. Each _____ member of the group gives an opinion about the product.

5. Several _____ my friends participated in a focus group recently.

6. Did any _____ these flavors appeal to you?

7. I haven't tried any _____ new flavors yet.

8. Plenty _____ products are introduced in this country every year.

9. Most _____ people in the group don't like this product.

10. Most _____ them don't think it will be successful.

17 Using Quantifiers: Market Research II

You have just gone to the supermarket to buy groceries. After you finished shopping, a market researcher gave you the list below and asked you to write a paragraph about your purchases. In your paragraph, tell about five items that you bought—three items on the list and two not on the list. Tell how much of each item you bought and why. In addition, mention three items on the list that you didn't buy and tell why you didn't buy them. Try to use a different general quantifier in each sentence about the items you bought. Use *not . . . any* in the sentences about the items you didn't buy.

Example: When I was shopping today, I bought a little coffee. I don't have coffee at home every day, so I didn't buy a lot. I bought several lobsters because I'm going to give a dinner party for my friends. All of my friends love lobsters. . . . I didn't get any peanut butter because I never eat it. . . .

Food Products List			
bananas	coffee	ice cream	peanut butter
candy	cookies	oranges	rice
carrots	frozen dinners	lobsters	spinach
cheese	fruit juice	potato chips	steaks

See the *Grammar Links* Website for a complete model paragraph for this assignment.

Check your progress! Go to the Self-Test for Chapter 8 on the *Grammar Links* Website.

Chapter 9

Modifiers, Pronouns, and Possessives

Introductory Task: What's Your Reaction?

A. Check the box before the sentence that describes your reaction to the particular food. If your reaction is somewhere in between, check the middle box.

1. ❏ Broccoli is a vitamin-filled green vegetable. It has a pleasant flavor.

   ❏

   ❏ Broccoli is an unpleasant vegetable. It has a very strong, bitter flavor.

2. ❏ Chocolate is my favorite candy. I can't resist eating lots of rich, wonderful chocolate.

   ❏

   ❏ Chocolate isn't an exciting food. I don't eat much chocolate.

3. ❏ I love to eat lobsters. I really enjoy their delicious, juicy white meat.

   ❏

   ❏ I refuse to eat lobsters. I have no desire to put a frightened lobster into boiling water.

4. ❏ Snails make a wonderful meal. I like them cooked with melted butter and fresh garlic.

   ❏

   ❏ I would never eat snails. They're slimy, disgusting animals.

B. Work in small groups. First, compare your reactions to the foods in the pictures. Were they similar or different? Then discuss other foods that you like or dislike very much. Why do you like or dislike these foods? Find two foods that everyone in the group likes and two foods that everyone in the group dislikes. As a class, compare likes and dislikes. Are there any foods that all the groups agree on?

Modifiers
■ Adjectives and Other Modifiers of Nouns

FORM and FUNCTION

A. Modifiers of Nouns

Modifiers of nouns describe and give more information about nouns.

(The modifiers in this grammar briefing come before nouns. Adjective clauses, modifiers that follow nouns, are discussed in Unit Five.)

> modifier   modifier   noun
> Fernando is the **tall**, **good-looking** boy
> modifier (adjective clause)
> **who always comes to class late**.

B. Adjectives

Adjectives are the most common modifiers of nouns. They describe nouns by telling their appearance and other qualities.

> **strong**, **black** Colombian coffee
>
> **long wooden** spoon
>
> **polite**, **well-behaved** children

-Ing and -ed Adjectives

Adjectives that end in -ing and -ed often describe feelings.* If the adjective ends in:

- -ing, the noun that it modifies causes the feeling.

- -ed, the noun that it modifies experiences the feeling.

*These adjectives have the same form as present and past participles. If the past participle doesn't end in -ed, the adjective doesn't either (e.g., broken, upset).

> What a **boring** woman! No one wants to talk to her.

> What a **bored** woman! She doesn't have anything to do.

Use of Intensifiers with Adjectives

Adjectives can be strengthened by intensifiers—words like really and very.

> She's a **really/very** good teacher.

(continued on next page)

C. Nouns as Modifiers

A noun can modify another noun. The noun modifier is singular.	There are several **steak restaurants** near our house. Let's go on the **bike path**.

D. Compound Modifiers

Compound modifiers have two words joined by a hyphen. Often the words are:

- Number + singular noun.

three-pound chicken
NOT: ~~three-pounds~~ chicken

- Noun
  Adjective
  Adverb } + -*ed* adjective, -*ing* adjective

sun-filled room, **time-wasting** activity

best-liked student, **good-looking** boy

well-known actor, **slow-moving** traffic

■ Order of Modifiers Before Nouns

FORM and FUNCTION

MODIFIERS								NOUN MODIFIED
ADJECTIVES							NOUN	
OPINION/ QUALITY	APPEARANCE (INCLUDING SIZE, HEIGHT, LENGTH)	AGE	SHAPE	COLOR	NATIONALITY/ ORIGIN	MATERIAL	NOUN	
lovely		new				silk		blouse
	big		round				fruit	bowl
good					French			food
ugly				gray			rain	clouds

1. When two or three adjectives modify a noun, they tend to occur in a certain order.

   He was a **mean old** man.
   NOT: He was an ~~old mean~~ man.

2. Use a comma between adjectives that seem to modify the noun equally. (Hint: These adjectives can be separated by *and*.)

   good, nutritious food (food that is good and nutritious)

   Do not use a comma if the last adjective + noun makes a combination, and the first adjective modifies that combination.

   good Italian food (Italian food that is good)

Modifiers

1 Identifying Modifiers: Another Look

Work with a partner. Go back to the introductory task on page 168. Find the modifiers in the sentences, underline them, and circle the noun that they modify.

Example: Broccoli is a <u>vitamin-filled</u> <u>green</u> (vegetable.) It has a <u>pleasant</u> (flavor.)

2 *-Ing* and *-ed* Adjectives: Food and Feelings

A. Use the adjectives to complete the sentences.

Satisfied

Satisfying

> satisfied/~~satisfying~~

Waiter: Did you enjoy your dinners?

Customer: Yes, we did. Please give our compliments to the chef. That was a really

<u>satisfying</u> meal.
           1

Waiter: I will. The chef likes to have _____ diners.
                                          2

comforted/comforting

Psychologist: When adults feel stressed, they want ＿＿＿＿＿＿＿＿＿＿ foods, often the foods
3

they loved as children. When they eat these foods, they feel less stressed. They feel

like ＿＿＿＿＿＿＿＿＿ children again.
4

relaxed/relaxing

Fitness Instructor: For relaxation, it's better to exercise than to eat. Sports and workouts at the

gym are ＿＿＿＿＿＿＿＿＿＿ activities. And a ＿＿＿＿＿＿＿＿＿＿
5   6

person may be able to handle stress without frequent visits to the refrigerator.

bored/boring

Vicky: I was thinking about boredom and food. Do you think that ＿＿＿＿＿＿＿＿＿＿
7

people sometimes eat just because they need stimulation?

Jennie: Yes, I do. Whenever I'm doing a ＿＿＿＿＿＿＿＿＿ assignment, I have a hard time
8

concentrating until I eat chocolate.

tempted/tempting

Meg: This bakery has the most ＿＿＿＿＿＿＿＿＿ pastries I've ever seen. Don't they
9

look delicious?

Terry: My feeling is that a ＿＿＿＿＿＿＿＿＿ person shouldn't resist temptation. Let's
10

try them!

> *stimulation* = an increase in physical or mental activity.

 B. Work with a partner. Write two sentences about each kind of person.

1. amusing people; amused people

   Amusing people tell jokes and funny stories. They're fun to be with.
   Amused people smile and laugh. They're having a good time.

2. annoying people; annoyed people

3. boring people; bored people

4. interesting people; interested people

5. shocking people; shocked people

3 **Noun Modifiers:** Food Safety

Change the words in parentheses to noun modifier + noun and complete the sentence.

1. Handle __steak knives__ carefully. They're very sharp.
   (knives for steaks)

2. There might be dirt or germs on fresh vegetables. Wash them before you cut them up for

   _____.
   (soup made of vegetables)

3. Don't let the _____ stay open too long. Warm food can spoil.
   (door to the refrigerator)

4. Don't let small children play with _____. The children could suffocate.
   (bags made of plastic)

5. Never try to dry a wet newspaper in the _____. It could catch fire.
   (oven powered by microwaves)

6. Accidents can happen. Keep a _____ in the kitchen.
   (extinguisher for fires)

7. Keep your fingers out of the _____. The blades are dangerous.
   (processor for food)

8. Do you think that we really need all this _____?
   (advice about safety)

4 **Compound Modifiers:** Long-Lasting Memories

Complete the sentences with a compound modifier formed by using the appropriate words from the sentence in parentheses.

1. Childhood memories stay with you. (They last a long time.) They're

   __long-lasting__ memories.

2. I used to visit my grandmother during vacations. (One vacation was two months.)

   Once I stayed with her for a _____ vacation.

3. My grandmother cooked on an old stove. (That kind of stove burns wood.) It was a

   _____ stove.

4. When I was young, we ate cookies on holidays. (They were baked at home.)

   They were _____ cookies.

5. My mother made all our meals. (They were cooked well.)

   They were _____ meals.

6. Every Thanksgiving my mother roasted a big turkey. (One weighed thirty pounds.)

   She once roasted a _____ turkey.

7. My mother doesn't do much cooking anymore. (The activity consumes time.)

   Cooking is a _____ activity.

8. But I still have memories of our kitchen. (It smells sweet.)

   I remember a _____ kitchen.

5 Order of Modifiers: What Are Your Food Cravings?

A. Write the modifiers under the blanks in an appropriate order. Include commas when they are indicated.

Hank: What am I craving right now? I'd like a <u>really big, thick</u> hamburger. But I
1 (big / , / really / thick)

don't crave the _____ hamburgers from fast-food restaurants.
2 (boring / little)

Greta: I crave ice cream constantly. At the moment, I want a _____
3 (round / big / very)

scoop of triple-fudge ice cream.

Rolf: I've been thinking about pizza. I'm going to have a _____ pizza
4 (mushroom / delicious)

as soon as I can. I'm going to get it at a(n) _____
5 (charming / Italian / old / ,)

restaurant in my neighborhood.

Patty: My favorite snack is _____ chips. I get the ones that
6 (corn / crunchy / very)

come in a _____ bag. And I dip them in a
7 (plastic / large / blue)

_____ sauce.
8 (chili / red / tasty)

Tanya: I'm trying to lose weight, so I've stopped eating butter. But I dream about the kind of

butter in the _____ box.
9 (cardboard / , / rectangular / yellow)

It has a picture of a _____ woman on it.
10 (Native American / young / beautiful)

> *food craving* = a very strong desire for a certain food.

B. 1. Write five sentences about foods that you crave or like best. In each sentence, use two or three modifiers to describe a noun. Use an intensifier in at least two sentences.

Example: I crave delicious, smooth milk chocolate. I like very strong, black Colombian coffee.

2. Read your sentences to the class. As a class discuss your cravings. Are people's cravings similar or different? What are some cravings that seem surprising or unusual?

6 Using Modifiers: Memories of the Past

Read the following story about Dino, who wanted to open a restaurant that would serve people's favorite foods—the ones they loved eating in their childhood. Use your imagination to rewrite the story, adding modifiers before nouns. It isn't necessary to add modifiers before all the nouns. Pay attention to modifier order. Include at least one of each of the following: *-ing* adjective, *-ed* adjective, noun modifier, and compound modifier. Change *a* to *an* where necessary.

Example: First, he talked to an amusing young Greek woman named Helen. . . . OR
First, he talked to a very short, good-looking woman named Helen. . . .

Dino asked various people to tell him about their memories. First, he talked to a woman named Helen. She told him stories about the meals her grandmother cooked. She described the fish, the vegetables, and the desserts. Then Dino talked to a teacher named Vinnie, who remembered some meals. Vinnie also talked a lot about the house and the garden where he lived and played as a child. After that, Dino heard from Evan, a man who loved music and art. But Evan didn't want to be reminded of his childhood. Finally, Dino met a woman named Cora. Cora had grown up in a family that lived in a city. She had memories of hot dogs and candy. Cora told Dino about the boyfriend she had just broken up with. In the end, Dino realized that his idea wouldn't work—people's feelings about food are too complicated. He decided to write stories instead. He married Cora and wrote her story first.

See the *Grammar Links* Website for a complete model story for this assignment.

GRAMMAR BRIEFING 2

Reflexive Pronouns; Reciprocal Pronouns; *Other*

FORM and FUNCTION

A. Pronouns

Pronouns replace noun phrases that have already been mentioned or that are clear from the context. (For a summary chart of pronouns, see Appendix 16.)	**Bob** isn't here now. But **he**'ll be back in a minute.

(continued on next page)

B. Reflexive Pronouns

1. The reflexive pronouns are *myself, yourself, himself, herself, itself, ourselves, yourselves,* and *themselves.*

   Use a reflexive pronoun instead of an object pronoun (*me, her,* etc.) when an object refers to the same person or thing as the sentence subject.

   > **The cook** burned **herself.** (herself = the cook)
   >
   > **They** have confidence in **themselves.** (themselves = they)
   > *Compare:* They have confidence in them. (*Them* and *they* refer to different people.)

2. Reflexive pronouns are also used to emphasize a noun. In this use, they often come right after the noun.

   > Go if you want. **I myself** wouldn't go. (emphasis to show the speaker feels strongly)
   >
   > The **principal herself** taught our class today. (emphasis because it's unexpected for a principal to teach a class)

3. Use *by* + reflexive pronoun to mean "alone" or "without help."

   > I was eating **by myself.**
   >
   > The children went to the store **by themselves.**

C. Reciprocal Pronouns

Each other and *one another* are reciprocal pronouns. They are used as objects when two or more people or things, mentioned in the subject, give and receive the same feelings or actions. The reciprocal pronouns refer to these people or things.

> **Tom and Paula** don't really trust **each other.** (Tom doesn't trust Paula, and Paula doesn't trust Tom.)
>
> **The children** cooperate well with **one another.** (Each child cooperates with the other children.)

D. *Other*

Other and *another* refer to an additional one or more of a noun that has been mentioned.

> A: Look! There's a baby robin. And there's **another.**
> B: And there are **others** under that tree.

The other and *the others* refer to all other instances of that noun.

> One of the boys in the class is my best student; **the other** is having a lot of problems. (There are only two boys in the class.)

Another and *others* refer to only some other instances of that noun.

> One of the boys in the class is my best student; **another** is having a lot of problems. (There are boys in addition to these two.)

Reflexive Pronouns; Reciprocal Pronouns; *Other*

7 Reflexive and Reciprocal Pronouns—Meaning: Seeing Differences

Work with a partner. Explain the difference in meaning or emphasis between the sentences in each pair.

1. a. Lewis saw himself in the mirror.
   b. Lewis saw him in the mirror.

   In (a), <u>himself</u> refers to Lewis. Lewis saw Lewis in the mirror. In (b), <u>him</u> doesn't refer to Lewis; it refers to some other man or boy. Lewis saw someone else in the mirror.

2. a. Lucy and Trevor ordered dinner for themselves.
   b. Lucy and Trevor ordered dinner for each other.

3. a. Monica and Howard were writing letters to them.
   b. Monica and Howard were writing letters to each other.

4. a. Eva was talking to her.
   b. Eva was talking to herself.

5. a. Dora served herself dinner.
   b. Dora herself served dinner.

6. a. I myself have gone to Paris.
   b. I've gone to Paris by myself.

7. a. I talked to the president himself.
   b. I talked to the president myself.

8 Reflexive and Reciprocal Pronouns: Movable Feasts

Circle the correct pronoun.

1. Today one out of 10 meals in the United States is eaten in a car, but when I was growing up, my family always ate at home. My mother put the food on the dining room table, but she didn't serve (us)/ ourselves the food. We served <u>us / ourselves</u>.

2. Whenever I was sick, my father myself / himself served me / myself breakfast in bed. This was unusual, though.

3. My sister has five-month-old twins, Yolanda and Yvonne. Right now she's busy feeding them / themselves. When the twins are old enough to feed them / themselves, my sister won't be so busy.

4. Yesterday my children ate in the car. They took turns feeding themselves / each other. First, Toby put a chicken nugget into Sam's mouth. Then Sam put a chicken nugget into Toby's mouth.

5. A: After we pick up our food, let's all sit in the car and listen to the radio while we eat.

    B: Let's talk to ourselves / one another instead. I want to hear what everyone's been doing.

6. Sometimes I like to be myself / by myself in my car, because then I can sing to me / myself and no one else can hear.

9 Forms of *Other*: Sharing

Complete the sentences by using *another*, *others*, *the other*, or *the others*.

1. A: Thanks for the cookie. It was delicious.

    B: There are plenty more. Do you want _another_____?

2. I have two cookies. I'm going to eat one. Do you want to eat _____?

3. A: I'm like a lot of young single people. I like living by myself. I don't want to share my food or space.

    B: I'm used to sharing everything with _____. I grew up in a big family.

    A: So did I. That's why I'm so happy being alone now. I got tired of sharing with all _____ in my family.

4. A: I brought back the CD you loaned me. Can I trade it for _____?

    B: Sure, but why just borrow one? I have a lot of CDs. If you want to borrow _____, you can pick out as many as you'd like.

5. A: Would you like something to eat or drink? I know how to make exactly five things. Tea and coffee are two of them; instant noodles and scrambled eggs are _____; and, believe it or not, lobster Newburg is _____.

   B: I'm sorry. I heard tea and coffee, but I didn't hear _____. Could you repeat them?

6. A: I like Irene because she has so many fine qualities. One is kindness. _____ is honesty.

   B: And _____ is generosity. She gave me her last piece of chocolate this morning.

Indefinite Pronouns

FORM and FUNCTION

A. Forming Indefinite Pronouns

	SOME-	ANY-	NO-	EVERY-
+ -ONE	someone	anyone	no one	everyone
+ -BODY	somebody	anybody	nobody	everybody
+ -THING	something	anything	nothing	everything

B. The Meaning of the Indefinite Pronouns

1. To say none (not any), use indefinite pronouns with *no-*.

   | There's **nothing** in the house to eat. |
   | **Nobody** told me. |

   However, following a negative, use indefinite pronouns with *any-*.

   | There isn't **anything** in the house to eat. |
   | I didn't tell **anybody**. |

2. To say all of a group, use indefinite pronouns with *every-*.

   | It was a good party. **Everyone** had fun. |
   | The guests loved the food. They ate **everything**. |

(continued on next page)

3. To talk about people and things in general, use indefinite pronouns with *any-* or *every-*.

Anyone/Everybody can learn to cook.

When you're hungry, **anything/everything** tastes good.

4. To talk about particular unspecified people and things, use indefinite pronouns with *some-*.

Someone/Somebody called for you.

I know I'm forgetting **something**.

In questions, pronouns with *any-* often have the same meaning as pronouns with *some-*.

Is **anyone** at the door? = Is **someone** at the door?

5. To talk about unspecified people or things but not particular ones, use indefinite pronouns with *any-*.

A: What do you want to do tonight?
B: You choose. I'll do **anything**.

GRAMMAR **HOT**SPOT!

When used as subjects, indefinite pronouns take singular verbs.

Everyone **is** hungry.

Nobody **was** home.

TALKING THE TALK

1. *They, them,* and *their* are often used with indefinite pronouns.

Anyone can do this if **they** really try.

Everyone needs to bring **their** book with **them**.

In formal writing, *he or she, him or her,* and *his or her* are usually used instead.

Everyone can improve **his or her** life.

2. In conversation, *you* is often used as an indefinite pronoun meaning "people in general."

You can't always believe the newspapers. (*you* = people in general)

Indefinite Pronouns

10 **Indefinite Pronouns:** Something for Everyone

Use combinations of the words in the box to complete the sentences. More than one answer may be possible.

some-		-one
any-	+	-body
no-		-thing
every-		

1. I need to answer all my e-mail messages. I haven't written back to __anyone/anybody__ for ages.

2. The drawer was empty. _____ was in it.

3. Harriet goes running with _____, but I don't know his name.

4. A: We can ask one more person to dinner. Who do you want to invite?

   B: You decide. I'll be happy with _____.

5. A: Is Otis a vegetarian?

   B: Yes, he is. He doesn't eat _____ with meat in it.

6. A: Do you know Cedric Lawton?

   B: No, I don't know _____ named Cedric.

7. A: When you go to the store, please get me _____ to eat.

   B: What do you want?

   A: I don't care. I just feel like having a snack. _____ will be fine.

8. A: Do you have all the ingredients for the soup?

   B: Yes, I do. I have _____ I need.

9. Finding recipes on the Internet is easy. _____ can do it.

10. A: You look worried. Is _____ wrong?

    B: No, _____ is wrong. I don't have any problems.

    _____ is okay.

11. A: _____ is knocking at the door. Are you expecting

    _____ to visit?

    B: No, _____ is supposed to be coming now.

12. You get to try a lot of different dishes at a potluck dinner because _____ brings a dish to share.

Possessives

FUNCTION

Use of Possessives

1. Possessives show ownership.

> **his** restaurant
> **the Smiths'** house

2. Possessives also show:

   • Amount (e.g., of time or money).

   > **10 dollars'** worth of gas
   > **two months'** salary

   • Origin.

   > the cheeses **of France**
   > **Shakespeare's** plays

   • That something is part of another thing.

   > **the restaurant's** kitchen
   > **my** leg

FORM

A. Possessive Determiners

1. The possessive determiners are *my, your, his, her, its, our,* and *their.*

   > **my** parents, **its** purpose, **our** party

2. Like articles and other determiners, these words come before the noun and any modifiers. They cannot be used with articles, since a noun has only one determiner.

   > **My** favorite movie is on TV tonight.
   > I gave him **my** sandwich.
   >   **NOT:** I gave him ~~the~~ my sandwich.

B. Possessive Nouns

1. A possessive noun can be made from any noun, by:

   • Adding an apostrophe to a plural noun that ends in *s.*

   > The **boys'** names are Paul and Jeremy.
   > The **Smiths'** party was fun.

   • Adding apostrophe + *-s* to all other nouns.
   (Names ending in an *s* are sometimes followed with just an apostrophe, e.g., *Charles', Mr. Jones'.*)

   > The **boy's** name is Michael.
   > *Sesame Street* is a popular **children's** show.
   > **Mr. Jones's** job pays well.

2. Possessive nouns are used with an article or another determiner.

   > **The/My boss's** office is large.

(continued on next page)

C. Possessive Pronouns

The possessive pronouns are *mine, yours, his, its, hers, ours,* and *theirs.* They take the place of a noun phrase.	She gave away her banana, but I ate **mine**. (= *my banana*)

D. Possessive Phrases

1. Possessive phrases are formed with *of* + a noun phrase. They follow the noun.	The seat **of the chair** needs to be fixed. (*of the chair = the chair's*)
2. Possessive phrases are usually used:	
• For things, rather than people. (For people, use possessive nouns instead.)	What's the color **of the walls**? (walls are things) **NOT USUALLY:** What's ~~the walls~~' color? **Myra's** office is over there.
• To avoid a long string of words before the noun.	She's a friend **of a roommate from college**. (avoids "a roommate from college's friend")

GRAMMAR PRACTICE 4

Possessives

11 **Possessives—Form and Uses:** Biology + Engineering = Bioengineering

Work with a partner. Underline the possessive forms in the sentences and mark each one with the letter of the meaning it indicates.

a. ownership   **b.** amount   **c.** part   **d.** origin

1. The scientist's microscope is on a table in the laboratory.
    a

2. The top of the table is covered with equipment.

3. A: How much new equipment did she buy for this experiment?

    B: She bought ten thousand dollars' worth.

4. The exports of the United States include bioengineered food products.

5. Have you seen bioengineered vegetables on the shelves of a grocery store?

6. The researcher made the discovery after four years' work.

7. Quite a few farmers have tried growing bioengineered potatoes in their fields.

8. I was interested in the researcher's ideas about how to increase food production.

> *bioengineering* = the combination of biology and engineering used to study, experiment with, and try to improve living things.

12 **Forming Possessive Determiners, Possessive Pronouns, and Possessive Nouns:** Technology and Food I

Complete the sentences with the correct possessive form of the pronoun or noun in parentheses.

1. Wait a minute, Richard. You put on ___my___
   (I)

   lab coat by mistake. ___Yours___ is over there.
   (You)

2. This laboratory has one director. The ___director's___
   (director)

   job is to plan the experiments. The company has nine

   directors. The _____ job is to decide what
   (directors)

   policies the company will follow. Our _____ goal is to develop foods that are easier
   (company)

   to grow and process. Several companies are doing this kind of research. The _____
   (companies)

   technology has created new types of plants.

3. A: Can you help me? I'm looking for the _____ office.
   (boss)

   B: I'm sorry, this office isn't _____. You want the office with
   (she)

   _____ name on the door. This is _____ office.
   (Ms. Tanaka)   (Ms. Harris)

   A: It isn't easy to find a _____ office in this building.
   (person)

   B: You can find _____ office numbers in _____ directory.
   (people)   (we)

4. In this laboratory, the _____ work involves changing the characteristics of plants by
   (scientists)

   changing _____ genes. That _____ experiment involved changing the
   (they)   (scientist)

   characteristics of a plant by putting genes from an animal into _____ cells.
   (it)

5. A: Where are Bella and Charles? Are these salads _____?
   (they)

   B: Yes, they are. This is _____ salad, and that one is _____.
   (she)   (he)

6. A: _____ salads look all right, but you should try some of _____.
   (you)   (I)

   It has a bioengineered tomato in it.

   B: That's okay. We don't really want _____. _____ are more natural.
   (you)   (we)

   C: Actually, I'm interested in that tomato. What's _____ flavor like? Does it taste
   (it)
   like chicken?

---

cell = the basic unit of living matter in plants and animals. *gene* = a cell part that determines a feature or characteristic of a plant or animal.

---

13 Possessive Nouns Versus Possessive Phrases: Food and Technology II

Complete the sentences by forming possessive nouns and possessive phrases from the words in parentheses. In each, use the preferred possessive form. Add *the* where necessary.

1. <u>Richard's laboratory</u> is using biotechnology to change plants and animals.
   (Richard / laboratory)

2. To find his lab, go through the door at the <u>end of the hall</u> and up the stairs.
   (hall / end)

3. The lab is at the _____.
   (stairs / top)

4. I have some questions about the new foods. Will they affect _____?
   (people / health)

5. I talked to the _____,
   (well-known biotechnology laboratory / director)

   and he explained his opinion.

6. Through bioengineering, _____ will be able to resist diseases and
   (farmers / crops)

   insects, and people everywhere will have more food.

7. Now Richard is looking into _____.
   (another scientist in the laboratory / microscope)

8. There's a problem with an experiment. They're looking for the _____.
   (problem / cause)

9. I'm still worried. Could bioengineers accidentally create something like

   _____?
   (Dr. Frankenstein / monster)

 To learn more about the pros and cons of bioengineering, go to the *Grammar Links* Website.

 **Check your progress! Go to the Self-Test for Chapter 9 on the *Grammar Links* Website.**

Wrap-up Activities

1 **A Restaurant Review:** EDITING

Correct the 20 errors in the restaurant review. There are errors in articles, quantifiers, modifiers, possessives, nouns, and pronouns. The first error is corrected for you.

Taste of the Town—
A Review of Magnificent Food

Last week, I had dinner at Magnificent Food, ~~a~~ *the* newest restaurant in town. I invited the friend to come with me. The owner of Magnificent Food is the famous chef. His name is Charles whitney. My friend and I were looking forward to eating delicious specialties prepared by Mr. Whitney hisself.

When we arrived at the restaurant, we had to wait, so we sat down and began to look at the four-pages menu. When our table was finally ready, we asked our waiter for some advice about what to order. Although he didn't seem to have a lot of knowledges about the menu, he made any suggestions. We ordered two appetizers; one was smoked fish, and another was vegetable soup. The smoked fish looked beautiful, but it's flavor was strange. A vegetable soup had too many salt in it. The other people in the restaurant got their main courses right away, but we had a long wait for our because of a problem in the kitchen. When our plates finally came, there was plenty food on them. I had ordered a regional specialty from South. It shouldn't have been a bored dish, but it was— every of the bites was tasteless. My friends' steak looked very good, but everything on her plate was cold. We decided to go to an excellent small European café across the street for coffee and dessert.

New restaurants often have few problems, so I wasn't expecting Magnificent Food to be perfect. But I wasn't expecting to be such a disappointing customer. I hope that this restaurant improves and becomes truly magnificent.

2 A Very Special Dinner Party—Who's Invited? SPEAKING/WRITING

Step 1 Work in small groups. Imagine that your group is going to give a very special dinner party. You can invite any seven famous people, living or dead—no one will refuse to come to your party. You can invite people like Elvis Presley, Bill Gates, Hillary Clinton, Michael Jordan, John F. Kennedy, Jennifer Lopez, Tiger Woods, Princess Diana, or anyone you choose. Think of people you would like to invite and discuss them. Decide on seven guests that you would all like to invite.

Step 2 Write two or more sentences about each person and the reasons the group wants to invite him or her. Pay attention to your use of articles, modifiers, and pronouns.

Example: Tiger Woods is a well-known, talented golfer. We hope that he will talk about himself and tell us the secrets of his success. OR Princess Diana was a beautiful young woman. She had an interesting life.

Step 3 Read your sentences to the class. Which group's dinner party will be the most interesting? Why?

3 Review a Restaurant: WRITING

Step 1 Work with a partner. Imagine that the two of you are restaurant reviewers for a newspaper. Decide what restaurant you want to review. The restaurant can be a real one or one that you make up, and it can be any kind of restaurant—ethnic, fast food, casual, or elegant. Talk about the food (how it looks and tastes), the service (what the waiters or waitresses are like, how well they do their job), and the décor (what the restaurant and its furniture look like).

Step 2 Make notes about the food, service, and décor of the restaurant.

Step 3 Write a three-paragraph review of the restaurant. Use at least one of each of the following: an *-ing* and *-ed* adjective, a noun modifier, a compound modifier, a possessive noun, a possessive determiner, and a possessive phrase. Pay attention to your use of articles and pronouns.

 See the *Grammar Links* Website for a model review for this activity.

4 **Create a Culture:** SPEAKING

Step 1 Work in groups of three. The three of you are members of an imaginary culture. Discuss the answers to these questions: What does your culture consider to be appropriate food for each meal? How much of each food do people eat at each meal? Are there separate courses, or do people eat all the food at the same time? Who does the cooking in families? Are there any prohibited foods (foods that people aren't allowed to eat)? What do people eat when they celebrate special occasions?

Step 2 Make notes on your answers to the questions.

Step 3 Describe your culture's food and food habits to the class. Refer to your notes if necessary. Pay attention to your use of count and noncount nouns, articles, quantifiers, and modifiers.

Example: In our culture, most people eat one small meal, one large meal, and several snacks each day. We eat the small meal as soon as we wake up in the morning. We usually have a few dill pickles, some apple pie or a little ice cream, and a lot of hot tea. . . . Our most important holiday is on June 21. On that day, everyone eats young green onions and hard-boiled eggs.

Adjective Clauses

TOPIC FOCUS
Personality

UNIT OBJECTIVES

■ **adjective clauses with subject relative pronouns (*that, who, which*)**

(Psychologists are scientists *who study thoughts, feelings, and behavior*. Psychology is a subject *that interests me*.)

■ **adjective clauses with object relative pronouns (*that, who[m], which*, [0])**

(The work *that they do* is interesting. Are you shy with people *who you don't know well*?)

■ **adjective clauses with relative pronouns that are objects of prepositions**

(Personality is a topic *that we are learning about*. The professor is someone *for whom I have a lot of respect*.)

■ **adjective clauses with possessive relative pronouns**

(That's the teacher *whose class I want to take*.)

■ **adjective clauses with *where* and *when***

(Tell me about the place *where you grew up*. I remember the day *when we met*.)

Grammar in Action

🎧 Reading and Listening: Alive in Our Times

Read and listen to this radio interview.

Host: Lorrie Kress
Guest: Professor Bruno Schiller

A: Hello, everyone. I'm Lorrie Kress, and this is "Alive in Our Times." My guest today is a (psychologist) **who does research on personality**. He's someone **whom I admire very much**. I'd like to welcome a man **whose ideas are always interesting**, Professor Bruno Schiller.

B: Thank you, Lorrie.

A: Professor Schiller, personality is something **that many of us want to know more about**. Can you tell us how we get our personalities?

B: Well, Lorrie, psychologists have developed many theories about this. Basically, there are two factors **which work together in childhood to form people's personalities**. The first is biology. Biology is responsible for the characteristics **that you are born with**. And the second is environment. Your environment includes your surroundings, your family and friends, and your experiences.

A: My sisters and I had the same parents and the same environment as children, but we have really different personalities now. Do you know why?

B: Actually, there is a theory **which might explain the differences among children in the same family**. According to this theory, your personality differences are a result of your birth order, in other words, your position as the oldest, a middle, or the youngest child in your family. A firstborn child experiences things differently than a laterborn child does. Only children, that is, children who have no brothers or sisters, are in many ways similar to firstborn children.

A: So, Professor Schiller, what are some characteristics **that birth order might be responsible for**?

B: Well, birth order might determine whether you are creative or practical. It could also determine whether you are the kind of person **that usually follows rules** or the kind of person **that sometimes breaks the rules**.

A: Can you guess my birth order?

B: Perhaps. Let me give you a test **whose results could tell me about your personality**.

---

factor = something that helps cause a certain result. *characteristic* = a feature or quality.
firstborn = the oldest child in a family. *laterborn* = a child born second, third, etc., in a family.

Think About Grammar

Work on your own to complete the task.

1. The boldfaced clauses in the radio interview are adjective clauses. Adjective clauses modify nouns and indefinite pronouns (e.g., *someone*). They give information about the noun or pronoun. An adjective clause comes after the noun or pronoun it modifies. Look at the boldfaced adjective clauses in the radio interview. Circle the noun or pronoun that each one modifies. The first one is circled for you.

2. Adjective clauses begin with relative pronouns. Look at the boldfaced adjective clauses.

   The relative pronouns are __who_____, _____,

   _____, _____, and _____.

3. Nouns and pronouns can refer to people (e.g., *man* and *someone*) or things, including abstract things and ideas (e.g., *factors* and *something*). The relative pronoun in an adjective clause refers to the same person or thing as the noun that it modifies. Look at the nouns and pronouns you circled and at the relative pronouns in the adjective clauses that modify them.

   a. The relative pronouns __who_____, _____,

      _____, and _____ can refer to people.

   b. The relative pronouns _____, _____, and

      _____ can refer to things.

10

Adjective Clauses

Introductory Task: The Birth-Order Theory of Personality Development—A Test

A. Complete the sentences by circling the letter, **a** or **b**, of the choice that describes you better.

1. I am someone who _____.
   a. doesn't like much change   b. likes new experiences

2. Other people see me as somebody who _____.
   a. is self-confident   b. is a little insecure

3. I am the type of person who _____.
   a. tries to dress and act as others do   b. tries to dress and act differently

4. In my work or studies, I'm the kind of person that _____.
   a. likes to be practical and realistic   b. likes to be imaginative and creative

5. I am a person who _____.
   a. enjoys being a leader   b. isn't interested in being a leader

6. Politically, I see myself as someone that _____.
   a. wants to keep things the same   b. wants to change things

7. I am the type of person that _____.
   a. usually follows rules   b. is sometimes willing to bend or break rules

B. Turn to page A-3 to find out what your answers mean. Then circle the appropriate choices:

According to the theory, I have the personality characteristics of [a firstborn child / a laterborn child]. In fact, I am [a firstborn child / a laterborn child] in my family.

C. Work as a class. Count the number of people who are firstborns **and** according to the theory have the personality characteristics of firstborns. Count the number of people who are laterborns **and** according to the theory have the personality characteristics of laterborns. Add these two groups to find out how many people the theory works for. Then count the number of people the theory does **not** work for. Does the theory work for most of the class members? Discuss your opinions of the theory.

For more information about birth order and personality, go to the *Grammar Links* Website.

Adjective Clauses

FORM and FUNCTION

A. Uses of Adjective Clauses

1. Adjective clauses modify nouns. They give information about the nouns. An adjective clause can modify any noun in a sentence. Put the adjective clause right after the noun it modifies.

   subject noun
   The **man who was at the party** seemed really nice.

   object noun
   I'm looking for an English **class that meets in the evening**.

2. Adjective clauses can also modify indefinite pronouns (*someone, anything*, etc.).

   I know **someone who can help you**.

   Anything that is worth doing is worth doing well.

3. Adjective clauses make it possible to combine two sentences. The sentences must have noun phrases referring to the same person or thing.

   Sentence 1: **A man** just moved next door to me.
   Sentence 2: **The man** is a professional tennis player.

   Combined sentence: A **man who is a professional tennis player** just moved next door to me.
   OR The **man who just moved next door to me** is a professional tennis player. (*a man* in Sentence 1 must = *the man* in Sentence 2; *the man/a man → who*)

B. Sentences with Adjective Clauses; Structure of Adjective Clauses

MAIN CLAUSE	ADJECTIVE CLAUSE		
	RELATIVE PRONOUN (= SUBJECT)	VERB	
I'm reading a book	**that**	**is**	**interesting.**
	RELATIVE PRONOUN (= OBJECT)	SUBJECT	VERB
I'm reading a book	**that**	**Lee**	**liked** a lot.

Adjective clauses are a kind of subordinate clause. That is, they cannot stand alone but must be used with a main clause.

main clause   adj clause   main clause
The man **who fixed the sink** is coming back tomorrow.

(continued on next page)

Relative Pronouns

1. An adjective clause begins with a relative pronoun.

> Paula is someone **that/who/whom** you would really like.
>
> The course **which/that** meets at eight in the morning is too early for me.

2. The relative pronouns presented in this chapter are *that, which, who,* and *whom.**

   Whose, also a relative pronoun, is discussed in Chapter 11.

> She's the teacher **that/who/whom** I like.
>
> The notebook **that/which** I need has a blue cover.

3. The relative pronoun and the noun modified refer to the same person or thing.

> The **teacher that/who/whom** I really liked isn't there this year. (*that/who/whom = the teacher*)

4. The relative pronouns do not change. They do not have masculine or feminine or singular or plural forms.

> I know {a boy / a girl / some people} **who** went to school there.
>
> (*who = a boy, a girl, some people*)

Subject and Verb

Like all clauses, adjective clauses must have a subject and a verb.

> subj   V
> I didn't see any people **that I knew**.

The subject of the clause:

- May be the relative pronoun. (See Grammar Briefing 2, page 196.)

> subj   V   obj
> He's the guy **who** likes Joan.

- May be another noun or pronoun in the clause. (See Grammar Briefing 3, page 199.)

> obj   subj V
> He's the guy **who/whom** Joan likes.

GRAMMAR **HOT**SPOT!

What is not a relative pronoun.

> Everything **that/which** he said is true.
> **NOT:** Everything ~~what~~ he said is true.

Adjective Clauses

1 Identifying Adjective Clauses: Psychologists and Mothers

In the following passage, underline each adjective clause and circle the noun or pronoun it modifies. Put a second line under the relative pronoun in the clause.

A re you a (person) who is shy? Or are you a person who is outgoing? And why are you shy or outgoing? Are these characteristics which you had at birth? Or are they characteristics which came from your life experiences? These are questions that psychologists have been trying to answer for a long time. According to modern psychologists, a combination of biological factors and experience shaped your personality. This is something that mothers know, too. Each child that a mother has seems different from the others, even as a newborn. And as her children grow, the mother can see differences in their experiences. She can see how the experiences that her children have help to shape their personalities. Sometimes the theories that psychologists develop express what mothers have always known!

2 Adjective Clauses: Same Family, Different Personalities

A. David is telling Julie about the people in the photo. Listen once for the main idea. Listen again and fill in the name of each person.

Alan   ~~Barbara~~   Cathy   Dennis   Jack   Joan   Kyle   Mary

Barbara

practical

B. Now listen again and fill in the characteristic that's used to describe each person.

adventurous   insecure   ~~practical~~   shy   creative   outgoing   self-confident   timid

3 **Position of Adjective Clauses:** Telling More

Complete the sentences with the adjective clauses in parentheses.
Write the adjective clauses after the nouns that they modify.

> *who are in the photo*

1. The people are older now. (who are in the photo)

2. The aunt lives in New Mexico now. (who likes to paint)

3. I've had some great vacations with the uncle. (who's a mountain climber)

4. My aunts and uncles have telephone conversations. (that last for hours)

5. The bird-watching book is very popular. (which my uncle wrote)

6. My aunt is someone. (whom you would really like)

7. My outgoing uncle has become a talk show host, so now he has a job.

    (that's perfect for his personality)

8. People often comment on the differences in their personalities and interests.

    (that know my mother and her brothers and sisters)

GRAMMAR BRIEFING 2

Adjective Clauses with Subject Relative Pronouns

FORM

A. Structure of Adjective Clauses with Subject Relative Pronouns

MAIN CLAUSE	ADJECTIVE CLAUSE		
	SUBJECT RELATIVE PRONOUN	VERB	OBJECT
I have a friend	**who**	**is studying**	**psychology.**
= I have a friend. + **The friend/She** is studying psychology.			

MAIN CLAUSE	ADJECTIVE CLAUSE			MAIN CLAUSE CONTINUED
	SUBJECT RELATIVE PRONOUN	VERB	OBJECT	
My friend	**who**	**studies**	**psychology**	is interested in personality.
= My friend is interested in personality. + **My friend/She** studies psychology.				

1. In these adjective clauses, the relative pronoun is the subject of the adjective clause.

    > subj V
    > Psychology is a topic **that** really interests her.
    > subj
    > = Psychology is a topic. + **The topic** really interests her. (*The topic → that*)

(continued on next page)

A. Structure of Adjective Clauses with Subject Relative Pronouns (continued)

2. The verb of the clause agrees with the noun that is modified. (Remember: This noun and the relative pronoun refer to the same person or thing.)

subj   V
She reads lots of **books that relate to psychology**.
(*relate* agrees with *books*; *that = books*)
NOT: She reads lots of books that ~~relates~~ to psychology.

B. Subject Relative Pronouns: *Who, That, Which*

1. For people, use *who* or *that*.

A **scientist who/that** studies personality has developed a new theory.

2. For things, ideas, and animals,* use *that* or *which*.

   *For pets, *who* can also be used (e.g., *I have a cat who's really affectionate*).

The scientist has developed a **theory that/which** explains personality.

Recently, there was a **conference that/which** was just about his theory.

GRAMMAR **HOT**SPOT!

Remember! The relative pronoun is the subject of the adjective clause. Do not include another subject pronoun.

Children who are the youngest are often creative.
NOT: Children who ~~they~~ are the youngest are often creative.

TALKING THE TALK

Who and *that* are often contracted in speech and informal writing.

She's someone **who's** creative.
She teaches a course **that's** really interesting.

GRAMMAR PRACTICE 2

Adjective Clauses with Subject Relative Pronouns

4 **Adjective Clauses with Subject Relative Pronouns; Combining Sentences: Relationships and Personalities I**

Combine the sentences. Use the second sentence to make an adjective clause. Use any appropriate relative pronoun.

1. a. A big family lives in the house. The house is next door to mine.

   A big family lives in the house that/which is next door to mine.

b. The little girls are very talkative. They are outgoing.

_____

c. The little girl takes longer to make new friends. She is shy.

_____

d. Have you met the people? They live next door.

_____

2. a. I talked to a person. The person knows my sisters.

_____

b. Sleeping until noon is an activity. The activity appeals to my lazy sister.

_____

c. An activity is going running at 6 a.m. The activity appeals to my energetic sister.

_____

3. a. Elvira's two brothers have very different personalities. Her brothers are interested in Africa.

_____

b. The timid brother collects stamps. The stamps come from countries in Africa.

_____

c. The adventurous brother wrestles with crocodiles. The crocodiles live in rivers in Africa.

_____

5 Forming Adjective Clauses with Subject Relative Pronouns: Defining Terms

Use the words given to complete the definitions with adjective clauses. Use *who* or *which* and the correct form of the verb.

1. refer / to a person's way of thinking, feeling, and acting

   Personality is a term _which refers to a person's way of thinking, feeling, and acting_ .

2. study / people's thoughts, feelings, and behavior

   Psychologists are scientists _____.

3. make / a careful study of a certain subject or problem

   A *researcher* is a person _____.

4. try / to explain situations or events

   Theories are statements _____.

5. be / part of your personality

   Traits are characteristics _____.

6. be / the oldest child in a family

   A *firstborn* is someone _____.

7. be / born second, third, and so on, in a family

   Laterborns are children _____.

8. help / cause a certain result

   A *factor* is something _____.

6 **Using *Someone* + *Who*:** Who Does It Better?

Work with a partner. Take turns asking and answering questions about people and their characteristics. Follow the example. Use *someone who* as in the example.

1. Hair stylist: creative or practical?

   Example: Student A: Should a hair stylist be someone who's creative or someone who's practical?
   Student B: I think a hair stylist should be someone who's creative.
   Student A: Why?
   Student B: I want to have a hair style that's new and unusual.

   OR: Student B: A hair stylist should be someone who's practical.
   Student A: Why?
   Student B: Hair stylists should think of hair styles that are easy to take care of.

2. Car mechanic: creative or practical?
3. Scientist: realistic or imaginative?
4. Soccer player: calm or excitable?
5. Mountain climber: adventurous or careful?
6. The leader of a country: optimistic or pessimistic?

> *optimistic* = tending to expect good things to happen. *pessimistic* = tending to expect bad things to happen.

GRAMMAR BRIEFING 3

Adjective Clauses with Object Relative Pronouns

FORM

A. Structure of Adjective Clauses with Object Relative Pronouns

MAIN CLAUSE	ADJECTIVE CLAUSE		
	OBJECT RELATIVE PRONOUN	SUBJECT	VERB
I've met lots of people	who	I	like.

= I've met lots of people. + I like **the people/them**.

MAIN CLAUSE	ADJECTIVE CLAUSE			MAIN CLAUSE CONTINUED
	OBJECT RELATIVE PRONOUN	SUBJECT	VERB	
The students	that	he	teaches	are very hard working.

= The students are very hard-working. + He teaches **the students/them**.

In these clauses, the relative pronoun is the object of the verb. (Notice that it is the object of the sentence that becomes the adjective clause.) The subject of the adjective clause follows the relative pronoun.

> obj subj V
> The work **that** he does is interesting. = The work is
> obj
> interesting. + He does **the work**. (*the work → that*)

(continued on next page)

B. Object Relative Pronouns: *Who, That, Which, Whom,* [0]

1. For people, use *who, whom,* or *that.*

   It's important to have **friends who/whom/ that** you trust.

2. For things, ideas, and animals,* use *that* or *which.*

   *For pets, *who* can also be used (e.g., *My brother has a dog who he takes everywhere*).

   I can talk to my friends about any **problem that/which** I have.

   My brother has a **dog that/which** he takes everywhere.

3. The object relative pronoun is often omitted ([0] = no relative pronoun).

   It's important to have friends **[0]** you trust.

   I can talk to my friends about any problem **[0]** I have.

GRAMMAR **HOT**SPOT!

1. The object relative pronoun is the object of the verb. Do not include another object pronoun.

   I have a friend **who** I often visit.
   NOT: I have a friend who I often visit ~~her~~.

2. Remember that [0] is only an object pronoun. Do not omit a **subject** relative pronoun.

   He's someone **who/[0]** my father knows.

   But: He's someone **who** knows my father.
   NOT: He's someone ~~[0]~~ knows my father.

TALKING THE TALK

In speech, [0], *that,* and *who* are usually used. *Whom* is used mainly in formal speech and in writing.

In writing, use *whom* or *that* or [0] as object relative pronouns. *Who* is generally considered incorrect.

She's a teacher **[0]/that/who** students admire. (more informal)

She's a teacher **whom** students admire. (more formal)

Adjective Clauses with Object Relative Pronouns

7 **Adjective Clauses with Object Relative Pronouns;**
Combining Sentences: Relationships and Personalities II

Combine the sentences. Use the second sentence to make an adjective clause.
Use any appropriate relative pronoun (*who, whom, which, that,* [0]).

1. a. The woman is creative. Jerry dates the woman.

    The woman who/whom/that/[0] Jerry dates is creative.

    b. The pickle ice cream was delicious. She made the ice cream.

    _____

2. a. The story was true. I heard it.

    _____

    b. I heard the story from a person. I trust the person.

    _____

3. a. Arthur isn't shy when he's around people. He knows them well.

    _____

    b. The discussion was very serious. Arthur and I had the discussion recently.

    _____

4. a. The most fun-loving person is Tony. I know the person.

    _____

    b. The jokes are really funny. He tells them.

    _____

5. a. The man is generous. Tiffany plans to marry him.

    _____

    b. Tiffany's boyfriend gave her a kitten. She loves the kitten.

    _____

8 **Object Relative Pronouns; Combining Sentences:** Tell Me About It

Combine the sentences. Use the second sentence to make an adjective clause. Show all
the relative pronouns (*who, whom, which, that,* [0]) that are possible.

1. Tell me about the psychology course. You're taking it.

    Tell me about the psychology course which you're taking.
    Tell me about the psychology course that you're taking.
    Tell me about the psychology course you're taking.

2. We have a teacher. Everyone admires her.

3. The students work very hard. She teaches them.

4. The topic is personality. We're discussing the topic.

5. Have you passed all the tests? The teacher has given the tests.

9 **Subject and Object Relative Pronouns:** Birth Order and Personality

Fill in the blanks with all the choices (*who, whom, which, that,* [0]) that are possible.

Are you someone _who/that_____ was a firstborn child? Or were you
                    ₁

a laterborn in your family? Some psychologists believe that your birth order and the

relationships _____ you had with the others in your family had
                  ₂

a lot to do with the personality _____ you have now.
                                      ₃

Children _____ are born first enjoy having all of their parents'
             ₄

attention. This attention is something _____ they want to keep.
                                            ₅

Children _____ are born later also want to get attention. Each
             ₆

laterborn wants to create a situation _____ is new and different
                                           ₇

and hopes to be the child _____ the parents notice most.
                               ₈

As a result of their early experiences, firstborns may become adults

_____ prefer to keep things as they are. Firstborns also tend to be
      ₉

natural leaders _____ have a great deal of self-confidence. Because
                     ₁₀

of their place in the family, laterborns may become adults _____
                                                                ₁₁

like to have new experiences. They tend to be imaginative and adventurous. Of course,

you may know laterborns _____ you consider to be self-
                             ₁₂

confident leaders. And you probably know firstborns _____
                                                          ₁₃

you regard as creative adventurers. This is because there are many factors

_____ can be important in forming personality.
      ₁₄

10 Subject and Object Relative Pronouns; Combining Sentences: Another Theory

Use the second sentence to form an adjective clause modifying the appropriate noun in the first sentence. Use any appropriate relative pronoun (*who, whom, which, that,* [0]).

1. Last week I read a book. It was about birth order and personality.

   Last week I read a book which was about birth order and personality.

   OR

   Last week I read a book that was about birth order and personality.

2. I talked to a scientist about it. She is a friend of mine.

   _____

3. My friend disagrees with the theory in the book. I read the book.

   _____

4. Other researchers have developed a more scientific theory. My friend respects them.

   _____

5. According to this theory, some personality characteristics have a source. The source is biological.

   _____

6. Chemicals can influence our personalities. The chemicals are in our brains and bodies.

   _____

7. These chemicals can affect our response to events. We experience the events.

   _____

8. What do you think of the theory? My friend believes it.

   _____

11 Completing Sentences with Adjective Clauses: An Alien Invasion?

 Last night you had a terrifying experience. Afterward, you weren't able to do your homework or even speak. As a result, you need to write a letter to your teacher explaining what happened. Complete the sentences with adjective clauses.

Dear _____,

I'm very sorry that I haven't done my homework, but I hope you will excuse me. Last night I was kidnapped by aliens, that is, people from another planet. There were three different types of strange-looking people on the spaceship. The first type were people who had huge dark eyes and bald heads _____.
                                                    1
The second type were people _____.
                                                    2
The third type were people _____.
                                                    3
They all wore clothes _____.
                                                    4
    The aliens spoke English to me, but among themselves they spoke a language _____. They took
                                                    5
me onto a spaceship _____.
                                                    6
On the spaceship, they told me they were interested in talking to humans
_____.
                                                    7
    While I was on their spaceship, I could hear music
_____. The aliens were eating
                                                    8
kinds of food _____.
                                                    9
They didn't give me any of the food, but they gave me a drink
_____. Early this
                                                    10
morning the aliens finally brought me back home. I know I have a creative imagination, but this is not science fiction!

    Your student,

    _____

12 **Using Adjective Clauses:** Describing Personalities

 A. Work with a partner. Choose one of the people in the photos. (Keep your choice a secret from other class members.) Discuss the person you have chosen: What do you think her personality is like? What are her likes and dislikes? What are her talents and interests? In your discussion, include sentences with adjective clauses.

> Example: Student A: *She looks like someone who's outgoing and friendly.*
> Student B: *I agree. I think she's a woman who likes sports and is very athletic. . . .*
> OR
> Student A: *I think she's the type of person that's very creative.*
> Student B: *She also seems to be someone who's quiet and serious. Some things that she doesn't like are noisy, crowded parties and . . .*

 B. Write a one-paragraph description of the person you chose, but **don't** include anything about her appearance. Use at least five adjective clauses.

C. Read your description to the class. Can the class guess which person you are describing?

See the *Grammar Links* Website for a model paragraph for this activity.

Check your progress! Go to the Self-Test for Chapter 10 on the *Grammar Links* Website.

More About Adjective Clauses

Introductory Task: Do You Agree or Disagree?

A. Read the statements about personality and circle your response, *a* or *b*, to each one.

---

1. Personality comes from a combination of two factors: the characteristics that you are born with and the environment you grow up in.

   a. I agree.   b. I disagree.

2. The other children with whom a child plays or goes to school are important influences on the child's personality.

   a. I agree.   b. I disagree.

3. The way that parents treat a child is an important influence on the type of personality the child will have. For example, children whose parents treat them with kindness and patience will grow up to be kind and patient adults.

   a. I agree.   b. I disagree.

4. Personality develops in childhood and doesn't change after that. That is, adulthood is a time when personality does not change.

   a. I agree.   b. I disagree.

5. In order to choose a job in which you will be happy and successful, you need to know your personality type. People whose personalities aren't good matches for their jobs can't find happiness or be effective in their work.

   a. I agree.   b. I disagree.

B. Work in small groups. Compare your responses to the statements. Tell why you agree or disagree with each statement.

---
environment = surroundings, family and friends, experiences, etc.

Adjective Clauses with Relative Pronouns That Are Objects of Prepositions

FORM

A. Structure of Adjective Clauses with Relative Pronouns That Are Objects of Prepositions

MAIN CLAUSE	ADJECTIVE CLAUSE			
	OBJECT RELATIVE PRONOUN	SUBJECT	VERB	PREPOSITION
Personality is a topic	**that**	**we**	**are learning**	**about**.

= Personality is a topic. + We are learning about **personality/it**.

MAIN CLAUSE	ADJECTIVE CLAUSE				MAIN CLAUSE CONTINUED
	OBJECT RELATIVE PRONOUN	SUBJECT	VERB	PREPOSITION	
The friend	**who**	**I**	**went**	**with**	is here.

= The friend is here. + I went with **the friend/him**.

1. In these relative clauses, the relative pronoun is the object of a preposition. (Prepositions include *about*, *for*, *in*, *on*, *with*, etc.)

                    obj of
               prep subj V
   She's someone **who** we have a lot of confidence
   prep
   in. = She is someone. + We have a lot of
                     obj of
                     prep
   confidence in her. (*her* → *who*)

2. The preposition can be put at the beginning of the adjective clause, before the relative pronoun.

                   obj of
            prep prep subj V
   She's someone **in whom** we have a lot of
   confidence.

B. Relative Pronouns That Are Objects of Prepositions: *Who, That, Which, Whom,* [0]

1. The same relative pronouns are used as for the objects of verbs:

   • *Who*, *whom*, *that*, and [0] for people.

   She's **someone who/whom/that/[0]** I don't like to argue with.

   • *Which*, *that*, and [0] for things and ideas.

   My children have some **ideas which/that/[0]** I don't fully agree with.

   That's a **class which/that/[0]** he does well in.

(continued on next page)

B. Relative Pronouns That Are Objects of Prepositions (continued)

2. If the preposition is at the beginning of the adjective clause, use only *whom* or *which*.

> He's someone **for whom** I have a lot of respect.
>
> Your company has several positions **for which** I'd like to apply.

TALKING THE TALK

In speech, the preposition usually occurs at the end of the adjective clause.

Prepositions at the beginning of the adjective clause are considered formal and used mainly in writing.

> The school offers some scholarships **which** I might qualify **for**. (more informal)
>
> I am writing to ask about scholarships **for which** I might qualify. (more formal)

GRAMMAR PRACTICE 1

Adjective Clauses with Relative Pronouns That Are Objects of Prepositions

1 **Adjective Clauses with Relative Pronouns That Are Objects of Prepositions; Combining Sentences:** Finding the Right Job I

Combine the pairs of sentences. Use the second sentence to make an adjective clause. Show all possible patterns.

1. The teacher explained personality types. We met with her.

   The teacher with whom we met explained personality types.
   The teacher whom we met with explained personality types.
   The teacher who we met with explained personality types.
   The teacher that we met with explained personality types.
   The teacher [0] we met with explained personality types.

2. The counselor discussed careers. We listened to him.

3. I learned about some jobs. I am suited for them.

2 **Informal and Formal Versions of Adjective Clauses with Relative Pronouns That Are Objects of Prepositions:** Writing About Jobs

Rewrite the sentences so that they are formal.

1. The counselor I talked to gave me some advice.

   The counselor to whom I talked gave me some advice.

2. We want to find jobs we will succeed in.

3. She is helpful to the students she works with.

4. The project they are working on will be finished soon.

5. The position he is applying for is in the sales department.

6. I am grateful to the person I got the information from.

3 Relative Pronouns as Objects of Prepositions: Your Preferences and Your Personality

Fill in the blanks with all the choices (*who*, *whom*, *which*, *that*, [0]) that are possible.

Psychology is a subject __which, that, [0]__ many people are
                                    1

interested in. And there are many people for _____
                                                            2

psychology can be useful. They include people who want to choose a job

_____ they are well suited for. By using psychology
            3

to understand their personality types, thes people can make choices with

_____ they will be satisfied.
            4

Psychologists often use a test to determine a person's personality type.

A personality test determines your type by asking you about your preferences.

For example, a personality test may ask you about the kinds of people

_____ you feel comfortable with. Do you like to
            5

be with a few people with _____ you have close
                                        6

friendships or with many people to _____ you aren't
                                                7

so close?

When you are trying to understand your type, there are some important points

_____ you should be aware of. One is that there are
            8

no "good" or "bad" preferences. People are different, and these differences are useful.

You can get along well with the people _____ you study
                                                        9

or work with when you try to understand and accept their different personality types.

If your future career is something about _____
                                                        10

you've been thinking, you may want to take a personality test. It could help you

understand your preferences and find a job _____ you
                                                        11

will be excited about.

 Check out the *Grammar Links* Website for links to an online personality test.

4 **Adjective Clauses with Relative Pronouns That Are Objects of Prepositions:** What Are Your Interests?

A. You have just been hired by a large corporation. They want to know more about your interests so they can decide which department to place you in. Answer the questions, using the cues in parentheses.

MYMIX Corporation Human Resources Department
1. Which corporation are you most enthusiastic about? ([0] . . . about) *The corporation [0] I am most enthusiastic about is MYMIX.*
2. What kind of work are you most interested in? (which . . . in)
3. What free-time activities are you involved in? ([0] . . . in)
4. Which school subject have you excelled in? (that . . . in)
5. Which person are you most grateful to? (to whom . . .)
6. Which world problem are you most concerned about? (about which . . .)

B. 1. Imagine that you work in the Human Resources Department at MYMIX Corporation. Use the cues to write more questions like those on the form in Part A.

1. (music / like to listen to)

   What kind of _____?

2. (sports / be interested in)

   Which _____?

3. (people / like to work with)

   What kind of _____?

4. (job / be best suited for)

   What kind of _____?

B. 2. Work with a partner. Student A: Interview Student B, asking the questions in Part A and the questions you wrote. Student B: Answer the questions, omitting the relative pronoun in each answer. Then reverse roles.

Example:
Student A: *Which corporation are you most enthusiastic about?*
Student B: *The corporation I'm most enthusiastic about is MYMIX.*

GRAMMAR BRIEFING 2

Adjective Clauses with Possessive Relative Pronouns

FORM

A. Structure of Adjective Clauses with Possessive Relative Pronouns

MAIN CLAUSE	ADJECTIVE CLAUSE		
	POSSESSIVE RELATIVE PRONOUN	NOUN	
I spoke to the teacher	**whose**	**class**	**is so popular**.

= I spoke to the teacher. + **The teacher's/Her** class is so popular.

MAIN CLAUSE	ADJECTIVE CLAUSE			MAIN CLAUSE CONTINUED
	POSSESSIVE RELATIVE PRONOUN	NOUN		
The teacher	**whose**	**class**	**I want to get into**	is going to help me.

= The teacher is going to help me. + I want to get into **the teacher's/her** class.

1. These adjective clauses begin with the possessive relative pronoun *whose* + noun.

    I need to find the person **whose umbrella** I took. = I need to find a person. + I took the person's umbrella. (*the person's → whose*)

2. *Whose* + noun may be:

    • The subject of the adjective clause.

    $$\text{I heard the scientist } \underset{\text{subj}}{\underline{\textbf{whose work}}} \text{ is attracting} \underset{\text{obj}}{\underline{\text{so much interest.}}}$$

    I heard the scientist **whose work** (subj) is attracting so much interest (obj).

    • The object of the adjective clause.

    I met the scientist **whose work** (obj) I (subj) admire (V).

    • The object of a preposition that is in the adjective clause.

    She is the scientist **whose work** (obj of prep) I (subj) told (V) you about (prep).

B. The Relative Pronoun *Whose*

1. *Whose* is a possessive like *my*, *his*, etc. Like those words, it must be followed by a noun.

    That's the woman **whose husband** I was talking to.
    Compare: I was talking to **her husband**.

2. *Whose* is usually used to modify people. However, it can be used to modify things.

    That's the **teacher whose class** I'm interested in.

    That's the **school whose programs** I'm interested in.

Adjective Clauses with Possessive Relative Pronouns

5 **Adjective Clauses with Possessive Relative Pronouns; Combining Sentences:** Finding the Right Job II

A. Combine the pairs of sentences. Use the second sentence to make an adjective clause with *whose*.

1. The teacher explained personality types. We heard her lecture.

   The teacher whose lecture we heard explained personality types.

2. She talked about people. Their personalities are well suited for the work they do.

3. People are usually happy. Their work gives them a lot of satisfaction.

4. There are several authors. We may read their books.

5. I found out about some job counselors. Their specialty is personality testing.

6. The teachers have all been helpful. We've taken their courses.

7. The counselor gave me a personality test. I went to his office.

8. I am an outgoing person. My personality is practical.

9. The counselor recommended a book. Its title is *What Color Is Your Parachute?*

10. Now I'm planning to visit the departments. I'm interested in their programs.

11. There are organizations. Their websites have online personality tests and career guidance.

B. Complete the sentences with adjective clauses with *whose*.

1. I enjoy being around people _whose backgrounds are different from mine_____.

2. I get along well with students _____.

3. I prefer to work with people _____.

4. People _____

   are interesting to me.

5. I'm the kind of person _____.

6. I read a book _____.

7. I'd like to work for a company _____.

 To find out more about personality and careers, visit the *Grammar Links* Website.

Adjective Clauses with *Where* and *When*

FORM

A. Adjective Clauses with *Where*

<table>
<tr>
<td>

1. *Where* can begin an adjective clause that modifies the noun *place* or a noun referring to a place—*country, city, building, house, room, street,* and so on.

</td>
<td>

For our anniversary, we're going to go back to the **place where** we met.

This is the **building where** I have my English class.

</td>
</tr>
<tr>
<td>

2. Instead of *where*, you can use an adjective clause with a relative pronoun that's an object of a preposition (see Grammar Briefing 1, page 207).

Remember: Use only *which* if the preposition is at the beginning of the adjective clause.

</td>
<td>

I really liked the **place that/which/[0]** Tom moved to.

This is the **building that/which/[0]** I have my English class **in**.

This is the building **in which** I have my English class.

</td>
</tr>
</table>

B. Adjective Clauses with *When*

<table>
<tr>
<td>

1. *When* can begin an adjective clause that modifies the noun *time* or a noun referring to a period of time—*century, year, day, night,* and so on.

</td>
<td>

I remember a **time when** I didn't have so much homework.

That was the **year when** we started college.

I'm looking forward to the **day when** I graduate.

</td>
</tr>
<tr>
<td>

2. Instead of *when*, you can use an adjective clause with a relative pronoun that's an object of a preposition such as *in* or *on*.

   • With *that* and [0], the preposition is often omitted.

   • With *which*, the preposition must be included.

</td>
<td>

That was the **year that/which/[0]** we started college **in**.

That was the year **that/[0]** we started college.

That was the year **which** we started college **in**. OR That was the year **in which** we started college.

</td>
</tr>
</table>

1. Do not use a preposition with *where* or *when*.

   This is the place where Nina lives.
   NOT: This is the place where Nina lives ~~at~~.

2. Do not use question word order if *where* or *when* introduces an adjective clause.

   Wh- *question*: Where is your house?
   Adjective clause: Please describe the place where **your house is**.
   NOT: Please describe the place where ~~is your house~~.

GRAMMAR PRACTICE 3

Adjective Clauses with *Where* and *When*

6 **Adjective Clauses with *Where*; Combining Sentences:** Memories of Places

> **A.** Combine the sentences. Use the second sentence to make a clause with *where*, omitting the unnecessary words.

1. These photos show the places. I spent my childhood in the places.
   These photos show the places where I spent my childhood.
2. That's the house. My family lived in the house.
3. The bedroom was painted blue. I slept in the bedroom.
4. The garden was behind the house. I played in the garden.
5. That's the hospital. My father worked at the hospital.
6. This is the school. I first studied English at the school.

B. Rewrite the sentences using a relative pronoun that's the object of a preposition. Show all the patterns.

1. This is the cabin where we spent a night.

   This is the cabin in which we spent a night.
   This is the cabin which we spent a night in.
   This is the cabin that we spent a night in.
   This is the cabin we spent a night in.

2. The lake where we swam was very cold.

3. Do you remember the place where we met?

7 **Adjective Clauses with *When*; Combining Sentences:** Memories of Times

A. Combine the sentences. Use the second sentence to make a clause with *when*, omitting the unnecessary words.

1. I remember the time. We lived in that house at that time.

   I remember the time when we lived in that house.

2. I remember the day. We moved into the house on that day.

3. There was a month. It rained constantly during that month.

4. That was the year. I started school in that year.

5. The week was exciting. We went to the mountains in that week.

6. There was one summer. The weather was unusually hot during that summer.

B. Rewrite the sentences using a relative pronoun that is the object of a preposition. Show all the patterns. Omit the preposition where appropriate.

1. I remember the morning. I left home (on that morning).

   I remember the morning on which I left home.
   I remember the morning which I left home on.
   I remember the morning that I left home.
   I remember the morning I left home.

2. That was the year. We started school (in that year).

3. Do you remember the day? We met (on that day).

8 **Using Adjective Clauses with *Where* and *When*:**
Describing Places and Remembering Times

A. Work with a partner. Tell each other about places that you remember from your childhood. Describe things like their location, appearance, or size. Use *where* and the following pairs of cues.

Example:
Student A: Tell me about the city where you lived.
Student B: The city where I lived is near the ocean/full of people and
              traffic/beautiful.

city or town : live	room : sleep	places : play
house or apartment : live	school : study	place : mother or father work

B. Now ask and answer questions about memories of events and your feelings about them. Follow the pattern in the example. Use *when* and the following cues.

Example:
Student A: Do you remember a time when you felt excited?
Student B: I felt excited on the day when I started school.

excited	frightened	happy	sad	disappointed	adventurous

9 **Relative Pronouns, *Where*, and *When*:** A Childhood Experience I

Complete the sentences with any appropriate relative pronoun (*who, that, which, [0], whose*), *where*, or *when*.

When I was three years old, my parents took me on the first long trip _that_ _____
                                                                              1

I had ever been on. I was very little, but I remember the details clearly. My parents were the kind of

people _____ daily routines didn't change much, so going on a trip
                    2

was an experience _____ was very exciting for me. I remember that we
                              3

took the trip at a time _____ the weather was very hot. We traveled
                                  4

for two days by car from the town _____ we lived to a big city. The hotel
                                              5

_____ we stayed in seemed huge, and the room
            6

_____ I slept was cool, comfortable, and much nicer than my
            7

bedroom at home. I didn't know how to read yet, but the waiters _____
                                                                                  8

worked in the hotel restaurant always gave me a menu. I pretended to read it and felt very grown-up.

We ate in other restaurants, too, and the food in every one _____ we
                                                                    9
went to was new, different, and delicious. I wanted that trip to last forever. Now, years later, I'm the

kind of person _____ likes change and new experiences. I also like to
                        10
get to know people _____ lives are very different from mine. The days
                             11
_____ I'm traveling are the best days of my life.
         12

10 Using Adjective Clauses: A Childhood Experience II

   Think about your childhood experiences. Choose one that had an important influence
on you. Write a paragraph about it. Use adjective clauses to help describe what
happened, the time, the place, the other people who were involved, and your feelings.
Use Exercise 9 as a model. Include adjective clauses with relative pronouns that are the
objects of prepositions, with *whose*, and with *where* and *when*.

See the *Grammar Links* Website for another model paragraph for this assignment.

Check your progress! Go to the Self-Test for
Chapter 11 on the *Grammar Links* Website.

Wrap-up Activities

1 **Another Theory:** EDITING

Correct the 11 errors in the passage. There are errors with in relative pronouns and adjective clauses. Some errors can be corrected in more than one way. The first error is corrected for you.

Your Blood Type and Your Personality

T here are people ~~which~~ *who* think your blood type reveals your personality. These people believe in the blood type theory of personality.

According to people who believes in the blood type theory, you can use your blood type to discover your natural talents and tendencies: Blood type is something what can help you find the right job or the right boyfriend or girlfriend.

The blood type that is most common is Type O. What are the characteristics that a Type O person has them? According to a book which explains the theory, people are optimistic that have Type O blood. Business is a field in that they are successful.

A person who his blood type is A usually has a good sense of order. He keeps the place where he lives in very neat. A Type A is also a person that tends to be patient, hard-working, and sensitive.

People whom have Type B blood are the most likely to be creative. They are people who's nature is to be flexible and full of new ideas. Some jobs that Type B people are suited for are artist, designer, and golfer.

Type AB is the rarest blood type. It was the blood type of John F. Kennedy. Kennedy was a man whom many Americans admired. The book describes Type AB people as natural leaders with characteristics that includes logical thinking and honesty.

2 The Category Game: SPEAKING

Step 1 Work in teams of two or three. Decide on a category for each group of words. Then express the category in a sentence containing an adjective clause.

1. creativity, bravery, shyness, generosity, optimism
   They're all personality characteristics which people can have.
2. the sun, an egg yolk, a school bus, a lemon, a dandelion
   They're all things that are yellow.
3. milk, gasoline, alcohol, blood, water
4. a robber, a murderer, a kidnapper, a burglar, a smuggler
5. a house, a bottle, a box, a backpack, a refrigerator
6. flood, flavor, flexible, flower, flip
7. birthday, wedding, anniversary, holiday, graduation
8. a court, an arena, a course, a field, a stadium
9. a nurse, an X-ray technician, a surgeon, a physical therapist, a dietician
10. ears, chopsticks, dice, stereo speakers, ice skates
11. a blanket, a stove, the sun, love, a bath
12. fish, frogs, humans, ducks, polar bears

Step 2 Now each team thinks of three groups of five words that somehow fit into categories like those above. The team reads its lists to the other teams. The other teams try to be the first to guess the category. Each guess must be in the form of a question containing an adjective clause, for example, *Are they all things that are yellow?* Keep score. The winner is the team that guesses the most categories correctly.

3 Making Up Definitions: WRITING

Imagine that the following nonsense words are real English nouns for people, animals, places, times, and things, including activities and feelings. Think of a possible meaning for each word and write a definition for it. Each definition should include at least two adjective clauses. Try to use all types of adjective clauses. You can be as creative as you wish.

Example: *A bowpam is an animal that has short pink fur, a fat body, and a long tail that drags on the ground. Bowpams live in countries where the weather is cold and wet. OR Bluther is a feeling people have at times when they're confused or nervous.*

1. bowpam	3. gyrgot	5. morokoves	7. termunter	9. strolth
2. bluther	4. plonkist	6. quingle	8. zenvidix	10. exmiants

4 What Are Your Preferences? WRITING

Your preferences, that is, your likes, dislikes, and interests, can tell someone a lot about your personality type. Imagine that a person you've never met has asked you to describe yourself. Write one paragraph about your preferences. You can include your preferences in
—people
—work and school
—free-time activities
—places and times
—movies, music, books, etc.

Use a variety of types of adjective clauses, including clauses with relative pronouns that are the objects of prepositions, with *whose*, and with *where* and *when*.

Example: I can describe myself best by telling you some of my likes, dislikes, and interests. I like to be around people who are calm and logical. People whose lives are disorganized make me a little nervous, so I prefer not to spend much time with them. The classes that I enjoy the most are math and science. In the future, I want to have a job in which I can work with numbers and computers. At times when I don't have to work or study, I like to be outdoors. I love going to places where it's quiet and the air is clean and fresh. . . .

 See the *Grammar Links* Website for a complete model paragraph for this assignment.

Gerunds and Infinitives

TOPIC FOCUS
Entertainment

UNIT OBJECTIVES

▪ **gerunds**
(*Singing* is her profession.)

▪ **infinitives**
(It's fun *to watch* television.)

▪ **verbs that take gerunds or infinitives or both**
(Jeff *enjoys listening* to music. He *wants to go* to the concert. He *remembered reading* about it. He *remembered to get* the tickets.)

▪ **performers of the actions of gerunds and infinitives**
(Leila didn't understand *their liking* horror movies. She asked *them to tell* her the reason.)

▪ **verbs followed by base forms**
(Our parents *let* us *go* to the concert. We *heard* the band *play*.)

Grammar in Action

🎧 **Reading and Listening:** A Popular Export?

Read and listen to this article.

A Popular Export?

The United States's biggest export is its popular culture. Popular culture includes forms of entertainment that appeal to large numbers of people—for example, television programs, movies, and popular music. These American entertainment products are extremely popular internationally, but they also cause controversy. Here are some opinions from people in various countries:

A: "I like **to listen** to American music because there are so many different styles. **Listening** to it gives me the opportunity **to experience** the cultural diversity of the United States. I'm studying English in order **to understand** the songs better."

B: "We need **to protect** our language and culture. We can do this by **not showing** so many American television programs and movies. Our goal is **to preserve** our cultural traditions."

C: "I dislike **having** so much American entertainment in this country and throughout the world.

It's the same everywhere, so it's causing cultural differences among countries **to disappear**. It's important for the world **not to lose** cultural diversity."

D: "I like **watching** Hollywood movies. The movie-makers are good at **telling** enjoyable stories that appeal to lots of different people. American movies have been popular internationally since the 1920s. I don't think we've lost our cultural identity as a result of **watching** them."

E: "My everyday life is pretty boring. **To escape** is a pleasure for me. So my favorite free-time activity is **watching** action-adventure movies. I can dream of **being** a hero."

F: "It's easy **to blame** American television programs and movies for **bringing** violence to this country. But the United States isn't the only source of the violent images we see."

export = something that is sent to another country for sale there. *controversy* = disagreement. *diversity* = quality of having differences, variety.

Think About Grammar

Work with a partner to complete the tasks.

A. In the article, the boldfaced words are

gerunds (the base form of a verb + -*ing*), e.g., *listening*, and

infinitives (*to* + the base form of a verb), e.g., to *listen*.

Look at the article, and underline the gerunds and circle the infinitives.

B. Gerunds and infinitives are similar in some uses but differ in others. Look at each of the gerunds and infinitives you marked in the article. When you find a use, check it off. Check each use off only once; leave a blank where you did not find a gerund or infinitive for a use.

Use	Gerund	Infinitive
1. subject of sentence	✓	✓
2. object of verb (i.e., verb + _____)	_____	_____
3. following an adjective (adjective + _____)	_____	_____
4. object of preposition (preposition + _____)	_____	_____
5. following a noun (noun + _____)	_____	_____

12

Gerunds and Infinitives

Introductory Task: A Good Decision?

A. Some verbs can be followed by infinitives (e.g., *to watch*), and some can be followed by gerunds (e.g., *watching*). Read the conversation between two roommates. Circle the forms that you think are correct. If you're not sure, try to guess. You will be able to check your answers in Part B.

Gil: It's almost eight o'clock. Do you **want** (to watch) / watching *Bulletproof*?
1

Ken: That's a police drama, isn't it? I don't really **enjoy** to watch / watching those kinds
2

of programs. Besides, I **need** to do / doing some more homework.
3

Gil: I just **finished** to do / doing the math assignment. Have you finished it yet?
4

Ken: Yes, I have. I **plan** to study / studying English next.
5

Gil: There's a situation comedy called *Buddies* on at eight, too. Let's watch it.

Ken: Gil, I'm sorry, but I **refuse** to watch / watching TV tonight. My education comes first.
6

I'm going to **keep** to study / studying.
7

Gil: Television can be educational. My teacher often **recommends** to watch / watching
8

Washington Affairs for information about the government and current events.

Ken: Does your teacher **suggest** to watch / watching situation comedies, too?
9

Gil: I'm not sure, but I think there are good reasons for us to watch them. For example,

by listening to the conversations, we can improve our comprehension skills.

Ken: Turn on the TV! I've **decided** to study / studying English by watching *Buddies*.
10

B. Listen to the conversation. Check your answers in Part A.

C. Look at the boldfaced verbs in the conversation. Complete the lists:

Verbs that are followed by an infinitive:

<u>want</u>   _____   _____   _____   _____

Verbs that are followed by a gerund:

_____   _____   _____   _____   _____

> *situation comedy* = a humorous television series with a regular cast of characters.

GRAMMAR BRIEFING 1

Gerunds

FORM

A. Forming Gerunds

1. Gerunds are formed from verbs. Use the base form of the verb + *-ing*. (See Appendix 3 for spelling rules for verbs + *-ing*.)	I enjoy **swimming**.
2. For negative gerunds, use *not* before the base form of the verb + *-ing*.	Thank you for **not smoking**.

B. Gerund Phrases

Gerunds can occur as part of a phrase.	Victor likes **running** in marathons. **Finding** a good job isn't easy.

FUNCTION

A. Gerunds as Subjects and Subject Complements

1. Gerunds are often used as subjects of sentences. When a gerund is the subject, use a singular verb.	**Planning** a party **takes** lots of time and effort.
2. Gerunds can also be subject complements.	My hobby is **singing**.

(continued on next page)

B. Gerunds as Objects

1. Certain verbs can have gerunds as their objects.

   These verbs include:

   | He **suggested not staying out** late. |
   | The whole family **enjoys skiing**. |

appreciate	deny	enjoy	mention	postpone	recommend	understand
avoid	discuss	finish	mind	quit	resent	
delay	dislike	keep	miss	recall	suggest	

   (For a more complete list, see Appendix 18. For verbs that can also take infinitives, see Chapter 13, Grammar Briefing 1, page 241.)

2. Gerunds can also be objects of certain phrasal verbs (e.g., *give up, put off*).

   (See Appendix 8 for common phrasal verbs that take objects.)

   | He's **given up looking** for a new apartment. |
   | I **put off telling** him the bad news. |

C. Gerunds as Objects of Prepositions

1. Gerunds can be objects of prepositions.

   | I gave him some tips **about studying**. |

2. They can therefore occur after:

   - Verb + preposition combinations (e.g., *look into, talk about, worry about*).

     (See Appendixes 9 and 10 for common verb/phrasal verb + preposition combinations.)

     | I'm **thinking about buying** tickets. |

   - *Be* (or a similar verb) + adjective + preposition combinations (e.g., *be afraid of, be good at, be happy about*).

     (See Appendix 17 for common *be* + adjective + preposition combinations.)

     | They **are interested in seeing** the concert. |
     | He **seems nervous about taking** the test. |

D. Expressions with Gerunds

1. Use *by* + gerund to tell how something is done.

   | You get tickets **by calling** the theater. |
   | They celebrated **by going** out to dinner. |

2. Use *go* + gerund to talk about doing recreational activities. Gerunds used with *go* include *bicycling, camping, dancing, fishing, hiking, jogging, running, shopping, skiing,* and *swimming*.

   | Let's **go camping** this weekend. |
   | We **went dancing** last night. |

(continued on next page)

D. Expressions with Gerunds (continued)

3. Gerunds are also used in other common expressions.

> We **had fun skiing**.
>
> **It's no use complaining**.
>
> Don't just **stand there doing** nothing.
>
> I **waste all my money eating** in restaurants.

These expressions include:

be busy	have fun (trouble/a problem/ problems/a good time, etc.)	sit/stand/lie + there
can't help	it's no use	spend/waste + time/money

GRAMMAR **HOT**SPOT!

Don't confuse gerunds with the present participle of verbs in the progressive tenses.

> My hobby is **singing**. (gerund *singing* as subject complement)
>
> Susan **is singing** in the rain. (present progressive of verb *sing*)

GRAMMAR PRACTICE 1

Gerunds

1 Identifying Gerunds and Present Participles: Culture Shock?

In the following text, underline the gerunds and present participles. Mark the gerunds *G* and the present participles *PP*.

>   *PP*
>   I'm an American student, and I'm <u>taking</u> my first trip outside the United States. Before
>   *G*
> I started <u>traveling</u>, I'd been looking forward to experiencing a completely different culture.
>
> But not all the experiences that I'm having are new and different. For example, at the
>
> moment, I'm listening to the radio. Willie Nelson is singing, "On the road again . . . The life I
>
> love is making music with my friends." I don't mind listening to country-and-western music
>
> at home, but hearing it in this country seems very strange. Watching television here is a
>
> surprise, too—many of the programs come from the United States. I'm experiencing a weird
>
> kind of culture shock!

2 Gerunds as Subjects and Subject Complements: Thinking About Entertainment

Complete the sentences with gerunds (single words or phrases). Use your ideas about different forms of entertainment.

1. <u>Dancing OR Playing the guitar</u> is a lot of fun.

2. A form of entertainment that I don't enjoy very much is _____.

3. _____ is a good way to escape from everyday life.

4. _____ is usually a waste of time.

5. An activity that is both educational and entertaining is _____.

6. My favorite entertainment is _____.

3 Gerunds as Objects of Verbs: Matching Up

A. American students starting college often live in dormitories. To find roommates who get along, colleges ask students to describe themselves. Complete the sentences with a gerund formed from the verb in parentheses.

> *Although my teachers recommend* <u>not waiting</u> *to do assignments,*
> 1 (not, wait)
>
> *I usually postpone* _____ *until late at night. I'm not very tidy,*
> 2 (study)
>
> *and I don't mind* _____ *in a messy room. I dislike*
> 3 (live)
>
> _____ *most kinds of TV shows, except for science fiction*
> 4 (watch)
>
> *dramas. I've never missed* _____ *an episode of* <u>Star Trek</u>.
> 5 (see)
>
> *I don't like rock music at all, but I really enjoy* _____ *to*
> 6 (listen)
>
> *my CDs of Broadway show tunes. I suggest* _____ *me with*
> 7 (not, pair)
>
> *a roommate who likes rock and doesn't like show tunes.*

B. Write a statement like the one in Part A about your preferences in studying, keeping your room, television, and music. Use at least six verbs followed by a gerund, for example: *avoid, can't imagine, dislike, (not) enjoy, finish, keep, (not) mind, miss, postpone, resent.*

See the *Grammar Links* Website for another model statement for this assignment.

C. Read your statements to the class. Try to decide which students would get along best as roommates. (Hint: Colleges have discovered that music preferences matter the most.)

4 Gerunds as Objects of Prepositions: The Roots of Rock and Roll

Complete the sentences with an appropriate preposition and a gerund formed from the verb in parentheses. (If necessary, look in Appendixes 9 and 17 for help with prepositions.)

In the 1950s, television and Elvis Presley were responsible <u>for making</u>
1 (make)

rock and roll popular. Elvis's voice had a special quality, and he was known

_____ in a unique way while
2 (move)

he sang and played the guitar. Although some people

strongly disapproved of his style, many others were

enthusiastic _____ his
3 (see)

performances. All over the country, people talked

_____ him on TV. Elvis
4 (watch)

succeeded _____ huge
5 (attract)

audiences.

How did Elvis create his style of rock and roll? One

influence was rhythm-and-blues music, developed by

African-American musicians. He was interested _____ like those
6 (play)

musicians did. Another influence was country-and-western music—the traditional music of the

South, which Elvis was used _____. Both rhythm-and-blues music and
7 (hear)

country-and-western music are good _____ common experiences
8 (express)

and feelings. Here are examples of lyrics from country-and-western songs: "I'm afraid

_____ you." "Don't you ever get tired _____ me?"
9 (lose)   10 (hurt)

 Check out the *Grammar Links* Website for information about Elvis Presley and links to song lyrics.

5 *By* + Gerund: Entertainment Challenges

A. Work with a partner. Think of at least two ways to answer the each of the following questions. Use *by* + gerund in your answers.

1. How can you play the guitar without using your hands?

    You can play the guitar by plucking the strings with your teeth or toes.
    You can do it by asking someone else to play it for you.

2. How can you find out when a TV program will be on if you don't have a schedule?

3. How can you operate a CD player without touching it with your fingers?

4. How can you get into a concert if all the tickets have already been sold?

5. How can you become more physically fit while watching TV?

B. As a class, compare answers. For each question, choose your favorite solution.

6 Gerunds with *Go* and in Other Expressions: Popular Culture in Two Generations

Use the words in parentheses and the expressions in the box above each paragraph to complete the sentences. Use each expression once.

> be busy   ~~go~~   ~~having a hard time~~   sits around   spends too much time   wastes his money

Parent: I'm ___having a hard time living___ with my teenage son these days. He used to
          1 (live)

  ___go bicycling___ with his friends, but now he just
          2 (bicycle)

  _____ loud, aggressive music.
          3 (listen to)

He _____ CDs by rappers and metal bands.
          4 (buy)

And he _____ to concerts when he should
          5 (go)

  _____ his homework.
          6 (do)

> can't help   go   have a good time   have problems   it's no use

Son: My parents _____ my interest in gangsta rap
          7 (understand)

  and hard rock music, and _____ it to them.
          8 (explain)

  They _____ to music that was popular
          9 (listen)

  before I was born. My mom and dad _____
          10 (dance)

  sometimes. My mom's favorite is disco music by the Bee Gees. I guess they

  _____ that old stuff.
          11 (like)

7 | Using Gerunds: The Music That We Keep Listening To

 A. Work in a small group.

1. Read the following information.

   A researcher, Robert M. Sapolsky, wondered why some people like listening to new kinds of music but others don't. He conducted a survey and concluded that age is the explanation: If you are over 35 when a style of popular music is introduced, you probably won't like it. Most people continue listening to styles of music that they first heard when they were 20 or younger.

2. Use the words and expressions in the box to talk about your own music preferences and those of people who are older or younger than you.

> **Verb**: *appreciate, avoid, enjoy, (dis)like, don't mind, keep, miss, understand, quit*
> **Verb–Preposition**: *care about, (dis)approve of, talk about, insist on*
> **Be + Adjective + Preposition**: *be accustomed to, be fond of, be interested in, be enthusiastic about, be used to*
> **Other Expressions**: *can't help, have trouble, have problems, spend time, it's no use*

> Example: I'm interested in trying new music, but my parents keep listening to music that was popular when they were young. They sometimes talk about not liking the music I listen to.

3. Decide whether you agree or disagree with the researcher's conclusions.

B. Use the words and expressions in the box to write sentences with gerunds.

1. Write three sentences about music preferences that you have in common with other members of your family or with friends.

   > Example: My mother and I both enjoy playing old Beatles records.

2. Write three sentences about differences of opinion about music that you have with other members of your family or with friends.

   > Example: I dislike hearing the music that my teenage children like, but it's no use complaining about it.

GRAMMAR BRIEFING 2

Infinitives I

FORM

A. Forming Infinitives

1. To form infinitives, use *to* + the base form of a verb.	I want **to dance**.
2. For negative infinitives, use *not* before *to* + the base form of the verb.	I must ask you **not to smoke**.

(continued on next page)

B. Infinitive Phrases

Infinitives can occur as part of a phrase.	I want **to dance** a tango.

A. Infinitives as Subjects and Subject Complements

1. Infinitives can be subjects.

   However, usually *it* is put in subject position and the infinitive is put at the end of the sentence. The meaning is the same.

   > **To dance** professionally became her dream. = **It** became her dream **to dance** professionally.

2. Infinitives can also be subject complements.

   > His preference was **to go** to a movie instead of a play.

B. Infinitives as Objects

Certain verbs can have infinitives as their objects. These verbs fall into three groups:*

- Verb + infinitive

  > He **agreed to sing**.

  Some verbs are followed directly by an infinitive. They include:

agree	can/can't afford	intend	offer	seem	wait
appear	decide	learn	plan	tend	

- Verb + noun phrase + infinitive

  > She **convinced John to sing**.

  Some verbs are followed by a noun phrase and then an infinitive. They include:

cause	force	invite	persuade	teach	trust
convince	hire	order	remind	tell	warn

- Verb (+ noun phrase) + infinitive

  > She **asked to sing**.
  >
  > She **asked him to sing**.

  Some verbs can be followed directly by an infinitive or can have a noun phrase before the infinitive. They include:

ask	choose	get	want
beg	expect	need	would like

*See Appendix 19 for more complete lists of these groups of verbs. For verbs that can also take gerunds, see Chapter 13, Grammar Briefing 1, page 241.

1. Infinitives cannot be objects of prepositions. Use gerunds instead.

   I'm thinking **about** **buying tickets**.
   NOT: I'm thinking about ~~to buy tickets~~.

2. *To* is part of some phrasal verb–preposition, verb–preposition, and *be* + adjective + preposition combinations (e.g., *look forward to, be used to*). This *to* is a preposition, not part of an infinitive, and it is followed by a gerund.

   I'll look forward to seeing you again.
   NOT: I'll look forward to ~~see~~ you again.

   We **were used to singing** in a group.
   NOT: We were used to ~~sing~~ in a group.

GRAMMAR PRACTICE 2

Infinitives I

8 **Infinitive as Subject; *It* + Infinitive:** Is It Your Dream to Be a Rock Star?

Restate each sentence in two ways using an infinitive phrase.

1. Becoming a rock star isn't easy.

   To become a rock star isn't easy.
   It isn't easy to become a rock star.

2. Becoming a successful rock musician takes hard work and creativity.

3. Developing a unique style is necessary.

4. Being able to compose music is essential.

5. Writing expressive song lyrics is important.

6. Creating artistic videos is a great challenge.

9 **Verb + Infinitive Patterns:** Our Band

Complete the sentences with *her*, [0], or *her*/[0].

1. a. We agreed _[0]_ to play in the band.

   b. We invited _her_ to play in the band.

   c. We wanted _her/[0]_ to play in the band.

   d. We hoped _____ to play in the band.

2. a. I told _____ to practice often.

   b. I expected _____ to practice often.

   c. I planned _____ to practice often.

   d. I persuaded _____ to practice often.

3. a. Ben offered _____ to sing the new song.

    b. Ben taught _____ to sing the new song.

    c. Ben would like _____ to sing the new song.

    d. Ben chose _____ to sing the new song.

4. a. We decided _____ to record the song.

    b. We asked _____ to record the song.

    c. We convinced _____ to record the song.

    d. We needed _____ to record the song.

10 **Verb + Infinitive Patterns:** **An Interview on the Music Channel**

Complete the sentences with an infinitive or an appropriate pronoun and infinitive.

A: Lucie, your latest video seems _to be_ _____ very popular with our
                                    1 (be)

    viewers all over the world. I want _you to know_ _____ how happy I am
                                        2 (know)

    that you are here tonight.

B: I would like _____ you for inviting me.
                   3 (thank)

A: First of all, I want _____ more about your background.
                          4 (know)

B: Well, my mother is a classical pianist, and she taught _____
                                                            5 (play)

    the piano. And I learned _____ songs by being around my
                              6 (write)

    father, who's a poet. My parents expected _____
                                                7 (continue)

    with classical music, but I chose _____ it. I needed
                                       8 (not, do)

    _____ my own style.
     9 (develop)

A: What's next? Do you intend _____ on another concert tour?
                                 10 (go)

B: I've decided _____ for a while because I want to
                   11 (not, perform)

    experiment with new forms of music.

A: As one of your greatest fans, I would like _____
                                                12 (know)

    how much I'm looking forward to hearing your new music.

11 Using Verbs with Infinitives: I Want (You) to Tell What's Going On

A. Work with a partner. Look at these scenes from four common types of television shows. Discuss what the characters might be doing. Use your imagination. Then write about three of the scenes. For each description, use at least three of the verbs given followed by infinitives (alone or as phrases).

1. Police Drama

warn, want, tell, offer, attempt, ask

Example: The police officer is warning
her not to go into the house.
She wants to know what happened. . . .

2. Situation Comedy

would like, tell, refuse, persuade, pretend, beg

3. Cooking Program

would like, teach, learn, invite, hope, ask

4. Hospital Drama

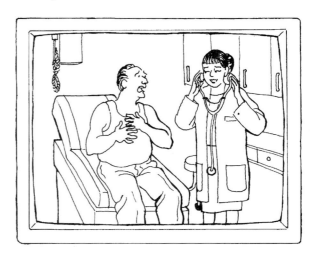

trust, tell, seem, need, expect, agree

B. Tell the class your description of one of the scenes.

Infinitives II

FUNCTION

A. Adjective + Infinitive

Certain adjectives can be followed by infinitives. Many of these adjectives describe feelings or attitudes.

He is **eager to help out**.

We were **lucky to get** tickets.

These adjectives include:

afraid	ashamed	determined	fortunate	hesitant	prepared	relieved	shocked
amazed	careful	disappointed	glad	lucky	proud	reluctant	sorry
anxious	delighted	eager	happy	pleased	ready	sad	willing

B. *In Order* + Infinitive

In order + infinitive expresses purpose. *In order* can be omitted with no change in meaning.

We're meeting next week (**in order**) **to discuss** the project.

(**In order**) **to get** the discount, you have to be a student.

C. *Too* and *Enough* with Infinitives

Infinitives are used with *too* and *enough* + adjective, adverb, and/or noun. This use of infinitives also expresses purpose. Use them as follows:

- *Too* + adjective/adverb + infinitive.

  (**Note:** *Too* often implies a negative feeling or situation.)

  The children are **too old to get in** for half price.

  We're walking **too slowly to catch up** with them.

- Adjective/adverb + *enough* + infinitive.

  The children are **young enough to get in** for half price.

  He plays **well enough to get on** the team.

- *Enough* + noun + infinitive.

  (**Note:** *Enough* often implies a positive feeling or situation.)

  I have **enough money to buy** tickets for everyone.

D. Infinitives as Noun Modifiers

Infinitives can modify a noun. An infinitive follows the noun that it modifies.

I heard about an easy **way to learn** languages.

Use the infinitive to express purpose. Do not use *for* + gerund.

We're here (**in order**) **to do** business.
NOT: We're here ~~for doing~~ business.

TALKING THE TALK

In speech and informal writing, infinitives are often shortened to *to* when the meaning is clear.

I've never visited Russia, but I'd like **to**. (*to* = to visit Russia)

A: Have you ever sung with a band?
B: No, I'm too lazy **to**. (*to* = to sing with a band)

GRAMMAR PRACTICE 3

Infinitives II

12 Adjectives + Infinitives: Soap Opera Scenes

Complete the sentences with an appropriate infinitive.

1. Warren told Nicola that his brother had been killed by a shark. Ever since then, he has been afraid _to swim_ in the ocean. Nicola thought that Warren's brother was still alive, so she was surprised _____ the story.

2. Danielle was frantic because she had lost her wedding ring. She was relieved _____ it in her purse, and she put it on. She didn't want Phillip to know that she'd taken her ring off, so she was reluctant _____ him what had happened.

3. Candace was ready _____ to a party with Shawn, but her father refused to let her go. Candace became determined _____ her parents' house and live on her own.

4. After his terrible accident, Griff was fortunate _____ alive. His girlfriend Trista was anxious _____ to the doctor about Griff's condition and their future together.

soap opera = kind of daytime TV drama with strong emotions and conflicts between characters.

13 Infinitive of Purpose: Why Did They Do It?

A. Complete the sentences with an appropriate infinitive of purpose.

1. Wendy turned on Channel 8 _(in order) to see the news_ .

2. Brian switched to the weather channel _____ .

3. Before Mike started watching TV, he went into the kitchen _____ _____ .

4. Luis got bored with the program he was watching, so he picked up the remote control _____ _____ .

5. While Zella was driving, she turned on the radio _____ _____ .

6. Instead of watching TV, Elina went to the library _____ _____ .

B. Work with a partner.

1. Make a list of the types of TV programs (e.g., situation comedies, talk shows, sports events) that you, your friends, and members of your family watch.

2. Tell your partner why you, your friends, or your family members watch each type of program you listed. Use infinitives of purpose to state the reasons.

Example: My dad watches baseball games in order to relax.
I watch situation comedies in order to laugh/to see my favorite actors.

14 Infinitives with *Too* and *Enough*: Changing Channels

Complete the sentences with *too* or *enough*, as appropriate, and an infinitive. Use the words in parentheses.

The Sports Show

Dan: Casey, I'd like your prediction on tonight's game. Will the Blues win?

Casey: The Blues are _good enough to beat_ any team. But they may be
                              1 (good, beat)

        _____ tonight. Harris has been injured.
                    2 (weak, win)

        He doesn't have _____ many minutes.
                                 3 (strength, play)

Dan: I've heard that Mihalic may join the Blues soon. Is he very talented?

Casey: Yes, he's _____ a top player. But it's
                          4 (talented, be)

        _____ if he'll live up to his talent. It would be great to
              5 (soon, know)

        have him on the team, though. I hope he can join _____
                                                                  6 (soon, help)

        the Blues this season.

Police Drama

Captain: Have you talked to the victim's wife?

Detective: Not yet. She's _____ what happened.

1 (upset, talk about)

Captain: Do you have a suspect?

Detective: Yeah, but I hope that it isn't _____ him. He stole a lot

2 (late, catch)

of money. He has _____ for a long time.

3 (money, live on)

Captain: Then we need to find him soon. I hope you're _____

4 (smart, figure out)

how to do it.

15 Infinitives as Noun Modifiers: The Value of Television

Television has both positive and negative aspects. Think of some positive aspects of television and different television programs. Write sentences with each of the following nouns + infinitive phrases: *ability, chance, opportunity, way.*

Example: *Television gives people a chance to learn about new and different things.* OR
Watching Moneyline is a good way to get information about business.

16 Using Infinitives; Infinitives Shortened to *To*: Your Own Talk Show

A. Imagine that you are the host of a television talk show. Your next guest will be a person who is well known in the world of entertainment—for example, a television or music star. Decide who the guest will be. What do you want to ask her or him? Complete the following *yes/no* questions with infinitive phrases.

1. Can you afford to buy a Rolls-Royce _____?

2. Have you ever wanted _____?

3. Are you afraid _____?

4. Do you feel fortunate _____?

5. Are you too _____?

6. Do you have enough _____?

7. Have you had an opportunity _____?

8. Would you like _____?

B. Work with a partner. Ask your partner the questions you wrote in Part A. Your partner plays the part of the star and uses his or her imagination to answer the questions. The answers should include some infinitives shortened to *to*. Then reverse roles. Present your interviews to the class.

Example: Student A: *Can you afford to buy a Rolls-Royce?*
            Student B: *Yes, I can afford to.* OR *Yes, I can afford to, but I don't want to.*

Check your progress! Go to the Self-Test for Chapter 12 on the *Grammar Links* Website.

Chapter 13

More About Gerunds and Infinitives

Introductory Task: A Crime Movie

A. Work with a partner. The sentences describe what happened in a crime movie. In each sentence, look at the boldfaced verb + infinitive or gerund. Decide which happened first—the action expressed by the verb or the action expressed by the infinitive or gerund. Mark the action that happened first with **1** and mark the action that happened second with **2** (e.g., in sentence 1, planning comes first, then stealing). If both actions happened at the same time, mark both with **1**.

1. A group of thieves **planned to steal** some jewels from a museum in Greece.

2. A burglar alarm was connected to the floor of the museum, so they **decided to enter** from the roof.

3. A witness ran to the police station and **reported seeing** someone on the roof.

4. The thieves **kept lifting** jewels out of the building.

5. They **wanted to finish** the job.

6. They **intended to sell** the jewels to a man in Amsterdam.

7. The police caught them several days later, but they **denied stealing** anything.

8. While they were in jail, the thieves got into an argument, and finally one of them **admitted stealing** the jewels.

> *burglar alarm* = a device that warns if thieves enter a building. *witness* = someone who sees a crime occur.

B. Complete the sentences with *gerund* or *infinitive*.

1. The action expressed by the _____ tends to occur after the action expressed by the verb.

2. The action expressed by the _____ tends to occur before or at the same time as the action expressed by the verb.

Verbs + Gerunds and Infinitives

FUNCTION

A. Verbs That Take Only Gerunds or Only Infinitives

1. Some verbs take only gerunds or only infinitives. (See Chapter 12 and Appendixes 18 and 19 for these verbs.)

   > I **finished studying**.
   > **NOT**: I finished ~~to study~~.
   >
   > I **planned to study**.
   > **NOT**: I planned ~~studying~~.

2. There is often a difference between verbs that take only gerunds and verbs that take only infinitives. Sometimes this difference can help you figure out whether to use a gerund or an infinitive:

   - Gerunds often follow verbs that indicate that an action is happening or has happened. That is, the action of the gerund happens before the action of the verb or at the same time.

     >   2nd   1st
     > I **miss jogging**. (The jogging happens first, then I miss it.)
     >
     >   same time
     > We **enjoy cooking**. (The cooking and our enjoyment happen at the same time.)

   - Infinitives often follow verbs that indicate that an action will or can happen. That is, the action of the infinitive happens after the action of the verb.

     >   1st   2nd
     > They **convinced** Dave **to jog**. (First they convinced him, then he jogged.)
     >
     >   1st   2nd
     > I **want to cook** tomorrow. (First I want to, then I cook.)

(continued on next page)

B. Verbs That Take Gerunds and Infinitives

1. Some verbs can take a gerund or an infinitive.

    > I **hate studying.** = I **hate to study.**
    >
    > They **continued working.** = They **continued to work.**

    These verbs include:

begin	hate	love	start
continue	like	prefer	

2. Some verbs can take a gerund or a noun phrase + infinitive. If the infinitive is used with a general noun phrase (e.g., *people*), the sentence has the same meaning as the sentence with the gerund.

    > We **advise not driving.** = We **advise people not to drive.**
    >
    > We **advised John not to drive.**

    These verbs include:

advise	encourage	require
allow	permit	urge

C. Verbs That Take Gerunds and Infinitives but with a Difference in Meaning

Some verbs take gerunds or infinitives but with a difference in meaning. The difference in meaning is related to the difference discussed in section A. These verbs include:

-   *Remember*:

    Remember + gerund—the action of the gerund comes before the action of remembering.

    >   2nd   1st
    > I **remember rehearsing** for the play. (I rehearsed in the past; I remember now.)

    Remember + infinitive—the action of remembering comes before the action of the infinitive.

    >   1st   2nd
    > I always **remember to go** to rehearsals. (First I remember, i.e., think of going; then I go.)

(continued on next page)

C. Verbs That Take Gerunds and Infinitives but with a Difference in Meaning (continued)

- *Forget*:

  Forget + gerund—the action of the gerund comes first.

	2nd	1st

  I'll never **forget meeting** you for the first time.
  (I met you in the past; I won't forget this event.)

  Forget + infinitive—the action of forgetting comes first, so the action of the infinitive doesn't happen.

	1st	2nd

  I'm sorry I **forgot to meet** you this morning.
  (First I forgot, so I didn't meet you.)

- *Stop*:

  Stop + gerund—the action of the gerund happens first and then stops.

	2nd	1st

  She **stopped smoking**. (She smoked in the past but then stopped.)

  Stop + infinitive—some other action stops and then the action of the infinitive happens.

	1st	2nd

  She **stopped to smoke**. (She stopped what she was doing in order to then smoke.)

- *Try*:

  Try + gerund—the attempted action, expressed by the gerund, occurred.

  I **tried calling** you, but you weren't home. (I did actually call.)

  Try + infinitive—the attempted action, expressed by the infinitive, did not occur.

  I **tried to call** you, but I couldn't find a phone. (I wanted to call but couldn't.)

GRAMMAR PRACTICE 1

Verbs + Gerunds and Infinitives

1 **Verbs That Take Only Gerunds or Only Infinitives:** A Film Festival

A. Use the words in parentheses to complete the sentences with an infinitive or gerund. (Hint: Does the action come after the action of the verb? Or does the action come before or at the same time as the action of the verb?)

1. The university film festival is going to show some famous Hollywood movies. I want

   _____to see_____ all of them.
        (see)

2. I saw several classic movies at the festival last year. I really enjoyed _____watching_____ them.
                                                                                                (watch)

3. We're staying at the library until nine tonight. Then we're going to quit

   _____ and go to *Citizen Kane*.
           (study)

4. A classmate and I were talking about *The Godfather*, and I promised

   _____ to it with her. It starts at seven tonight.
   (go)

5. I went to *Close Encounters of the Third Kind* last night. When I finished

   _____ it, I believed that aliens really had visited Earth.
   (watch)

6. I'm looking forward to *Some Like It Hot*. I've been working hard all week, and I need

   _____ a funny movie.
   (see)

7. I haven't seen *North by Northwest* yet, but I've read about it. I expect

   _____ it a lot.
   (like)

8. Have you seen *Gone with the Wind*? While you're watching it, you can imagine

   _____ in the South during the time of the Civil War.
   (live)

9. The film festival is great. I appreciate _____ this chance to escape
   (have)

   into a fantasy world.

10. I can't go to this festival, but I hope _____ it next year. It sounds
    (attend)

    like fun.

B. Work with a partner. Write answers to the following questions. In each sentence, include an infinitive phrase or gerund phrase and one of these verbs: *appreciate, can imagine, enjoy, hope, need, want.*

1. People watch movies for many different reasons. What are three reasons that they watch them?

   Example: They enjoy escaping from reality.

2. Choose three of the following types of movies: action-adventure movies, animated movies, comedies, crime movies, disaster movies, horror movies, musicals, romances, science fiction, thrillers, Westerns. What is a reason that people like watching each type of movie?

   Example: comedies—They enjoy seeing other people in embarrassing situations.

2 | **Using Verbs That Take Gerunds and Infinitives:** What's Your Opinion?

A. Work with a partner. American movies are popular all over the world, but they also cause controversy in many places (see page 222). What kinds of reactions do people in other countries have to American movies? Are their preferences going to change in the future? Write four sentences with gerunds and infinitives using the following verbs: (not) like, love, prefer, hate, begin, continue.

Example: People like watching American movies because they like to see something new and different. OR In many countries people don't like having so many American movies in their theaters. They won't continue going to them.

B. Read your sentences to the class. As a class, discuss your opinions about this topic.

3 | **Verbs That Take Gerunds and Noun Phrase + Infinitives:** Entertainment and More

A. Use the words in parentheses to complete the sentences with a gerund or an infinitive.

1. Seeing movies allows you ___to experience___ other cultures.
   (experience)

2. Some people advise _____ to movies for education as well as entertainment.
   (go)

3. Teachers sometimes encourage their students _____ movies to improve their
   (watch)

   listening skills.

4. Getting information from a movie doesn't require _____ all the words.
   (understand)

5. There are some very good old movies that I advise you _____ at the video store.
   (rent)

6. For example, I urge you _____ *Breaking Away*. It's funny, and you can get a sense
   (see)

   of life in an American college town in the 1970s.

B. Work alone and then with a partner.

1. Think of two movies you would advise your partner to see. For each movie write two sentences, giving your advice and the reason for it. Use *advise* (or *encourage* or *urge*) with an infinitive. Then tell your partner what you have written.

Example: I advise you to see 2001: A Space Odyssey. It has great special effects, and you can imagine being in another world.

2. Decide on two movies that you and your partner both like. Give advice to the class about them. Use *advise* with a gerund.

Example: We advise seeing Casablanca. It has romance and suspense.

To find out more about old movies, check out the *Grammar Links* Website.

4 *Remember, Forget, Stop,* **and** *Try*: Slapstick Comedy

 A. Stan Laurel and Oliver (Ollie) Hardy were famous slapstick comedians. Listen to the descriptions of typical slapstick situations involving Stan and Ollie. Then listen again and circle the correct answers.

1.	Did Ollie put his hat on his head?	(Yes) / No
2.	Did Stan take the cake off the seat of the car?	Yes / No
3.	Did Stan leave the roller skate at the top of the stairs?	Yes / No
4.	Did Ollie turn on the water?	Yes / No
5.	Did Stan leave the ladder leaning against the house?	Yes / No
6.	Did Ollie and Stan carry the sofa?	Yes / No
7.	Did Ollie and Stan put up the sail?	Yes / No
8.	Did Ollie go out with Stan now?	Yes / No
9.	Did Stan go out with his wife now?	Yes / No

B. Listen again. This time you will hear an explanation of what happened. Check your answers in Part A.

> *slapstick* = type of comedy with lots of silly mistakes, collisions, falls, and arguments.

5 **Remember, Forget, Stop,** and **Try**: The Hughes Brothers

Use the words in parentheses to complete the sentences with gerunds or infinitives.

Background: *Rollo and Lucky Hughes's neighbor Mrs. Gray is an elderly widow. She deposited $5,000 in the bank, but the bank made a mistake and didn't credit her account. Now she can't pay her bills and is desperate. Rollo and Lucky have decided to rob the bank to get her money back.*

Scene I: *The living room in Rollo and Lucky's small house*

Rollo: Stop ___watching___ TV, Lucky. It's time to go. Did you remember
 1 (watch)

 ___to put___ gas in the car?
 2 (put)

Lucky: Yeah, I did. I was going to wash the car, too, but I forgot _____ it.
 3 (do)

Rollo: That's not important now. Where's my comb? It was here earlier. I remember

 _____ it on the table.
 4 (see)

(Lucky leaves for a moment and returns.)

Lucky: I tried _____ for it in the bathroom, and it's not there.
 5 (look)

Rollo: Never mind. We'll stop _____ one on the way to the bank.
 6 (buy)

Lucky: Your hair looks okay. Why do you need a comb?

Rollo: Don't you remember _____ the robbery? I'm going to have a
 7 (plan)

 comb in my pocket and pretend it's a gun.

Lucky: Oh, now I remember. Then the teller will give us the money.

Scene II: *At the bank*

Lucky: I'm really nervous about doing this, Rollo. I can't stop _____.
 8 (shake)

Rollo: Don't worry. Just remember _____ the note to the teller. . . .
 9 (hand)

(Lucky hands the teller a note that says, "Give us $5,000 and nobody will get hurt.")

Teller: I recognize you. You're Lucky Hughes! You were in my class in high school.

 I'll never forget _____ to school with you.
 10 (go)

Lucky: Please don't call the police! We're only trying _____ poor
 11 (help)

 Mrs. Gray.

Teller: You haven't gotten any smarter, have you? I know you mean well, but you need

 to learn: Crime never pays.

6 **Using Gerunds and Infinitives:** Your Movie Script

A. Work in small groups. Write a short script for a scene from any kind of movie (e.g., action-adventure, comedy, disaster, horror, romance, science fiction). There should be a role for each person in the group. In your script, use at least three of these verbs followed by a gerund or by an infinitive: *forget, remember, stop,* and *try.* Also, use at least two verbs that are followed only by gerunds and at least two that are followed only by infinitives. You can choose from the following list or use any others: *admit, agree, deny, enjoy, finish, hope, intend, keep, need,* and *plan.*

B. Perform your movie scene for the class.

See the *Grammar Links* Website for a model script for this assignment.

GRAMMAR BRIEFING 2

Performers of the Actions of Gerunds and Infinitives

FORM and FUNCTION

A. Performers of the Actions of Gerunds

1. In the sentences we've seen so far, the action of the gerund is performed by:

   - The subject of the sentence.

     > I hate **taking** the keys. (I perform the action of taking the keys.)
     >
     > The assistant finished **setting up** the cameras. (The assistant performs the action of setting up the cameras.)

   - People in general, rather than specific performers.

     > **Swimming** is a lot of fun. (People in general perform the action of swimming and find it fun.)
     >
     > I can't understand **giving up** without trying. (I can't understand when people in general perform the action of giving up.)

2. Sometimes, however, there is a specific performer that is **not** the subject of the sentence. This performer of the gerund action is expressed by a possessive noun or possessive determiner.

     > I hate **my brother's/his taking** the keys. (My brother performs the action of taking the keys.)
     >
     > I can't understand **Megan's/her giving up** without trying. (Megan performs the action of giving up.)

(continued on next page)

B. Performers of the Actions of Infinitives

1. In the sentences we've seen so far, the action of the infinitive is performed by:

   - The subject of the sentence.

     Barbara plans **to cook** dinner for you. (Barbara performs the action of cooking.)

     Phil is always eager **to please** people. (Phil performs the action of pleasing.)

   - The people or things in the noun phrase that comes before the infinitive (with verbs that take noun phrase + infinitive).

     I convinced **John to go** to the party. (John performs the action of going.)

     I expect **them to help** us. (They perform the action of helping.)

   - People in general.

     These days, it isn't easy **to find** a job. (for people in general)

2. Sometimes there is no noun phrase and the performer of the infinitive action is not the sentence subject or people in general. In such cases, the performer is expressed with *for* + noun phrase.

   I'll wait **for Jack/him to come** home. (Jack performs the action of coming home.)

   These days it isn't easy **for recent graduates to find** a job. (Recent graduates perform the action of finding jobs.)

TALKING THE TALK

In speech, the performer of the gerund action is often indicated by a nonpossessive noun or an object pronoun, instead of by possessive forms.

I really appreciate **Don/him** doing that for me. *Compare*: I really appreciate Don's/his doing that for me. (more formal)

Performers of the Actions of Gerunds and Infinitives

7 Performers of Gerunds: Indiana's Adventures

A. *Raiders of the Lost Ark* and the other Indiana Jones movies are among the most popular action-adventure movies ever made. Combine the sentences. Replace the boldfaced word in the second sentence with a gerund phrase based on the first sentence. In combining, change the first sentence in any way needed. Include a possessive form for the performer of the gerund where needed.

1. Indiana went to find the lost Ark of the Covenant. Indiana was excited about **this**.

   Indiana was excited about going to find the lost Ark of the Covenant.

2. Indiana found his former girlfriend Marion in Nepal. Marion didn't appreciate **this**.

   Marion didn't appreciate Indiana's/his finding her in Nepal.

3. Marion disappeared in Cairo. Indiana was upset about **this**.

4. Indiana found her in a tent where she had been tied up. Indiana was happy about **this**.

5. He didn't untie her. She resented **this**.

6. Indiana dropped into a pit full of poisonous snakes. Indiana hated **this**.

7. The villains pushed Marion into the pit, too. Marion was terrified by **this**.

8. Indiana found the lost ark. **This** made the villains very angry.

9. They captured Marion. **This** infuriated Indiana.

10. Indiana told her not to look at the evil spirits coming from the ark. Indiana saved Marion's life by **this**.

> *Ark of the Covenant* = an ancient religious object. *pit* = a deep hole. *villain* = an evil person. *infuriate* = make extremely angry.

B. Work with a partner. Use the sentences you wrote in Part A to tell each other about *Raiders of the Lost Ark*. Use nonpossessive forms.

Example: Marion didn't appreciate Indiana [OR him] finding her in Nepal.

8 Performers of Infinitives: Remaking King Kong

A. Use the information in the first sentence to complete the second sentence. Use *for* with a noun phrase when necessary.

1. The director asked Adam, "Will you act in the movie?" The director asked

   Adam to act in the movie _____.

2. Adam asked the director, "Can I play the leading role?" Adam asked

   to play the leading role _____.

3. The director said to Adam, "If you'll play the leading role, I'll be happy." The director will be happy <u>for Adam to play the leading role</u>.

4. Adam said, "If I play the leading role, I'll be happy." Adam will be happy

   _____ .

5. Then the director talked to Adam for a long time, and finally Adam said, "Okay. I'll wear a gorilla costume." The director persuaded _____ .

6. Then the director said to Adam, "You're going to climb to the top of the Empire State Building." The director planned _____

   _____ .

7. Adam said, "No problem. I'll climb to the top of the building." Adam wasn't afraid

   _____ .

8. Adam's girlfriend Suki said to him, "Adam, please don't climb to the top!" Suki was afraid

   _____ .

9. Adam said, "I'm going to win an Academy Award." Adam intended

   _____ .

10. Suki said to Adam, "In that case, you can do it!" Suki was willing

    _____ .

 B. Imagine that you're going to direct a movie in which your classmates play roles. Write six sentences about your plans. Include at least two sentences with *for* + noun or pronoun. Use any of the following verbs: *expect, persuade, plan, want, would like.* Use *be* + *eager, happy, pleased,* or other adjectives.

Example: I want to make a science-fiction movie. I'm eager for Lena to play the part of an alien. I'm going to ask her to pilot the alien space ship.

GRAMMAR BRIEFING 3

Verbs Followed by Base Forms

FORM

A. *Have, Make, Let*

Have, make, and *let* are causative verbs. That is, their meaning relates to causing (in the case of *let,* allowing) someone to do something.

These verbs are always followed by noun phrase + base form of verb. Do **not** use an infinitive after these verbs.

>   V   NP   base form
> **I'll have my assistant call** you.
>
>   V   NP base form
> I **made them leave**, so I could be alone.
>
>   V NP base form
> The boss **let us leave** early, because it's Friday.

(continued on next page)

B. Verbs of Perception

1. *Hear*, *notice*, *observe*, *see*, and *watch* are verbs of perception. These verbs are followed by a noun phrase + the base form of a verb. Do **not** use the infinitive.

   >   V   NP   base form
   > I **heard Professor Smith give** a talk on French poetry.
   >
   >   V   NP   base form
   > We **saw them perform**.

2. These verbs can also be followed by a noun phrase + the *-ing* form.

   Do not use a possessive before the *-ing* form.

   >   V   NP   *-ing* form
   > I **heard Professor Smith giving** a talk on French poetry.
   >
   >   V   NP   *-ing* form
   > We **saw them performing**.
   > **NOT**: We saw ~~their~~ performing.

GRAMMAR **HOT**SPOT!

The verb *help* can take an infinitive or a base form. In speech the base form is more common. *Help* can occur with or without a noun phrase.

> I **helped** (**them**) **to clean up** after the party.
> OR I **helped** (**them**) **clean up** after the party.

GRAMMAR PRACTICE 3

Verbs Followed by Base Forms

9 **Forms Following Causative Verbs, Verbs of Perception, and Other Verbs:** The Wizard of Oz

The following is a summary of *The Wizard of Oz*, a movie classic from 1939.* Complete the sentences with the base, infinitive, or *-ing* forms of the verbs in parentheses. If two forms are correct, show both forms.

At the beginning of the movie, we hear Dorothy <u>singing/sing</u> "Somewhere

                                           1 (sing)

Over the Rainbow." She is at home in Kansas with her little dog, Toto. A sudden tornado comes, and

Dorothy and Toto are carried over the rainbow into the land of the Munchkins. Dorothy watches the

little Munchkins _____. Soon she wants _____
                          2 (dance)   3 (go)

*The summary is in the simple present, a tense often used in telling stories.

back to Kansas. The Good Witch gives her a pair of red slippers and tells her

_____ a yellow brick road to the Emerald City, where she will find the
4 (follow)

Wizard of Oz. The Wizard will help her _____ her way back home. Soon
5 (find)

after she starts down the road, Dorothy discovers the Scarecrow. She has him _____
6 (come)

with her so that he can ask the Wizard _____ him a brain. Next, they find
7 (give)

the Tin Man, who is rusty. Dorothy helps him _____ again by oiling him.
8 (move)

She lets the Tin Man _____ them on their journey, because he hopes
9 (join)

_____ a heart. They meet the Cowardly Lion and allow him
10 (get)

_____, too. He wants the Wizard _____ him
11 (come)   12 (give)

courage. After the Wizard finally lets them _____ the Emerald City, they tell
13 (enter)

him why they are there. The Wizard makes them _____ to the castle of
14 (go)

the Wicked Witch. When the Witch sets fire to the Scarecrow, Dorothy throws water at the flames.

The water kills the witch. We hear her _____ and see her
15 (scream)

_____. Later the Good Witch reappears. She tells Dorothy and her friends
16 (melt)

that they always had what they were looking for, but that they had to find it out for themselves. She

has Dorothy _____ the heels of her slippers three times, and Dorothy and
17 (click)

Toto are back in Kansas.

---

tornado = a violent windstorm.

 Learn more about *The Wizard of Oz* by going to the *Grammar Links* Website.

> **Check your progress! Go to the Self-Test for Chapter 13 on the *Grammar Links* Website.**

Wrap-up Activities

1 Going to Graceland: EDITING

Correct the 10 errors in the passage. There are errors in gerunds and infinitives and related forms. Some errors can be corrected in more than one way. The first error is corrected for you.

Elvis Presley
Fan Site

Every year, thousands of people from all over the world travel to Memphis, Tennessee,
                    to visit
~~for visiting~~ Graceland, Elvis Presley's home. I've never been to Graceland, but I want going

there. I look forward to do it someday because Elvis has a very important place in the history

of American popular culture. I wasn't enough old to see Elvis when he was alive, but I'll never

forget to hear "Love Me Tender" for the first time. I've watched his movies, and I've talked to

people who saw his performing in the 1950s.

People who are my age sometimes have

problems to understand why he shocked

people so much.

I think that Elvis was an example of the

American dream—a poor boy who became

successful by using his talent and energy.

Elvis's home, Graceland

When he was young, he dreamed about to be rich someday. But later it was difficult for him

to deal with his success. He was very generous, and he often went to the store for buying

Cadillacs and other expensive gifts for people. Being so generous caused him to have financial

problems, though. He started taking too many pills, and he became famous for eating lots of

fried food. Now we are used to think of Elvis as a troubled person who lost control of his

life—an American tragedy. But I prefer to keep remembering his musical achievements.

2 A Game Show Pre-Test: WRITING

Step 1 Work in small groups. Imagine that you work for a cable television channel, English Language Learning Network. You produce a game show called *Grammar Challenge*. Many people would like to be contestants on the show. In order to select the best contestants, you have decided to test their ability to use gerunds and infinitives and to use verbs that take base forms. Write a fill-in-the-blanks test with 10 items.

Example:

1. I tried _____ for help, but no one heard me.
    (scream)

2. That car is *too expensive for me* _____ .
    (buy)

Step 2 After your teacher has checked your test, make copies of it for the other students in the class. After they have completed it, check their answers.

3 A Fan Letter: WRITING

Write a letter to an actor or singer whom you admire. Include at least five of the following:

a verb + gerund	an adjective + infinitive
a verb + preposition + gerund	a noun modified by an infinitive
a verb + infinitive	an infinitive of purpose
a verb + NP + base or *-ing* form	*too* or *enough* + infinitive

Example:
Dear Bob,
I'm writing to express my admiration for your singing. I had a chance to hear your latest album recently, and I want you to know how much I liked listening to it. . . .

 See the *Grammar Links* Website for a complete model letter for this assignment.

4   What's Your Opinion?   SPEAKING/WRITING

Step 1 Work in small groups. Read the following statement:

American entertainment products—especially music, television programs, and movies—will continue to be popular and successful internationally for many years.

Step 2 Discuss whether you agree or disagree with the statement and why. In your discussion, use some of the words listed in sentences with gerunds and infinitives.

Verbs: *appreciate, (dis)approve of, avoid, continue, enjoy, keep, like, love, need, prefer, refuse, start, stop, try, would like*

Expressions: *have fun, spend time*

Be + **Adjective** + **Preposition:** *concerned about, critical of, enthusiastic about, interested in, responsible for*

Example: I agree. People prefer to watch American television programs, and they will continue watching them. OR I disagree. People are going to become more enthusiastic about seeing programs from their own countries, and they're going to stop watching so many American programs.

Step 3 Write a paragraph explaining why you agree or disagree with the statement. Use at least six sentences with gerunds and infinitives.

Example:
American entertainment products will continue to be popular and successful internationally for several reasons. First, for some small countries, producing their own TV programs costs too much. But not making their own programs isn't a problem, because they can get American programs that people enjoy watching. . . .

 See the *Grammar Links* Website for a complete model paragraph for this assignment.

Modals

Courtship and Marriage

UNIT OBJECTIVES

- **modals of ability**
  (A typical three-year-old *can* talk.)

- **belief modals used to talk about the present and future**
  (She has *MD* after her name, so she *must* be a doctor. She *will* probably be happy to meet him.)

- **social modals**
  (*May* I help you? What *should* I wear to the wedding?)

- **perfect modals**
  (Things *might have* gone better for them.)

- **belief modals used to talk about the past**
  (They *must have* been married for a long time.)

- **social modals used to talk about the past**
  (You *could have* found Mr. Right long ago.)

Grammar in Action

🎧 Reading and Listening: In Class

Read and listen to this discussion from a cultural anthropology class.

Teacher: Before class ends, I want to remind you that the midterm exam is next week. You **should** read the information that I've written on the blackboard about it. **Can** everyone see the blackboard?

Student A: **Is** the exam **going to** be difficult?

Teacher: It **shouldn't be** too difficult. Students who have come to every class and done all the reading **should** do well on it. Of course, you **must** review the material. A review is always necessary. And I have a suggestion: You **might** work together in study groups.

Student B: **May** I ask one more question? **Could** you repeat the definition of *courtship*?

Teacher: Of course. Courtship is part of the process of choosing a mate, that is, a husband or wife. Courtship refers to social activities between males and females that **might** lead to marriage. Dating **can** be a part of courtship, as it often is in this country, but it **doesn't have to** be—courtship customs are different in different cultures. And the ways of choosing a mate differ, too. There are various possibilities. For example, the individuals themselves **may** find their mates. Or their family members **could** be the ones who find suitable mates for them. Or they **might** ask a matchmaker, or go-between, to identify potential mates. But even if families or matchmakers arrange an introduction, this doesn't necessarily mean that the individuals **must** marry one another. In most cases, the individuals **are allowed** to make the final decision.

Student C: In this culture, most people think that a decision to marry **ought to** be based on romantic love—that you **shouldn't** marry someone unless you're strongly attracted to them. How important is romantic love as a basis for choosing a mate in other cultures?

Teacher: Well, cultural anthropologists who have done research on this topic believe that romantic love **must** be nearly universal. That is, they're certain that it occurs almost everywhere. But they have found it isn't universally important as a basis of marriage. In many cultures, family considerations are more important. I know you're interested in this topic, so we **will** discuss it more next week, but we've run out of time. You **may** go now.

---

cultural anthropology = the study of humans' beliefs, patterns of behavior, and customs.

Think About Grammar

The boldfaced words in the discussion are one-word modals, phrasal modals, and modal-like expressions. Modals are used to express belief that something is certain, likely, or just possible. They are also used to express ability and to do other things like give advice or permission and to make requests or suggestions. Most modals have more than one use.

Work with a partner. In each of the following pairs of sentences from the discussion, a modal occurs as a belief modal and in another use. Complete the sentence that follows the pair with *a* and *b*. (If you need help in deciding how a modal is used, go back to the discussion and read the sentence in its context.)

1. a. You **should** read the information that I've written on the blackboard.
    b. Students who have come to every class and done all the reading **should** do well on the exam.

    Should is used to say that something is likely in <u>b</u> and to give someone advice in <u>a</u>.

2. a. **Can** everyone see the blackboard?
    b. Dating **can** be a part of courtship.

    Can is used to say that something is possible in _____ and to ask about ability in _____.

3. a. **Could** you repeat the definition of *courtship*?
    b. Their family members **could** be the ones who find suitable mates for them.

    Could is used to say that something is possible in _____ and to make a request for someone

    to do something in _____.

4. a. Individuals themselves **may** find their mates.
    b. You **may** go now.

    May is used to say that something is possible in _____ and to give someone permission to

    do something in _____.

5. a. Courtship refers to social activities that **might** lead to marriage.
    b. You **might** work together in study groups.

    Might is used to say that something is possible in _____ and to make a suggestion to

    someone in _____.

6. a. You **must** review the material.
    b. Cultural anthropologists believe that romantic love **must** be nearly universal.

    Must is used to say that something is certain in _____ and to express the necessity for

    someone to do something in _____.

14

Modals

Introductory Task: How Certain Is She?

Work with a partner. Read each group of statements made by Andrea and answer the questions.

1. a. Theresa **is** married. She introduced me to her husband.
   b. Dale **might be** married. It's possible that he is, but I really don't know.
   c. Brian **must be** married. He wears a wedding ring.
   d. Dana **could be** married. Maybe she is, maybe she isn't.

   Which boldfaced verb or modal + verb combination(s) did Andrea use when she was

   fully certain about the situation? _is_____

   very certain about the situation? _____

   not very certain about the situation? _____ _____

2. a. Tamika **might not be** married. It's possible that she isn't, but I don't have any way of knowing for sure.
   b. Elliot **must not be** married. I've seen him at movies and restaurants with several different women.
   c. Sheila **isn't** married. I know for a fact that she is single.
   d. Marco **couldn't be** married. He's only 16, and he lives with his parents.

   Which boldfaced verb or modal + verb combination(s) did Andrea use when she was

   fully certain about the situation? _____

   very certain about the situation? _____ _____

   not very certain about the situation? _____

3. The sentences in 1 are affirmative sentences. The sentences in 2 are negative sentences. One modal expresses a different degree of certainty in negative sentences than it does in affirmative sentences.

   Circle the modal:　　could　　might　　must

Overview of Modals
■ One-Word Modals

FORM

A. Overview

Modals are auxiliary verbs.	They **should be** home now.
Unlike auxiliary verbs *have* and *be*, one-word modals don't change form and are followed by the base form of the verb.	He **can help** you, and we **can help**, too.
One-word modals include *can, could, may, might, must, should, will,* and *would*.	

B. Affirmative Statements

SUBJECT	MODAL	BASE FORM OF VERB	
I	**can**	**speak**	English.
He	**should**	**call**	her.

C. Negative Statements

SUBJECT	MODAL + *NOT**	BASE FORM OF VERB	
Lauren	**cannot**	**go.**	
They	**will not**	**listen**	to me.

D. *Yes/No* Questions and Short Answers

QUESTIONS	SHORT ANSWERS
Should they **come**?	Yes, they **should**.
Will he **be** there?	No, he **won't**.

E. *Wh-* Questions

WH- QUESTIONS ABOUT THE SUBJECT	OTHER *WH-* QUESTIONS
Who might come?	**What can** he **do**?

***CONTRACTIONS**

can + not → can't
could + not → couldn't
might + not → mightn't
must + not → mustn't
should + not → shouldn't
will + not → won't
would + not → wouldn't

(continued on next page)

Phrasal Modals

A. Overview

Phrasal modals begin with *be* or *have* and end with *to*. The *be* and *have* change form. Phrasal modals are followed by the base form of the verb.

Phrasal modals include *be able to, be allowed to, be going to, be supposed to, be to, have to,* and *have got to.*

> She **was supposed to go** yesterday, and I'm **supposed to go** today.
>
> He **has to leave** now, and we **have to leave**, too.

B. Affirmative Statements

SUBJECT	PHRASAL MODAL	BASE FORM OF VERB	
She	**is able to**	**speak**	English.
He	**has to**	**leave**	now.

C. Negative Statements

SUBJECT	PHRASAL MODAL + *NOT**	BASE FORM OF VERB	
They	**were not to**	**be**	here.
She	**does not have to**	**go**	home.

D. *Yes/No* Questions and Short Answers

QUESTIONS	SHORT ANSWERS
Are we **supposed to study** now?	Yes, you **are**.
Do they **have to leave** yet?	No, they **don't**.

E. *Wh-* Questions

WH- QUESTIONS ABOUT THE SUBJECT	OTHER *WH-* QUESTIONS
Who is supposed to come?	**What do** we **have to bring?**

*For contractions with *be* and *do*, see Chapter 1, Grammar Briefing 1, page 5.

One-Word Modals and Phrasal Modals

A. Overview

1. Most modals have more than one meaning.

> He **could** swim well. (past ability)
>
> The phone **could** be busy. (present possibility)

2. Different modals often express similar meanings.

> He **could** be here. = He **might** be here. = He **may** be here.

(continued on next page)

B. Combining Modal Meanings

To express two modal meanings, use a one-word modal + a phrasal modal or use two phrasal modals. (One-word modals cannot be used together.)	You **must be able to** swim in order to go. OR You **have to be able to** swim in order to go. **NOT:** You ~~must can~~ swim in order to go.

■ Modal-like Expressions

FORM and FUNCTION

Overview

1. In this unit, the term *modal* includes modal-like expressions *ought to* and *had better*. Modal-like expressions are similar to modals in meaning and use. They are followed by the base form of the verb. Like one-word modals, they don't change form.	You **ought to go**, and he **ought to go**, too. You **had better be** careful, and he **had better be** careful, too.
2. *Ought to* and *had better* are used in affirmative statements. *Ought to* is not usually used in negatives. *Ought to* and *had better* are not usually used in questions.	He **ought to tell/had better tell** someone. He **had better not** tell anyone.

GRAMMAR **HOT**SPOT!

1. One-word modals: • *Can + not* is written as one word even if not contracted.	She **cannot/can't** go.
• *May + not* is not contracted.	You **may not** smoke in here. **NOT:** You ~~mayn't~~ smoke in here.

2. Phrasal modals:
   • *Have to* does not contract with the subject.
	I **have to** study.
	  NOT: ~~I've to~~ study.

• *Have to* occurs with *do* in negatives and questions. *Have got to* doesn't occur in negatives and questions.	**Do** I **have to** study?
	  NOT: ~~Have I to/Have I got to~~ study?
	I **don't have to** study tonight.
	  NOT: I ~~haven't to/haven't got to~~ study tonight.

Overview of Modals

1 **Identifying One-Word Modals, Phrasal Modals, and Modal-like Expressions:** A Study Group

Work with a partner. Read the exchange of instant messages between two students. Underline the modals and circle the verbs that follow them. Including the example, there are 16 modals.

● ● ●   Instant Message with   **"Bo23"**

Bo23
Last message received at: [M]

Bo23: Hi, Darryl. We ought to meet soon. The midterm exam is going to include questions about marriage customs in other cultures, so we have to review that topic. We've got to review the definitions of the terms in the textbook, too.

DK: I have everything in my notes. For example, in most cultures men must not have more than one wife at a time. It's prohibited. But there are a few cultures in which men are allowed to have more than one wife. That's called *polygyny*.

Bo23: Could I borrow your notes?

DK: Of course. I can bring them to the study group. Do you want to meet at eight tomorrow night?

Bo23: I haven't made any other plans, so I should be able to meet at eight. I'm not sure about Andre, though. He might not be free then. We'd better check with him before we decide for sure.

DK: He isn't available now. When is he supposed to be home?

Bo23: He had to work tonight, so he may not be home until later. I will send you a message after I talk to him. Bye for now.

---

2 One-Word Modals, Phrasal Modals, and Modal-like Expressions—
Form: A Student–Teacher Conference

Complete the sentences using the correct form of the words in parentheses.
Use contractions where possible.

S: I'm sorry that I __couldn't come_____ to class last Friday.

1 (could / not / come)

   I _____ home because I was sick.

2 (have to / stay)

   _____ you some questions?

3 (I / may / ask)

T: Yes, of course.

S: When _____ our term papers?

4 (we / have to / turn in)

T: Everyone _____ their papers by the day of the final

5 (be supposed to / turn in)

   exam. Students _____ them to me earlier, but they

6 (can / give)

   _____ after the exam.

7 (may / not / turn them in)

S: _____ any topic related to courtship?

8 (we / be allowed to / choose)

T: Yes, you are, but you _____ it carefully. Your paper

9 (ought to / think about)

   _____ examples to illustrate your ideas, but it

10 (have got to / include)

   _____ too long, so choose a topic that's not too

11 (must / not / be)

   broad. But don't pick a topic that you _____ enough

12 (can / not / find)

   information about.

S: I'm interested in personality characteristics that attract people when they're choosing

   a mate.

T: You _____ some interesting information on that in

13 (might / be able to / find)

   the library.

S: I'll go look now, since I _____ to class yet. Thanks

14 (have to / not / go)

   very much.

Modals of Ability

FORM and FUNCTION

A. Can

Use *can* to express ability in the present or in general.	I **can** hear the TV in the other room. Dogs **can** hear sounds that humans **can't** hear.

B. Could

Use *could* to express past ability (but see C2).	When I was younger, I **could** stay up all night without feeling tired.

C. Be Able To

1. Because *be* changes form, you can use *be able to* to express ability:

   - In the present or in general.

     I can't speak Spanish, but **I'm able to** understand it.

   - In the past.

     I couldn't speak Spanish when I was young, but I **was able to** understand it.

   - In the future.

     After I go to Mexico, **I'll be able to** understand Spanish.

   - With other tenses, such as the present perfect. (Do not use *could*.)

     I've been able to swim since I was six.
     NOT: I ~~could~~ swim since I was six.

2. To talk about **past ability connected to single events**, use *be able to*, not *could*.

   Last night, the police **were able to** catch the thief.
   NOT: Last night, the police ~~could~~ catch the thief.

   However, if the sentence is negative, either *be able to* or *could* can be used.

   Last night, the police **weren't able to** catch the thief. OR Last night the police **couldn't** catch the thief.

Modals of Ability

3 **Present, Past, and Future Ability:** Developing Survival Skills

Complete the sentences with an appropriate form of
be able to. Where *can* or *could* is possible, write it as well.
Use negatives where indicated. Use contractions with *not.*

1. When people are choosing a mate, they want someone

   that they __*can/are able to*__ get along with well.
   ⎯⎯⎯⎯⎯⎯⎯⎯
             a

   There might be a special reason for this: Children

   __*can't/aren't able to*__ survive without a great deal of attention. Of course, a mother may
   ⎯⎯⎯⎯⎯⎯⎯⎯⎯⎯
        b (not)

   _____ take care of her children on her own. But children might
           c

   have an easier time when they grow up with two parents who

   _____ get along well and cooperate in raising them.
           d

2. Eli is a four-year-old child. His parents are very proud of his rapid development. For example,

   when he was 18 months old, he _____ speak in complete
                    a

   sentences. When he was three, although he _____ write yet, he
                       b (not)

   _____ read simple books. He _____
           c   d

   do simple arithmetic problems since he was three and a half.

3. Eli's parents take turns looking after him. Last Monday, for example, his father stayed home with

   him, and his mother _____ finish an important project at her
                  a

   office. Yesterday, his father _____ stay home, but his mother
                  b (not)

   stayed with him. She took Eli to the library, and he _____ find
                      c

   some good books to read. Tomorrow his mother might _____
                            d

   take him to her office.

4. Even though Eli is a very capable child, he _____ take care of
                    a (not)

   himself at any time in the near future. Someday, he _____ survive
                       b

   on his own, but until then he will need his parents' care and cooperation.

4   Present, Past, and Future Ability: Your Skills

Read the following statements. For each one, write a sentence that gives an example of the statement. Use *can*, *can't*, *could*, or *couldn't* where possible. Use a form of *be able to* otherwise.

1. Ten years ago, I was able to do things that I'm not able to do now.

   Example: I could learn to speak foreign languages easily.

2. Ten years ago, I wasn't able to do things that I'm able to do now.

3. Ten years from now, I'll be able to do things that I'm not able to do now.

4. There are things that I might be able to do soon.

5. There are many things I've been able to do for a long time.

6. I have many useful abilities now.

GRAMMAR BRIEFING 3

Belief Modals Used to Talk About the Present

FORM and FUNCTION

A. Overview

Speakers use belief modals to express different degrees of certainty. The following modals are used to express different degrees of certainty about the present:

DEGREE OF CERTAINTY	MODALS IN AFFIRMATIVE SENTENCES	MODALS IN NEGATIVE SENTENCES
very certain ↓ not very certain	**must, have to, have got to**	**must not (mustn't), could not (couldn't), cannot (can't)**
	should, ought to	**should not (shouldn't)**
	may, might, could	**may not, might not (mightn't)**

1. Modals in affirmative sentences express degrees of certainty about what is.

   > He **must** be here. (= I'm strongly certain that he is here.)

2. Modals in negative sentences express degrees of certainty about what is not.

   > He **must not** be here. (= I'm strongly certain that he is not here.)

3. If speakers are entirely certain, they do not use a modal.

   > He **is** here. (= I know he is here.)

4. *Could* and *might* are the belief modals used in questions about the present.

   > **Could/Might** they be at the party?

(continued on next page)

B. Expressing Degrees of Certainty in Affirmative Sentences

Must, Have To, Have Got To

1. Use *must*, *have to*, and *have got to* when you feel that something is almost certainly true—that there are no other real possibilities.	He **must** be on the way. He didn't answer the phone. She**'s got to** be here. Her books are on the desk.

Should, Ought To

1. Use *should* and *ought to* when you feel that something is the most likely possibility.	He **should** be home. He's usually home at this time. The food here **ought to** be good. The restaurant is crowded.
2. *Should* and *ought to* are **not** usually used to express possibilities that are undesirable.	The food here is probably bad. **NOT**: The food here ~~ought to/should~~ be bad.

May, Might, Could

Use *may*, *might*, and *could* when you feel that a possibility isn't necessarily more likely than other possibilities.	The kids **may** be tired. I don't know. He **might** be at school now. Or he **could** be at work.

C. Expressing Degrees of Certainty in Negative Sentences

In negative sentences, use *must*, *should*, *may*, and *might* the same way as in affirmative sentences.	He **mustn't** be there. He didn't answer the phone. He **shouldn't** be home yet. He usually works late. The baseball game **may not/mightn't** be over yet. I don't know.
However: • Use *could* and *can* when you are very certain.	He **couldn't/can't** be in Colombia. I saw him yesterday.
In negative sentences *could* and *can* also often express surprise, especially about something that is not pleasant.	The food **couldn't/can't** be gone. The party just started.

• Do not use *have to*, *have got to*, or *ought to*.	He **mustn't/couldn't/can't** be here yet.
	    NOT: He ~~doesn't have to~~ be here yet.
	
	He **shouldn't** be home yet.
	    NOT: He ~~ought not to~~ be home yet.

(continued on next page)

D. Other Ways of Expressing Degrees of Certainty

You can sometimes use adverbs and adjectives
instead of belief modals:

- Adverbs used in this way include *certainly*,
  probably, *possibly*, and *maybe*.

  Dinner is **probably** ready now. (= Dinner
  should be ready now.)

  Maybe dinner is ready now. (= Dinner might be
  ready now.)

- Adjectives used in this way include *certain*,
  probable, *likely*, and (*im*)*possible*.

  They're **certain** to be ready now. (= They must
  be ready now.)

  He's **likely** to be home. (= He should be home.)

GRAMMAR **HOT**SPOT!

Remember! *Can't* is a belief modal, but *can* is not.

The food **can't** be gone.

There **may/might/could** be more food in the
kitchen.
NOT: There ~~can~~ be more food in the kitchen.

TALKING THE TALK

Have/has to, have/has got to, and *ought to* are often
pronounced "hafta, hasta," "'ve gotta, 's gotta," and
"oughta."

"He hasta be tired."

"Dinner oughta be ready."

Belief Modals Used to Talk About the Present

5 Belief Modals About the Present—Form and Meaning: The Family Connection

Chitra's aunts are having a get-together. Complete their sentences with the appropriate form of the choice that is correct or better expresses the meaning. Use contractions where possible.

1. Chitra __must__ be interested in getting married. She's asked
   (must / might)
   everyone in the family to help her find a husband.

2. We _____ have several friends whose sons would be suitable
   (must / should)
   husbands for her. We have quite a few friends, so I think it's a likely possibility.

3. Jaya's son _____ be interested in meeting Chitra. I haven't
   (have to / may)
   asked Jaya, so I'm not very certain.

4. Sonia's son _____ be a teacher now. I think it's possible
   (must / could)
   that he is.

5. Rita's son _____ be a lawyer now. He finished law school
   (have to / might)
   a couple of years ago, and he works for a law firm.

6. Harry _____ live with his parents now. I'm not certain.
   (may + not / could + not)

7. Tara _____ have any sons. She's never mentioned any
   (have got to + not / must + not)
   to me.

8. Reema has two sons. _____ one of them be ready to
   (Might / May)
   get married?

9. The young man in this picture _____ be Anjali's son.
   (have got to / ought to)
   I'm very certain because he looks *exactly* like her.

10. It _____ be too early to call Shoba. She's usually up by
    (should + not / ought to + not)
    this time.

11. Sanjay _____ be away on a trip. I saw him this morning.
    (can + not / might + not)

6 **Belief Modals about the Present:** Making Guesses

Rob has received an e-mail message from a woman he's interested in meeting, but his computer is not working right, and information is missing. Read his thoughts about the message. Use information in the message to complete the sentences with *must*, *have to*, *have got to*, *should*, *ought to*, *may*, *might*, *could*, and, in negative sentences only, *can*. In each blank, write all the forms that you think express the intended meaning. Use *not* where necessary. Use contractions with *not* where possible.

Here's some information about me. My name is Nicola Long, MD

In my work, I care for both adults and children

I was born on May 19, 19

In addition to all water sports, I enjoy

You can reach me at home most evenings by calling (604)-447-3914

I'm usually at home after 7 p.m.

It ___shouldn't___ be difficult to figure out more about
    ₁

Nicola. There are clues in the message. For example, there's an *MD* after her name. She

___must/has to/has got to___ be a doctor. It's the only logical possibility.
    ₂

But what kind of doctor is she? She _____ be
    ₃

just a children's doctor. There are lots of possibilities, though.

_____ she be a surgeon? An eye doctor? Or . . . ?
    ₄

I wonder how old she is. People don't finish medical school before at least their late 20s.

So she _____ be older than 25, but she
    ₅

_____ be older than 30 yet.
    ₆

Based on the e-mail, it looks like Nicola _____
    ₇

enjoy swimming and sailing, which are my favorite sports. Apart from that, I'm not very

certain that we both enjoy the same things. We _____
    ₈

have a lot in common—I hope so—or we _____
    ₉

have a lot in common—that would be too bad.

Her telephone area code is the same as mine. This area code is now used only for my city,

so she _____ live in another city. It's 8:30 now.
    ₁₀

Based on the e-mail, she _____ be at home now.
    ₁₁

Since she's probably there, I think I'll try calling her.

7 **Using Belief Modals About the Present:** Singles Seeking Mates

One way to find a mate is to advertise in a newspaper.

1. Work with a partner. Read the following ads and the questions about them. Discuss possible answers, using belief modals.

   Example: Pat's a medical professional. Could Pat be a dentist? OR
   Pat doesn't want to meet anyone who has a pet. Pat mustn't like pets.

2. Write sentences to answer the questions. In each sentence, use one of the following modals: *must, have to, have got to, may, might, can,* or *could.* For each person include at least two sentences with negative modals.

Medical professional.

In my free time, I read *Sports Illustrated, Car and Driver, Gourmet,* and *Fine Cooking.* I'm very tall, and I play a team sport.

I drive a red Japanese car, wear red clothing, often have quiet dinners at home, and avoid going to restaurants.

Please don't respond if you have a pet. My name is Pat.

---

1. What's Pat's profession?

   a. Pat may be a dentist. _____

   b. _____

2. What sport does Pat play? _____

3. What brand of car does Pat drive? _____

4. What are some of Pat's likes, dislikes, and interests?

   a. _____

   b. _____

   c. _____

5. What is Pat's personality like? _____

6. Is Pat a man or a woman? _____

Scientist.

(I've published a book, *Distant Galaxies*, and many articles in *Sky and Telescope*.)

In my free time, I read detective stories, *Travel*, and *Art and Architecture*. I play a racquet sport.

I listen to music by Bach and Mozart and have visited museums in many countries.

I'm interested in meeting a vegetarian who is willing to walk or take public transportation everywhere we go. No rock and roll fans, please! My name is Chris.

1. What's Chris's profession? _____

2. What sport does Chris play? _____

3. Does Chris have a car? _____

4. What are some of Chris's likes, dislikes, and interests?

   a. _____

   b. _____

   c. _____

5. What is Chris's personality like? _____

6. Is Chris a man or a woman? _____

GRAMMAR BRIEFING 4

Belief Modals Used to Talk About the Future

FORM and FUNCTION

A. Overview

Speakers use the following modals to express different degrees of certainty about their predictions:

DEGREE OF CERTAINTY	MODALS IN AFFIRMATIVE SENTENCES	MODALS IN NEGATIVE SENTENCES
very certain ↓ not very certain	**will, be going to**	**will not (won't), be going to + not**
	should, ought to	**should not (shouldn't)**
	may, might, could	**may not, might not (mightn't)**

Will and *be going to* are the belief modals most often used in questions about the future. Do not use *may*.

Will he/**Is** he **going to** be here tomorrow?
NOT: ~~May~~ he be here tomorrow?

(continued on next page)

B. Expressing Degrees of Certainty in Affirmative Sentences

1. Use *will* and *be going to* if you are very certain about your prediction.

   | It'**ll** rain tomorrow. |

   You can weaken the certainty by using an adverb like *probably*.

   | It'**ll probably** rain tomorrow. |

2. Use *should* and *ought to* if you are somewhat certain about your prediction.

   | The 10:00 train **ought to** be pretty empty. |
   | We **should** be able to get there on time. |

3. Use *may*, *might*, and *could* if you are not very certain about your prediction.

   | The economy **may/might** improve soon. |
   | We **could** see economic growth by the end of the year. |

C. Expressing Degrees of Certainty in Negative Sentences

Use *will*, *be going to*, *should*, *may*, and *might* as in affirmative sentences.

| Tina probably **won't/isn't going to** have dinner with us. |

Ought to and *could* are not used in negative sentences.

| My courses next semester **shouldn't** be hard. |
| **NOT:** My courses next semester ~~ought not to~~ be hard. |

| They **may not/might not** come tomorrow. |
| **NOT:** They ~~could not~~ come tomorrow. |

GRAMMAR **HOT**SPOT!

Notice! *Must*, *have to*, and *have got to* are not used to express certainty about the future. They are **present** belief modals.

| It'**s going to** snow a lot this winter. |
| **NOT:** It ~~must~~ snow a lot this winter. |

Belief Modals Used to Talk About the Future

8 Belief Modals About the Future: Finding Mr. or Ms. Right

A. Complete the sentences in the interview using the information in brackets. Use *will*, *be going to*, *should*, *ought to*, *may*, *might*, and *could*. In each blank write all the possible forms. Use *not* where necessary. Use contractions with *not* where possible.

Liz: Helen, you've studied recent courtship trends. What are your predictions? Will we see changes in the methods Americans use to find mates?

Helen: Things have been changing. And they __will/are going to__ continue to change.
 1 [very certainly]
These changes __mightn't/may not__ happen everywhere in the country, though.
 2 [possibly not]

Liz: What kinds of changes do you expect to see?

Helen: In the past, many Americans just waited to meet a suitable person. This method

_____ be the most common way for people to find
 3 [probably not]
mates in the future, though. A lot of them are just too busy to meet suitable mates by

chance. This situation _____ change soon.
 4 [certainly not]

Liz: Advertising on the Internet _____ become a more
 5 [possibly]
popular way of finding a mate.

Helen: Yes. But advertising _____ become as popular as
 6 [possibly not]
another strategy that has been used in many cultures—going to a matchmaker. In the

future, we _____ see more people using professional
 7 [probably]
matchmakers. With matchmakers, people _____ have
 8 [very certainly]
a better chance of finding Mr. or Ms. Right.

B. These are some ways in which people find mates: waiting to meet a suitable person by chance, advertising in the newspaper, advertising on the Internet, using matchmakers, and using family connections.

1. As a class, discuss your predictions about how common it will be for people to use each of these methods in the future. What other methods might become common? Why will each method become more or less common?

2. On your own, write five predictions using modals that express your degree of certainty. Include *not* in at least one sentence. Use *probably* with *will* or *be going to* where appropriate to weaken your prediction. Give a reason for each one.

Example: Advertising for a mate on the Internet could become much more common. People will probably be too busy to search in other ways.

9 Belief Modals About the Present and Future: Matchmakers in Action

Rose and Vera are matchmakers. They are trying to find a suitable mate for Lola. Circle the correct form; if both forms are correct, circle both.

Rose: Lola is talented and intelligent. It ought not to /(shouldn't) be difficult to find

       1

       suitable men for her.

Vera: Yes, but Lola is very demanding. It (is going to)/(will) take a lot of searching to find

                      2

       just the right man.

Rose: Lola is studying engineering. Eddie's an engineer. They should / must get along

                               3

       well if we introduce them to each other.

Vera: Rose, look at Eddie's picture. He must / has to be at least 60 years old. I think he

                           4

       might / should be too old for her.

         5

Rose: What about Chad? He's a handsome 25-year-old. Oh, but he's a vegetarian, and Lola

       loves steaks. He mayn't / mightn't be right for her. . . . say—Sky's a young, steak-

             6

       eating engineer. He could / may have all the qualities that Lola wants. He travels

              7

       occasionally, so he couldn't / may not be home now, but I'm going to call him.

                 8

Vera: And what about Lola? May / Will she check with us soon?

                     9

Rose: Let me call her. . . . There's no answer. She mustn't / doesn't have to be home now.

                           10

       And she may not / could not check with us until next week. . . . But when she

            11

       does and she hears about Sky, she has to / is going to be very happy.

                       12

GRAMMAR BRIEFING 5

Social Modals I: Modals for Permission, Requests, and Offers

FORM and FUNCTION

A. Overview

Modals for permission, requests, and/or offers include *can, could, may,* and *will.* Some modals are considered more formal or polite. So the situation and the relationship between the speaker and listener can influence the choice of modal. However, usually you can use any of the possible modals. You can also use *please* to show politeness.

Student to teacher: **Could** you (**please**) explain this example?

Student to student: **Can** you (**please**) lend me your pen?

(continued on next page)

B. Requesting and Giving Permission

more formal ↓ less formal	**may**
	could
	can

Requesting Permission

To ask for permission, use *may*, *could*, or *can*.	*Request for permission:* **May/Could/Can** I (please) use your phone?
	Possible response: Sure, you **can**. It's on the table.

Giving Permission

To give (or refuse) permission, use *may* or *can*. *Could* is not used.	You **may/can** leave when you finish. You **may not/cannot** leave until you finish. **NOT**: You ~~could~~ leave when you finish. OR You ~~could not~~ leave until you finish.
May in this use is considered very formal. It is often used in public announcements.	Passengers in rows 1–10 **may** board now.

C. Making Requests

more formal ↓ less formal	**would, could**
	will, can

To make a request (i.e., ask someone to do something), use *would*, *could*, *will*, or *can*.	*Request:* **Would/Could/Will/Can** you (please) open the door for me?
To respond to a request, use *will* or *can*. *Would* and *could* are not usually used.	*Possible response:* Of course I **will/can**. **NOT USUALLY**: Of course I ~~would/could~~.

(continued on next page)

D. Making Offers

more formal	**shall**
↓	**may**
	could
less formal	**can**, **will**

1. To make an offer in a **question**, use *shall*, *may*, *could*, or *can*.

   Shall is used only with *I* or *we* and is not very common.

   > *Offer*: **Shall/May/Could/Can** I bring you the menu?
   >
   > *Possible response*: Yes, thank you.

2. To make an offer in a **statement**, use *can* or *will*.

   > *Offer*: I **can/will** help you with those bags.
   >
   > *Possible response*: Thanks.

E. Alternative Responses to Requests for Permission, Requests, and Offers

Responses can take the form of answers to *yes/no* questions. However:

> A: Could I (please) borrow a pen?
> B: Yes, you can.

- Affirmative responses are often made friendlier with expressions such as *certainly*, *of course*, and *sure*.

  > B: Sure. I have another one.

- Negative responses are often softened with expressions such as *I'm sorry, but . . .* and *I'm afraid . . . .*

  > B: I'm sorry, but I don't have one. OR I'm afraid I don't have mine.

Social Modals I: Modals for Permission, Requests, and Offers

10 Modals for Permission: Situations and Relationships I

Work with a partner. Write dialogues with questions and responses for the following situations. Use each modal in the box in one question, choosing modals appropriate to the situations. Your responses can include an appropriate modal and can be made friendlier or softened.

| can | ~~could~~ | may |

1. You're on an airplane that has several empty seats. You want to move to a window seat.

   You: _Could I move to a window seat_ ?

   Flight attendant: _Yes, of course you can./I'm sorry, but you can't._ .

2. You're sitting with your sister in her kitchen. You want to get a drink of water.

   You: _____?

   Your sister: _____.

3. You're at a formal party at the home of an older woman whom you don't know well. You want to look at her garden.

   You: _____?

   The hostess: _____.

11 Modals for Requests: Situations and Relationships II

Work with a partner. Write dialogues with questions and responses for the following situations. Use each modal in the box in one question, choosing modals appropriate to the situations. Your responses can include an appropriate modal and can be made friendlier or softened.

| ~~will~~ | would |

1. You're in class. You ask a friend to lend you his calculator for a few minutes.

   You: _Will you lend me your calculator for a few minutes_ ?

   Your classmate: _Sure, I will./I'm afraid I left it at home_

2. You're in class. Your math professor has just explained a problem. You ask her to go over that problem again.

   You: _____?

   The professor: _____.

| can | could |

3. You're at a party. You ask a good friend to give you a ride home.

   You: _____?

   Your friend: _____.

4. You're at the doctor's office. You ask the doctor to sign your health insurance form.

   You: _____?

   The doctor: _____.

12 Modals for Offers: Situations and Relationships III

Work with a partner. Write dialogues with questions or statements and responses for the following situations. Use each modal in the box in one question or statement, choosing modals appropriate to the situations. Give any appropriate response.

> can   ~~could~~   may

1. You are in an office at the school where you are a student. The secretary has some letters ready to mail. You offer to mail them for her.

   You: _Could I mail those letters for you_____?

   The secretary: _Yes, thank you./No, thanks. I can do it_____.

2. You are walking across the campus of the school where you are a student. You see a professor who is much older than you struggling with the heavy books he's carrying. You offer to carry them for him.

   You: _____?

   The professor: _____.

3. Your friend just got a new computer program. You offer to show her how to use it.

   You: _____?

   Your friend: _____.

> will   shall   can

4. You're at work. Your boss mentions that the office feels a little warm. You offer to turn on the air conditioner.

   You: _____?

   Your boss: _____.

5. You've just finished dinner at your brother's house. You offer to help him wash the dishes.

   You: _____?

   Your brother: _____.

6. Your younger sister's friend calls. Your sister isn't home. You offer to take a message for her.

   You: _____?

   Your sister's friend: _____.

13 Modals for Permission, Requests, and Offers: Another Matchmaker

Jin has decided to ask a matchmaker to search for a wife for him. Circle the correct form.

Secretary: Good morning, sir. (May) / Will I help you?
                                         1

Jin: Yes, thank you. I have an appointment with Ms. Mota.

Secretary: Might / Will you have a seat, please? Ms. Mota will be with you in a few minutes.
              2

          May / Would you fill out this form for her?
           3

Jin: Certainly, I <u>will / would</u>. I'm sorry, I don't have a pen. <u>Could / Would</u> I please
                     4   5
            borrow one?

Secretary: Of course You <u>could / can</u> use this one. <u>Shall / Will</u> I make you a cup of tea to drink while
                              6   7
            you're waiting?

Jin: Yes, thank you. . . .

Ms. Mota: I <u>may / will</u> help you now.
                   8

Jin: Thank you. <u>May / Will</u> I introduce myself? I'm Jin Tanaka.
                           9

Ms. Mota: You're a very polite young man. I'm sure we'll find you a bride very soon.

14 **Permission, Requests, and Offers:** Practicing Politeness

Work with a partner. Think of situations—for example, at school, home, a shop, a
restaurant, or a party—in which people need to ask permission, make a request, and
make an offer. Make up three dialogues (one asking for permission, one with a
request, and one with an offer) similar to those in Exercises 10, 11, and 12. Present
your dialogues to the class.

GRAMMAR BRIEFING 6

Social Modals II: Modals for Suggestions, Advice, Expectations, Warnings, and Necessity

FORM and FUNCTION

A. Overview

Modals can be used in telling listeners what to do. Different modals express different strengths; the
speaker can be making a suggestion (weak) or stating a necessity or prohibition (strong):

STRENGTH	USE	ONE-WORD MODALS	PHRASAL MODALS; MODAL-LIKE EXPRESSIONS
weak	Suggestion	**could, might, shall**	
	Advice/opinion	**should, should not (shouldn't)**	**ought to**
	Expectation		**be supposed to, not be supposed to; be to, not be to**
	Warning		**had better, had better not**
strong	Necessity/obligation	**must**	**have to, have got to**
	Prohibition	**must not (mustn't), cannot (can't)**	**not be allowed to**
	Lack of necessity		**not have to**

(continued on next page)

B. Suggestions

1. *Could* and *might* are the modals generally used to make suggestions.

   However, in questions and negative statements, *should* is usually used instead of *could* or *might*.

   > If Allison is being unfriendly, you **could/might** try talking to her about it.

   > What **should** I do if she doesn't want to talk?
   > You probably **shouldn't** push her to talk.

2. *Shall* is used mainly in questions with *we*. It is used to make suggestions about possible actions and activities. *Shall* is considered formal and is not very common.

   > **Shall** we go now?

C. Advice and Opinions

Use *should* and *ought to* to give advice and state opinions.

> You **should/ought to** go home if you aren't feeling well. (advice)

> The city **should/ought to** fix the holes in this road. (opinion)

In negatives and in questions, *should* is usually used.

> We **shouldn't** go there. Where **should** we go?

D. Expectations

Be supposed to and *be to* are used to express expectations, for example, about correct behavior. The expectations are sometimes based on rules or instructions.

> We**'re supposed to/'re to** bring a gift to the party.

> You**'re supposed to/'re to** take two teaspoons of the medicine twice a day.

> We**'re not supposed to/'re not to** be there until nine o'clock.

E. Warnings

Had better is used to give warnings. It implies there will be bad consequences if the warning isn't followed.

Had better is often contracted (*'d better*). It is not usually used in questions.

> You**'d better not** be late for dinner.

> You **had better** hand that paper in today, or the teacher will lower your grade.

(continued on next page)

F. Necessity and Obligation; Lack of Necessity; Prohibition

Necessity and Obligation

Use *must, have to,* and *have got to* to express necessity or obligation. The necessity or obligation is sometimes based on rules or laws.

Although all three can be used:

- *Must* is considered stronger and more formal. It is used more often in written rules and less often in speech.

> You **must/have to/have got to** be 18 to vote. (law: in writing, *must* more common; in speech, *have to/have got to* more common)
>
> You **must/have to/have got to** send in your transcript in order to apply. (rule: in writing, *must* more common; in speech, *have to/have got to* more common)
>
> He **has to/has got to/must** work this weekend. (*have to/have got to* more common)

- In questions, *have to* is used. *Have got to* cannot be used. *Must* in questions is used to make a complaint.

> **Do** you **have to** work this weekend?
> NOT: ~~Have you got to~~ work this weekend?
>
> **Must** you play your music so loud? (complaint)

Lack of Necessity; Prohibition

1. Use *not have to* to say that something is not necessary.

> You **don't have to** eat in the cafeteria, but you can if you want to.

2. Use *must not* to say something is prohibited.

> You **must not** eat or drink on the bus.

   Prohibition can also be expressed by *cannot* and *not be allowed to.*

> You **can't/are not allowed to** eat or drink on the bus.

TALKING THE TALK

Should and *ought* to are usually used by someone who has the authority to give advice.

> *Teacher:* For homework, you **should** study for the test. Is there anything I can do to help you prepare for it?

When a person doesn't have this authority, *should* and *ought to* can sound impolite. Instead, *could* and *might* are used to offer suggestions.

> *Student:* You **could** give us a study guide.

Social Modals II: Modals for Suggestions, Advice, Expectations, Warnings, and Necessity

15 Modals for Suggestions, Advice, Expectations, Warning, and Necessity: Wedding Customs

A. Hiro, who is a Japanese visitor to the United States, has been invited to a wedding. He has never been to an American wedding, so he's asking a friend for advice. Complete the sentences with the form that is correct or more appropriate. Use contractions where possible.

Hiro: Laura, I need your advice. What ___should___ I wear to the wedding?
1 (might / should)

Laura: Well, that depends on the kind of wedding it is. You _____
2 (should not / might not)

wear clothes that are too casual. In my opinion, you _____
3 (could / ought to)

find out if it's a formal wedding. Men _____ wear dark
4 (be supposed to / might)

suits to formal weddings. That's expected, so they all do.

Hiro: I need a suggestion for a gift. What

_____ give the bride and groom?
5 (ought I to / should I)

Laura: There are lots of possibilities. You

_____ give them something special from Japan, but that's
6 (might / must)

just a suggestion.

Hiro: What are my obligations at the wedding reception? _____ I _____
7 (have got to / have to)

make a speech?

Laura: No, you don't. After the reception begins, you _____ wait
8 (be to / could)

in line and give the bride and groom your best wishes, because that's correct behavior.

Later, some of the guests may offer toasts, or short speeches, to the newlyweds. If they do,

you _____ offer one, too, but it isn't an obligation. If you
9 (must / could)

want to dance with the bride, you can ask her by saying,

"_____ we dance?"
10 (Shall / Must)

Hiro: I'm worried about being able to do everything

properly. You _____
11 (have got to / be supposed to)

come to the wedding with me. I'll need you there.

Laura: Oh no, Hiro. You _____ take uninvited guests to a
12 (could not / not be allowed to)

wedding. It isn't permitted. But don't worry. You _____
13 (must not / not have to)

know much about the customs. It isn't necessary. Oh, there is one thing I need to warn

you about. Weddings usually begin on time, so you _____
14 (had better not / not have to)

be late.

Hiro: I'll go early, but I'm still going to worry.

Laura: _____ you worry so much, Hiro? Just have a good time!
15 (Shall / Must)

B. Work with a partner—if possible, someone who knows about wedding customs in a culture that you're not familiar with. You've been invited to a wedding. Ask your partner for advice and suggestions, and ask about expectations for clothing, gifts, behavior, and customs. In the questions and answers include *should*, *ought to*, *could*, *might*, and *be supposed to*, as appropriate. Then reverse roles.

To learn about wedding customs in the United States and other countries, go to the *Grammar Links* Website.

16 Modals for Opinion, Obligation, Lack of Necessity, and Prohibition: The Roles of Marriage Partners I

A. Kim is leading an international students' discussion on the responsibilities of husbands and wives. Complete the sentences using *should* or *ought to*. If both are possible, write both. Use contractions with *not* where possible.

Kim: What are your opinions? Which tasks

should a husband do? Which tasks
1 (a husband)

_____ do?
2 (a wife)

Dana: I think a marriage _____
3

be a partnership with both people doing everything.

Lesley: Well, there's one thing a husband probably

_____ do—decorate
4 (not)

the house.

Nate: I agree, and I think there's one more thing.

A husband _____ shop
5 (not)

for his wife's clothes!

Tasks
Earning the money to support the family
Caring for the children
Housework
Cooking
Repairing and maintaining the house and car
Managing the money
Shopping
Decorating the house

B. Complete the sentences using *have to, have got to,* and *must*. Use contractions with *not* where possible. Write all correct forms.

Kim: What about obligations? <u>Does</u> a wife <u>have to</u> do certain tasks?
                                                                1

Lee: No, I don't think so. These are all things that couples <u>have to/have got to/must</u> talk
                                                       2

about and share the responsibility for. The important thing is that if you promise to do

something, you _____ forget to do it. Of course,
                                 3 (not)

if people are very rich, they _____ do the
                                   4 (not)

cooking and cleaning themselves, because they can pay someone else. But in general, one

person _____ make a decision without discussing
                                 5 (not)

it with the other one.

Kim: Does everyone agree? _____ a couple _____
                                 6

share in these responsibilities?

Kiko: I think that a wife _____ manage all the money.
                                 7

It's her responsibility. She can tell her husband how she's managing it, but she

_____ tell him.
                             8

Adel: In my culture, a woman _____ drive a car—it
                                 9 (not)

isn't allowed. So a husband _____ take care of
                                 10

the car and do a lot of the shopping.

Kelly: In my culture, things have changed. In the past, husbands earned the money to support their

families. Now a lot of women _____ share that
                                 11

responsibility because one salary isn't enough.

17 Modals for Opinion, Obligation, Lack of Necessity, and Prohibition: The Roles of Marriage Partners II

Work in small groups. Use the list of tasks in Exercise 16 as the basis for a discussion. One student should act as the leader and ask the others to discuss the following questions.

1. In your opinion, are there certain tasks that a husband or a wife should do?

2. Are there certain tasks that a husband or a wife has an obligation to do?

3. Are there tasks that either of them shouldn't or mustn't do?

4. What other responsibilities and obligations do husbands and wives have?

5. Is it necessary for couples to discuss their expectations and opinions about responsibilities and obligations before they marry?

18 Using Ability, Belief, and Social Modals: Points of View

 A. As a class, discuss the following statements. Do you agree with either one?
Do you have a different point of view?

1.

> *Marriage partners should find each other on their own. They ought to make a decision to marry based on their romantic love for each other. I can't imagine letting my family influence my choice of a partner. They can't understand my situation—or what I need in a partner—as well as I do.*

2.

> *My family should be involved in finding a suitable partner for me. My decision to marry is going to be influenced more by family considerations than by romantic love. My family can understand me better than anyone else. They will suggest possible partners with whom I will be able to get along well. Romantic love may develop later.*

 B. Write a paragraph explaining your point of view about finding and deciding on a marriage partner. Use at least two of each of the following types of modals: ability (e.g., *be able to, can*), belief (e.g., *could, will, may, might, must*), and social (e.g., *be supposed to, must, have to, should*).

See the *Grammar Links* Website for a model paragraph for this assignment.

Check your progress! Go to the Self-Test for Chapter 14 on the *Grammar Links* Website.

15

More About Modals

Introductory Task: Giving Advice

A. You are Addy Viser, the writer of a newspaper advice column. You have received the following letter.

> Dear Addy Viser,
>
>   I'm 25 years old. A year ago I fell in love with a woman named Irene. Irene and I wanted to get married, but when my parents found out, they didn't approve because they've never gotten along with her family. My friends thought that I should follow my heart and marry Irene. But I listened to my family's advice and decided not to marry her. Irene married another man yesterday. Now I realize that I can never love anyone else as much as I love Irene, and I feel regretful. I **should have listened** to my friends instead of my family. Do you agree?
>
>   Regretful

Read the following possible responses to "Regretful." Check the one that you think is best.

_____ Yes, you **should have listened** to your friends. You **shouldn't have let** your parents' opinion influence you. You **ought to have done** what was right for you.

_____ No, you **shouldn't have followed** your friends' advice. Marriages between people whose families don't get along can be very difficult. Besides, you say that Irene married another man. She **couldn't have loved** you as much as you loved her.

_____ You **should have gotten** advice from a professional counselor. With a counselor's help, you **might have worked** things out with your family. Things **could have turned** out more happily for you.

B. As a class, discuss your responses. Does anyone have other ideas about what "Regretful" should have done in this situation? Use *should have* and *shouldn't have* to give your opinion.

Example: *"Regretful" should have asked a sympathetic aunt or grandmother to talk to his parents.*

Perfect Modals

FORM

A. Overview

Perfect modals are formed by adding *have* to many of the modals from Chapter 14. They are followed by the past participle of the verb. Perfect modals include:

- *Could have, may have, might have, must have,* and *should have,* formed from one-word modals.

  You **should have known** better.

- *Have to have* and *have got to have,* formed from phrasal modals with *have.*

  He **has to have finished**.

- *Ought to have* and *had better have,* formed from modal-like expressions.

  She **ought to have asked** us.

B. Affirmative Statements

SUBJECT	MODAL + *HAVE*	PAST PARTICIPLE	
They	**might have**	**left**.	
She	**has to have**	**helped**	him.

C. Negative Statements

SUBJECT	MODAL + *NOT* + *HAVE**	PAST PARTICIPLE	
He	**must not have**	**known**.	
You	**should not have**	**done**	that.

The perfect modals formed from phrasal modals and modal-like expressions are not commonly used, except for *had better not have.*

You **had better not have** told him.

*For contractions of modals with *not*, see Chapter 14, Grammar Briefing 1, page 261.

D. Questions

Yes/No *Questions and Short Answers*

QUESTIONS	SHORT ANSWERS
Could they **have gone**?	Yes, they **could have**.
Should we **have helped** him?	No, we **shouldn't have**.

(continued on next page)

D. Questions (continued)

Wh- *Questions*

WH- QUESTIONS ABOUT THE SUBJECT	**OTHER *WH-* QUESTIONS**
Who could have told him?	**What should** I **have done**?

Questions generally use only perfect modals formed from one-word modals.

When **could** he **have** been here?

TALKING THE TALK

Have in the perfect modal is often pronounced "of" or "a."

"We should-of/shoulda tried harder."

"He couldn't-of/couldn'ta gone there."

GRAMMAR PRACTICE 1

Perfect Modals

1 **Perfect Modals—Form: The Dangers of Romantic Love**

Use the words in parentheses to complete the sentences.
Use contractions with *not* where possible.

Stella: The story of Romeo and Juliet was such a tragedy, but I

think that things <u>might have turned out</u>

                                    1 (might / turn out)

differently for Juliet. A happier ending

_____ possible.

                   2 (have to / be)

Maria: But how? Their families were enemies, and Juliet's

father had arranged for her to marry another man,

Count Paris. _____ her father?

                                3 (Juliet / should / obey)

Stella: No, but Romeo and Juliet _____ smarter.

                                       4 (should / be)

First of all, Romeo _____ himself.

                              5 (should / not / kill)

Maria: But he thought that Juliet had died.

Stella: Well, she _____ to be alive, but she
                    6 (may / not / seem)

        was. Romeo _____ to find out for sure.
                         7 (might / try)

        He _____ her.
                8 (ought to / rescue)

Maria: What _____ when she discovered that Romeo
                  9 (Juliet / should / do)

        was dead? Without him, she _____ living.
                                        10 (could / not / go on)

Stella: She _____ him very much. But Juliet was
                 11 (must / love)

        only 13. She _____ someone else.
                          12 (might / meet)

Maria: How _____? Remember, she had to marry
                  13 (that / could / happen)

        Count Paris.

Stella: Poor Juliet! Romantic love really can lead to tragedy, can't it?

🌐 Go to the *Grammar Links* Website to find out more about the story of Romeo and Juliet.

2 Perfect Modals—Contracted and Full Forms: A Communication Problem?

🎧 Frank is the host of a radio program, *Speaking Frankly*. People call him for advice
about relationships. Listen to the dialogue once for the main ideas. Then listen again
and fill in the blanks with the words that you hear. You will hear contracted forms, but
you should write full forms.

Frank: Hello! You're on the air. What's your relationship problem?

Elise: Hi, Frank. This is Elise from California. I had a problem with my boyfriend the other night,

        and I want to know what I <u>should have</u> _____ done about it.
                                                      1

        We were driving to our friends' new house, and we got lost. We finally found the house,

        but it <u>should not have</u> _____ taken us two hours to do it.
                                  2

Frank: Let me guess. Your boyfriend _____ been driving. He
                                                    3

        _____ asked someone for directions, but he didn't do it.
                    4

Frank: Let me guess. Your boyfriend _____ been driving. He
                                                    3

        _____ asked someone for directions, but he didn't do it.
                    4

Elise: Right! How did you know? There were several times when he

        _____ stopped to ask someone, but he didn't.
                    5

Frank: Elise, try to think of the situation from your boyfriend's point of view. Imagine that he had stopped to ask someone. You _____ thought that
6

he wasn't fully in control of the situation.

Elise: He wasn't fully in control of the situation. He _____
7

asked someone.

Frank: You _____ found the house any faster that way.
8

That person _____ known where it was but
9

_____ tried to be helpful and given wrong directions.
10

Elise: When we finally found the house, our friends had gone out without us. They

_____ wanted to keep waiting. I guess I
11

_____ complained, but I did.
12

Frank: You _____ been upset. But your boyfriend probably
13

_____ done anything differently. A lot of men just have
14

a very hard time asking for directions.

Elise: I understand that now. Thanks, Frank.

Belief Modals Used to Talk About the Past

FUNCTION

A. Overview

Speakers use perfect modals to express different degrees of certainty about events and situations in the past:

DEGREE OF CERTAINTY	MODALS IN AFFIRMATIVE SENTENCES	MODALS IN NEGATIVE SENTENCES
very certain ↓ not very certain	**must have, have to have, have got to have**	**could not have (couldn't have), cannot have (can't have), must not have (musn't have)**
	should have, ought to have	**should not have**
	may have, might have, could have	**may not have, might not have (mightn't have)**

(continued on next page)

A. Overview (continued)

1. The belief modals in the past express the same degrees of certainty they do in the present.

    Past: Ted **could have** been at the party (weak certainty), but Megan **must not have** been (strong certainty).

    Present: Ted could be at the party (weak certainty), but Megan must not be (strong certainty).

2. *Could have* is the modal most often used in questions. *Might have* can also be used.

    Could he **have** been at the party?

B. Expressing Degrees of Certainty in Affirmative Sentences

1. *Must have, have to have,* and *have got to have* express very strong certainty about the past.

    He **must have/has to have/has got to have** been at the party on Friday. Kim saw him there.

2. *Should have* and *ought to have* express somewhat strong certainty about the past.

    He **should have/ought to have** been at the party on Friday. He told me he was going.

3. *May have, might have,* and *could have* express weak certainty about the past.

    He **may have/might have/could have** been at the party on Friday. I know he was invited.

C. Expressing Degrees of Certainty in Negative Sentences

In negative sentences, use *must have, should have, may have,* and *might have* the same way as in affirmative sentences.

He **must not have** been at the party. No one saw him.

He **shouldn't have** been at the party. He said he wasn't going to go.

He **may not have/might not have** been at the party. But he might have been.

However:

*   Use *could have* and *can have* when you are very certain.

    He **couldn't have/can't have** been at the party. No one saw him.

*   *Have to have, have got to have,* and *ought to have* are not used.

    He **shouldn't have** been at the party. **NOT:** He ~~ought not to have~~ been at the party.

Belief Modals Used to Talk About the Past

3 **Belief Modals About the Past—Form and Meaning:** Your Parents' Wedding

Complete the conversation with the appropriate form of the choice that is correct or better expresses the meaning. Use contractions where possible.

Mira: Your parents' wedding _____must have_____ been in St. Anne's Church.
          _{1 (must have / might have)}

If you look closely at one of the photos, you can see a sign that says "St. Anne's."

Who performed their wedding ceremony?

Tony: It _____ been Father Ruiz. He didn't work at St. Anne's then.
          _{2 (must have + not / have to have + not)}

It _____ been Father Malley. That's possible.
          _{3 (must have / could have)}

Mira: Was the church full of people?

Tony: The church _____
          _{4 (should have + not / ought to have + not)}

been full. It's very big, so it probably wasn't.

Mira: Was the ceremony long?

Tony: It _____ been long.
          _{5 (may have + not / could have + not)}

I'm not sure.

Mira: Your mother's wedding dress was beautiful. Did she

sew it herself?

Tony: She _____ sewed it. She doesn't know how to sew.
          _{6 (can have + not / may have + not)}

Mira: Where did she get the pearl necklace she wore for the wedding?

Tony: She _____ borrowed it from someone. I'm certain that she's
          _{7 (have to have / should have)}

never owned a pearl necklace.

Mira: There aren't any pictures of the reception. Do you think they had a white cake?

Tony: They _____ had a white cake. That was the tradition, and
          _{8 (have got to have / might have)}

everyone had one.

Mira: Your mom's sister _____ been happy about saying goodbye
          _{9 (must have + not / should have + not)}

to her. She's crying in this picture. Did anyone take a video of your parents' wedding?

Tony: They _____ taken a video! Videos didn't exist yet.
          _{10 (could have + not / might have + not)}

4 Belief Modals About the Past: The Mystery of a Long-Term Marriage I

Don's elderly parents live in a small town far from Don. On June 8, he called the captain of the town's police department. Complete the sentences with *must have, have to have, have got to have, should have, ought to have, may have, might have, could have,* and, in negative sentences only, *can have.* In each blank, write all the modals that work best in the context. Use *not* where necessary. Use contractions with *not* where possible.

Don: I'm very worried about my parents, Captain. Something strange

<u>must have/has to have/has got to have</u> happened to them. There isn't any other
   1

explanation for the situation. I tried calling them at noon. They

<u>shouldn't have</u> been out then. They almost always have
                   2

lunch together at home at noon. But no one answered.

Captain: I wouldn't worry. There are lots of possibilities.

They _____ gone for a drive.
              3

Don: I called the neighbors. They said that my parents' car is in the driveway.

Captain: In that case, they _____ have gone for a
                          4

drive in their car. Did the neighbors go inside the house to look around?

Don: No. The door was locked. And they couldn't see inside—my parents

_____ left the curtains closed.
              5

Captain: Did the neighbors see anything in the mailbox?

Don: They didn't say, but there probably wasn't any mail. At least, there

_____ been mail, because it usually isn't
              6

delivered until later. Also, the neighbors told me that my mother missed the meeting at the

Senior Center this morning.

Captain: There are possible explanations for that.

She _____ remembered about the meeting.
             7

Don: My mother writes notes to remind herself of things. My parents have disappeared.

Captain: That's unlikely, but since you're so worried, I'll go over and take a look.

Don: Thank you. They _____ left a key under the
                      8

doormat. I know that they usually do.

5 **Belief Modals About the Past:** The Mystery of a Long-Term Marriage II

The police captain didn't find Don's parents, but he did find evidence. He thought about possibilities and drew conclusions. Write sentences using *must have*, *have to have*, *have got to have*, *could have*, *may have*, *might have*, and, for negative sentences only, *can have*. You can write any sentence that fits with the information. Use *not* where necessary.

1. Everything was very orderly in the house.

   He thought: _They must not have left in a hurry._

2. Then he found a note that said, "Call travel agency again."

   He thought: _They may have gone on a trip._

3. He saw a brochure from a travel agency, "Antarctic Adventures for Seniors."

   He thought: _____

4. All their warm clothes were still in the closets, and it's winter in Antarctica in June.

   He thought: _____

5. He found a box labeled "Beach Umbrellas." It was empty.

   He thought: _____

6. He found a receipt in the desk for two tickets to Honolulu on June 8 at 5 a.m.

   He thought: _____

7. He found a note that said, "Don't forget to tell Don about our 50th wedding anniversary trip."

   He thought: _____

   The captain called Don. What did he tell him?

6 **Using Belief Modals About the Past:** Married Couples

1.   2.   3.

Work with a partner. Look at the couples in the photographs. What are your impressions of their marriages and lives? Use belief modals in the past to describe their life together before the photo was taken.

Example: They must have been married for a long time. They might not have had an easy life. They may have had to work very hard.

Social Modals Used to Talk About the Past

FORM and FUNCTION

A. Overview

Modals used to talk about the past express degrees of strength similar to those used to talk about the present:

STRENGTH	USE	ONE-WORD MODALS	PHRASAL MODALS; MODAL-LIKE EXPRESSIONS
weak	Suggestion	**could have, might have**	
	Advice/opinion	**should have, should not have (shouldn't have)**	**ought to have**
	Expectation		**be supposed to, not be supposed to; be to, not be to**
	Warning		**had better have, had better not have**
strong	Necessity/obligation		**have to**
	Prohibition	**could not (couldn't)**	**not be allowed to**
	Lack of necessity		**not have to**

B. Perfect Forms and Other Forms

1. One-word modals occur as perfect modals (*could have, might have, should [not] have*).

   The only exception is *could not*.

   > You **could have** given them a ride.

   > He **couldn't** get his driver's license until he was 18.

2. Modal-like expressions occur as perfect modals (*ought to have, had better [not] have*).

   > You**'d better have** done well on the test.

3. Phrasal modals occur with *be* and *have* in their past form (*was/were [not] supposed, was/were [not] to, had better [not] have, was/were not allowed to, had to/didn't have to*).

   > You **were supposed to** mail this last week.

   > We **weren't allowed to** go in early.

   > We **didn't have to** write a paper.

(continued on next page)

A. Suggestions

Could have and *might have* suggest possibilities that did not occur:

- *Could have*, which is used more, often implies that an opportunity was lost.

  We **could have** gotten free tickets, but we didn't know about it.

- Both modals often imply a criticism.

  You're late. You **could have/might have** called.

B. Advice

Should have and *ought to have* are often used to say that:

- Something was a good idea but didn't happen.

  You **should have/ought to have** gone home as soon as you felt sick. (a good idea but you didn't do it; implied criticism)

- Something that was a bad idea happened (in negative sentences with *should*).

  I **shouldn't have** stayed up so late last night. (a bad idea and I did it; implied regret).

Both modals imply criticism or regret.

C. Expectations

Be supposed to and *be to* are used to say that:

- Something was expected or planned but didn't happen.

  You're late. You **were supposed to/were to** get here at nine o'clock.

- Something wasn't expected or planned but happened (in negative sentences).

  Mom's going to be mad at us. We **weren't supposed to/weren't to** leave without telling her.

D. Warnings

Had better have is used, in affirmative and negative sentences, to give warnings about past actions.

He**'d better have** told me the truth.

You**'d better not have** left all the lights on.

(continued on next page)

E. Necessity: Lack of Necessity; Prohibition

1. Use *have to* to express past necessity.	He **had to** work last weekend.
2. Use *not have to* to express lack of necessity.	We **didn't have to** go to class while we were studying for exams.
3. Use *couldn't* or *not be allowed to* to express prohibition in the past.	As a child, I **couldn't/wasn't allowed to** watch TV until I finished my homework.

GRAMMAR **HOT**SPOT!

Do not use *must* (*not*) *have* to express necessity and prohibition. Unlike *must*, it is only a belief modal.	Yesterday I **had to** take my brother to the airport. **NOT:** Yesterday I ~~must have taken~~ my brother to the airport. He **couldn't** take more than two bags. **NOT:** He ~~must not have taken~~ more than two bags.

Social Modals Used to Talk About the Past

7 Social Modals About the Past: An Odd but Happy Couple

Use the expressions given to complete the sentences. Use each expression once.
Use contractions where possible.

~~be supposed to~~	not be allowed to	have to	ought to have	should not have

Roxie <u>was supposed to</u> _____ marry an older man. When she broke her
1

engagement to him, a friend said, "What a mistake! You _____
2

broken your engagement. You _____ married him." Roxie
3

replied, "I _____ end it. It became necessary because he was
4

always telling me what to do. I _____ make my own decisions—
5

he never let me." Then Roxie found Jim, who's five years younger than she is. Jim admired her and

gave her confidence.

could have	could not	had better have	have to	not have to

After a few months, Jim and Roxie were sure of their love, but they weren't sure of their families'

approval, so they decided to have a secret wedding. They wanted to get married as soon as possible,

but they _____ get married without a marriage license. So they
6

_____ wait for a few days. After their wedding, Jim told his
7

family what had happened. Jim's sister complained, "You _____
8

told me. Roxie may be older, but she's perfect for you. You _____
9

keep your love a secret." Then she warned him, "You _____ given
10

her a beautiful wedding ring." Jim assured her that Roxie was very happy with the wedding ring and

with him.

8 Social Modals About the Past: Nana's Rules

Rachel is talking to her grandmother, Nana. The sentences in brackets tell you what they are thinking. Complete each sentence with all the modals appropriate to expressing their thoughts. Use *could have, might have, should have, ought to have, be supposed to, be to, had better have, have to, could,* and *be allowed to.* Use *not* where necessary. Use contractions where possible.

Nana: Rachel, you're 35 years old, and you're not married yet. You <u>should have/ought to have</u>

                                                                 1

found Mr. Right by now. [This was a good idea, but you haven't done it.]

Rachel: I've tried, Nana. For example, I met a man named Owen at a party. I went up to him and introduced myself.

Nana: You <u>shouldn't have</u> talked to him first. [It was a bad idea, but you did it.]

                         2

You _____ waited for him to introduce

                                     3

himself. [This was a good idea, but you didn't do it.]

Rachel: Owen _____ call me the next day. [This was

                                          4

what we planned and what I expected.] But he didn't, so I called him and invited him out.

Nana: You _____ called him. [This was a bad idea,

                                     5

but you did it.] You _____ waited longer.

                                          6

[This is one suggestion.] Or you _____ just

                                              7

forgotten about him. [This is another suggestion.] There are plenty of other nice men.

Rachel: Anyway, it turned out that Owen already had a girlfriend. He

_____ told me that at the party. [This was a

                                     8

possibility but it didn't occur, and I'm complaining.] But then I met Eric.

Nana: Rachel, you _____ invited him out, too.

                                     9

[This is a warning.]

Rachel: I did. He was shy, so I _____ do it. [It was a
                                            10
necessity.] But things didn't work out with him, either.

Nana: Rachel, you _____ found Mr. Right by now,
                                 11
but you didn't follow the rules. [You lost the opportunity.] When I was young, women

_____ speak to men first or invite them out.
          12

[It was prohibited.] But this was good. We _____
                                                        13

worry about getting involved with men who weren't interested. [It wasn't a necessity.] Also,

men like to take the lead. If you follow the old rules, Mr. Right will come to you.

9 Using Social Modals About the Past: Communication Problems?

You're Addy Viser. Work with a partner. Read and discuss the following two letters, which people have written to your newspaper advice column. In your opinion, did they do the right thing or should they have done things differently? Write a short paragraph in response to each letter. Use *could have, might have, ought to have,* and *should have* in your sentences. Include some sentences with *not*.

1.
Dear Addy Viser,

    My wife and I recently celebrated our fifth anniversary. As a surprise for my wife, I got tickets to a Dar Williams concert, because I thought that was her favorite singer. I kept our destination a secret until we got to the concert. After we sat down, she told me that the singer she likes is Lucinda Williams. The evening wasn't perfect, because my wife was disappointed. I didn't feel so good, either.

                        Peter

2.
Dear Addy Viser,

    My boyfriend asked me to look after his houseplants for a month while he was gone. I agreed to do it, although I wasn't really sure what to do. I drove ten miles to his house every day to water them, and I put lots of fertilizer on them. I don't know why, but the plants are nearly dead now. My boyfriend came back yesterday. He didn't thank me for looking after the plants, and he hasn't been as cheerful as he usually is.

                        Barbara

Example:
Dear Peter, Your wife ought to have appreciated the special effort you made to surprise her. . . . OR You shouldn't have bought tickets before you made sure of the name of your wife's favorite singer. . . .

 See the *Grammar Links* Website for complete model letters for this assignment.

10 Belief and Social Modals About the Past: Which Words Should Addy Viser Have Used?

Circle the correct choice. If both are correct, circle both.

Dear Addy Viser,

I met a woman named Rachel last month and called her the next Saturday afternoon for a date that night. She said that she couldn't go out with me because she (had to help)/ must have helped her grandmother. The next week I called her office and left a message for her to call me. I know that she had to get / must have gotten the message because her secretary told me she put it on her desk.
I didn't have to work / mustn't have worked that weekend, so I waited at home for her to call, but she never did. I was disappointed. Should I have called her again?

Wondering

Dear Wondering,

Yes, you ought to have called / should have called Rachel again. You know she has to have gotten / must have gotten the message, but you don't know why she didn't respond. Maybe she's decided to follow the old social rules. In the past, women had to let / must have let men take the lead. They couldn't telephone / couldn't have telephoned a man to tell him they wanted to go out. They have to have waited / had to wait for men to call them. And there's another possibility: Rachel might not have wanted / could not have wanted to seem too eager. It was a way to keep you interested in her, and it seems to have worked.

P.S. Why did you wait until Saturday afternoon to call for a date on Saturday night? You might have asked / could have asked her for a date for the following Saturday instead. Next time, don't call later than Wednesday!

Check your progress! Go to the Self-Test for Chapter 15 on the *Grammar Links* Website.

Wrap-up Activities

1 Should Ms. Monish Give Advice? EDITING

Correct the 11 errors in the passage. There are errors in modals and phrasal modals. Some errors can be corrected in more than one way. The first error is corrected for you.

> *must have heard*
> By now, you ~~must hear~~ of Ms. Monish, the marriage counselor whose advice column appears in hundreds of newspapers. Every day thousands of people write to Ms. Monish. They ask her, "May you give me some advice?" or "I was confused. What should I have done?" When people tell her they are considering divorce, she responds, "You shouldn't get a divorce. You are able to work out your marriage problems in the future." Recently, she criticized a divorced woman by telling her, "You mustn't have divorced your husband. You should have try harder." Sometimes she writes, "A man's way of communicating can be different from a woman's. You ought to try to understand your husband better."
>
> Because so many people read Ms. Monish's column and follow her advice, I wanted to know more about her background and qualifications. I finally could interview her one day. But when I talked to her, I mustn't find out much because she refused to answer my questions about her past. In order to learn more, I must ask other people. One of her friends told me that Ms. Monish has been married and divorced twice. When I heard this, I thought, "Ms. Monish has to have had marriage problems of her own in the past. She mustn't have worked those problems out very well." Her friend told me, "Ms. Monish's first marriage mustn't break up. And her second marriage hadn't got to break up, either. She couldn't communicate well with her husbands, and now she regrets it. But she must of learned a lot from those experiences."

2 Describing Yourself and Your Ideal Mate: WRITING

Imagine that you have gone to a matchmaker to find your ideal husband or wife. The matchmaker needs some information from you. Write a paragraph responding to the questions in 1 and a paragraph responding to the questions in 2.

1. What abilities do you or don't you have now? What abilities do you expect to have in the future? (Use *can* and *be able to*.)

   Example: I can't cook very well, but I can wash dishes. . . . Two years from now, I'll be able to program computers.

2. What abilities does your ideal mate have? (Use *can* and *be able to*.) What qualities are possible, necessary, or not necessary in your ideal mate? (Use *can, might, could, should, ought to, must, have to*, and *have got to*.)

   Example: My ideal husband is someone who can cook very well. . . . He doesn't have to be handsome, but he must have a sense of humor. . . .

 See the *Grammar Links* Website for complete model paragraphs for this assignment.

3 Join the Politeness Patrol: WRITING/SPEAKING

Step 1 Work with a partner. As members of the "Politeness Patrol," your task is to change impolite (i.e., abrupt or inappropriate) requests, offers, and responses into polite ones, using modals and other polite expressions.

Impolite	Polite
1. Young student: *Hey, there. I need change for a dollar. Give me some.*	Young student: Excuse me. Could you please give me change for a dollar?
Older stranger: *Here.*	Older stranger: Certainly I can.
2. Man, asking for a date: *Want to go to a movie with me?*	Man, asking for a date: _____ _____
Woman: *No way. I'm busy.*	Woman: _____
3. Student: *I'm going to carry your books for you.*	Student: _____ _____
Teacher: *Do it.*	Teacher: _____
4. Guest: *Those apples look good. You're going to let me have one.*	Guest: _____ _____
Host: *Take it.*	Host: _____

Step 2 Now think of typical situations where people ask permission, make requests, or make offers. Write two "impolite" dialogues like those in Part A. Then write the same dialogues in a polite version, using modals and polite expressions. Present both versions to the class. Use the tone of your voice to make the impolite dialogues sound very impolite and the polite dialogues sound very polite.

4 Love-Life Dilemmas: SPEAKING/WRITING

Step 1 Work in groups of three. Discuss the following difficult situations. Use belief and social modals in the past—for example, *may (not) have* and *should (not) have*. Use belief modals to make predictions about the future—for example, *might (not)* and *will (not)*. Then decide what actions are possible, advisable or not advisable, and necessary or not necessary for Pauline and Carol to take. Use social modals—for example, *could, should (not), must (not)*, and *(not) have to*.

1.

> _Pauline_: I have a good friend named Marcia, who has been married for a year to a man named Bruce. Last Friday night, I went to a movie alone. While I was in the theater, I noticed that Bruce was sitting in the row ahead of me. (I'm sure that Bruce didn't see me.) I was very surprised to see that he was at the movie with a woman that I didn't recognize. I haven't told Marcia about this. I've been worrying about it, and I'm not sure what to do.

2.

> _Carol_: Six months ago, Michael asked me to marry him, and I accepted his proposal because he is a very kind and responsible man. Everyone in my family likes Michael very much. We have invited 300 people to our wedding, which is scheduled to take place in two weeks. Last week I ran into Austin. I had fallen in love with Austin in high school, but we hadn't seen each other for a long time, because we went to colleges in different cities. He was disappointed to hear about my marriage plans. Now all of my old feelings for Austin are coming back.

Step 2 On your own, choose one of the two situations. Write a paragraph about it, discussing the actions you think were and are possible, advisable, or necessary for Pauline or Carol to take. Use any appropriate modals, including at least five of the following: *could (have)*, *may (have)*, *might (have)*, *have to (have)*, *must (have)*, *should (have)*, *and ought to (have)*.

 See the *Grammar Links* Website for a model paragraph for this assignment.

Passives

TOPIC FOCUS
World of Sports

UNIT OBJECTIVES

▧ **passive sentences in simple present and simple past**
(Medals *are awarded* in every Olympics. A Canadian *was awarded* the first Olympic medal for snowboarding.)

▧ **passive sentences versus active sentences**
(The ball was caught by the center fielder. The center fielder caught the ball.)

▧ **passive sentences with and without agents**
(Sports are played *by professional and amateur athletes*. Sports are played in many different places.)

▧ **passive sentences in progressive and perfect tenses**
(A new stadium *is being built*. The old one *has* already *been torn down*.)

▧ **passive sentences with modals**
(The stadium *must be completed* before the next football season.)

▧ ***get* passives**
(Professional athletes *get paid* large salaries.)

▧ **passive causatives**
(The team *had* new seats *installed* in the stadium.)

Grammar in Action

Read and listen to this article.

The World of Sports

Sports **are played** by increasing numbers of professional athletes. Moreover, many new records **have been set** in recent years. Nowadays records **are being broken** at a faster pace by stronger and better athletes. Some old records **haven't been broken** yet but likely **will be broken** in the not-too-distant future.

Sports have become a huge entertainment industry. Sports events **are attended** by millions of fans. Many more fans **can be found** in front of their televisions on the days that their teams play.

Sports **are** often **played** in large, modern facilities. Arenas and stadiums that **were built** many years ago **are being replaced**, and more new facilities **will be built** in the future.

Millions of dollars **are spent** on sports every year. Modern stadiums are expensive, and large salaries **are paid** to top professional athletes. Many people believe that too much money **is being spent** on new stadiums and that such large salaries **shouldn't be paid** to professional athletes. **Can** fans **be expected** to share the costs through paying higher ticket prices? Tickets for some sports events have become so expensive that many fans can't afford them. **Will** these fans **be forgotten** by the sports industry as it goes after larger profits elsewhere?

What is the future of sports? Some experts predict that the costs of salaries and stadiums will become greater than the money a team can raise. This may cause problems for one of the world's top entertainment industries.

Think About Grammar

A. Look at the following active and passive sentences. Underline the subject of each sentence, and circle the object of the active sentence. Then complete the statements below.

Active sentence: The goalie threw the ball.

Passive sentence: The ball was thrown by the goalie.

1. The object of the active sentence becomes the _____ of the passive sentence.

    The subject of the active sentence appears in the passive sentence following the word

    _____ .

2. In the passive sentence, the main verb, _____, is in its past participle form,

    and a form of the verb _____ comes before it.

3. In an active sentence, the subject *performs* the action of the verb and the object *receives*

    (is affected or changed by) the action of the verb. In a passive sentence, in contrast, the

    _____ *receives* the action of the verb.

B. In the passage, the sentences with boldfaced verbs are passive. Find an example of each of the following. Write the boldfaced verb.

1. a passive in the simple present _are played_____

2. a passive in the simple past _____

3. a negative passive _____

4. a passive in the present progressive _____

5. a passive in the present perfect _____

6. a passive in the future _____

7. a passive with a modal _____

Chapter 16

Introduction to the Passive

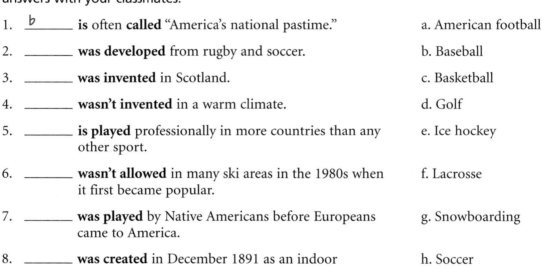

Introductory Task: Sports Trivia

A. Fill in each blank with the letter of the sport that completes the sentence. See how many answers you can get right! Compare answers with your classmates.

1. ___b___ is often **called** "America's national pastime."

2. _____ **was developed** from rugby and soccer.

3. _____ **was invented** in Scotland.

4. _____ **wasn't invented** in a warm climate.

5. _____ **is played** professionally in more countries than any other sport.

6. _____ **wasn't allowed** in many ski areas in the 1980s when it first became popular.

7. _____ **was played** by Native Americans before Europeans came to America.

8. _____ **was created** in December 1891 as an indoor winter sport.

a. American football

b. Baseball

c. Basketball

d. Golf

e. Ice hockey

f. Lacrosse

g. Snowboarding

h. Soccer

Check your answers on page A-4.

B. Work with a partner. Take turns asking and answering the following questions. In your answers, include the sports in Part A and other sports you know about.

1. Which sports **are played** at this time of the year?

2. Which sports **are played** by teams?

3. Which sports **are** usually **considered** individual sports?

4. Which sports **are watched** by many people?

5. Which sports **are televised**?

6. Which sports **were invented** fairly recently?

The Passive I
■ Passives in the Simple Present and Simple Past

FORM

A. Affirmative Statements

SUBJECT	*BE*	PAST PARTICIPLE OF MAIN VERB*	(PREPOSITIONAL PHRASE [*BY . . .*])	
Graduation	**is**	**held**	(by the school)	each May.
The graduation ceremony	**was**	**planned**	(by the students themselves)	months ago.

B. Negative Statements

SUBJECT	*BE + NOT/N'T*	PAST PARTICIPLE OF MAIN VERB*	(PREPOSITIONAL PHRASE [*BY . . .*])	
The payments	**aren't**	**recorded**	(by our office)	right away.
The bills	**weren't**	**sent out**	(by the assistant)	on time.

C. *Yes/No* Questions

BE	SUBJECT	PAST PARTICIPLE OF MAIN VERB*	(PREPOSITIONAL PHRASE [*BY . . .*])	
Is	day care	**provided**	(by the company)	for employees?
Was	the doctor's visit	**covered**	(by your insurance)?	

D. *Wh-* Questions

WH- WORD	*BE*	SUBJECT	PAST PARTICIPLE OF MAIN VERB*	(PREPOSITIONAL PHRASE [*BY . . .*])	
Who	**was**		**suspended**	(by the principal)	yesterday?
When	**are**	new students	**admitted**	(by the school)?	

*See Appendix 7 for the past participles of irregular verbs.

(continued on next page)

Passive Sentences Versus Active Sentences

FORM

ACTIVE SENTENCES			
SUBJECT	VERB	OBJECT	
The committee	**wrote**	new rules	last week.

PASSIVE SENTENCES				
SUBJECT	*BE*	PAST PARTICIPLE OF MAIN VERB	(PREPOSITIONAL PHRASE [*BY . . .*])	
New rules	**were**	**written**	(by the committee)	last week.

1. A passive sentence differs from an active sentence in these ways:

subject   verb
Active: Professor Smith teaches
     object
Psychology 101 every semester.
              subject   verb
Passive: Psychology 101 is taught
   prepositional phrase
(by Professor Smith) every semester.

   - The passive sentence adds *be* and has the main verb in its past participle form.

     Active: **teaches**

     Passive: **is taught**

   - The object of the active sentence is the subject of the passive sentence.

     Active: **Psychology 101** = object

     Passive: **Psychology 101** = subject

   - The subject of the active sentence, if included in the passive sentence, is in a prepositional phrase with *by*. It can be omitted.

     Active: **Professor Smith** = subject

     Passive: **Professor Smith** is in prepositional phrase with *by*

2. Active sentences can have any verb. Passive sentences can have only **transitive verbs**—verbs that, in active sentences, take an object. (Remember, an active sentence object is the passive sentence subject.)

   Passive sentences are not possible with **intransitive verbs**—verbs that don't take an object. Common intransitive verbs include *appear, be, belong, come, die, go, happen, look, occur, seem, sleep, stay,* and *walk*.

   Active: A truck **hit** my car. (*hit* is a transitive verb; *my car* = object)

   Active: The two vehicles **collided**. (*collide* is an intransitive verb; no object)

   Passive: My car **was hit** by a truck. **BUT NOT**: My car ~~was collided~~.

Remember! Verbs like *happen* and *seem* are not transitive and are not used in passive sentences.

An accident **happened**.
 NOT: An accident ~~was happened~~.

They **seemed** happy.
 NOT: They ~~were seemed happy~~.

GRAMMAR PRACTICE 1

The Passive I

1 **Passive Sentences in the Simple Present:** Baseball Uniforms I

Complete this discussion from a sports history class. Use the words in parentheses to complete passive sentences in the simple present. Use contractions where possible.

Professor: Let's talk for a moment about why a baseball team might adopt a different uniform. After

all, uniforms __aren't worn__ forever. New styles __are adopted__ for some fairly
         1 (not, wear)   2 (adopt)

specific reasons. For example, often a change _____ when a team
                                                   3 (make)

moves to another city.

Lauren: If a team is losing, _____ to change the uniforms?
                                  4 (something, do)

Professor: Yes, often different caps _____, or the style of the shirt
                                          5 (use)

_____. Not surprisingly, this kind of design change usually
     6 (modify)

_____ when a team is winning.
     7 (not, consider)

Sammy: What happens when new owners buy a team?

_____?
             8 (the old uniforms, keep)

Professor: Not usually, and new uniforms _____ when a new stadium
                                               9 (often, design)

_____.
     10 (build)

Mark: What _____ with the old uniforms?
                11 (do)

Professor: Some _____ in museums, some _____
                     12 (put)   13 (keep)

by the players, and some _____ to fans or collectors.
                              14 (sell)

Mark: Cool! Maybe I can find some for sale on the Internet.

2 Passive Sentences in the Simple Past: Baseball Uniforms II

Complete the class discussion. Use the words in parentheses to complete passive sentences in the simple past. Use contractions where possible.

Professor: Another interesting fact is that players __weren't always identified__ by names or
1 (not, always, identify)

numbers on their uniforms. Players _____ identical uniforms,
2 (give)

and a fan _____ to recognize the players by their faces and
3 (expect)

positions. In the early 1900s, some teams experimented with using numbers on uniforms,

but numbers _____ by any team for a whole season until 1929.
4 (not, wear)

Ruth: Did all the teams wear numbers that season?

Professor: No, and teams _____ to use them until 1933. The New York
5 (not, require)

Yankees wore numbered uniforms in the 1929 season, and the numbers

_____ on the basis of the batting order.
6 (assign)

Sammy: But, wait a minute. _____ to play
7 (one player, ever, send in)

for another player? What happened then?

Professor: Good point. That was a problem since two players couldn't have the same number. So then

the numbers didn't match the batting order. That numbering system was also a problem

when a player _____ to another team or when a player
8 (trade)

_____ from a team. In these cases, the batting order
9 (drop)

_____, so players couldn't keep their numbers
10 (often, change)

from one season to the next. Because of all these problems, this system

_____ for very long. Okay, let's move on from numbers to
11 (not, use)

names. When _____ to the uniforms?
12 (players' names, add)

Sammy: I know! Names _____ on uniforms in 1960 by the Chicago
                              13 (first, put)

              White Sox.

Professor: You're right. The decision to use names _____ by the fact
                                                              14 (probably, influence)

              that more and more games _____ on TV. However, the use of
                                              15 (show)

              names _____ by a number of teams because they wanted fans to
                        16 (oppose)

              buy programs to find out who the players were.

> *batting order* = the order that baseball players take a turn at hitting the ball. *send in
> for* = replace or substitute one player for another. *program* = a list of players and
> other information for a sports event.

To find out more about sports uniforms, go to the *Grammar Links* Website.

3 Forming Passive Sentences: Names for Sports Facilities

Underline the objects in the active sentences. Remember to underline the entire noun
phrase. Complete the passive sentences. Do not include a *by* phrase.

1. Today sports teams earn <u>a lot of money</u> from the places where sports are played.

    Today <u>a lot of money is earned</u> from the places where sports are played.

2. In many cases, teams name sports facilities for sponsors such as airlines or soft drink companies.

    In many cases, _____ for sponsors such as airlines

    or soft drink companies.

3. In the past, teams didn't name sports facilities for sponsors.

    In the past, _____ for sponsors.

4. They named sports facilities for famous players and coaches.

    _____ for famous players and coaches.

5. Why do teams give sponsors' names to sports facilities?

    Why _____ to sports facilities?

6. Sponsors pay large fees to teams to advertise sponsors' names on sports facilities.

    _____ to teams to advertise sponsors' names on

    sports facilities.

7. When sponsors support teams, the large fees cover some of the teams' expenses.

    When sponsors support teams, _____ .

> *sponsors* = companies that pay some of the costs of an event, a facility, etc., in
> return for advertising.

4 **Passive Sentences—Questions and Answers:** Stadiums

Work with a partner. Student A asks questions with simple present and simple past passives to complete the chart about Invesco Field at Mile High. Use the words given. When no *wh-* word is given, ask a *yes/no* question. Student B uses the information on page A-4 to answer with passive sentences. Then Student B asks questions to complete the chart about the Skydome and Student A answers with the information on page A-4.

Example: Student A: When was Invesco Field at Mile High first opened to the public?
Student B: Invesco Field at Mile High was first opened to the public in 2001.

Invesco Field at Mile High Denver, Colorado	The Skydome Toronto, Canada
First year: _2001_	First year: _____
Uses: _____	Uses: _____
Playing surface: _____	Playing surface: _____
Other fact: _____ _____ _____	Other fact: _____ _____ _____
Other fact: _____ _____ _____	Other fact: _____ _____ _____

Invesco Field at Mile High

1. when/open/to the public
2. what/use/for
3. games/play/on grass
4. why/computerized system/put/under the grass
5. how/money/raise/for art work at the stadium

The Skydome

1. when/open/to the public
2. what/use/for
3. games/play/on grass
4. how/roof/design/to open
5. what/use/to fasten the artificial turf

artificial turf = a substitute surface to grass, as on a playing field.

 To find out more about these stadiums, go to the *Grammar Links* Website.

5 Transitive and Intransitive Verbs; Writing Passive Sentences: Player Salaries

A. Label the boldfaced verbs with a *T* for transitive or an *I* for intransitive. All of the sentences are active. There are six transitive verbs and six intransitive verbs.

Sports teams **pay** some of the highest salaries in the world to their top athletes.
^{T}
$_1$

These athletes **work** hard, but are they worth the money they receive?
$_2$

Players' salaries **reflect** the popularity of a sport. For example, in the past hockey
$_3$

players didn't earn as much money as football players. Recently, hockey **seems** to have
$_4$

become a more popular sport. Now, nearly all sports fans **recognize** the names of the
$_5$

top hockey players. As a consequence, these players **earn** higher salaries. But
$_6$

basketball players still **appear** to be the top earners in sports year after year. The
$_7$

average salary of a professional basketball player **was** $3.5 million in 2001 compared
$_8$

to $1.1 million for a hockey player.

According to one financial expert, paying high salaries **hurts** sports teams. Top
$_9$

players **attract** fans. However, what **happens** when ticket prices are so high that fans
$_{10}$ $\quad\quad\quad\quad\quad\quad\quad\quad\quad$ $_{11}$

can't afford to buy them? When fans **don't come** to watch the teams, will athletes'
$\quad\quad\quad\quad\quad\quad\quad\quad\quad\quad\quad\quad\quad$ $_{12}$

salaries change?

B. Six of the sentences in the passage can be rewritten as passive sentences. Rewrite these sentences. In each, include a prepositional phrase with *by*.

Example: *Some of the highest salaries in the world are paid by sports teams to their top athletes.*

The Passive II

A. Active Sentences Versus Passive Sentences

ACTIVE SENTENCES

AGENT	VERB	RECEIVER OF ACTION	
The janitors	cleaned	**the school**	from top to bottom.

PASSIVE SENTENCES

RECEIVER OF ACTION	VERB	AGENT	
The school	was cleaned	**by the janitors**	from top to bottom.

1. An **agent** is the noun that performs the action of the verb.

   In active sentences, the subject is usually an agent.

   In passive sentences, the agent, if included, is usually in a *by* phrase.

   The cat scratched the child.

   The child was scratched by **the cat**.

2. A **receiver** is the noun that the action of the verb affects.

   In active sentences, the receiver is usually the object of the verb.

   In passive sentences, the receiver is usually the subject.

   The cat scratched **the child**.

   The child was scratched by the cat.

B. Using Passives Without *By* to Omit the Agent

1. Sometimes, we don't want to mention the agent. In passives, the agent is an optional *by* phrase. So we can omit the agent by using a passive without a *by* phrase.

   The school was cleaned from top to bottom. (*The school* is the receiver; there is no agent.)

2. Speakers may want to omit the agent because:

   • The agent is unknown, unimportant, or unnecessary.

   The Olympics were started in Greece. (The agent is unknown.)

   When it started getting dark, the stadium lights were turned on. (The agent is unimportant.)

   The students were taught fractions this year. (It is unnecessary to mention the agent— obviously, teachers did the teaching.)

(continued on next page)

B. Using Passives Without *By* to Omit the Agent (continued)

• The agent is a general subject (*people, anyone, everyone,* etc.).	Customs are developed over the years. (i.e., by people) The origins of some customs aren't understood. (i.e., by anyone)

C. Using Passives in Writing

Passives are used more in writing than in speech. They are common in news reports and, especially, in scientific and other academic writing, where agents are often less important than processes and results.	Samples of the flies' eggs **are taken**, and the larvae that emerge from the eggs **are grown** in bottles. The fully grown larvae **are** then **examined**. (The scientists who perform these processes are not important; the processes and their results are important.)

GRAMMAR PRACTICE 2

The Passive II

6 **Meaning of Passive Sentences:** Can the Cougars Win?

Listen to the radio broadcast of a basketball game. Then listen again and put a check next to the sentence that gives the information that is in the broadcast.

1. _____ a. Carson expects to lead his team.

   __✓__ b. People expect Carson to lead his team.

2. _____ a. Other players passed the ball to Carson.

   _____ b. Carson passed the ball to other players.

3. _____ a. Peterson is playing in the second half.

   _____ b. Young is playing in the second half.

4. _____ a. Thomas hit the ball.

   _____ b. Sanchez hit the ball.

5. _____ a. Phillips tripped Sanchez.

   _____ b. Sanchez tripped Phillips.

6. _____ a. Phillips hurt someone in the last play.

   _____ b. Someone hurt Phillips in the last play.

7. _____ a. The players encourage the fans.

   _____ b. The fans encourage the players.

8. _____ a. Stanley Brown is the coach.

   _____ b. Stanley Brown is a player.

7 Receivers in Active and Passive Sentences: Babe Didrikson Zaharias

Underline the receiver of the action of the verbs in boldface. Circle the performer of the action, if it is given.

1. (Most athletes) **outshine** their competitors in only one sport.

2. In contrast, many sports **were played** well by the great (Mildred "Babe" Didrikson Zaharias.)

3. Babe **hit** balls hard like Babe Ruth, the famous baseball player. (This explains her nickname.)

4. In high school, she **achieved** recognition as an All-American basketball player.

5. In the 1932 U.S. track and field championship, more points **were scored** by Didrikson alone than by any team.

6. Two track and field records **were set** by Didrikson in the 1932 Summer Olympics.

7. She **won** two gold medals and a silver medal in the 1932 Olympics.

8. Didrikson **earned** 35 victories in her 21-year golf career.

9. From April 1946 to August 1947, she **defeated** all her opponents, winning 17 consecutive golf tournaments.

10. Many competitions in tennis and bowling **were won** by Didrikson, too.

11. The title "Greatest Female Athlete of the First Half of the Twentieth Century" **was awarded** to Babe Didrikson Zaharias in 1950.

8 Omitting the *By* Phrase: Catch a Wave

Circle the verbs in the following passive sentences. (Some sentences have more than one verb.) Cross out *by* phrases if the agent isn't important or necessary.

1. Some sports, like surfing, (are done) by individuals, not teams.

2. Surfing (is done) with or without a surfboard ~~by surfers~~.

3. The sport was popularized by Duke Kahanamoku in the early twentieth century.

4. Kahanamoku, an Olympic swimmer, was recognized by people as an accomplished surfer.

5. This happened when surfing exhibitions were included in swimming competitions by some competition organizers.

6. Today, many people surf, partly because formal training isn't needed by surfers.

7. More and more women are seen on surfboards by other surfers.

8. Women, especially, are inspired by champion surfer Lisa Andersen.

9. They are motivated by her surfboarding skill and her accomplishments.

---

exhibition = a special, noncompetitive part of a sports event.

---

9 **Writing Passives; the *By* Phrase:** Individual Sports

Write passive sentences with the information given. Include the agent in a *by* phrase only if the agent is important or necessary information. Use appropriate tenses.

I. *Snowboarding*

	Agent	Action	Receiver	Other Information
1.	people	often describe	snowboarding	as surfing on snow
2.	Jake Burton and Tom Sims	start	the first snowboard companies	in the late 1970s
3.	organizers	first include	snowboarding	in Olympic competition in 1998

1. Snowboarding is often described as surfing on snow.
2. The first snowboard companies were started by Jake Burton and Tom Sims in the late 1970s.

II. *Cycling*

	Agent	Action	Receiver	Other Information
4.	the French	hold	the first road race	in 1869
5.	millions of people	watch	the Tour de France	every year
6.	Henri Desgranges	organize	the first Tour de France	in 1903

III. *Marathon Running*

	Agent	Action	Receiver	Other Information
7.	officials	define	the length of a marathon	as 42 km, 195 m
8.	athletes	originally run	this distance	in the 1908 Olympic Games
9.	African runners	dominate	the sport	in the 1990s

10 Passives in Academic Writing: Arthroscopic Surgery for Sports Injuries

A. Read the passage on arthroscopic surgery. Find the sentences that have one or more passives and underline the verbs in passive form. Then go back and work with a partner to answer the following questions.

1. How many sentences in the passage have one or more passives? **7**
2. How many times is the passive used?
3. In how many of the passives is an agent included in a *by* phrase?
4. Why is the *by* phrase omitted in so many of the passive sentences?
5. Why is the passive used so often in the passage?

Arthroscopic Surgery

Injuries occur in all sports, and injuries to joints, especially the knee, are common. Surgery for these injuries has become simpler because of the advances in arthroscopic surgery, one of the most common procedures in sports medicine today. Arthroscopic surgery <u>was</u> first <u>performed</u> in the mid-1950s by a Japanese doctor, Masaaki Watanabe, who also designed one of the first widely used arthroscopes. The procedure <u>was</u> <u>brought</u> to North America in 1965 by a Canadian doctor, Robert W. Jackson.

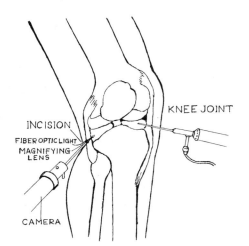

Using an arthroscope, a surgeon can examine and treat joint problems that used to require extensive surgery and long recovery periods. An arthroscope is a thin tool containing a fiber-optic light, a magnifying lens, and a video camera. In arthroscopic surgery, a small incision, or cut, is made and the arthroscope is inserted into the incision. Sterile fluid is injected into the joint space to enlarge the space, and the tissues are examined. Repairs are made to the injury through another small incision. Usually, because the incisions are so small, stitches are not required, and surgical tape is used to close them instead. When injuries are treated with arthroscopic surgery, they heal faster, so little time is needed for recovery, and normal activity is resumed by the patient within a short time.

---

joint = a place where two or more body parts are joined. *fiber-optic* = using glass or plastic fibers that are capable of transmitting light around curves. *magnify* = make something appear larger than it really is. *sterile fluid* = a liquid that is free from living microorganisms, especially those that cause disease. *tissue* = the substance that plants and animals are made of. *stitch* = a piece of thread used to close an incision in surgery.

B. Write a paragraph that explains a process or procedure like the one in Part A. Possibilities include biological, chemical, mechanical, mental, physical, and social processes, or any other process you know or can find out about. Use at least five passive sentences in your paragraph. Use the simple present and simple past tense and at least one negative. Make sure to use the passive appropriately.

See the *Grammar Links* Website for a model paragraph for this assignment.

Check your progress! Go to the Self-Test for Chapter 16 on the *Grammar Links* Website.

Chapter 17

More About Passives

Introductory Task: The Things Fans Do

A. Sports fans do some strange things to support their teams and bring them good luck. Put a check next to each statement that you think is true.

___✓___ 1. Fans **got** their faces **painted** red, white, and blue to support the U.S. soccer team.

_____ 2. A barrel (and very little else) **was being worn** by one football fan to every game, even when the weather was cold.

_____ 3. A couple with World Cup tickets **got married** in the stadium an hour before the game started.

_____ 4. A fan **got** his hair **cut** and **colored** to look like a soccer ball.

_____ 5. A fan **had** a soccer-ball dress **made** for the World Cup.

_____ 6. Stuffed animals, even very big ones, **get taken** to games for good luck.

_____ 7. Rubber rats **were being thrown** on the ice at hockey games until officials stopped this for safety reasons.

_____ 8. A fan **won't have** his lucky shirt **washed** and wears it to all his team's games.

Then turn to page A-4 for the answers.

B. Read the three items, and then complete them.

1. Two of the sentences in Part A are passives with *be* + past participle. That is, they are like the passives in Chapter 16, although they are not in the simple present or simple past. The passive forms are: __was being worn_____ and _____.

2. Two of the sentences in Part A are passives that are not formed with *be*. Instead, they include the verb _____ + past participle. These passive forms are

_____ and _____.

3. Four of the sentences in Part A are passive causatives. Passive causatives include an object. They are formed with the verb _____ or _____ + object + past participle. The examples here (verb + object + past participle) are

_____, _____,

_____, and _____.

Passives in Progressive and Perfect Tenses

■ Passives in the Present and Past Progressive Tenses

FORM

A. Affirmative Statements

SUBJECT	BE	PRESENT PARTICIPLE OF *BE*	PAST PARTICIPLE OF MAIN VERB*	
The package	is was	**being**	**sent**	by our office.

B. Negative Statements

SUBJECT	BE	NOT	PRESENT PARTICIPLE OF *BE*	PAST PARTICIPLE OF MAIN VERB*	
The notices	are were	**not**	**being**	**delivered**	on time.

C. *Yes/No* Questions

BE	SUBJECT	PRESENT PARTICIPLE OF *BE*	PAST PARTICIPLE OF MAIN VERB*	
Is **Was**	that sofa	**being**	**thrown out?**	

D. *Wh-* Questions

WH- WORD	BE	(SUBJECT)	PRESENT PARTICIPLE OF *BE*	PAST PARTICIPLE OF MAIN VERB*	
Why	is was	the problem	**being**	**ignored?**	
What	is was		**being**	**done**	about the problem?

*See Appendix 7 for past participles of irregular verbs.

■ Passives in the Present and Past Perfect Tenses

FORM

A. Affirmative Statements

SUBJECT	HAVE	PAST PARTICIPLE OF *BE*	PAST PARTICIPLE OF MAIN VERB*	
The bills	have had	**been**	**paid.**	

(continued on next page)

B. Negative Statements

SUBJECT	*HAVE*	NOT	PAST PARTICIPLE OF *BE*	PAST PARTICIPLE OF MAIN VERB*	
The grass	has / had	not	been	watered	for days.

C. Yes/No Questions

HAVE	SUBJECT	PAST PARTICIPLE OF *BE*	PAST PARTICIPLE OF MAIN VERB*	
Have / Had	new plans	been	made	yet?

D. *Wh-* Questions

WH- WORD	*HAVE*	(SUBJECT)	PAST PARTICIPLE OF *BE*	PAST PARTICIPLE OF MAIN VERB*	
When	have / had	those issues	been	discussed	before?
What	has / had		been	discussed?	

*See Appendix 7 for past participles of irregular verbs.

GRAMMAR PRACTICE 1

Passives in Progressive and Perfect Tenses

1 Passive Sentences in Progressive Tenses: A Baseball Stadium Is Being Built

Complete the passive sentences in the sports radio interview from 2003. Use the words in parentheses and the present progressive and past progressive tenses.

Eric: Bob, what's the latest news on Petco Ballpark here in San Diego?

Bob: Eric, I'm happy to report that lots of work _is being done_ _____ on the ballpark right
                                                          1 (do)

now. As everyone knows, work on the stadium stopped in late 2000. The money that was needed

to pay for the work _____, as a result of legal
                              2 (not, raise)

problems. Although significant progress _____ before
                                                  3 (make)

work stopped, nothing was done for more than a year, so the ballpark won't be ready when

originally scheduled.

Eric: Yes, the delay was unfortunate, but we were thrilled to learn that last week the construction

crews _____ the go-ahead, so now work has
4 (give)

started again. Tell us about some of the features of the new ballpark. The plans

_____ by the experts as exciting and different.
5 (describe)

Bob: It will be great, Eric. When it _____ back in 1998,
6 (plan)

the architects wanted to give all fans the best possible view. They felt that this just

_____ in many ballparks of the 1980s and 1990s.
7 (not, do)

Eric: How does their plan solve the problem?

Bob: It solves it partly by a special design involving "neighborhoods." These neighborhoods

_____ because seats _____
8 (create)   9 (install)

in sections that are clearly separated from each other. Also, all of the seats

_____ at an angle so they'll all face the pitcher's mound.
10 (put in)

Eric: What other features _____ in the design of the stadium?
11 (include)

Bob: In early 2000, as the plans for the seating _____, the
12 (finalize)

designers turned their attention to fans who might not be able to afford the best seats. As a

result, now several areas _____ around the ballpark
13 (place)

where fans who pay a small admission fee can stand and watch the game. In addition, a unique

"Park at the Park" area _____ where people can sit
14 (design)

on the grass instead of in a seat.

Eric: It sounds like a fun experience _____ for every fan in
15 (plan)

every price range. We're going to have a great new ballpark. Thanks for talking to us today.

> raise money = collect money. pitcher's mound = the place on a baseball field where the pitcher stands to throw the ball.

To find out more about stadiums and arenas, go to the *Grammar Links* Website.

2 Passive Sentences in Perfect Tenses: Sports Records Have Been Broken

Complete the passive sentences about sports records. Use the words in parentheses
and the present perfect and past perfect tenses.

1. The Masters golf tournament ___has been won_____ six times by Jack Nicklaus.
(win)

2. A mile ___hadn't been run_____ in under four minutes until Roger Bannister ran a
(not, run)

3-minute-59-second mile in England on May 6, 1954.

3. A 63-yard field goal _____ by New Orleans Saints kicker
(kick)

Tom Dempsey in 1970 before Denver Broncos kicker Jason Elam tied the record in 1998.

4. A perfect ten _____ by a gymnast until Nadia Comaneci of
(not, achieve)

Romania did it in the 1976 Olympic games.

5. Twenty-six touchdowns _____ in a
(make)

season by running back Marshall Faulk of the St. Louis Rams.

6. Seventy home runs _____ by
(hit)

Mark McGwire, of the St. Louis Cardinals in 1998 before Barry Bonds

of the San Francisco Giants hit 73 in 2001.

7. A 12-stroke lead _____ by the
(not, reach)

winner of the Masters golf tournament until Tiger Woods did it in 1997.

Tiger Woods

8. Two gold medals _____ in the heptathlon by
(earn)

Jackie Joyner-Kersey, one of the top women athletes of the twentieth century.

9. Ninety-two goals _____ in a hockey season by
(score)

Wayne Gretzky of the Edmonton Oilers.

10. More than 100 points _____ by a basketball player in a
(not, score)

single game, but Philadelphia basketball center Wilt Chamberlain scored 100 points in a game

against the New York Knicks on March 2, 1962.

11. The record of 2,130 consecutive baseball games played

_____ by Lou Gehrig of the
(set)

New York Yankees but was broken by Cal Ripken of the Baltimore

Orioles, who played 2,632 consecutive games.

Nolan Ryan

12. Three hundred eighty-three batters _____
(struck out)

in a single season by Nolan Ryan of the California Angels.

13. The record for the most losses to the same opponent in Grand Slam

tennis tournament finals _____
(set)

by Venus Williams. Interestingly, her opponent was her sister

Serena Williams.

Venus and Serena Williams

Passives with Modals

FORM

A. Overview

Passive sentences can include modals, phrasal modals, and modal-like expressions.

It **might be discussed.**
It **has to be discussed.**
It **ought to be discussed.**

B. Affirmative Statements

SUBJECT	MODAL	BASE FORM OF *BE*	PAST PARTICIPLE OF MAIN VERB*	
The new plan	**might**	be	discussed	at the meeting.
The packages	**had better**	be	mailed	today.

C. Negative Statements

SUBJECT	MODAL + *NOT*	BASE FORM OF *BE*	PAST PARTICIPLE OF MAIN VERB*	
The package	**will not**	be	delivered	today.
The lawn	**isn't supposed to**	be	watered	again yet.

D. *Yes/No* Questions

MODAL + SUBJECT	BASE FORM OF *BE*	PAST PARTICIPLE OF MAIN VERB*	
Should the files	be	reorganized?	
Are the awards **going to**	be	announced	tonight?

E. *Wh-* Questions

WH- WORD	MODAL (+ SUBJECT)	BASE FORM OF *BE*	PAST PARTICIPLE OF MAIN VERB*	
Who	should	be	invited	to the ceremony?
When	**do** the applications **have to**	be	submitted?	

*See Appendix 7 for past participles of irregular verbs.

Passives with Modals

3 **Passives with Modals:** Should a New Stadium Be Built?

Complete the passive sentences in the sports article. Use the words in parentheses.

Many sports teams want new stadiums. For a stadium to be built, it

__must be funded__ _____. Sports teams believe that to be successful, a
             1 (must, fund)

stadium project _____ by the teams alone and that it
                2 (can, not, pay for)

_____ by the public—that is, by a city and its taxpayers—
          3 (ought to, finance)

as well as by the teams that will play there. For this to happen, stadium funding usually

_____ by voters. Teams therefore try to convince voters
          4 (has to, approve)

that a new stadium will be good for the city because, for example, new jobs

_____ as a result.
          5 (are going to be, create)

Recently, financial experts have begun to question whether stadiums are good investments

for cities. Many believe that the benefits that teams promise

_____ by constructing a new stadium. These experts argue
          6 (will, not, bring about)

that the money for a stadium _____ mainly or entirely
                7 (should, pay)

by the teams that will profit from playing there. They don't believe that the money a city spends

_____ by the teams. For example, the money
          8 (will, pay back)

_____ if the teams don't sell enough tickets. Teams
          9 (might, not, pay back)

argue back by saying that the pleasure that stadiums bring to fans

_____.
          10 (can, not, measure)

_____? As long as teams want new stadiums and
          11 (should, a stadium, build)

ask cities for funds, the question _____.
                12 (will, debate)

_____ to make a stadium project work for both the teams
          13 (can, something, do)

and the cities? For one thing, a limit _____ on the city's
                14 (can, place)

contribution. Additional costs _____ by the teams. Other
                15 (could, absorb)

uses for the stadium _____ by both the teams and the
          16 (might, consider)

cities. When sports teams and cities work together, a profitable stadium project can be a reality.

4 **Using Passives with Modals:** Can This Problem Be Solved?

Think of a problem at your school or in your community. In small groups discuss this problem. Use modals with passives to express an opinion about what could be done, should be done, is supposed to be done, and must be done to correct the problem. Report your problem and solutions to the class.

Example: *Our school doesn't have a place for students to eat lunch together, and there isn't enough time to go out. Students need a place to eat together. A place of some kind should be provided. An office might be converted. If space can't be found, more time for lunch ought to be given so students can go out to eat.*

5 **Passives in Different Verb Tenses:** What a Place!

Find information on a public place you are interested in. It can be a sports stadium or arena or any other building or monument anywhere in the world. Write a paragraph telling about the place—when and where it was built, who it was designed by, what it is being used for, who it is visited by, and other interesting facts. Use at least three passive sentences in different tenses and two passive sentences with modals.

Example: *The Roman Coliseum was the world's largest early sports arena for 18 centuries after it was constructed. It was built over a 10-year period starting in AD 72. It had eighty entrances and could hold 50,000 spectators. Public events such as gladiator fights and wild animal hunts were held at the Coliseum. At times in its history, stones were removed to build other buildings. It is visited every year by many tourists from all over the world. . . .*

To find information on famous world monuments, go to the *Grammar Links* Website. See the *Grammar Links* Website for a complete model paragraph for this assignment.

Get Passives

FORM and FUNCTION

A. Passive Sentences with *Get*

Passive sentences can be formed with *get* instead of *be*, including:

• Affirmative sentences.	She **gets teased** by the other kids. That player **got sent** to another team.
• Negative sentences.*	The soup **didn't get eaten**. Those notices **haven't gotten sent out** yet.
• *Yes/no* questions.*	**Does** the mail **get picked up** on Sundays? **Have** those bills **gotten paid** yet?
• *Wh-* questions.*	When **did** your bike **get stolen**? Who **got fired**?
• Sentences in any tense.	We **are getting cheated**. My car **has gotten broken into** several times.
• Sentences with modals.	You **could get arrested** for doing that. All the students **are going to get promoted**.

*Do is used in negatives and questions in the simple present and simple past.

B. *Get* Passives Versus *Be* Passives

1. *Get* passives are used mainly in conversation and informal writing. They are not usually used in formal writing.

   Be passives can be used in informal or formal contexts.

   The mayor **got reelected**. (informal—e.g., conversation, informal letter)
   Compare: The mayor **was reelected**. (more formal—e.g., TV or newspaper story, as well as conversation, informal letter)

2. *Get* passives are used just with certain verbs—mainly verbs that emphasize some change, especially bad change.

   Be passives can be used with any verbs that allow the passive.

   The cake **got eaten** before we arrived. (emphasis on change) OR The cake **was eaten** before we arrived.

   My bike **got stolen**. (bad change) OR My bike **was stolen**.

   But:

   Protective clothing **must be worn** here.
     NOT: Protective clothing ~~must get worn~~ here.

   We **haven't been told** the truth.
     NOT: We ~~have gotten~~ told the truth.

Be or *get* followed by an *-ed* adjective can look like a passive. (In fact, this structure is sometimes called "stative passive.") Here is how to tell the difference:

- With **be/get** + **-ed adjective**, the *-ed* word is an adjective, so:

  The sentence is about a feeling or quality (e.g., the feeling of worry).

  | We were/got worried. |

  The intensifier *very* can be put before it.

  | We were/got very worried. |

- With **passive with be/get**, the *-ed* word is a verb, so:

  The sentence is about an action (e.g., the action of robbing).

  | We were/got robbed. |

  The intensifier *very* cannot be put before it.

  | **NOT**: We were/got ~~very~~ robbed. |

GRAMMAR PRACTICE 3

Get Passives

6 *Get* Passives: **Bad Things Can Happen to Good Players!**

Use the words in parentheses to complete the *get* passive sentences. Use appropriate tenses.

Playing professional sports is the ambition of many young athletes. These youngsters dream

of one day being as famous as Shaquille O'Neal, and they hope that they __will get paid_____
                                                                                    1 (pay)

a salary like his. But playing professional sports isn't easy, and it can be dangerous.

Professional athletes often get hurt. Over the years, many baseball players

_____ by pitched balls. Few quarterbacks
                    2 (hit)

_____ by much bigger football players at various points in
          3 (not, injure)

their careers. Basketball players _____ while
                                              4 (probably, will, knock down)

playing, too. Hockey players often _____ by other players'
                                                    5 (cut)

sticks and soccer players _____.
                                      6 (can, kick)

Behavior on and off the field can also lead to problems and to lost playing time. Players

_____ for bad behavior during games and as a
                  7 (may, suspend)

result may have to sit out for several games. Hockey players are notorious for fighting. They often

_____ of the game. Unfortunately, these days more and more
8 (kick out)

professional athletes _____ for their behavior off the field.
9 (arrest)

Finally, a professional athlete's career is often short. When their performance begins to decline,

players _____ to other teams. Sometimes they simply
10 (trade)

_____ for the next season.
11 (not, hire)

None of this stops young athletes from hoping they _____
12 (choose)

to play professionally.

> *ambition* = a strong desire to achieve something. *pitched* = thrown toward
> a batter in baseball. *notorious* = known widely and regarded unfavorably.
> *kick out* = make someone leave. *decline* = become less good.

7 *Get* **Passives:** Lucky Larry and Poor Pete

Work with a partner. Look at the chart about Lucky Larry and Poor Pete. Student A
reads sentence 1 about Lucky Larry to Student B. Student A asks Student B a *yes/no*
question about Poor Pete based on this sentence and using the same tense. Student B
should use the information about Poor Pete to answer. After sentence 4, Student B
reads about Poor Pete and asks Student A questions about Lucky Larry. Student A
answers with the information given.

Example: Student A: Lucky Larry got hired by the top team in his league. Did Poor Pete
get hired by the top team in his league?
Student B: No, he didn't. He got hired by the worst team in the league.

Lucky Larry	Poor Pete
1. Lucky Larry got hired by the top team in his league.	1. (hire) by the worst team in his league
2. Lucky Larry is getting promoted to head coach.	2. (demote) to assistant coach
3. Lucky Larry gets recognized by the fans.	3. (confuse with) the equipment manager
4. Lucky Larry is going to get paid to write a book.	4. (charge) for his parking space
5. (praise) for his team's success	5. Poor Pete has gotten blamed for his team's failure.
6. (invite) to many social events	6. Poor Pete gets ignored by his friends.
7. (elect) to the Sports Hall of Fame	7. Poor Pete may get ejected from the game for bad behavior.
8. (choose) to be coach of the year	8. Poor Pete will get fired at the end of the year.

> *demote* = reduce somebody in rank or status. *confuse with* = be unable to tell
> the difference between two people. *eject* = make someone leave; throw out.

8 Using Passive Sentences: The Games We Play

A. Read the paragraph. Underline the *be* and *get* passives.

Baseball <u>is played</u> on a field by two teams. A point (or "run") is scored when a batter-runner safely touches all four bases. Sometimes a runner can run only to the next base, but when the ball gets hit out of the ballpark, the player who hit it is allowed to run to all the bases and score.

B. Write a paragraph like the one in Part A about a game that you know how to play (a sport, a card game, a board game, etc.). Focus on the actions or the receivers of the actions, not on the agents. Use at least two passive sentences with *be* and one *get* passive.

9 True Passives Versus Stative Passives: Fan Superstitions

Read the passages. Label the boldfaced verbs with a *P* if they are true passives or an *S* if they are stative passives. (Remember, stative passives can take the intensifier *very*.)

I. *The Sock Monkey*

Brett Morris lost his sock monkey when he was 10, but he never forgot it. So
                                                            P
when Brett, who is now an adult, **was given** another sock monkey by a friend,
        S   1
he **was delighted**. While watching a football game involving his favorite
        2
team, Brett put the sock monkey in front of the TV. Brett **is devoted** to his
                                                              3
team, and when his team won, he and his friends decided the sock monkey was
responsible. Now, they make sure that the sock monkey **gets put** in front of the
                                                          4
TV before every game!

II. *Pulled-up Socks*

Cleveland Indian baseball fans believed pulled-up socks made their team win.
This practice **got started** because player Jim Thome wore his socks that way in
                  5
games. On Thome's birthday, the other players on the team wore their socks
pulled up in his honor, and the Indians won the game. Fans **were excited**. They
                                                              6
believed that pulling up their socks would help the team win, so at Indians games
many fans **could be seen** wearing pulled-up socks.
              7

---

devoted = showing strong affection for; loving.

 To find out more about funny fan behavior, go to the *Grammar Links* Website.

Passive Causatives

FORM

A. Overview

Passive causatives can occur in any tense and with modals. *Get* or *have* is followed by an object + a past participle. The form of *get* or *have* depends on the tense.

I **got/had** the washing machine **fixed.**

I **haven't gotten/had** the washing machine **fixed** yet.

When **are** you **going to get/have** the washing machine **fixed?**

B. Affirmative Statements

SUBJECT	(AUXILIARY)	*GET/HAVE*	OBJECT	PAST PARTICIPLE OF MAIN VERB*	(*BY* PHRASE)	
Emily		**gets/has**	her hair	**done**		every week.
I	**am**	**getting/having**	my hair	**done**	by a professional	next time.

C. Negative Statements

SUBJECT	AUXILIARY + *NOT*	*GET/HAVE*	OBJECT	PAST PARTICIPLE OF MAIN VERB*	(*BY* PHRASE)	
We	**didn't**	**get/have**	our house	**painted**	by the company that usually does it.	
We	**haven't**	**gotten/had**	our house	**painted**		since 2000.

D. *Yes/No* Statements

AUXILIARY	SUBJECT	*GET/HAVE*	OBJECT	PAST PARTICIPLE OF MAIN VERB*	(*BY* PHRASE)	
Did	you	**get/have**	your car	**repaired**	by the new mechanic?	
Are	you	**getting/having**	your car	**repaired**		this week?

E. *Wh-* Questions

WH- WORD	AUXILIARY	(SUBJECT)	*GET/HAVE*	OBJECT	PAST PARTICIPLE OF MAIN VERB*	(*BY* PHRASE)
Why	**did**	you	**get/have**	your cabinets	**built**	by that carpenter?
Who	**is**		**getting/having**	a cabinet	**built?**	

F. Passive Causatives with Modals

SUBJECT	MODAL	*GET/HAVE*	OBJECT	PAST PARTICIPLE OF MAIN VERB*	(*BY* PHRASE)
You	**should**	**get/have**	your groceries	**delivered**	by the store.
We	**are going to**	**get/have**	these groceries	**delivered.**	

*See Appendix 7 for past participles of irregular verbs.

Meaning and Use

1. Passive causatives express the idea that someone "causes" someone else to perform a service.

   I **got/had** the food for the party **prepared** by a restaurant. (I "caused" the restaurant to prepare the food.)

   A *by* phrase can be included to tell who performs the service.

   I got/had my car repaired **by a new mechanic**. (*by a new mechanic* included because information is not obvious)

   Often, however, a *by* phrase is not included, if this information is obvious or unimportant.

   I got/had my car repaired (by a mechanic). (*by a mechanic* often not included because information is obvious)

2. With passive causatives, the sentence is about the person receiving the service, not the person performing the service or the service itself.

   I'm getting a new phone **put in**. (sentence is about the person getting the phone)
   Compare:
   The phone company is putting in a new phone. (active sentence; sentence is about the phone company—the performer of the action)
   A new phone is being put in (for me). (passive; sentence is about the new phone)

GRAMMAR PRACTICE 4

Passive Causatives

10 Passive Causatives: Supporting the Team

A. The Cougars basketball team is very good, but the players are very lazy. As a result, people do things to support the team. Match the agents in List A with their actions in List B. Then write five sentences with passive causatives, using *get* or *have*, telling how the agents support the team. Use *the players* as the subject of each sentence.

List A		List B
1. an athletic trainer	_____	a. make their travel arrangements
2. a gourmet chef	_____	b. wash their uniforms
3. the coach	_____	c. cut their hair
4. a travel agent	_____	d. choose their positions
5. a laundry service	_____	e. cook their meals
6. a hairstylist	1 _____	f. tape their ankles

Example: The players get/have their ankles taped by an athletic trainer.

B. Change the sentences in Part A by adding one of the following time expressions: *last year*, *next year*, *since they won the championship*, *right now*, *before they became famous*, *by the time the game starts*. Use an appropriate verb tense.

Example: The players had a travel agent make their travel arrangements last year.

C. Mismatch the agents in List A with the actions in List B. Then write **three** sentences with a passive causative that tell how the agents don't support the team. Use *the players* as the subject of each sentence.

Example: The players don't get their ankles taped by a gourmet chef.

11 Using Passive Causatives: Getting Things Done

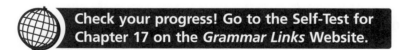 Work with a partner. Student A asks Student B *wh-* and *yes/no* questions about things he/she has done by someone else. Each question should include a passive causative with *get* or *have*. Student B answers Student A's question and adds more information. Use a variety of tenses in both the questions and answers. Use items in the box and your own ideas.

> hair/cut; shoes/shine; clothes/dryclean; apartment, room, house/paint; car/repair; pet/feed; TV, watch, etc./repair; dinner, groceries, etc./deliver; gift/wrap

Example: Do you get your hair cut by a hairdresser? Yes, I do. How often do you have your hair cut? I have my hair cut every two months. I had it cut last week, but I'm not very happy with it.

Have you ever gotten your shoes shined? No, I haven't, but I'd like to get them shined sometime. Maybe when I visit New York I can get them shined.

Check your progress! Go to the Self-Test for Chapter 17 on the *Grammar Links* Website.

Wrap-up Activities

1 **Sports Nicknames:** EDITING

Correct the 10 errors in these true stories. There are errors with passives. Some errors can be corrected in more than one way. The first error is corrected for you.

are given/have been given

There are many nicknames in sports. Some athletes ~~given~~ interesting nicknames as a result of their actions in games. One such athlete was "Wrong-Way" Riegels, who played in the 1929 Rose Bowl. The Rose Bowl is an important college football game that is play on January 1st every year. In the 1929 game, the football was dropped by a player from Georgia Tech, and Roy Riegels, from the University of California, picked it up and began to run. It was seemed that Riegels would score easily. But, for some reason, he got confused and ran 65 yards the wrong way. By the time he got turn around by a teammate, the other team had also run down the field, and Riegels got tackled on the one-yard line on the wrong end of the field. Because of Riegels' run down the field, his team was lost the game 8–7, and he was nicknamed "Wrong-Way" Riegels.

Sometimes the play, not the player, gets the nickname. A famous soccer goal knows by its nickname, the "Hand of God" goal. This goal was scored by Argentinean superstar Diego Maradona against the English in the 1986 World Cup. When the ball kicked over the heads of the English defense by another Argentinean player, both Maradona and the English goalkeeper, Peter Shilton, jumped for it. Maradona was appeared to have hit the ball into the goal with his head, but Shilton protested that Maradona had been hit it with his hand. The goal was permitted to stand, and the game was won by Argentina, 2–1. When the television replays proved that Shilton was correct, Maradona was declared that the goal had been "a little bit Maradona, a little bit the hand of God."

2 **Guess That Sport:** SPEAKING

Student A thinks of a game or a sport. The other students in the class ask *yes/no* questions about the game or sport, using the passive when possible. The first person who guesses the game or sport gets to think of the next game or sport.

Example: Is this game played professionally in the United States? Is a ball used in this game?

3 **"Get" the Answer:** SPEAKING

Step 1 Work with a partner. Write eight interview questions to find out interesting things about your classmates. Include a *get* passive in four of the questions and a passive causative (with *get* or *have*) in the other four. You can use the phrases in the box or your own ideas.

> *Get* passives: get hired for an unusual job, get invited somewhere special, get charged for something you didn't buy, get offered something for free, get chosen for an award, get fired from a job, get elected to an office or position
>
> Passive causatives: get/have special clothing made for you, get/have your hair cut in a style you hated, get/have your picture taken with someone famous, get/have something special done for you, get/have something valuable stolen

Example: Have you ever gotten hired for an unusual job?

Step 2 On your own, interview someone other than your partner, using the questions you wrote. When the person answers *yes* to a question, ask for details. Report the most interesting answers to the class.

4 **All About . . . :** WRITING

Step 1 Find out about a sport on the Internet or from encyclopedias, books, or magazines. Find out about when, where, and by whom it was invented; who it is played by; when and where it is played; what records have been set; and what is predicted for the future of the sport. You might also look for interesting stories about the sport and successes and failures.

Step 2 Write two paragraphs of at least six sentences each about the sport. Use at least five passives in several tenses, including one negative passive and one passive with a modal.

Example: The inventor of golf isn't known, but the game was probably developed in Scotland. However, in 1457, the Scots were forbidden to play golf by the King of Scotland because he thought that young men were wasting time on the golf courses instead of practicing with bows and arrows. . . .

Golf is played on specially designed courses. . . .

 See the *Grammar Links* Website for complete model paragraphs for this assignment.

Conditionals

Natural Disasters

UNIT OBJECTIVES

- **factual conditionals**
  (*If* the temperature *falls* below 32°F, water *freezes*. *If* she *saw* the weather report, she *knew* about the storm.)

- **future conditionals**
  (*If* it *continues* to rain, there *will be* a flood.)

- **present unreal conditionals**
  (*If* I *were* you, I *would watch* the weather forecast.)

- **past unreal conditionals**
  (*If* an earthquake *hadn't occurred*, the building *wouldn't have collapsed*.

- **sentences with *hope* or *wish***
  (I *hope* the storm *will stop* soon. I *wish* the storm *would stop* soon.)

343

Grammar in Action

🎧 Reading and Listening: The Two Faces of Nature

Read and listen to this passage from a book.

<u>**If you were looking at the earth from a satellite now, you would see a beautiful and peaceful-looking planet.**</u> But the peaceful appearance of the earth from space is misleading. Within the earth's atmosphere and beneath its surface, there are powerful, and often violent, forces at work. **If it's a late afternoon in the early summer, a tornado is probably forming somewhere in North America. If it's late summer, a hurricane is probably moving across an ocean toward land.** And, regardless of time of year, an earthquake may occur and a volcano may erupt.

A Tornado

These events—severe weather, earthquakes, and volcanoes—are part of the cycles of nature and the forces that shaped the earth. **The earth would be a very different place if these events didn't occur.** For example, **the Hawaiian islands wouldn't have formed if volcanoes hadn't erupted in the middle of the Pacific Ocean.** Severe natural events continue to have beneficial effects for life on the earth. For example, both volcanoes and floods make the soil more fertile, which is good for farming. However, **these natural events**

A Volcano Erupting

can become natural disasters if they negatively affect people and their property.

A Hurricane Coming Ashore

More and more people are being affected by violent natural events because the population is increasing in areas where these events are most likely to occur. More and more, then, natural events are causing disasters. Our ability to predict some natural events—hurricanes and blizzards, for example—is relatively good, so we have time to escape from them or to prepare for them. But others—earthquakes, for example—occur without warning. **If earthquakes could be predicted, many lives could be saved.** In short, even though our scientific knowledge has increased, at this point humans still can't defend themselves against some of the most powerful forces of nature.

After an Earthquake

If we can learn more about prediction of natural events, then perhaps someday we'll be able to keep more of these events from becoming natural disasters.

Adapted from Kendrick Frazier, *The Violent Face of Nature: Severe Phenomena and Natural Disasters.* New York: Morrow, 1979.

---

satellite = a mechanical device going around earth in space. *misleading* = giving a false idea. *erupt* = release melted rock, steam, etc. *severe* = extreme. *beneficial* = good, helpful. *fertile* = favorable to the growth of plants and crops.

Think About Grammar

The boldfaced sentences in the passage are conditional sentences. These sentences contain a condition clause, sometimes called an *if* clause, which expresses a condition, and a result clause, which expresses the result of the condition.

A. Look again at the conditional sentences in the passage. For each one, underline the condition (*if*) clause once and the result clause twice. The first one has been underlined for you.

B. Mark these statements *T* for true or *F* for false.

1. __F__ The author of the passage believes that you are looking at the earth from a satellite now.

2. _____ It's possible for tornadoes to form in North America in the early summer.

3. _____ The Hawaiian islands formed because volcanoes erupted in the middle of the Pacific Ocean.

4. _____ It's possible for people to predict earthquakes now.

5. _____ The author of the passage believes that it might be possible for us to learn more about prediction of natural events.

18

Factual Conditionals; Future Conditionals

Introductory Task: Hazardous Conditions and Results

A. Work with a partner. Fill in each blank in the conditions column with the letter of the result that best completes the sentence.

<table>
<tr><td align="center">Conditions</td><td align="center">Results</td></tr>
<tr>
<td>

1. If we have a *thunderstorm*, <u>g</u>
2. If it rains heavily for several days, _____
3. If you see a funnel-shaped column of rapidly spinning wind, _____
4. If the winds of a tropical storm reach 74 miles (120 km) per hour, _____
5. If a severe snowstorm with high winds is expected, _____
6. If there is a long period with no rainfall, _____
7. If the ground is moving violently, _____
8. If a *volcano* erupts, _____

</td>
<td>

a. a *blizzard* warning will be issued.

b. a *flood* might occur.

c. the result is a *drought*.

d. a major *earthquake* is probably occurring.

e. the storm is officially classified as a *hurricane*.

f. it's probably a *tornado*.

g. we will experience hard rain with noise and flashes of lightning.

h. lava, ash, and steam come out of the ground.

</td>
</tr>
</table>

B. The sentences in Part A describe various natural events. Discuss them as a class. Which ones have you experienced? Where do or might they occur? Then use a sentence with an *if* clause to tell your classmates about a natural event they might experience in a particular place. Use the simple present in the *if* clause and use *will* or *might* in the result clause.

Example: Thunderstorms are frequent in the summer here. If you stay here in the summer, you will experience a thunderstorm. OR Major earthquakes have occurred in California. If you go to California, you might experience an earthquake.

---

hazardous = full of danger. *funnel-shaped* = with a wide top and long, narrow bottom.
tropical storm = a storm that begins in a warm-weather region. *lava* = melted rock.

Overview of Conditionals*

FORM and FUNCTION

A. Conditional Sentences

1. A conditional sentence has two clauses: an *if* clause and a result clause. The clauses can come in either order. When the *if* clause is first, use a comma between clauses.

if clause	result clause
If the sun shines,	water evaporates more quickly.

result clause	*if* clause
Water evaporates more quickly	if the sun shines.

2. A conditional sentence expresses a condition and a result: Something might happen (the condition). That will make something else happen (the result).

condition	result
If the sun shines,	water evaporates more quickly.

B. Statements

AFFIRMATIVE STATEMENTS

IF CLAUSE	RESULT CLAUSE
If it snows,	(then) we'll go skiing this weekend.

NEGATIVE STATEMENTS

IF CLAUSE	RESULT CLAUSE
If it doesn't snow,	(then) we won't go skiing.

1. The result clause can begin with *then*. There is no difference in meaning. Use *then* only if the result clause comes second.

   If the air is cold enough, **then** rain turns to snow.
   NOT: ~~Then~~ rain turns to snow if the air is cold enough.

2. The negative can be:

   - In the *if* clause.

     If it **doesn't** rain, I'll water the lawn.

   - In the result clause.

     If it rains, I **won't** water the lawn.

   - In both clauses.

     If it **doesn't** rain, the lawn **won't** get enough water.

*The example sentences are factual conditionals and future conditionals. For factual conditionals, see Grammar Briefing 2, page 350. For future conditionals, see Grammar Briefing 3, page 355. This overview also applies to unreal conditionals (Chapter 19, Grammar Briefings 1 and 2, pages 361 and 369).

(continued on next page)

C. Questions

YES/NO QUESTIONS		SHORT ANSWERS

IF CLAUSE	RESULT CLAUSE	
If it snows,	will the schools be closed?	No, they won't. OR Yes, they will.

WH- QUESTIONS

IF CLAUSE	RESULT CLAUSE
If it rains tomorrow,	when will we have the picnic?

Use question word order only in the result clause. **Will you go** if I go?

GRAMMAR PRACTICE 1

Overview of Conditionals

1 **Conditional Questions and Statements—Form:** Temperature Facts and Figures

A. Use the words given in parentheses to write *yes/no* questions, short answers, and statements in the simple present tense. Write the *if* and result clauses in the order given, in the questions and answers. Use *then* in the answers where possible. Use commas where necessary.

1. (if/you/heat/water/to 100°C) (it/boil)

   Q: _If you heat water to 100°C, does it boil_____?

   A: Yes, _it does_____. _If you heat water to 100°C, then it boils_____.

2. (water/boil) (if/you/heat/it/to 100°F)

   Q: _____?

   A: No, _____. _____.

3. (if/water/be heated/to 212°F) (it/boil)

   Q: _____?

   A: Yes, _____. _____.

4. (water/freeze) (if/its temperature/be/32°C)

   Q: _____?

   A: No, _____. _____.

B. Use the words given in parentheses to write *wh-* questions and answers in the simple present tense. In each item, write the *if* and result clauses in the order given, and use the same order in the answer. Use *then* in the answers where possible. Use commas where necessary.

1. Q: <u>What happens to water if its temperature is 32°F</u>?
   (what / happen / to water) (if / its temperature / be / 32°F)

   A: <u>Water begins to freeze if its temperature is 32°F</u>.
   (begin / to freeze)

2. Q: _____?
   (if / the temperature / be / 20°C in their classroom) (how / students / feel)

   A: _____.
   (feel / comfortable)

3. Q: _____?
   (how / students / feel) (if / the temperature / be / 20°F in their classroom)

   A: _____.
   (not / feel / at all comfortable)

4. Q: _____?
   (if / you / want / to convert temperatures from Celsius to Fahrenheit) (what / you / do)

   A: _____.
   (use / this formula: $F = 9C/5 + 32$)

> C = Celsius. F = Fahrenheit.

Factual Conditionals

FORM

A. Factual Conditional Sentences*

IF CLAUSE	RESULT CLAUSE
If you **mix** blue and yellow,	you **get** green.
If you **are** hungry,	we **should get** lunch now.
If the Indian restaurant **was** closed,	they probably **went** to the Chinese restaurant.

*For general information on the form of conditional sentences, see Grammar Briefing 1, page 347.

B. Factual Conditionals with Present Tense Verbs

Factual conditionals often have present tense verbs. The verbs may be simple and/or progressive.

If I **have** money, I **spend** it.

If they**'re skiing**, they**'re having** a good time.

If the children **are getting** tired, it**'s** time to leave.

C. Factual Conditionals with Past Tense Verbs

Factual conditionals often have past tense verbs. These may be simple and/or progressive.

The teachers always **helped** us if we **needed** help.

If he **was missing** class a lot, he **wasn't learning** much.

If I **was having** trouble with my homework, I **asked** for help.

D. Modals in Factual Conditionals

Modals can be used in:

- The *if* clause.

  We often take the five o'clock train if we <u>**can get** to the station on time</u>.

- The result clause.

  If you're leaving now, <u>**can** I **go** with you</u>?

- Both clauses.

  You <u>**should make** a lot of money if you **can work** a lot this month</u>.

(continued on next page)

E. Imperatives in Factual Conditionals

The imperative can be used in the result clause.	If you need $20, **take** it from my wallet. **Turn off** the TV if you have homework to do.

FUNCTION

A. General Truths and Habits

1. Factual conditionals can express general truths. These conditionals usually use the simple present.	If it**'s** five o'clock in New York, it**'s** two o'clock in California. If clouds **cover** the sun, then the temperature **goes** down.
2. Factual conditionals can express habits. These can be present or past habits. The simple tenses are most often used.	If I **get** up early, I **take** the eight o'clock bus to work. If I **cooked**, my roommate **washed** the dishes.
3. In factual conditionals that express general truths or habits, you can use *when* or *whenever* instead of *if*. There is little or no difference in meaning.	**When**(**ever**) it's five o'clock in New York, it's two o'clock in California. **When**(**ever**) I cooked, my roommate washed the dishes.

B. Possibility, Certainty, Ability, and Other Modal Meanings

Factual conditionals can express possibility, certainty, ability, advice, and other meanings connected with modals. These conditionals often use modals.	If he's not in his office, he **might be** at the gym. (present possibility) If he was talking on the phone all day, then he wasn't doing much work. (certainty about the past) If he **can't do** the work, you **should talk** to the teacher. (ability, advice)

C. Commands

Factual conditionals with imperatives can be used for commands.	If you're not feeling well, **stay** in bed.

Factual Conditionals

2 Factual Conditionals with Present Tense Verbs and Modals: The Nature of a Tornado

A. Combine the sentences in parentheses to form one sentence with an *if* clause and a result clause. Use the sentences in the order they are given. Decide which sentence should become which clause. Use *then* where possible. Use commas where needed.

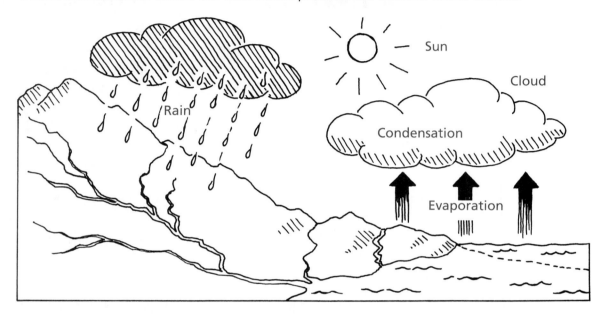

Storms occur as a result of natural processes involving the sun, air, water, and gravity. The sun heats the earth and the air around it. _Air rises if it is heated._ The sun heats the water on earth,

1 (Air rises. It is heated.)

too. _If the sun shines on water, then the water evaporates._ This means that the

2 (The sun shines on water. The water evaporates.)

water goes into the air as vapor. As warm air and the water vapor in it rise, the warm air becomes

cooler. _____

3 (The air cools. The water vapor in it condenses.)

That is, the vapor becomes tiny drops of water and forms clouds. The drops may join other drops.

_____

4 (The drops become too heavy for the air to hold. They fall to earth.)

The temperature determines the form in which the drops fall to earth.

_____

5 (The drops fall as rain. The temperature isn't below the freezing point.)

Thunderstorms occur under certain conditions.

_____

6 (A mass of warm, moist air is rising very rapidly. A thunderstorm can occur.)

Tornadoes are funnel-shaped windstorms that occur only under one condition.

_____
7 (A tornado can't occur. There is no thunderstorm.)

An area that includes Texas, Oklahoma, and Kansas is known as "Tornado Alley"

because tornadoes are most frequent there.

_____
8 (Thunderstorms are moving across Tornado Alley at this moment. A tornado is probably forming.)

Tornadoes can be extremely destructive.

_____
9 (A house is hit by a tornado. The house might explode.)

> *gravity* = the natural force that causes objects to move toward earth. *vapor* = water
> in the form of a gas. *destructive* = causing great damage; able to destroy.

B. Look at the sentences you wrote in Part A. In which sentence is it **not possible** to

use *when* in place of *if*? _____

To learn more about thunderstorms and tornadoes, click on the *Grammar Links* Website.

3 Factual Conditionals with Past Tense Verbs: The Making of a Television Meteorologist

A. In his book *Weathering the Storm*, Gary England describes his experiences growing
up in Oklahoma. Use the words given to write factual conditionals with past tense
verbs. Write the words in the order in which they are given. Decide which group of
words should become the *if* clause and which should become the result clause. Use
commas where needed.

1. Before the 1950s, people often had no warning of approaching tornadoes.

   If people didn't have warning, disasters occurred.
   _____
   (people / not / have / warning) (disasters / occur)

2. England's parents and grandparents often told stories about life in the old days.

   _____
   (he / listen / with fascination) (they / tell / stories about terrible tornadoes)

3. As a child, England learned to be cautious about severe weather. Sometimes he would see a
   thunderstorm approaching.

   _____
   (he / play / outside) (he / race / into the house)

4. In those days, weather radar and television didn't exist yet.

   _____
   (people / see / threatening clouds or tornadoes) (they / report / them to the sheriff)

5. The sheriff would then sound a warning siren.

   _____
   (everyone in England's family / run / into the cellar) (they / hear / the siren)

6. In the 1950s, TV weather forecasts began, and England could sometimes watch them.

_____
(the weatherman / predict / a snowstorm) (he / look forward / to it)

7. He spent all his time waiting for the storm.

_____
(he / be / disappointed) (the storm / not / begin / before his bedtime)

8. As soon as he woke up, he looked out the window, hoping that it was snowing.

_____
(it / snow) (he / be / very excited)

> *meteorologist* = weather scientist. *sheriff* = a kind of police officer.
> *cellar* = a storage room beneath a house.

 B. Write five sentences about what you often did in storms or other weather situations when you were a child. Use a progressive in at least one sentence.

Example: If it was snowing, I built a snowman. OR I stayed inside if it was very hot.

4 Using Factual Conditionals with Modals and Imperatives: The Weather Helpline

 A. Work with a partner. Your task is to respond to calls to the Weather Helpline. Read the situations and think of at least two factual conditionals to say in response to each one. Use the caller's last sentence to form the *if* clause and use a modal or imperative in the result clause. You can give advice or suggestions with *must, should, ought to, may, might, could,* or *can.* You can give commands with imperatives.

1. I'm outside. I can see dark clouds and lightning nearby.
   If you can see dark clouds and lightning nearby, it could be dangerous for you to be outside.
   If you can see dark clouds and lightning nearby, go inside as soon as possible.
   You shouldn't stay outside if you can see dark clouds and lightning nearby.

2. My English class starts in a few minutes. I'm in another building, so I have to walk across the campus to get to it. It's raining hard and lightning.

3. I've been on the beach in my swimming suit for a couple of hours. My skin is beginning to turn red.

4. I'm in my car on the highway, driving through a terrible rainstorm. I can't see where I'm going.

5. The weather is very cold and wet. I have a sore throat and a headache.

6. My plane is supposed to leave in two hours, so I need to drive to the airport soon. It's snowing hard.

7. The weather has been extremely hot and dry recently, and I'm worried about my garden. The flowers are turning brown.

 B. For each situation in Part A, write at least one factual conditional with a modal or imperative in the result clause.

Future Conditionals

FORM

A. Future Conditional Sentences*

IF CLAUSE	RESULT CLAUSE
If I**'m** in the neighborhood,	I**'ll stop** by to see you.
If I **have** time this weekend,	I**'m going to clean** the house.
If you **can wait** until next week,	the doctor **can see** you in the evening.

*For general information on the form of conditional sentences, see Grammar Briefing 1, page 347.

B. *If* Clause

1. In future conditionals, the *if* clause generally has a present tense verb—simple present or present progressive.

   If it **rains/is raining** tomorrow, we'll reschedule the picnic.

   If we **reschedule** the picnic, the students will be disappointed.

2. The ability modal *can* is sometimes used.

   We'll reschedule for Sunday if everyone **can come** then.

C. Result Clause

1. The result clause usually has *will* or *be going to.* (*Will* is more common than *be going to.*)

   If it rains tomorrow, we**'ll reschedule/'re going to reschedule** the picnic.

2. Instead of *will* or *be going to,* you can use:

   • Another modal.

   If I go to the picnic, **can** you **give** me a ride home?

   • An imperative.

   If you're coming to the picnic, **bring** a main dish or a dessert.

(continued on next page)

FUNCTION

A. Predictions

Future conditionals express what will happen in the future if certain conditions occur. They are therefore often used to make predictions.

| If you study for the test, you'll do well. |

B. Other Common Uses

Other common uses include:

- Plans.

  If you come when the weather is warm, we'll go to the beach.

- Offers.

  We can take you to the airport tomorrow if you need a ride.

- Suggestions and advice.

  If your boss doesn't give you a raise soon, you should talk to him.

- Requests.

  If you finish your work early today, can you help me with mine?

- Threats.

  If you don't obey the baby sitter, then you're not going to go to the party tomorrow.

- Commands.

  Lock the door if you're the last one to leave.

GRAMMAR PRACTICE 3

Future Conditionals

5 **Future Conditionals—Form:
The Hurricanes of the Future**

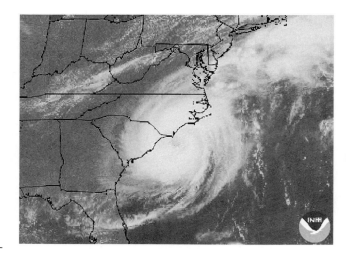

Use the words in parentheses to complete the future conditionals. You can use *will* or *be going to*.

1. The weather everywhere on Earth

   <u>will/is going to change</u>
                 (change)

   if global temperatures <u>continue</u>   to rise.
                                 (continue)

2. If the climate _____ warmer, the water in the
                           (become)

   Atlantic Ocean _____ warmer.
                      (get)

3. If the water in the Atlantic _____ warmer, hurricanes
(become)

    _____ in number and severity.
    (increase)

4. Also, hurricanes _____ more people if the population
    (affect)

    along the coastlines _____ to grow.
    (continue)

5. But people _____ injured by hurricanes if they
    (not / be)

    _____ precautions.
    (take)

6. People who live where hurricanes are common should have a weather radio which they can tune in

    at any time. They _____ warnings and
    (hear)

    instructions on the radio if a hurricane _____
    (come)

    toward land at the time they tune in.

7. If meteorologists' forecasts _____ accurate,
    (be)

    during the next hurricane season seven hurricanes _____
    (form)

    over the Atlantic.

8. To find out how the National Hurricane Center follows hurricanes, visit its website. If a hurricane

    _____ at that time, you
    (form)

    _____ satellite images of it on your computer screen.
    (be able to see)

    > *coastlines* = land areas next to the ocean. *precaution* = an action taken to guard against danger.

Visit the *Grammar Links* Website for links to information about and images of hurricanes.

6 **Future Conditionals—Uses:** If You Come Visit Me . . .

A friend or relative who lives in another place has written that she or he might be able to come visit you. The following sentences are part of your response. Complete the sentences. In each sentence, use *will* or another modal or an imperative. The content should be appropriate for the function in brackets.

1. *If you come visit me,* we'll have a great time _____.
    [prediction]

2. *If you can come when the weather is warm,* _____.
    [plan]

3. *If you want to spend a lot of time outdoors here,* _____.
    [command]

4. *If you would like to do some shopping here,* _____.
    [suggestion]

5. *If I can't be with you all the time,* _____.
   [prediction]

6. *If you need a ride from the airport,* _____.
   [offer]

7. *If you have any questions about what to expect,* _____.
   [command]

8. *If you have time,* _____?
   [request]

9. *I'm really looking forward to seeing you. If you don't come visit me,*

   _____.
   [threat]

7 Using Factual and Future Conditionals: If You Like Cold/Warm Weather . . .

International Falls, Minnesota

Average high temperature in January: 14°F
Outdoor activities:

Ice Fishing   Ice Skating   Snowmobiling   Cross-Country Skiing

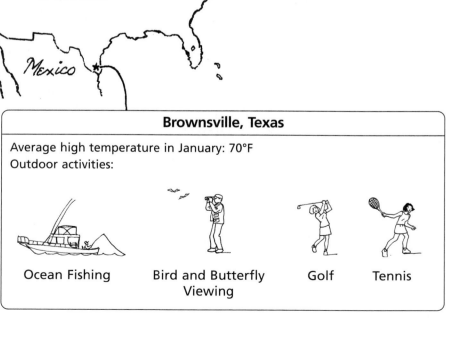

Brownsville, Texas

Average high temperature in January: 70°F
Outdoor activities:

Ocean Fishing   Bird and Butterfly Viewing   Golf   Tennis

You are a writer for IfYouGo.net, a travel and weather website. Your assignment is to write a one-paragraph article about January vacations in International Falls and Brownsville. Use the information given on page 358 and your imagination to write about the places, the weather, and what visitors can do there. Use at least five conditionals, including conditionals with modals and imperatives.

Example: If you want to take a vacation in January, then you might want to visit International Falls or Brownsville. If you like cold weather, you'll have a great time in International Falls. . . . When you're in International Falls, it's easy to visit Canada.

 See the *Grammar Links* Website for a complete model paragraph for this assignment.

 Check your progress! Go to the Self-Test for Chapter 18 on the *Grammar Links* Website.

Chapter 19

Present and Past Unreal Conditionals; *Hope* and *Wish*

Introductory Task: At Home in the Storm

A. The pairs of pictures show different situations. In the space before each sentence, write the letter of the more logical choice.

1.

2.

a. We don't have any bread.
b. It's possible that we have some bread.

3.

4.

a. It's possible that the storm is over.
b. The storm isn't over yet.

B. The sentences given in pictures 1 and 3 are factual conditionals. The sentences given in 2 and 4 are present unreal conditionals.

1. Complete the sentences with *factual* and *unreal*.

   a. In _____ conditionals, the *if* clause expresses a condition that is possible.

   b. In _____ conditionals, the *if* clause expresses a condition that is impossible, untrue, or very unlikely.

2. Complete the sentences with *present* or *past*.

   The sentences in 2 and 4 are different from those in 1 and 3 because the sentences in 2 and 4

   use _____ tense forms instead of _____ tense forms.

   But all four sentences take place in the _____ time.

GRAMMAR BRIEFING 1

Present Unreal Conditionals

FORM

A. Present Unreal Conditional Sentences*

IF CLAUSE	RESULT CLAUSE
If we **had** a car,	we **would drive** to the mall.
If I **were working** more hours at my job,	I **couldn't do** all my school work.
If I **could live** anywhere,	I **might live** near the ocean.

* For general information on the form of conditional sentences, see Chapter 18, Grammar Briefing 1, page 347.

B. *If* Clause

1. In present unreal conditionals, the *if* clause has a **past tense** verb—simple or progressive.

   > If I **knew** the answer, I would tell you.
   >
   > If I **were leaving** now, I would give you a ride.

2. *Were* is used with all persons of *be*, including first and third person singular.

   > If **I were working** on a computer, I could finish more quickly.
   >
   > If **he were** here, we could finish more quickly.

3. *Could* to express ability is sometimes used.

   > If she **could sing**, she would take voice lessons.

C. Result Clause

In the result clause, use *would*, *could*, or *might*.

> If you studied more, you **would/could/might get** better grades.

(continued on next page)

A. Talking About What Is Impossible or Unlikely in the Present

1. The *if* clause of a present unreal conditional expresses a condition that is unreal at the present time.

   The result clause tells what would happen if this condition were real.

   The sentence expresses an unreal condition and an unreal result.

   The unreal condition may be:

   - Impossible or definitely untrue.

unreal condition	unreal result

     If your grandparents were alive, they would be very proud of you.

unreal condition	unreal result

     If I were the teacher, I'd give a lot less homework.

   - Very unlikely but still possible.

unreal result	unreal condition

     Ray would call us if he were in town.

2. Instead of *would* in the result clause, you can:

   - Use *could* or *might* to say that, if the unreal condition were true, the unreal result would be only possible, not certain.

     If I had money, I **might/could travel** around the world. (a possibility if I had money)
     Compare: If I had money, I **would travel** around the world. (a definite plan if I had money)

   - Use *could* to express ability.

     If you were here, we **could talk** more.

B. Talking About What Is Impossible or Unlikely in the Future

Present unreal conditionals can be used to talk about the future. In this use, they express an unreal condition and unreal result in the future.

unreal condition	unreal result

If wars were never fought again, the world would be a much better place.

unreal condition	unreal result

If they were coming tonight, we could go to a movie. (They probably or definitely aren't coming.)

The unreal condition may be impossible or very unlikely.

Could and *might* have the same meanings as when these conditionals are used to talk about the present.

These sentences differ from future conditionals (Chapter 18, Grammar Briefing 3, page 355) because they are about what is impossible or unlikely in the future.

Compare: If they're coming tonight, we can go to a movie. (It's quite possible that they are coming.)

C. Giving Advice

Present unreal conditionals with *if I were you* are used to give advice.

If I were you, I would be more careful. (= You should be more careful.)

GRAMMAR **HOT**SPOT!

Remember! In present unreal conditionals, past forms do not express past time. They express the idea that something in the present or future is not real.

If I **asked** him for help now, he would help me. (present unreal conditional: I'm not asking him for help)
Compare: If I **asked** him for help when we worked together, he always helped me. (factual conditional: in the past I asked him for help)

TALKING THE TALK

1. In spoken English and informal writing, *would* is often contracted as *'d*.

   I'd have a talk with him if I were you.

2. In informal spoken English, *was* is sometimes used with first and third person singular subjects. This use is **not** considered acceptable in formal English.

   If he **was** a real friend, he'd be here helping you. (informal speech only)

   If he **were** a real friend, he would be here helping you.

Present Unreal Conditionals

1 **Present Unreal Conditionals—Form:**
Natural Hazards in the U.S. Pacific Region

Complete the present unreal conditionals, using the
words in parentheses. Use *might* in the result clause
where given. Use progressives where appropriate.

Mount St. Helens and Mount Rainier

1. Mount Ranier is a volcano near Seattle, Washington. If it _erupted_ without
   (erupt)

   warning, many people _would be_ in danger.
   (be)

2. Mount Ranier isn't expected to erupt soon. I _____ worried if I
   (not, feel)

   _____ near it.
   (be)

3. Mount St. Helens is another volcano in Washington. It could erupt again, so scientists are

   monitoring it continuously. People who live around it _____
   (be)

   concerned about their safety if scientists _____ it.
   (not, monitor)

4. Mount St. Helens isn't erupting now. If it _____ at this
   (erupt)

   moment, lava and mud _____ down its sides, and gases and
   (flow)

   ash _____ into the air.
   (shoot)

5. The top of Mount St. Helens is steep and icy, so climbing it is difficult. If it _____
   (be)

   easy to climb to the top, I _____ it next summer.
   (might, do)

6. More and stronger earthquakes occur in Alaska than in any other state, but Alaska isn't densely

   populated. If it _____ more densely populated, future Alaskan
   (become)

   earthquakes _____ very destructive.
   (might, be)

7. Tectonic plates are the thick pieces of solid rock that rest on the melted rock of earth's mantle.

   Two tectonic plates meet along the San Andreas Fault in California. If two tectonic plates

   _____ there, earthquakes _____ so
   (not, meet)   (not, be)

   common in that region.

8. My home is not close to the San Andreas Fault. But I _____ precautions against earthquakes if my home _____ close to it.
   (take)
   (be)

9. Tsunami are waves caused by volcanoes or earthquakes near or under the sea. If a giant tsunami _____ ashore in Hawaii, it _____ a great deal of damage.
   (come)
   (cause)

10. Tsunami, earthquakes, and volcanoes are hazards in Hawaii. If you _____ in Hawaii now, _____ you _____ the hazards?
    (vacation)
    (think about)

> *densely populated* = having many people living close together.
> *mantle* = a layer beneath the earth's surface.

2 Present Unreal Conditionals—Meaning: Visiting Hawaii's Volcanoes

Work with a partner. Read each sentence and mark the sentences that follow it *T* (true) or *F* (false).

1. If Mount Kilauea in Hawaii Volcanoes National Park weren't erupting, I wouldn't be so interested in visiting the park.

   __F__ Mount Kilauea isn't erupting.

   __T__ I'm interested in visiting the park.

2. If it were dangerous to observe the lava flows, the park rangers wouldn't let visitors do it.

   _____ It isn't dangerous to observe the lava flows.

   _____ The park rangers let visitors do it.

3. If flowing lava weren't so hot, you could touch it.

   _____ Flowing lava isn't very hot.

   _____ You can touch it.

4. The flowing lava would appear to be red if it were night.

   _____ The flowing lava doesn't appear to be red.

   _____ It's night.

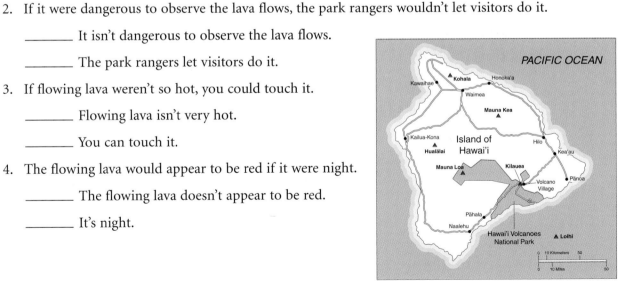

5. I might drive around the island if I had time.

_____ I definitely want to drive around the island.

_____ I don't have time to drive around the island.

6. If there weren't a "hot spot" in the earth's crust underneath Hawaii, volcanoes couldn't form new islands there.

_____ There is a "hot spot" in the earth's crust underneath Hawaii.

_____ It's possible for volcanoes to form new islands there.

> *crust* = outer layer.

3 Present Unreal Conditionals with *Would* and *Could*: Waiting to Be Rescued

Suppose that all the statements below are true. Use each pair of statements to write present unreal conditionals. Use *would* or *could* in the result clause, as appropriate. Use *could* in the *if* clause where appropriate.

1. We're trapped inside our house. We need to use our disaster supplies.

   If we weren't trapped inside our house, we wouldn't need to use our disaster supplies.

2. We don't have electricity. We can't cook.

3. We have plenty of canned food. We're not hungry.

4. We don't have hot water. I can't take a bath.

5. I have a flashlight. I can find my way in the dark.

6. Our battery-powered radio is working. We can listen to news reports.

7. We can play card games. We're not bored.

8. Our sleeping bags are keeping us warm at night. We're sleeping very well.

9. I'm prepared for disasters. I'm not worried.

4 Factual Versus Unreal Conditionals: Earthquakes

Complete the factual conditionals and unreal conditionals with the correct form of the verbs in parentheses. Use *would* in the result clause of the unreal conditionals.

A Seismologist and a Seismograph

1. The earth's crust moves. As a result, earthquakes occur. If the earth's crust <u>didn't move</u>,
(not, move)
earthquakes <u>wouldn't occur</u>.
(not, occur)

2. Seismographs are instruments used to record the movements of the earth's crust. If an earthquake <u>occurs</u>, a seismograph
(occur)
<u>records</u> its strength.
(record)

3. Seismologists study the movements of the earth's crust. I'm not a seismologist. But I

   _____ a lot about earthquakes if I
   (know)

   _____ a seismologist.
   (be)

4. Seismologists use the Richter Scale (0–9.0) to measure the intensity of earthquakes. Earthquakes

   _____ classified as "moderate" if they
   (be)

   _____ 5–5.9 on the Richter Scale.
   (measure)

5. Many very minor earthquakes occur every day. If someone _____
   (pay)

   you a dollar for every earthquake, you _____ about $9,000 per day.
   (earn)

6. People build earthquake-resistant structures in areas where earthquakes are frequent. Earthquakes

   _____ less damage if people _____
   (cause) (build)

   these structures.

7. Earthquakes are a hazard in California, so people build earthquake-resistant structures there.

   If they _____ these structures, earthquakes
   (not, build)

   _____ more damage.
   (cause)

> *earthquake-resistant* = able to withstand an earthquake without much damage.

Check out the *Grammar Links* Website for more information about volcanoes, earthquakes, and seismology.

5 Using Present Unreal Conditionals to Give Advice: Avoiding Risk

Work with a partner. For 1–5, read each situation to your partner and get your partner's advice. The advice should be phrased as *If I were you, ...* For 6–9, reverse roles.

1. A big storm just blew a power line down next to my house.

   If I were you, I wouldn't touch the power line. OR If I were you, I'd call the power company.

2. I'm outside playing soccer. Dark clouds are moving in, and I can see lightning.

3. I recently moved from Florida to Vermont, where the winters are very cold and snowy. It's October, and I don't have any warm clothes.

4. I'm driving to school through a heavy rainstorm. The underpass ahead of me is flooded.

5. I'm in Hawaii. I want to hike to the top of a volcano, but I'm not sure whether it's safe or not.

6. Because of a storm, the power has been off since yesterday. The food in my refrigerator is getting warm.

7. When I drove to school this morning, the weather was fine, but it's been snowing hard all day. Now it's time to go home. I've never driven in snow before.

8. I'm on vacation in California. I don't know what to do in case of an earthquake.

9. I want to move to a place where natural disasters are rare.

6 Using Unreal Present Conditionals: Things Would Be Different If . . .

A. Use the following statements and your own ideas to write unreal present conditionals. Include at least two conditionals with *could* or *might* in the result clauses.

1. There are thunderstorms.

   If there were no thunderstorms, parts of the earth might be very dry. OR I could spend more time playing soccer if there were no thunderstorms.

2. The weather isn't the same everywhere.

3. There are weather forecasts on the radio and television.

4. The weather isn't nice every day.

5. People talk about the weather a lot.

6. Earthquakes can't be predicted.

7. We can't control nature.

B. As a class, compare sentences.

Past Unreal Conditionals

FORM

A. Past Unreal Conditional Sentences*

IF CLAUSE	RESULT CLAUSE
If I **had known** about the concert,	I **would have gone** to it.
If he **hadn't failed** the final,	he **could have gotten** a B for the course.
If he **had been telling** the truth,	he **wouldn't have gotten** in trouble.

* For general information on the form of conditional sentences, see Chapter 18, Grammar Briefing 1, page 347.

B. *If* Clause

1. In past unreal conditionals, the *if* clause has a past perfect verb—simple or progressive.

    We would have had a better vacation if it **hadn't rained** every day.

    He wouldn't have had that accident if he **had been paying** attention.

2. *Could* to express ability is sometimes used.

    We would have been happy if they **could have come**.

C. Result Clause

In the result clause, use *would*, *could*, or *might* + *have* + a past participle.

If there hadn't been so much traffic, we **would have gotten/might have gotten** there on time.

If you had told me you needed help, I **could have helped** you.

(continued on next page)

FUNCTION

A. Talking About What Was Not Real in the Past

1. The *if* clause of a past unreal conditional expresses a condition that was not real in the past.

   The result clause tells what would have happened if the condition had been real.

   The sentence expresses an unreal condition in the past and its unreal result.

unreal condition	unreal result

   If Lou had come earlier, you would have met him. (Lou didn't come earlier, so you didn't meet him.)

unreal condition	unreal result

   If you hadn't spoken up, the situation wouldn't have changed. (You spoke up, so the situation changed.)

2. Instead of *would* in the result clause, you can:

   - Use *could* or *might* to express that the result would have been possible, instead of certain.

     If you had explained things to your boss, she **could/might have changed** her mind.

   - Use *could* to express ability.

     If I had studied algebra, I **could have solved** those problems.

B. Expressing Regret

Because they are about what could have happened but didn't happen, past unreal conditionals often express regret.

If I had studied, I could have done a lot better in school.

If the car hadn't been in the repair shop, we could have helped you with your move.

GRAMMAR **HOT**SPOT!

Although some native speakers use *would* in the *if* clause, this is considered incorrect.

If you **had told** me, I would have done something. **NOT**: If you ~~would have~~ told me, I would have done something.

Past Unreal Conditionals

7 Past Unreal Conditionals—Form: The Dust Bowl

Use the words in parentheses to complete the past unreal conditionals. Use *could* or *might* where given.

In the 1930s, an environmental disaster occurred in the southwestern Great Plains. This area became known as the Dust Bowl. In the 1920s, the price of wheat was very high. If the price for wheat __hadn't been__ so high, thousands of

1 (not, be)

people __wouldn't have moved__ to the Great Plains to start farms. In the 1920s,

(not, move)

a great deal of rain fell in the region. If the rainfall __hadn't been__

2 (not, be)

unusually good, people __might have known__ not to start farms there.

(might / know)

A terrible drought began in 1931. This drought _____ such

3 (not, have)

serious consequences if the farmers _____ the land more carefully. If the

(manage)

farmers _____ the natural grass to grow wheat, the soil

4 (not, plow up)

_____ so dry. If the farmers _____ trees

(not, get)   5 (plant)

around their farms, they _____ the soil from the wind.

(could / protect)

Terrible windstorms began in 1932. These storms blew the soil away and

were dangerous to people's health. You _____

6 (might / get)

"dust pneumonia" if you _____ in the Dust

(live)

Bowl. The dust blew all the way across the country. If you

_____ in New York City on May 21, 1934,

7 (be)

you _____ huge clouds of dust in the air.

(could / see)

The farms in the Dust Bowl were ruined. In the 1930s, the United States experienced economic depression.

If the economy _____ better, the situation in the Dust Bowl

8 (be)

_____ so tragic. Thousands of farmers moved to California. If the

(not, be)

government _____ jobs to many who stayed, they

9 (not, give)

_____. Finally, in the late 1930s, rain began to fall again.

(might / starve)

Colorado   Kansas

New Mexico   Oklahoma

Texas

economic depression = a period of severe decline in the economy, with many people unemployed.

 Visit the *Grammar Links* Website to learn more about the Dust Bowl.

8 Present Versus Past Unreal Conditionals: The Weather Here and There, Then and Now

Use the information given to complete the present and past unreal conditionals.

1. We had a heat wave last summer. The heat was unbearable, so I bought a new air conditioner.

   If the heat __hadn't been_____ unbearable, I __wouldn't have bought_____

   a new air conditioner.

2. It's extremely dry here. We're having a drought, so the grass isn't green. If we

   _____ a drought, the grass _____ green.

3. An ice storm broke all the power lines last winter. Some people didn't have electricity, so they had

   to go to emergency shelters to keep warm. If they _____ electricity,

   they _____ go to the shelters.

4. It's been raining for days, and houses near the river are being flooded. My house isn't near the

   river, so it isn't full of water. If my house _____ near the river, it

   _____ full of water.

5. This thunderstorm is violent and dangerous. The storm isn't over, so it isn't safe to go outside.

   If the storm _____ over, it _____ safe to

   go outside.

6. After the blizzard last month, we couldn't leave our house for three days. We didn't run out of

   food because I went to the store before the storm started. We _____

   food if I _____ to the store before the storm started.

7. A hurricane was moving in this direction last summer. It didn't come ashore, so it didn't cause a

   lot of damage. If it _____ ashore, it _____

   a lot of damage.

9 Past Unreal Conditionals: Weather Pleasures

Suppose that all the statements below are true. Use each pair of statements to write past unreal conditionals. Use *would* in the result clause except where *could* is given.

1. We swam across the lake so often because the weather was unusually hot.

   We wouldn't have swum across the lake so often if the weather hadn't been unusually hot.

2. You could skate on the pond all winter because the ice didn't melt.

3. The vegetables in our garden grew so fast because it rained every afternoon last summer.

4. People could go skiing in the park because the snow was so deep.

5. We could fly kites because the wind was blowing so hard.

6. I sat by the fire drinking cocoa and reading because I couldn't get to my office.

7. I got to know my neighbors because they needed help after the storm.

10 **Past Unreal Conditionals—Meaning:** Johnstown, Pennsylvania, 1889

Listen to the description of a disaster. You will hear each item twice. Decide whether the written statement given for an item is similar in meaning to what you heard. If it is similar, mark it with an *S*; if it is different, mark it with a *D*.

In 1852, a dam was built across the Little Conemaugh River, 15 miles above Johnstown, Pennsylvania. Thirty years later, the dam and the lake created by it were sold to new owners. These owners wanted to develop the lake into a fishing resort for people on vacation.

1. __*S*__ The fish didn't escape because wire screens were installed in front of the lake's natural outlets.

2. _____ The screens didn't become filled with dirt and plants, so the water could go through them.

3. _____ The water wasn't able to go through the screens, so it created a lot of pressure on the dam.

4. _____ The dam was strong because they repaired it properly.

5. _____ It didn't rain very hard in the spring of 1889, so the lake didn't overfill.

6. _____ People in Johnstown had been warned about the danger of flood often, so they didn't pay attention to the warning they got on May 31, 1889.

7. _____ People jumped onto the pile in front of the bridge, so they had a chance to survive.

8. _____ The pile didn't burst into flames, so hundreds of lives were saved.

9. _____ The deadliest flood in American history wasn't avoided because people didn't pay attention to the warnings.

> *dam* = wall built across a river to create a lake.

11 **Expressing Regret with Past Unreal Conditionals:** If I Had Known . . .

Use your own ideas to complete the past unreal conditionals. Use *would*, *could*, and *might* at least once each in the result clauses. Use commas where needed.

1. If I had known about your problem , I would have tried to help you. OR I might have been able to think of a solution. OR I could have helped you solve it.

2. If I had had more time yesterday _____

3. I might have gotten a better grade _____

4. If I had been more careful _____

5. I could have gone to the party _____

6. If I hadn't made a mistake _____

7. I would have felt better _____

8. I might not have had a problem _____

9. Would things have turned out differently for me _____

12 Using Past Unreal Conditionals: My Life Might Have Been Different If . . .

 A. Write four true statements about important events or situations in your life in the past. Then write a past unreal conditional sentence about each of the events or situations.

   Example: When I was six years old, my family got a piano. If my family hadn't gotten a piano, I wouldn't have been able to take music lessons.

B. Write four true statements about things that you didn't do or that didn't happen to you. Then write a past unreal conditional sentence about each thing.

   Example: I didn't study enough for the entrance examination. If I had studied enough, I wouldn't have had to take it again.

GRAMMAR BRIEFING 3

Sentences with *Hope* or *Wish*
■ Overview; Sentences with *Hope*

FORM and FUNCTION

A. Overview

1. Sentences with *hope* and sentences with *wish* express desires. The difference is:

   • Sentences with *hope*, like real conditionals, are about what is possible.

   | I **hope** Mary is here. (Mary might be here.) |

   • Sentences with *wish*, like unreal conditionals, are about what is impossible or highly unlikely.

   | I **wish** Mary were here. (Mary isn't here.) |

2. These sentences have a main clause followed by a noun clause that can begin with *that*. (For noun clauses, see Chapter 20.)

   main clause   noun clause
   I hope (that) I did well on the test.

   main clause   noun clause
   I wish (that) I had done well on the test.

B. Sentences with *Hope*

Sentences with *hope* express desires that something that is possible did happen, is happening, or will happen.

The verb forms used correspond to the time the hope is about.

I hope you **were having** a good time.

I hope he**'s enjoying** his vacation now.

I hope you**'ll be able to get** a lot done tomorrow.

(continued on next page)

■ Sentences with *Wish*

A. Sentences About the Present

In wishes about the present, you can use:

• A past tense verb—simple or progressive. (Use *were* with all persons of *be*.)	He wishes (that) he **had** more money. We wish (that) she **were spending** more time with us.
• *Could* to express ability.	I wish (that) I **could be** with you now.

B. Sentences About the Future

In wishes about the future, you can use:

• *Would*.	It never snows here—I wish it **would snow** this winter.
• *Could* to express ability.	I wish I **could study** full time next semester.
• *Were going to*.	They wish he **weren't going to miss** the party.
• The past progressive.	I wish I **were taking** a trip this summer.

C. Sentences About the Past

In wishes about the past, you can use:

• The past perfect.	We wish you **had been** there. I wish I **hadn't said** that.
• *Could have* to express ability.	I wish I **could have helped** you.

A. Sentences About the Present or Future

1. Sentences about the present or future express a desire for something that is impossible or unlikely.	I wish I could earn more money soon. (The speaker sees this as impossible or unlikely.) *Compare*: I hope I can earn more money soon. (The speaker sees this as possible.)
2. Sometimes they express:	
• A complaint.	I wish my neighbor would stop playing the piano.
• A regret.	I wish I could go on the trip with you.

(continued on next page)

B. Sentences About the Past

Sentences about the past express a desire for a situation that did not occur. They often express regrets.	I wish that I'd traveled a lot when I was young. (I didn't, and I regret it.) I wish I hadn't spent so much money. (I did, and I regret it.)

Sentences with *Hope* or *Wish*

13 **Sentences with *Hope* and *Wish*:** Delayed Due to Weather

Use the information given to complete the sentences with *hope* and *wish*.

1. a. Maybe the weather is good there. I hope *(that) the weather is good there* _____ .

   b. The weather isn't good there. I wish *(that) the weather were good there* _____ .

2. a. Maybe he's having a good time. I hope _____ .

   b. He isn't having a good time. I wish _____ .

3. a. Maybe the storm will end soon. I hope _____ .

   b. The storm won't end soon. I wish _____ .

4. a. Maybe his plane can take off soon. I hope _____ .

   b. His plane can't take off soon. I wish _____ .

5. a. Maybe he's coming home tomorrow. I hope _____ .

   b. He isn't coming home tomorrow. I wish _____ .

6. a. Maybe he heard the forecast. I hope _____ .

   b. He didn't hear the forecast. I wish _____ .

14 *Hope* and *Wish* About the Present and Future: Natural Disasters Make TV News

Complete the sentences by using the information given. Where more than one form is possible, use any appropriate form.

Hurricane on the Coast of Texas

Reporter: The hurricane is approaching your home. How do you feel about this?

Resident: Well, of course, I wish that the hurricane ___weren't approaching___ my home. But it's
1
possible that my house won't be badly damaged.

Reporter: I hope that your house ___won't be badly damaged___. The emergency officials are going to ask
2
everyone to go to a shelter soon.

Resident: I wish they ___weren't going to ask___ everyone to go. I'm not ready.
3

Reporter: It seems that the eye of the hurricane, with the strongest winds around it, will come ashore here.

Resident: That doesn't sound good. I wish that the eye of the hurricane

_____ ashore here.
4

Reporter: Unfortunately, we can't control hurricanes.

Resident: Right now I wish that we _____
5
them. But maybe I'll be able to come back home soon.

Reporter: I hope that you _____ back home soon.
6
Good luck!

Flood in Ohio

Reporter: As a result of heavy rain, the river has flowed over its banks, causing serious flooding. Is the water level going down now?

Resident: No, it isn't. I wish that it _____ now, because the first floor of my house
7
is covered with water.

Reporter: Do you have flood insurance?

Resident: No, I don't. I wish that I _____ flood insurance. But that's not my only
8
problem. My cat is lost. Maybe she's in a safe place, though.

Reporter: I hope that your cat _____ in a safe place. . . . It's possible that the
9
president will make disaster aid available.

Resident: That's good news. I hope that the president _____ disaster aid available
10
soon, so we can clean up and repair the damage.

Reporter: Unfortunately, floods happen often along this river. Of course, we wish that they

_____ so often. But whenever they happen, we'll be here to give you
11
the news.

Blizzard in Baltimore

Reporter: This evening I'm talking to people about the blizzard that's headed toward Baltimore. It's going to snow very hard.

Snowplow Operator: I wish it _____ very hard. Because of this storm,
12
I can't spend the evening with my family.

Reporter: Big storms can really disrupt family life. Notice how crowded this supermarket is.

Shopper: I wish it _____ so crowded.
13

Reporter: Let's find out how your son feels about the storm.

Child: I'm looking forward to it. But it isn't snowing now. I wish it _____.
14

Reporter: The storm won't start until later this evening.

Child: I wish the storm _____ soon. If we get a lot of snow, school will be
15
canceled.

Reporter: I see. The blizzard won't be a disaster for the children of Baltimore!

---

15 *Hope* and *Wish* About the Past: Talking About the News

Complete the sentences by using the correct forms of the words in parentheses to express wishes or hopes about the past.

Vicky: Did you watch television last night?

Joe: No, I didn't, because I had to work. I wish I __had had__ a chance to watch television
1 (have)

last night. I hope I __didn't miss__ anything important.
2 (not, miss)

Vicky: You missed a news program about natural disasters. I wish I _____
3 (know)

how they were going to present the stories. If I had known, I wouldn't have watched.

Joe: What do you mean? How did they present the stories?

Vicky: The reporters kept making the situations as dramatic as possible. I wish they

_____ asking people to talk about their feelings. First, they
4 (not, keep)

interviewed a man in Texas. I hope that hurricane _____ his house.
5 (not, destroy)

Then they interviewed a woman in Ohio. She was really upset because her house was flooded

and she'd lost her cat. She probably wishes she _____ about
6 (not, have to talk)

her problems on national television.

Joe: I hope the poor woman _____ her cat.
7 (find)

Vicky: Then they talked to people about a blizzard that hadn't even started yet. Of course, I hope the

blizzard _____ serious problems, but the report was really silly. I
8 (not, cause)

wish you _____ it. Why do you think reporters try to make the
9 (could, see)

weather news so dramatic?

Joe: They know that if the weather news is dramatic, more people watch television.

16 Using *Hope* and *Wish*: Questions and Answers

A. Use the words given to write questions.

1. What is something that you wish/you/experience/in the past?

   What is something that you wish you had experienced in the past?

2. What is something that you/hope/happen/yesterday?

   _____

3. What is something that you/wish/happen/yesterday?

   _____

4. What is something that you hope/not/happen/now?

   _____

5. What do you wish that you/do/now?

   _____

6. What is something that you hope/happen/soon?

   _____

7. What do you wish that you/do/tomorrow?

   _____

B. Work with a partner. Ask your partner the questions you wrote in Part A. Your partner answers, beginning each answer with *I wish* or *I hope*.

   Example: Student A: What is something that you wish you had experienced in the past?
   Student B: I wish that I had seen Brazil win the World Cup in 2002.

17 Using Unreal Conditionals, *Hope*, and *Wish*: What Are Your Regrets? What Are Your Dreams?

We all have regrets about the past. We also have fantasies about how our lives might be different in the present and future. Write two paragraphs.

1. In the first paragraph, tell about something that you did or didn't do that you now regret. Use *wish* and past unreal conditionals.

Example: When I was in high school, I got a job at a fast-food restaurant in order to earn money to buy a car. I spent every night at work. Now I wish I hadn't spent those nights at work. I wish I had spent that time studying. If I had had more time to study, I might have gotten much better grades. I could have taken advanced chemistry and physics if I hadn't been serving fried chicken until midnight every night.

2. In the second paragraph, tell about your hopes and wishes, including those that seem impossible, for the present and future. Use *hope*, *wish*, and present and future unreal conditionals.

Example: I'm happy with my life, but I sometimes wish that it were different. For example, I often wish that I were rich. If I were rich, my life would be easier. . . . I have dreams about the future, too. I wish that I could become a famous musician. If I could become a famous musician, I would give concerts all over the world. . . . I hope that at least some of my wishes come true.

 See the *Grammar Links* Website for complete model paragraphs for this assignment.

 **Check your progress! Go to the Self-Test for Chapter 19 on the *Grammar Links* Website.**

Wrap-up Activities

1 **A Disastrous Prediction:** EDITING

Correct the nine errors in the following passage. There are errors in conditional sentences and in sentences with *wish* and *hope*. Some errors can be corrected in more than one way. The first error is corrected for you.

In 1811–1812, the small town of New Madrid, Missouri, was the center of some of the biggest earthquakes ever recorded in the United States. ~~When~~ If the area had been densely populated then, the earthquakes would have caused great devastation. The shock waves from the earthquakes traveled for hundreds of miles. If you had lived in Boston at the time, you could of felt them. The area around New Madrid is still a dangerous earthquake zone. If the area wasn't so dangerous, people who live there might not take earthquake predictions so seriously.

In 1989, Iben Browning, a business consultant, made this announcement: "If my calculations are correct there is a 50 percent chance of a destructive earthquake striking New Madrid on December 3, 1990." Because many people believed that Browning had predicted previous earthquakes, hundreds of news reporters went to New Madrid. One reporter said, "If an earthquake will occur, it will be the best-recorded event in Missouri history. If nothing happens, people's reaction to the prediction will make an interesting news story." New Madrid experienced an "earthquake hysteria." Thousands of people bought disaster supplies, many residents decided to spend the week elsewhere, and the schools closed.

December 3 came and went. No earthquake occurred. Many people blamed the reporters for the hysteria. A physicist said, "Browning had not accurately predicted previous earthquakes. The reporters would have found this out if they would have investigated. Earthquakes cannot be predicted. I wish we can predict them!" Red Cross officials were glad that the prediction raised awareness about earthquakes, but they wished the hysteria wouldn't have happened. A government official said, "I hope an earthquake wouldn't ever come. But now we will be better prepared if one comes."

2 The Chain Reactions Game: SPEAKING

Step 1 Play this game as a class. Use your imagination to describe the possible results of the past unreal conditions given in the box. One student gives a result for the first condition. Then the next student changes that result into a condition and gives a result for it. Continue until everyone has contributed a sentence to the chain of events.

Example: Student A: *If it had snowed yesterday, I wouldn't have come to class.*
Student B: *If I hadn't come to class, I would have spent the day at home.*
Student C: *If I had spent the day at home, I might have baked a cake.*
Student D: *If I had baked a cake, . . .*

> 1. If it had snowed yesterday, . . .
> 2. If I had been alive a hundred years ago, . . .
> 3. If everyone in our class had gone to Hawaii last month, . . .

Step 2 To continue the game, think of your own conditions to start the chain of events.

3 A Guide to Disaster Preparation: WRITING

Step 1 Work in small groups. Each group should choose a natural disaster, for example, hurricanes or earthquakes. Get information from the library or the Internet about preparing for that kind of disaster.

Step 2 Write a one-page guide to inform your classmates about how to prepare for the disaster and advise them about where to go and what to do if it occurs or is about to occur. Use at least five factual conditionals.

Example: *If you live in an area with earthquakes, remove all heavy objects from high shelves. If you leave these objects on shelves, they might fall during an earthquake and injure someone. . . . If an earthquake occurs, do not go outside.*

 For links to information on disaster preparation, see the *Grammar Links* Website. See the *Grammar Links* Website for a complete model guide for this activity.

4 A Disaster Movie: WRITING/SPEAKING

Step 1 Work in groups of three. Write a script for a dramatic scene in a movie about a volcano eruption, a tornado, a blizzard, or any other natural disaster. The scene should include a part for each member of the group. Use each of the following at least once: *hope*, *wish*, future conditionals, present unreal conditionals, and past unreal conditionals.

Example:
Sabrina: *I wish we hadn't climbed to the top of the volcano. I hope it doesn't erupt before we can escape.*
Shinji: *If the helicopter can land here, it might be able to rescue us. . . .*

Step 2 Present your scene to the class.

 See the *Grammar Links* Website for a complete model scene for this activity.

Noun Clauses

TOPIC FOCUS
Popular Fiction

UNIT OBJECTIVES

- **noun clauses with *that***
  (I think *that those stories are by Agatha Christie.*)

- **noun clauses with *wh-* words**
  (She wonders *when they will fall in love.*)

- **noun clauses with *if/whether***
  (Can you tell me *if/whether you have the new Catherine Coulter romance?*)

- **quoted speech and reported speech**
  (Brent said, *"I'm in love with Katie."* Brent said *that he was in love with Katie.*)

- **changes in reported speech**
  (I'm leaving and I'll be there tomorrow. ➔ He said that *he was leaving* and *he would* be *here today.*)

- **reported questions, commands, and requests**
  (David asked *if we had homework.* The teacher told us *to write a paper.* Tanya asked us *to help her.*)

Grammar in Action

🎧 Reading and Listening: Explaining Popular Fiction

Read and listen to this lecture about popular fiction.

In almost any bookstore, you'll see a large Fiction/Literature section. You'll probably also see **(that) many works of fiction are in other sections instead**. These sections have labels such as *Romance*, *Mystery*, *Science Fiction*, *Horror*, and *Westerns*. You might wonder **how these books are different from the books you find under *Fiction/Literature***.

The answer is **that these books belong to genres** (pronounced JAHN-ruhz), types of fiction that follow certain formulas, or rules. If you pick up an unfamiliar novel from the Fiction/Literature section, you won't know **what kind of story it tells**. But if you pick up a novel from the Romance section, you can be pretty sure **that it's about a young woman who falls in love**. The reason is **that books in the romance genre almost always follow a certain formula**.

That genre fiction is popular is something no one would question. Booksellers say **that two-thirds of *all* books sold are genre fiction**. In fact, another name for genre fiction is "popular fiction."

However, experts wonder **why genre fiction is so popular**. Experts also wonder **whether books based on formulas can be considered literature the way, for example, Shakespeare's plays are literature**.

The first question might not be very hard to answer. A careful look at genre fiction shows **that it's like real life but much better**. The hero, man or woman, of a work of genre fiction has an important goal—whether it's to save the world from creatures from outer space, find the murderer before he strikes again, or marry the handsome millionaire. Readers are afraid **that the hero will fail**. When they close the book for the last time, they are relieved and gratified **that the hero has succeeded**. They care about **what happens to the hero** because they can identify with the hero and his or her goal. The second question is probably a harder one. See **if you can come up with an answer**.

---

work of fiction = a book that tells a story based on the imagination, not fact.
novel = a book-length work of fiction. *relieved* = not worried anymore.
gratified = pleased, satisfied. *identify with* = feel sympathy for.

Think About Grammar

A. Look at the pair of sentences from the lecture. Complete the statements that follow with words from the box.

noun phrase

a. In almost any bookstore, you'll see **a large Fiction/Literature section**.

noun clause

b. You'll probably also see **that many works of fiction are in other sections instead**.

| a clause   a subject and a verb   a word such as *that*   the object of a verb |

1. A noun clause functions like a noun or a noun phrase, because it can be, for example,

   _____.

2. A noun clause is _____ because it includes _____.

   It is linked to the rest of the sentence with _____.

B. Look at each boldfaced noun clause in the lecture and circle the word that it begins with. List these words. (List each word just once.)

that _____   _____   _____

_____   _____   _____

C. There are three types of noun clauses: *that*, *wh-*, and *if/whether*. Write two examples of each from the lecture.

1. *that* noun clauses: that many works of fiction are in other sections instead _____

   _____

2. *wh-* noun clauses: _____

   _____

3. *if/whether* noun clauses: _____

   _____

20

Noun Clauses

Introductory Task: Judging a Book by Its Cover

A. Look at the four book covers. What kinds of stories do these books tell? Each of the sentences with a noun clause on page 387 is about one of the books. Write the number of the book that the sentence is about.

Book 1

Book 2

Book 3

Book 4

1. I think

    a. that this book is a horror story. ____4____

    b. that this book is a mystery. _____

    c. that this book is a romance. _____

    d. that this book is science fiction. _____

2. She is telling him

    a. that they must report what they've seen to the commander of the Space Fleet. _____

    b. that she knows that he prefers someone from his own social class. _____

    c. that, if he knows anything about the crime, he'd better talk now. _____

    d. that he can't make her into a monster like him. _____

3. The reader will keep turning the pages to find out

    a. whether the man and woman will discover each other's true feelings. _____

    b. whether the murderer will be caught. _____

    c. whether people will learn the truth before creatures from another planet take over the world. _____

    d. whether the unnatural evil that has lasted for centuries will be destroyed. _____

B. Compare answers in a group. What other ideas do you have about these books from their covers? Which one of these books do you think that you'd like to read? Why? Discuss these questions. Use *I think that . . .* and *I think that I'd read . . . because . . . .*

Example: I think that she becomes a prisoner in his castle. . . . I think that I'd read the horror story because I like to feel scared. . . .

GRAMMAR BRIEFING 1

Overview of Noun Clauses

FORM and FUNCTION

A. Sentence and Clause Structure

MAIN CLAUSE	NOUN CLAUSE			
		SUBJECT	VERB	
He realizes	that	the work	isn't	easy.
I wonder	where	they	are going.	
We don't know	if	she	arrived	yet.

(continued on next page)

A. Sentence and Clause Structure (continued)

1. A noun clause occurs in a sentence with a main clause.

main
clause   noun clause
I think **that the movie started**.

2. Like any clause, a noun clause must have a subject and a verb.

subject   verb
I think that **the movie started**.

3. Noun clauses begin with:

- *That* (see Grammar Briefing 2, page 390).

I think **that** the movie started.

- A *wh-* word (see Grammar Briefing 3, page 394).

I don't know **when** the movie started.

- *If* or *whether* (see Grammar Briefing 4, page 397).

I wonder **if/whether** the movie started.

B. Uses of Noun Clauses

1. Like nouns, noun clauses can be used as:

- Subjects.

What she said isn't true.

- Subject complements.

My opinion is **that they won't care**.

- Objects of verbs.

I **wonder** **whether they are coming**.

- Objects of prepositions.

I will think **about** **how you can help us**.

2. Noun clauses can follow certain adjectives.

I am **sure** **that they talked to her**.

3. The verbs and adjectives that noun clauses follow usually express mental activities or feelings.* (For lists of these verbs and adjectives, see Grammar Briefing 2, page 390.)

We **agree/feel/think** that you should come with us.

I am **afraid/angry/convinced/surprised** that he didn't tell them about our plans.

*Noun clauses also follow verbs that report speech— for example, *say*, *ask*, and *tell* (see Chapter 21).

GRAMMAR **HOT**SPOT!

Do not confuse *that* noun clauses with adjective clauses with *that*. Noun clauses can occur where nouns occur. Adjective clauses modify, and follow, nouns.

I **know that the restaurant is good**. (noun clause; object of verb *know*)

I'm looking for a **restaurant that is good**. (adjective clause; modifies noun *restaurant*)

Overview of Noun Clauses

1 **Identifying Noun Clauses and Their Uses:** Two Views of Popular Fiction

A. Work with a partner. Read the following letters sent to a literary magazine. Underline each noun clause (*that, wh-, if/whether*) and circle the word that introduces it. (Remember: Do not confuse noun clauses with adjective clauses.) Including the examples, there are 11 noun clauses.

Dear Editor:

I am extremely disappointed (that) you included an article about genre fiction in your magazine last month. (That) this inclusion is inappropriate is obvious to any serious reader.

A literary magazine is supposed to be about literature—written works of art. Literature is fiction that is original and uses poetic language. With literature, you must read carefully and think about whether you understand the meaning.

It is clear that genre fiction is the opposite of literature. Genre fiction just follows formulas: for example, boy meets girl, and boy and girl fall in love and get married. Reading genre fiction is like watching TV.

My position is that you should stick to literature from now on.

Professor Harold Burton

Dear Editor:

As a writer of genre fiction, I feel that I must respond to Professor Burton.

First, 90 percent of all new fiction published is genre fiction. I don't know why the professor wants us to ignore 90 percent of all new fiction.

Second, I'm not sure if any fiction is fully original. Even Shakespeare got most of his stories from other sources!

Third, genre fiction deals with the same issues that the greatest works of literature deal with. Undoubtedly, the professor admires Dostoyevsky's *Crime and Punishment.* Doesn't he realize that mysteries are about crime and punishment?

Finally, I don't understand why the professor thinks watching TV is so bad. Perhaps he's a snob. That TV and genre fiction can bring people pleasure seems obvious and important.

Lydia Burgess

> *literary magazine* = a magazine with literature and articles about literature. *Crime and Punishment* = a famous novel by nineteenth-century Russian writer Fyodor Dostoyevsky.

B. Look at the noun clauses that you underlined in Part A. Label the function of each noun clause: *S* (= subject); *O* (= object); *O Prep* (= object of preposition); *SC* (= subject complement); *adj + NC* (= noun clause following adjective).

Example:

        adj + NC

   I am extremely disappointed (that) you included an article about genre fiction in your magazine last month.

Noun Clauses with *That*

FORM and FUNCTION

A. Structure of Noun Clauses with *That*

MAIN CLAUSE	NOUN CLAUSE	
	(*THAT*)	
I think	(**that**)	**this book will be interesting.**
I am sure	(**that**)	**class is canceled tomorrow.**

Noun clauses with *that* are introduced with the word *that*. *That* can usually be omitted.	We hope **that you will come.** = We hope **you will come.**

B. Uses of Noun Clauses with *That*

1. Noun clauses with *that* can be the subject of a sentence.

   That he's late doesn't surprise me.

   However, usually *it* is put in subject position and the *that* clause is put at the end of the sentence.

   It doesn't surprise me (**that**) he's late.

   The only time *that* **cannot** be omitted is when the noun clause is in subject position.

   NOT: ~~He's late~~ doesn't surprise me.

2. *That* noun clauses can be subject complements.

   The truth is (**that**) she's not a very happy person.

3. *That* noun clauses can be the object of the verb.

   I **hope** (**that**) <u>you'll like my friends</u>.

   Verbs that can be followed by *that* clauses include:

agree	doubt	guess	imagine	realize	show	understand
believe	feel	hear	know	remember	suppose	
decide	forget	hope	notice	see	think	

4. *That* noun clauses can follow an adjective.

   I'm **happy** (<u>that</u>) <u>you like my friends</u>.

   Adjectives that can be followed by *that* clauses include:

afraid	certain	glad	positive	sure
angry	convinced	happy	sad	surprised
aware	disappointed	pleased	sorry	worried

1. Unlike other noun clauses, a *that* clause **cannot** be the object of a preposition. Omit the preposition if possible or use a gerund phrase instead.

> I **heard** that they have problems. OR I heard **about** their having problems.
> **NOT**: I heard about ~~they have problems~~.

2. Be careful! Some verbs are used with gerunds and/or infinitives but not with noun clauses.

> I **want** you **to help** me.
> **NOT**: I want ~~that you help me~~.

3. If the main clause verb is past tense, the noun clause:

   • Has a past tense verb if the action of the main clause and the noun clause occur at the same time.

> Around noon, I suddenly **realized** that she **wasn't** with us.
> **NOT**: Around noon, I suddenly realized that she ~~isn't~~ with us.

   • Has *would* or *was/were going to* if the action of the noun clause occurs after that of the main clause.

> I **didn't think** that we **would find** her.
> **NOT**: I didn't think that we ~~will~~ find her.

GRAMMAR PRACTICE 2

Noun Clauses with *That*

2 *That* Noun Clauses—Form: The Rules of the Game

Use the words in parentheses to complete the sentences with *that* clauses. Include *that*. Use appropriate tenses.

It's obvious <u>that each genre has its own formula, or "rules"</u>. For mysteries, a main rule is
  1 (each genre / have / its own formula, or "rules")

_____—for example, a murder. When readers begin
  2 (the crime / must / be / important)

a mystery book, they know _____ but also "red
  3 (they / find / clues)

herrings," or false clues.

   It's equally obvious, however, _____.
  4 (all genres / share / certain rules)

An important shared rule is authenticity: Even minor details must seem vivid and real. One well-

known publisher of Westerns often refused to publish books because he felt

_____. In many cases, he actually
  5 (they / not / be / authentic enough)

thought _____, but he was disappointed
  6 (the books / be / good)

_____.
  7 (he / not / "smell the gunsmoke")

> *authenticity* = seeming real. *publish* = print and sell books.

3 **Forming Sentences with *That* Clauses: And Then There Are Subgenres—
A Tale of Two Detectives**

A. Combine the two sentences to form a sentence with a *that* clause. When possible, write the sentence in two ways. Include *that*. Do not omit any words other than *this*.

Every genre can be divided into subgenres.

1. For example, readers of mysteries know **this**. There are "classic" mysteries and "hard-boiled" mysteries.

   For example, readers of mysteries know that there are "classic" mysteries and "hard-boiled" mysteries.

2. **This** is a well-known fact. There are great differences between the two kinds of mysteries.

   It is a well-known fact that there are great differences between the two kinds of mysteries.

   That there are great differences between the two kinds of mysteries is a well-known fact.

3. One of the first things a reader notices is **this**. The tone of the writing is very different.

4. The reader of classic mysteries, like Agatha Christie's, expects **this**. The crime will take place in an upper-class setting, like a mansion in England.

5. The detective in these mysteries, for example, Christie's Hercule Poirot, knows **this**. He'll be able to solve the crime through logical thinking.

6. **This** is usually the case. The classic detective is an amateur with an interest in crime.

7. Experts have shown **this**. The hard-boiled mystery developed in the United States as authors tried to write more authentically about crime.

8. The reader of hard-boiled mysteries expects **this**. The action will occur in the streets of a city and will involve tough "lowlifes" as well as the rich.

9. The detective, like Raymond Chandler's Philip Marlowe, is a professional who knows **this**.
   He may need to use his weapon as well as his brains.

10. **This** doesn't surprise me. Many people read one kind of mystery but not the other.

---

tone = sound, style. *mansion* = a very large house, usually of a rich person. *amateur* = not a professional. *lowlife* = someone who does not have a good moral character.

B. Work with a partner. Read the following quotes. Two are from a hard-boiled detective novel by Raymond Chandler. Two are from classic detective stories by Agatha Christie. Use the tips in the box to discuss which quotes are from which author and why you think this. Use noun clauses after verbs such as *think*, *believe*, *agree*, *decide*, and *doubt* and after adjectives such as *certain*, *convinced*, and *sure*. When you have decided, compare answers with your classmates.

Example: I (don't) think that the quote in *a* is from a hard-boiled detective book because the woman seems . . . and because . . . I (don't) agree that the quotes in *a* and *b* are by the same writer, because I'm convinced that . . .

a. I [the detective] went on up the street and parked and walked back. In the daylight it seemed an exposed and dangerous thing to do. . . . She stood there straight and silent against the locked front door. One hand went up to her teeth and her teeth bit at her funny thumb. There were purple smears under her eyes.

b. "So you're tough tonight," Eddie Mars' voice said.
"Big, fast, tough, and full of prickles. What can I do for you?" [said the detective.]
"Cops over there—you know where. You keep me out of it?"
"Why should I?"
"I'm nice to be nice to, soldier. I'm not nice not to be nice to."
"Listen hard and you'll hear my teeth chattering."

c. "Mrs. Robinson did not seem to notice anything amiss. Very curious, is it not? Did she impress you as being a truthful woman, Hastings?" [asked the detective.]
"She was a delightful creature!"
"[Evidently,] since she renders you incapable of replying to my question. Describe her to me, then."
"Well, she's tall and fair; her hair's really a beautiful shade of auburn—"

d. . . . The side door in question was a small one in the angle of the wall, not more than a dozen yards from the scene of the tragedy. As we reached it, I [the detective] gave a cry. There. . . lay the glittering necklace, evidently dropped by the thief in the panic of his flight. I swooped joyously down on it. Then I uttered another cry which Lord Yardly echoed. For in the middle of the necklace was a great gap. The Star of the East was missing!

Sources: Agatha Christie, *Poirot Investigates* (Harper Paperbacks, 1992); Raymond Chandler, *The Big Sleep* (Vintage, 1976).

 Go to the *Grammar Links* Website find out more about Agatha Christie, Raymond Chandler, and their detectives.

4 *That* Clauses—Editing: He Said, She Said

Correct the errors involving *that* clauses. Including the example, there are six errors.

That
∧ Conversation adds interest to our daily life is something we all know. And all readers know that dialogue—the conversations of characters in a book—adds interest to fiction. Dialogue brings characters to life for readers. Good writers realize dialogue can also be a way of introducing information without taking up much space. There are limits to this use of dialogue to provide information. One writer decided that he will start a book with the following line: "Oh, Uncle, if you had come into my life years ago, I wouldn't have been alone, then in the orphanage, then with that cruel family, and then . . ." (And this writer was surprised about that nobody publishes his book!)

Dialogue should be like real conversation—but not too much like it. Listen to a real conversation. It is filled with *ums* and pauses is the first thing you will notice. You will probably also notice it is often boring and hard to understand. Readers would wonder about a book that had lines like this: "Um, . . . those canned tomatoes on the shopping list . . . uh, never mind." If writers want that people enjoy their books, they shouldn't have their characters sound exactly the way we do!

<aside>
Tips
- Characters: tough lowlifes? upper class?
- Language/characters' language: tough tone? formal tone?
- Setting: in the streets? an upper-class setting?
- Detective: thinking a lot? involved in dangerous action?
</aside>

Noun Clauses with *Wh-* Words

FORM and FUNCTION

A. Structure of Noun Clauses with *Wh-* Words

MAIN CLAUSE	NOUN CLAUSE	
	WH- WORD	
I understand	**why**	**they can't come.**
I don't remember	**when**	**the concert starts.**

1. Noun clauses with *wh-* words begin with a *wh-* word (*who, what, why, when, where, how*).

   I wonder **why/when/how** they came.

   I wonder **who/what** he knows.

2. *Wh-* noun clauses have statement word order, even when they are used in questions.

   I don't know what **he is** doing.
   NOT: I don't know what ~~is he~~ doing.

   Can you see where **they are**?
   NOT: Can you see where ~~are they~~?

B. Uses of Noun Clauses with *Wh-* Words

1. Noun clauses with *wh-* words have all the possible uses of noun clauses:

   • Subject.

   Why the meeting was canceled isn't clear to me.

   • Subject complement.

   The question is **how we can finish on time.**

   • Object of a verb.

   I **didn't notice when they left.**

   However, *wh-* noun clauses can follow only some of the verbs that *that* noun clauses can follow. These include:

decide	hear	notice	remember	understand
forget	know	realize	see	wonder

   • Object of a preposition.

   We finally decided **on when to take our trip.**

   • After an adjective.

   However, *wh-* noun clauses can follow only a few of the adjectives that *that* noun clauses can follow. These include *certain* and *sure*.

   I'm not **certain what the teacher told us about that.**

(continued on next page)

B. Uses of Noun Clauses with *Wh-* Words (continued)

2. *Wh-* clauses are often used in statements that express uncertainty.

   These statements are often negative.

   > I **wonder** <u>how he knows that</u>.

   > I **don't remember** <u>how the teacher explained those sentences</u>.
   >
   > I'm **not sure** <u>when the assignment is due</u>.

3. *Wh-* clauses are often used in indirect requests for information. These requests begin with *Do you know* or *Can/Could you tell me*. They are considered polite.

   > Do you know **what time it is**?
   > Could you tell me **where the post office is**?

GRAMMAR **HOT**SPOT!

1. Remember! Use statement word order in *wh-* noun clauses.

   > I wonder when **Mark will** get here.
   > **NOT:** I wonder when ~~will Mark~~ get here.

2. Remember! If the main clause verb is past tense, in the noun clause use past tense verbs instead of present tense verbs and *would* or *was/were going to* instead of *will* or *am/is/are going to*.

   > I **wondered** why she **wasn't** with us.
   > **NOT:** I wondered why she ~~isn't~~ with us.
   >
   > I **wondered** when we **would** see her.
   > **NOT:** I wondered when we ~~will~~ see her.

GRAMMAR PRACTICE 3

Noun Clauses with *Wh-* Words

5 Noun Clauses with *Wh-* Words—Form: Page Turners

Complete the noun clauses with the words in parentheses. Use appropriate tenses.

1. <u>Why books like mysteries are called "page turners"</u> isn't much of a puzzle.

(why / books like mysteries / be called / "page turners")

2. When Evelyn recently read her first Agatha Christie book, she was surprised at

   _____.
   (how / she / not be able to / put the book down)

3. She knew who was murdered, but she didn't know _____.
   (who / the murderer / be)

4. As she read, she tried to notice _____.
   (what / the clues / be)

5. But it was hard for her to notice the clues because she kept turning the pages to find out

   _____.
   (how / the book / end)

6. If readers are familiar with the genre, they understand _____.
   (why / characters / behave / the way they do)

7. The heroine in a romance novel is confused about _____,
   (why / the hero / seem / unfriendly)

   but the reader knows it's because he's falling in love!

heroine = female hero.

6 Indirect Requests for Information: Can You Tell Me Why He Is Asking These Questions?

Make each question more polite by including it in an indirect request.

1. Where is the Martha Blikenstrop Library?

   Can you tell me <u>where the Martha Blikenstrop Library is</u> ?

2. Who is Martha Blikenstrop? Do you know _____?

3. When does the library close today? Can you tell me _____?

4. What time is it now? Do you know _____?

5. How do I get downstairs? Can you tell me _____?

6. Where can I find a good place for lunch?

   Do you know _____?

7 Using Noun Clauses with *Wh-* Words: I Wonder Wh- . . .

1. Work with a partner. In a few sentences, tell your partner the basic plot (story) of a book, movie, or TV program he or she isn't familiar with. Don't reveal any details or the ending.

   Example: A man and a woman send each other e-mail messages but have never met. They think they have a lot in common and they want to meet. But they live far from each other.

2. Your partner should think of some things he or she would like to know about the book, movie, or program and express these in statements beginning *I wonder* + *wh-* word. Satisfy your partner's curiosity.

   Example: I wonder what they look like. . . . I wonder when and how they finally meet.

3. Reverse roles. Your partner tells you the plot of a book, movie, or program. Find out about the things you'd like to know about it, by making statements beginning with *I wonder* + *wh-* word.

Noun Clauses with *If/Whether*

FORM and FUNCTION

A. Noun Clauses with *If/Whether*

MAIN CLAUSE	NOUN CLAUSE	
	IF/WHETHER	
I don't know	if/whether	my flight will leave on time.
I wonder	if/whether	Laura is home now.

Noun clauses with *if/whether* begin with *if* or *whether*. They always have statement word order, even when they are in questions.

I'm not sure **if/whether** he is coming.

Have you heard **if/whether he is coming**?
  NOT: Have you heard if/whether ~~is he~~ coming?

B. Uses of Noun Clauses with *If/Whether*

1. Noun clauses with *if/whether* have all the possible uses of noun clauses:

   • Subject.

   Whether he was here isn't obvious.

   • Subject complement.

   The question is **whether the work will be done on time.**

   • Object of verb (the verbs are the same as for clauses with *wh-* words; see Grammar Briefing 2, page 390).

   I **wonder if/whether Sean and Dave know each other.**

   • Object of preposition.

   I often think **about whether I should change my major.**

   • After an adjective (as for clauses with *wh-* words, these include *certain* and *sure*).

   She's not **certain if/whether they left yet.**

   Use *if* **only** in clauses that are objects of verbs or follow an adjective. (*Whether* can always be used.)

   I **don't know if/whether** he's home.

   I'm not **sure if/whether** he's home.

   NOT: ~~If~~ he's home isn't obvious.

   NOT: I'm not sure about ~~if~~ he's home.

(continued on next page)

B. Uses of Noun Clauses with *If/Whether* (continued)

2. Like *wh-* clauses, *if/whether* clauses are often used:

   • In statements that express uncertainty.

   > I **wonder if/whether it's going to rain**.
   >
   > I **don't know if/whether my aunt will visit this year**.

   • In indirect requests for information, after *Do you know* or *Could/Can you tell me*.

   > Do you know **if/whether the bus stops here**?
   >
   > Can you tell me **if/whether the financial aid office is in this building**?

GRAMMAR **HOT**SPOT!

1. Remember! Use statement word order in *if/whether* noun clauses.

   > Do you know if **they are** planning to come?
   > **NOT**: Do you know if ~~are they~~ planning to come?

2. Remember! If the main clause verb is past tense, in the noun clause use past tense verbs instead of present tense verbs and *would* or *was/were going to* instead of *will* or *am/is/are going to*.

   > I **wondered** if she **wasn't** here.
   > **NOT**: I wondered if she ~~isn't~~ here.
   >
   > I **wondered if we would** see her.
   > **NOT**: I wondered if we ~~will~~ see her.

GRAMMAR PRACTICE 4

Noun Clauses with *If/Whether*

8 **Noun Clauses with *If/Whether*—Form: I Wonder If . . . ?**

Stuart Forrester is wondering whether he can write a book. Use the questions to complete his sentences with *if/whether* noun clauses. If both *if* and *whether* are possible, use both. Make only necessary changes.

1. Do I have enough talent to write fiction?

   I often think about <u>whether I have enough talent to write fiction</u>.

2. Could I write the story of my own life as a book?

   I wonder <u>if/whether I could write the story of my own life as a book</u>.

3. Would my story fit into the romance genre?

   I can't make up my mind about _____.

4. Would I find readers who are interested in my story?

   I'm not sure _____.

5. Can readers accept something a little bit different?

   _____ is the main issue.

   (*983 pages later . . .*) There's a writers' conference coming up. My favorite author, Lydia Burgess, will be there.

6. Should I go?

   I wonder _____.

7. Would Lydia Burgess have time to read the manuscript for my book?

   It's not clear _____. I hope so!

   > *manuscript* = papers intended for publication.

9 | Indirect Requests and Statements of Uncertainty: Do You Know If . . . ?

Use the questions to complete the indirect requests for information with noun clauses. Use *whether* in the noun clauses. Use the words in parentheses to answer with statements expressing uncertainty.

At the writers' conference:

1. Would you have time to read my manuscript?

   Stuart: Ms. Burgess, it's a privilege to meet you. I've written a book. Do you know

   whether you would have time to read my manuscript ?

   LB: **I don't know whether I would have time to read your manuscript** _____.
   (don't know)

2. Does your book belong to the romance genre?

   LB: Well, can you tell me _____?

   Stuart: _____.
   (not certain)

   I think so.

3. Would your story interest readers?

   LB: Well, can you tell me _____?

   Stuart: _____.
   (not sure)

   Maybe it would interest them because it's the story of my life. I went to work for a nice

   boss. I liked her a lot. But she fired me. . . . Let me give you my manuscript.

Next year, in a bookstore:

4. Do you have that new romance by Stuart Forrester?

Woman: Do you know _____?

Owner: _____. Everyone's been buying it!

(don't know)

 Go to the *Grammar Links* Website find out more about romance novels and writing romance novels.

10 Using Noun Clauses: I Think That . . . I Wonder If . . .

 A. Work in a small group. Pick two of the following topics. Discuss what you think about the topics, and discuss something that you would like to know about them. Use *that* clauses, *wh-* clauses, and *if/whether* clauses. Include negatives. Use verbs including *agree, believe, doubt, guess, know, realize, think, understand,* and *wonder.* Use adjectives including *certain, convinced, sure,* and *surprised.*

Topics:

1. Whether popular fiction can be considered literature

2. Why people read popular fiction in general and why they read particular genres (romance fiction, mysteries, horror fiction, science fiction, Westerns)

3. How reading genre fiction is similar to watching romances, mysteries, etc., on TV and how it is different

4. Whether fiction can be educational and what people can learn by reading it

5. Whether writing fiction would be hard or easy

Example: *I think it would be hard to write fiction. . . . I wonder how writers get the information that they need for their stories. . . .*

 B. Write a paragraph on one of the topics that your group discussed. Use each type of noun clause at least once.

Example: *I think that people can learn a lot by reading fiction. They can find out about how people live in different parts of the world and how people lived in different times. They can see whether other people would do the same things they would do in difficult situations. . . .*

 See the *Grammar Links* Website for a complete model paragraph for this assignment.

 Check your progress! Go to the Self-Test for Chapter 20 on the *Grammar Links* Website.

Quoted Speech; Noun Clauses with Reported Speech

Introductory Task: Passing Along a Message

A. Work with a partner. Read the following lines from two telephone conversations.

Claire to Miriam: I will be in San Francisco Wednesday on my way to Tokyo. Can Carlos and you meet me for dinner? I really am sorry I didn't call sooner.

Miriam to Carlos, the next day: Claire said that she would be here tomorrow on her way to Tokyo. She asked if you and I could meet her for dinner. She said that she really was sorry she hadn't called sooner.

The lines from the second conversation are reported speech: Miriam reports what Claire said. The reported speech adds some words and replaces some words. Underline all the new or different words. Answer these questions.

1. In reported speech, verbs that were present tense in the original speech become

   _____ tense verbs. Past tense verbs become _____ tense verbs.

2. What are the two modals in Claire's original speech? _____ _____

   What modals do they become in the reported speech? _____ _____

3. In addition to verbs, modals, and time and place words, what other kind of words can change

   in reported speech? _____

B. Read what Carlos told Miriam. Then complete Miriam's message to Claire.

Carlos to Miriam: I'm glad, and I can't wait to see her. I will pick her up at the airport. . . .

Miriam to Claire: Carlos said that _____

   and that _____. He said that

   _____ at the airport. . . .

Quoted Speech and Reported Speech
■ Overview of Quoted Speech and Reported Speech

QUOTED SPEECH	REPORTED SPEECH
Betty said, "You are in love with Mary."	Betty said (that) I was in love with Mary.
Betty asked, "Why do you love Mary?"	Betty asked why I loved Mary.
Betty asked, "Does Mary love you?"	Betty asked if/whether Mary loved me.

1. Quoted and reported speech differ in function:

    - Quoted speech is used to give the **exact words** that someone said, thought, or wrote.

      Betty said, "**You are in love with Mary.**" (Betty's exact words)

    - Reported speech is used to tell what someone said, thought, or wrote. It usually does not give the exact words.

      Betty said **I was in love with Mary.** (not Betty's exact words)

2. Quoted and reported speech differ in form:

    - Quoted speech occurs in a sentence between quotation marks.

      sentence
      Betty asked, "**Why do you love Mary?**"

    - Reported speech occurs in a noun clause (*that*, *wh-*, or *if/whether*; see Chapter 20).

      noun clause
      Betty asked **why I loved Mary.**

■ Quoted Speech

INTRODUCTORY WORDS	QUOTED SPEECH
The police officer asked,	"Did you see it happen?"

QUOTED SPEECH	INTRODUCTORY WORDS
"Yes, I did,"	she replied.

1. Quoted speech can come before or follow the words introducing it. Even when it follows, quoted speech begins with a capital letter.

    Dad said, "**M**aybe we should stop soon."

    "**A**re you tired?" Mom asked. "**T**he kids look tired."

2. If the introductory words come first, use a comma before the quoted speech.

    Dad said**,** "I *am* tired."

3. If the quoted speech comes first, use a comma before the introductory words instead of a period. (Questions end with a question mark; exclamations end with an exclamation point.)

    "Let's stop for the night**,**" Mom said.

    "Does this motel look OK**?**" Dad asked.

    "It looks great**!**" Mom replied.

(continued on next page)

Verbs Introducing Quoted or Reported Speech

FORM

INTRODUCTORY WORDS	SPEECH
She said (to him),	"They have problems."
She said (to him)	that they had problems.

Say, *tell*, and *ask* are the verbs most commonly used to introduce quoted or reported speech.

Verbs introducing speech follow four patterns:

- V (+ *to* + noun phrase): *admit, comment, complain, explain, mention, reply, say.*

  He **said** (**to her**), "Tom is unhappy."

  He **said** (**to her**) (that) Tom was unhappy.

- V + noun phrase: *remind, tell.*

  He **told her,** "Tom is unhappy."

  He **told her** (that) Tom was unhappy.

- V (+ noun phrase): *answer, ask, promise, warn.*

  He **asked** (**her**), "Why is Tom unhappy?"

  He **asked** (**her**) why Tom was unhappy.

- V only: *think.*

  He **thought,** "Tom is unhappy."

  He **thought** (that) Tom was unhappy.

GRAMMAR PRACTICE 1

Quoted Speech and Reported Speech

1 **Punctuating Quoted Speech; Identifying Reported Speech:** A Woman from His Past

A. Add the missing punctuation to the following quoted speech.

> Brent grabbed his coat and, glancing at his watch, said, "I'm leaving, Tom. I've told my clients that they can reach me tomorrow."
>
> Are you off to another night on the town, Brent Tom asked You told me that you'd reformed. Who are you going out with this time
>
> Live your life the way you want Brent replied Let me do what I want with mine
>
> Sure, you're the boss Tom said Hey, do you know who's back in town? That secretary of yours who left so suddenly. When she left, I thought that was too bad. But you said you were glad she was gone. . . . What was her name
>
> In a strange voice, Brent replied Katie

night on the town = a night out having a good time. *reform* = improve one's behavior.

B. Underline the sentences in Part A that include reported speech.

2 Verbs Introducing Speech: Brent and Katie

A. Work with a partner. Complete the sentences with the verbs in the box. Use each verb once. Include a noun or pronoun after the verb only if necessary.

admit	ask	promise	say	think
answer	~~explain~~	remind	~~tell~~	

1. "Katie, you look as beautiful as ever—but somehow more mature and sophisticated," Brent
   <u>told Katie/her</u>.

2. "I've traveled," Katie <u>explained</u>. "I've gone to school."

3. "Would you have dinner with me tonight, Katie?" Brent _____.

4. "No. I can't. I'm sorry," Katie _____.

5. "Come on, Katie," Brent _____. "You've got to. I won't take no for an answer."

6. "Remember what I told you the last time we spoke," Katie _____.

   "I said that I never wanted to have anything to do with you again."

7. "I remember," Brent _____.

   Katie looked away.

8. "But I'll never be like that again," Brent _____. "I love you, Katie, and I'm a changed man."

9. Katie didn't answer. She _____, "Can I believe him? I wish I knew!"

B. Look at the sentences in Part A. Add a noun or a pronoun after the verb where possible. Include *to* if it is needed.

2. "I've traveled," <u>Katie explained</u>ᴧ ^{to him/Brent} "I've gone to school."

3 Writing Quoted Speech: What Happened? What Will Happen?

 1. Work with a partner. Think of a scene between Brent and Katie that happens before or after the conversation in Exercise 2. Discuss the scene. What is happening in this scene and why? What are Brent and Katie thinking, and what do they say?

 2. Work together to write a short conversation for your scene. Use quoted speech introduced by *said*, *told*, and several other verbs. Each character should speak four or five times.

GRAMMAR BRIEFING 2

Changes in Reported Speech; Verb Tense in Reported Speech
■ Changes in Reported Speech

FORM and FUNCTION

Overview

Reported speech usually occurs in a different situation from the speech it reports: The speaker, listener(s), time, and place might be different. Therefore, often some changes in wording are needed.

Original speech: Josh to Liz, Monday, on the street: I don't know if I can meet you at school on Wednesday.

Reported speech: Liz to Paul, Wednesday, at school: Josh said that **he didn't know** if **he could meet me here today**.

These changes involve:

- Verbs (see below).

  don't know → didn't know

- Modals (see Grammar Briefing 3, page 410).

  can → could

- Pronouns (see Grammar Briefing 4, page 412).

  I → he; you → me

- Time and place expressions (see Grammar Briefing 4, page 412).

  on Wednesday → today; at school → here

■ Verb Tense in Reported Speech*

FORM

A. Verb Tense with a Present Tense Introducing Verb

Sometimes the verb that introduces reported speech is a present tense verb. In this case, the verb tense does not change in reported speech.

He **is** very bored with school.

John's parents **say** (that) he **is** very bored with school.

*Contractions can be used in reported speech (e.g., *John's parents say (that)* **he's** *very bored with school.*).

(continued on next page)

B. Verb Tense with a Past Tense Introducing Verb

1. Usually, the introducing verb is a past tense verb. In this case, the tense of the verbs in the reported speech often changes, as follows:

• Simple present → simple past.	She **writes** every day. → He said (that) she **wrote** every day.
• Present progressive → past progressive.	She **is writing** a letter. → He said (that) she **was writing** a letter.
• Present perfect → past perfect.	She **has written** many letters. → He said (that) she **had written** many letters.
• Present perfect progressive → past perfect progressive.	She **has been writing** many letters. → He said (that) she **had been writing** many letters.
• Simple past → past perfect.	I **wrote** a letter last week. → He said (that) she **had written** a letter last week.
• Past progressive → past perfect progressive.	She **was writing** a letter this morning. → He said (that) she **had been writing** a letter this morning.

2. However, there is **no** change if the verbs are:

• Past perfect verbs.	He **had traveled** to India before. → She said (that) he **had traveled** to India before.
• In unreal conditionals:	
Present unreal conditionals.	If Ted **loved** Mary, he **would marry** her. → She said (that) if Ted **loved** Mary, he **would marry** her.
Past unreal conditionals.	If Ted **had loved** Mary, he **would have married** her. → She said (that) if Ted **had loved** Mary, he **would have married** her.

C. Optional Changes in Verb Tense

The verb tense changes mentioned above are **optional** when the reported speech:

• Expresses a general truth.	The earth **revolves** around the sun. → The teacher said (that) the earth **revolved/revolves** around the sun.
	Hard work **pays off**. → My mom always said (that) hard work **paid/pays off**.
• Expresses a situation that is still true.	Bob **has** a new car. → She said (that) Bob **had/has** a new car.
• Is about future events.	Kirsten **is starting** college in the fall. → She said (that) Kirsten **was starting/is starting** college in the fall.

Changes in Reported Speech; Verb Tense in Reported Speech

Old Barkley
and Mrs. Barkley

John Small

Niles and
Victoria Pierson

**Background Information for the
Mystery Story in Exercises 4–9**

On the evening of Monday, May 4, in the dining room of her country mansion, old Mrs. Pierson fell over dead, apparently from a heart attack. Present on the sad occasion were:

- **Old Barkley** and **Mrs. Barkley**, butler and housekeeper to Mrs. Pierson for nearly 50 years.

- **John Small**, house guest, a young man who ran many charities and had become a close friend of Mrs. Pierson's since he met her last year.

The occasion turned from sad to potentially ugly when the doctor examined the dead woman and said he feared that she'd been poisoned. He immediately contacted the police and **Professor Wendell**, a retired history professor whose hobby was solving crimes. He also contacted Mrs. Pierson's nephew, **Niles**, and Niles's wife, **Victoria**.

In working on Exercises 4–9, see if you can arrive at the solution with Professor Wendell. Look for clues and try not to get fooled by red herrings (false clues)!

butler = a male servant in charge of managing a house. *charity* = an organization to help people.

4 **Changes in Verb Tense in Reported Speech:** The Doctor and the Lawyer Speak

The following quotes are from Professor Wendell's interviews with Mrs. Pierson's doctor and lawyer. Finish changing them to reported speech by filling in the appropriate forms of the verbs. Make all changes, including those that are optional. Where a change is not possible, fill in the verb form given in the original speech.

1. *Doctor*: We have been having flu epidemics here every year, yet I don't remember Mrs. Pierson ever getting sick.

    The doctor said that they __had been having__ flu epidemics there every year yet he __didn't remember__ Mrs. Pierson ever getting sick.

2. *Doctor*: If everyone were that healthy, I would be out of a job.

    He said that if everyone _____ that healthy, he _____ out of a job.

3. *Doctor*: She'd been really sick only once—about three months ago, she was getting weaker over a period of several weeks, but then suddenly she recovered.

    He said that she _____ really sick only once—about three months ago,

    she _____ weaker over a period of several weeks but then suddenly she

    _____.

4. *Doctor*: Someone poisoned her. I feel sure of it since her health was so good.

    He said that someone _____ her—that he _____

    sure of it since her health _____ so good.

5. *Lawyer*: I've been reviewing Mrs. Pierson's will, which she had recently changed.

    The lawyer said that he _____ Mrs. Pierson's will, which she

    _____ recently _____.

6. *Lawyer*: If she hadn't changed her will, nearly all her money would have gone to her nephew, Niles, and his wife, Victoria.

    He said that if she _____ her will, nearly all her money

    _____ to her nephew, Niles, and his wife, Victoria.

7. *Lawyer*: In the new will, nearly all her money is going to her friend John Small.

    He said that in the new will nearly all her money _____ to her friend John Small.

8. *Lawyer*: Under both wills, Mr. and Mrs. Barkley receive a cottage and a pension.

    He said that under both wills Mr. and Mrs. Barkley _____ a cottage and a pension.

> *cottage* = a small house. *pension* = money a person receives when retired.

5 Optional Changes in Verb Tense: The Money Angle

In the following statements, tense changes in the underlined verbs are optional. For each statement, decide why the change is optional. Choose one of the following reasons: *a general truth*; *situation still true*; *future event*.

	Original Speech	Reported Speech	
1.	*John Small*: I <u>am not</u> interested in the money for myself but for my charities.	John Small said that he <u>is not</u> interested in the money for himself.	*situation still true*
2.	*John Small*: Mrs. Pierson's faults? It <u>is</u> unkind for people to speak ill of the dead.	John Small said that it <u>is</u> unkind for people to speak ill of the dead.	_____
3.	*Niles Pierson*: In hard times, people <u>spend</u> on necessities, not on things like charity.	Niles Pierson said that in hard times people <u>spend</u> on necessities.	_____
4.	*Niles Pierson*: John Small <u>is starting</u> a new charity soon, when he gets Aunt's money.	Niles Pierson said that John Small <u>is starting</u> a new charity soon.	_____
5.	*Niles Pierson*: I <u>run</u> a successful art gallery.	Niles Pierson said that he <u>runs</u> a successful art gallery.	_____
6.	*Old Barkley*: Next week, we <u>move</u> into our new cottage.	Old Barkley said that next week they <u>move</u> into their new cottage.	_____

> *speak ill of* = say bad things about.

Modals in Reported Speech

FORM

A. Modals That Change Form in Reported Speech

When the verb introducing the reported speech is past tense, many modals change form. These include:

- *Can → could.*

  He **can** try it. → She said (that) he **could** try it.

- *May → might.*

  He **may** be there now. → She said (that) he **might** be there now.

- *Will → would.*

  They **will** go to the theater next week. → She said (that) they **would** go to the theater next week.

- *Have to, must → had to.*

  He **must/has to** know the answer. → She said (that) he **had to** know the answer.

- Phrasal modals with *be*, for example:
  Am/is/are going to → was/were going to.
  Am/is/are able to → was/were able to.

  They **are going to** buy a car. → She said (that) they **were going to** buy a car

B. Modals That Do Not Change Form in Reported Speech

Modals that do not change form include:

- *Could, might, should, would, ought to,* and *had better.*

  It **might** be too late. → She said (that) it **might** be too late.

- The perfect modals (e.g., *could have, may have, might have, must have, should have, would have*).

  They **should have** bought it. → She said (that) they **should have** bought it.

C. Optional Changes in Modals

As with changes in verb tense, the changes in modals are optional when the reported speech:

- Expresses a general truth.

  You **have to** have a well-balanced diet to be healthy. → She said (that) you **had to/have to** have a well-balanced diet to be healthy.

- Expresses a situation that is still true.

  Megan **can** play the piano well. → She said (that) Megan **could/can** play the piano well.

- Is about the future.

  They **will** go to the theater next week. → She said (that) they **will/would** go to the theater next week.

  They **are going to** buy a car. → She said (that) they **were going to/are going to** buy a car.

Modals in Reported Speech

6 **Changes in Modals in Reported Speech:** More Clues Emerge

Finish changing the speech to reported speech by filling in each modal + verb. Make all possible changes. Where a change is not possible, fill in as in the original speech.

1. *Mrs. Barkley:* Finally my husband and I will relax a bit, because people ought to relax when they're old.

   Mrs. Barkley said that finally her husband and she <u>would relax</u> a bit because people <u>ought to relax</u> when they were old.

2. *John Small:* I can't talk now because I have to meet with the director of the orphanage.

   John Small said that he _____ then because he _____ with the director of the orphanage.

3. *Police Inspector:* Someone must have poisoned Mrs. Pierson.

   The police inspector said that someone _____ Mrs. Pierson.

4. *Police Inspector:* Anyone could be the murderer, so no one should leave.

   He said that anyone _____ the murderer, so no one _____.

5. *Lawyer:* As a young man, Niles did some things he shouldn't have done—mainly gambling.

   The lawyer said that, as a young man, Niles had done some things he _____.

6. *Lawyer:* But now he's quite wonderful. He must be disappointed about his aunt's will, but he didn't complain.

   He said that he _____ disappointed about his aunt's will but he hadn't complained.

7. *Niles Pierson:* I may talk to a lawyer about the will—but then again I might not since I am able to live well on money from my art gallery.

   Niles Pierson said that he _____ to a lawyer about the will but that he _____ not since he _____ well on money from his art gallery.

Pronouns and Time and Place Expressions in Reported Speech
■ Pronouns in Reported Speech

FORM

A. Changes in Subject, Object, and Reflexive Pronouns and Possessives

Reported speech often requires changes in:

- Subject, object, and reflexive pronouns.

- Possesive pronouns and possessive determiners.

The changes occur when the speaker(s) and/or listener(s) are not those of the original speech.

Original speech:
Abby: I'm not going to do **your** work for **you**.
Phil: I'll do it **myself**.

Reported by Phil: Abby said (that) **she** wasn't going to do **my** work for **me**. I said (that) **I**'d do it **myself**.

Reported by Ben: Abby told Phil (that) **she** wasn't going to do **his** work for **him**. He said (that) **he**'d do it **himself**.

B. Changes in Demonstratives

Demonstratives often change, especially for objects that were nearby during the original speech but are not nearby during the reported speech.

I've read **this** (book). → She said (that) she'd read **that** book.

I've read **those** (books). → She said (that) she'd read **those** books.

■ Time and Place Expressions in Reported Speech

FORM

A. Changes in Time Expressions

1. Time expressions often change when the time of the original and reported speech differ.

   Original speech, Sunday: My sister is coming **today** to stay with me for a while.

   The next week: Sara said (that) her sister was coming **last Sunday** to stay with her for a while.

2. Common changes include:

   - *Now* → *then.*

   - *Today* → *that day, then.*

   - *Tomorrow* → *the next day.*

   - *Yesterday* → *the day before.*

   - *Next week* → *the following week.*

   It's starting **now**. → He said (that) it was starting **then**.

   I saw her **yesterday**. → He said (that) he had seen her **the day before**.

(continued on next page)

A. Changes in Time Expressions (continued)

3. There are many different possibilities, depending on when the reported speech occurs.

> *Monday*: The exam is **two weeks from today.**
>
> *Later that day*: The teacher said (that) the exam is **two weeks from today.**
>
> *The next day*: The teacher said (that) the exam is **two weeks from yesterday.**
>
> *One week later*: The teacher said (that) the exam is **next Monday.**

B. Changes in Place Expressions

Place expressions often change when the place of the original and reported speech differ. Common changes include:

- *Here → there* (at school, in Chicago, etc.).
- *There → here* (at school, in Chicago, etc.).

> I'll meet you **here.** → She said (that) she would meet me **there/in her office.**
>
> I'll be **there** soon. → She said (that) she would be **here/at school** soon.

GRAMMAR PRACTICE 4

Pronouns and Time and Place Expressions in Reported Speech

7 **Changes in Pronouns in Reported Speech:** Poisoned Grape Juice?

Professor Wendell's assistant has conducted some interviews and is reporting to the professor. Complete the speech as reported by the assistant to the professor by filling in the pronouns. Where no change is needed, fill in the pronoun from the original speech.

1. *Wendell's assistant*: I would like to hear about anything you or your husband remember only Mrs. Pierson eating or drinking.

   I told Mrs. Barkley that __I_____ would like to hear about anything

   __she_____ or __her_____ husband remembered only Mrs. Pierson eating

   or drinking.

2. *Mrs. Barkley*: Oh! Mrs. Pierson never had dinner without her special organic grape juice from Switzerland, and she never let us or anyone else touch a drop.

   Mrs. Barkley said that Mrs. Pierson had never had dinner without _____ special

   organic grape juice from Switzerland and _____ had never let _____

   or anyone else touch a drop.

3. *Mrs. Barkley*: So, when Mrs. Pierson asked me, I poured it for her myself from this very same bottle that I am showing you.

   Mrs. Barkley told me that when Mrs. Pierson asked _____, _____ had poured _____ for _____ _____ from _____ very same bottle that _____ was showing _____.

4. *Old Barkley*: You mean when Mrs. Pierson *ordered* you—she wasn't very polite to us; we put up with a lot from her.

   Mr. Barkley told his wife that _____ meant when Mrs. Pierson had *ordered* _____—that _____ hadn't been very polite to _____ and _____ had put up with a lot from _____.

5. *Mrs. Barkley*: I got a new bottle that night from a locked pantry that can be opened only with my key.

   Mrs. Barkley said that _____ had gotten a new bottle _____ night from a locked pantry that could be opened only with _____ key.

6. *Mrs. Barkley*: Oh, no! You'd better call the professor. You need to tell him something important: The new bottle of grape juice had already been opened.

   Mrs. Barkley cried out to me that _____ had better call _____ and that _____ needed to tell _____ something important: The new bottle of grape juice had already been opened.

8 Changes in Time and Place Words in Reported Speech: Getting at the When and Where of It

The assistant is reporting to Professor Wendell about other interviews. Read the information about the times and places of this report and the interviews. Then complete the reported speech by filling in time and place words. Make appropriate changes (some words can be changed in several ways). If no change is needed, fill in the words as they appear in the original speech.

Item 1: The assistant interviewed John Small on **Tuesday, May 6**, at the **country mansion**. He is reporting this interview to Professor Wendell on **Wednesday, May 7**, in the **city**.

1. *John Small*: I was <u>here</u> all <u>last weekend</u> and then returned <u>last night</u> for dinner.

   John Small said that he had been <u>there</u> all <u>last weekend</u> and then had returned <u>Monday night</u> for dinner.

Items 2–4: The assistant interviewed Victoria Pierson on **Tuesday, May 6**, at the **country mansion**. He is reporting this interview to Professor Wendell on **Wednesday, May 7**, in the **city**.

2. *Victoria Pierson*: My husband and I were <u>here</u> for the weekend and then returned <u>to the city</u> <u>Sunday night</u> after dinner.

   Victoria Pierson said that she and her husband had been _____ for the weekend and then had returned _____ _____ after dinner.

3. *Victoria Pierson*: We came back <u>this morning</u> as soon as we heard she had died.

   Victoria Pierson said that they had come back _____ as soon as they'd heard she had died.

4. *Victoria Pierson*: Niles had to leave <u>this evening</u> because he has some important meeting about the gallery <u>tomorrow</u>, but I've stayed until <u>now</u>.

   She said that Niles had had to leave _____ because he had some important meeting about the gallery _____ but that she had stayed until _____.

Item 5: The assistant interviewed Niles Pierson **just now**, on **Wednesday, May 7**, in the **city**. He is reporting this interview to Professor Wendell on **Wednesday, May 7**, in the **city**.

5. *Niles*: I have a meeting in a few minutes, so I can't talk <u>now</u>, but everything seemed fine <u>there</u> <u>Sunday evening</u>, although when I came back from my walk they'd been looking for a thief.

   Niles said that he has a meeting in a few minutes so he can't talk _____ but that everything had seemed fine _____ _____.

9 Changes That Occur in Reported Speech: Putting It All Together

A. Rewrite the sentences as speech that is reported by someone else at a later time in a different place. Make all possible changes.

1. *Professor Wendell*: It may be important for us to learn more about the man in the garden.

   Professor Wendell said that <u>it might be important for them to learn more about the man</u> <u>in the garden</u>_____.

2. *Mrs. Barkley*: After dinner Victoria Pierson was helping me put things away in the pantry.

   Mrs. Barkley said that _____

   _____.

3. *Victoria Pierson*: Suddenly I saw someone creeping behind the bushes and I screamed.

   Victoria Pierson said that _____

   _____.

4. *Mrs. Barkley*: I ran into the garden, but I wasn't able to get a good look at him.

   Mrs. Barkley said that _____

   _____.

5. *Old Barkley*: Later that evening we looked through the house, but nothing seemed to be missing.

   Old Barkley said that _____

   _____.

6. *Police Officer (to Police Inspector, showing him a small bottle)*: We've just now found a bottle of nitroglycerin.

   The police officer told the police inspector that _____

   _____.

7. *Police Inspector*: If a person takes too much nitroglycerin, it can cause death.

   The police inspector said that _____

   _____.

8. *Police Officer*: We found it in the trash can in the bedroom that Mr. Small has been using.

   The police officer said that _____

   _____.

B. 1. Who murdered Mrs. Pierson? Work in a small group. Look for clues in Exercises 4–9. You might want to take notes on a piece of paper. Discuss why and how the various characters might have murdered Mrs. Pierson. Use reported speech to talk about the evidence.

Example: The Barkleys might have murdered Mrs. Pierson. Mr. Barkley said that they had put up with a lot from Mrs. Pierson and that she wasn't very polite to them.

2. As a group, decide who you think murdered Mrs. Pierson. Write down your solution and explanation, and tell the class what you decided. Then turn to page A-4 for Professor Wendell's solution.

10 Relationship Between Original and Reported Speech: What Exactly Did They Say?

Listen to each conversation twice. The second speaker uses reported speech. Decide what the original speaker said. Circle *a* or *b*.

1. (a.) Marcia said, "He's doing fine."

   b. Marcia said, "He was doing fine."

2. a. Shana's sister said, "Shana is going to move back here in the fall."

   b. Shana's sister said, "Shana was going to move back here in the fall."

3. a. Brad said, "We might sell all the tickets."

   b. Brad said, "We might have sold all the tickets."

4. a. Lee said, "I'll be here tonight."

   b. Lee said, "I'll be there tomorrow night."

5. a. Heather said, "I don't want to speak to her anymore."

   b. Heather said, "She doesn't want to speak to me anymore."

6. a. Maria said, "I teach Spanish."

   b. Maria said, "I taught Spanish."

7. a. Ilya said, "I'll lend it to you."

   b. Ilya said, "I would lend it to you."

8. a. Paul said, "If I started my own business, I would hire you."

   b. Paul said, "If I had started my own business, I would have hired you."

GRAMMAR BRIEFING 5

Reported Questions, Commands, and Requests
■ Reported Questions

FORM and FUNCTION

A. Clauses for *Wh-* and *Yes/No* Reported Questions

1. Like statements, questions are reported in noun clauses. All the changes for reported speech discussed in Grammar Briefings 2–4 apply to reported questions.	Were **you here last night?** → She asked noun clause **if/whether I had been there Friday night.**
2. To report *wh-* questions, use *wh-* noun clauses.* (See Chapter 20, Grammar Briefing 3, page 394.)	When does the next train come? → He asked **when the next train comes.** What are you reading? → He asked **what I was reading.**
3. To report *yes/no* questions use *if/whether* noun clauses.* (See Chapter 20, Grammar Briefing 4, page 397.)	Is the train here yet? → He asked **if/whether the train was here yet.** Is your book good? → He asked **if/whether my book was good.**

*Remember! *Wh-* and *if/whether* noun clauses have statement word order.

(continued on next page)

1. Reported questions are usually introduced by *ask*. *Ask* may be followed by a noun phrase.

   Where are you going? → He **asked** (**me**) where I was going.

2. The expression *want to know* can also be used to introduce reported questions. *Wonder* can be used, too, especially for thoughts.

   He **wanted to know** where I was going.

   He **wondered** where I was going.

Reported Commands and Requests

FORM and FUNCTION

A. Overview of Reported Commands and Requests

Commands and requests are reported using **infinitives**, not noun clauses.

Reported commands and requests have the same changes in pronouns and time and place expressions as other reported speech (see Grammar Briefing 4, page 412).

Command: Sit down! → He said **to sit down**.

Request: Could **you** help **me tomorrow**? → He asked **me** to help **him today**.

B. Reported Commands

1. Reported commands are introduced by *tell* + noun phrase, *say*, or *ask* + noun phrase.

She	told us	to go.
	said	
	asked us	

2. If the command is a negative, put *not* before the *to* of the infinitive.

   Don't go yet. → She told us **not to go** yet.

C. Reported Requests

1. Reported requests are introduced by *ask* + noun phrase.

   Could you give me a ride? → He **asked us** to give him a ride.

2. You can also report a request in an *if/whether* noun clause with a modal.

   He asked (us) **if we could** give him a ride.

Reported Questions, Commands, and Requests

11 Reported Questions: Brainstorming

The students in Mrs. Blair's English class met in groups to brainstorm questions for a paper about reading. Carrie is reporting to the class about her group's questions. Rewrite the speech as questions reported by Carrie. Make all possible changes.

1. *Angela*: What kinds of books do people like to read? (ask)

   Angela asked what kinds of books people liked to read.

2. Paul: Do more men or women buy books? (want to know)

   _____

   _____

3. *Tim*: How many books does the average person in the United States read each year? (want to know)

   _____

   _____

4. *Carrie*: Can reading books change people's lives? (wonder)

   _____

   _____

5. *Tanya*: Have people been reading fewer books because of TV and the Internet? (wonder)

   _____

   _____

6. *Paul*: What reasons do people give for reading books? (ask)

   _____

   _____

7. *Angela*: Will children who read a lot continue to read a lot when they are adults? (wonder)

   _____

   _____

8. *Carrie*: What can be done to encourage people to read more? (ask)

   _____

   _____

> *brainstorm* = come up with ideas, especially in a group.

 Go to the *Grammar Links* Website to find out more about reading habits.

12 Reported Commands and Requests: She Told Us to Write

David is in Carrie's group but was absent yesterday, so Carrie is telling him what happened. Rewrite the speech as commands and requests reported by Carrie. Include the original listener if given in parentheses. Rewrite requests in two ways. Make all possible changes.

1. *Mrs. Blair* (to Carrie): Could you tell David about everything we discussed today? (ask)

   Mrs. Blair asked me to tell you about everything we discussed yesterday.

   Mrs. Blair asked me if I could tell you about everything we discussed yesterday.

2. *Mrs. Blair* (to class): Write a paper on a topic related to reading books. (tell)

   Mrs. Blair told us to write a paper on a topic related to reading books.

3. *Mrs. Blair* (to class): First think about questions you have about reading. (tell)

4. *Mrs. Blair* (to class): Could you help me get everyone started by sharing your questions with each other? (ask)

5. *Mrs. Blair*: Use the questions for ideas about topics. (say)

6. *Mrs. Blair* (to class): Don't use just your own ideas for this paper. (tell)

7. *Mrs. Blair*: Work on the paper in groups. (say)

8. *Tanya and Paul* (to Carrie): Could you and David do some research for the paper? (ask)

9. *Tanya and Paul* (to Carrie): Will you and David also edit the final paper? (ask)

10. *Mrs. Blair* (to class): Don't write more than five pages because I don't want to have too much reading to do. (tell)

13 Using Noun Clauses and Reported Speech: A Survey About Reading

A. Work with a partner. Ask your partner the following questions, and write down your partner's answers.

1. Do you read more often for information, more often for pleasure, or equally for both reasons?

2. Do you read more often in English or in another language?

3. What have you been reading lately (fiction books, textbooks and other nonfiction books, newspapers, magazines, comic books, other)?

4. Where and when do you read (on the bus? in the library? on weekends? in the evening? before going to bed? other?)?

5. When you were a child, did you read more or less than you do now?

6. Would you like to spend more time reading? Why or why not?

B. Join with two other pairs. Report on some of the questions you asked and on your partner's answers. Use some of the following verbs: *ask, add, admit, answer, comment, explain, mention, say, tell, think.*

Example: I asked Betty whether she reads more often for information or for pleasure. She said she reads more for information. She explained that she has been reading lots of magazine articles about taking care of babies. . . .

Discuss the questions and answers as a group. Were people's answers similar or different?

 C. Write a paragraph about the reading habits of people you surveyed. You can either write about the people in your group or use the questions to survey other people. Tell about what, why, when, and how much people read. Use noun clauses with reported speech.

Example: The people I surveyed have very different reading habits. Some people said that they read a lot. Other people said that they didn't read much or that they just read things for work or school. One woman said that she wanted to read more but never had enough time. . . .

See the *Grammar Links* Website for a complete model paragraph for this assignment.

Check your progress! Go to the Self-Test for Chapter 21 on the *Grammar Links* Website.

Wrap-up Activities

1 The Business of Romance Fiction: EDITING

Correct the 12 errors in the passage. There are errors in noun clauses and in quoted and reported speech. Some errors can be corrected in more than one way. The first error is corrected for you.

For my assignment, I decided to interview Alexa Smith, president of

Forever Yours Publishers. I wondered ~~that~~ *whether* I could get an interview with

her, because I know that she's very busy. I was surprised at that her

secretary said there would be no problem.

As soon as I met Ms. Smith, I told to her how much I enjoy reading

Forever Yours romances. I added that I had a whole bookcase of them

and asked if this was unusual. She answered that some women bought

every Forever Yours romance that was published. Then she told me to

don't be shy about asking my questions.

I started by asking Ms. Smith how did she decide which books to

publish. Computer analyses could be useful seemed obvious to me, so

I asked her whether she used computers. Ms. Smith replied that she

preferred to use Madge. She explained me that Madge was a secretary

who always guessed right about if a book would be a success.

I asked her whether she read manuscripts by first-time writers. She told

me that she has just looked at one. It began like this: "Oh, Uncle, if you

had come into my life years ago, I wouldn't have been alone." Maggie

said. According to Ms. Smith, after that first line she wasn't sure if to

read any more. But she pointed out that some inexperienced writers had

become very successful. For this reason, she always tells her workers that

they had to read each manuscript. After this, Ms. Smith ended the

interview by giving me a copy of the latest Forever Yours romance.

2 **A** _____ **Story:** SPEAKING/WRITING

Step 1 Work with a partner. Read the paragraphs and think about what kind of story they might be the beginning of. Use noun clauses in discussing your ideas.

Step 2 Complete the sentences with quoted speech, reported speech, and other noun clauses, as appropriate. Then read your paragraphs to the class.

All night long, I'd been unable to sleep because I was thinking about _____
_____. I was worried
_____. Now the phone was
ringing, and I knew _____. I picked it
up. As I'd expected, it was Craig. I wondered _____.
    " _____?" I asked.
    " _____," he answered.
_____ was obvious to me. Craig said
that it was urgent _____. And he told
me not _____. Trying hard to control
my voice, I asked him _____, but he
had hung up. For the first time, I realized _____.
I could only hope _____.

3 **Reporting a Scene:** WRITING

Step 1 Watch a TV show or a video. You can watch a movie or any kind of show in which people are talking—a comedy, a drama, a talk show, etc. While you are watching the movie or show, choose a scene or a part of a scene that is about three to five minutes long to tell the class about using reported speech. Take notes on what the people say. Don't write everything down—just a few things that are important— and don't try to write down the exact words. If you are watching a video, you can watch the scene again.

Step 2 When the show is finished, use your notes to write a paragraph. In your first two or three sentences, tell what the show was about. Then use reported speech to tell about the scene.

Example: In the movie I saw, a man wanted to marry a woman he didn't love. She was plain and clumsy, but she had a lot of money. In one scene, she spilled coffee all over the rug and said that she was sorry. He said that it didn't matter because only she mattered. He added that he had something to ask her. He wanted to ask her to marry him, but he couldn't quite manage to. So he asked her what time it was. Then he asked her if she'd like more coffee. Finally, he asked her if she would marry him. She answered that she would.

4 **Write Your Own Story:** SPEAKING/WRITING

Step 1 Work in a small group. Write a one-page story—a romance, science-fiction, horror, or mystery story or any other kind of story. You can use one of the beginnings below or make up your own beginning. Plan and discuss your story carefully before you start writing. Who are your characters? What happens and what will they do? How will the story end?

Step 2 Write your story. Include *that, wh-,* and *if/whether* noun clauses, quoted speech (start a new paragraph each time a different character speaks), and reported speech. When you have written your story, read it to the class.

A.
> The big house on the hill had been empty for longer than anyone could remember. It was overgrown with plants, and its broken shutters banged in the wind. The people in town all avoided the house. They said it had a terrible secret. But no one seemed to know what that secret was. One day in late summer, my brother and I decided to find out. . . .

B.
> We were driving home from a movie late one night when we saw it. Edgar saw it first and pointed it out to us. Al brought the car to a screeching stop.
>
> "It's just a weird plane," I said. "It's just some plane from the Air Force base."
>
> But I knew that wasn't true. As we watched, the strangely lit disk became larger and brighter. With a whirring noise, it touched down in the cornfield. . . .

C.
> Miss Watson looked like a sweet old lady. But everyone knew that she was a great detective—capable of outwitting the most brilliant criminal minds. Mrs. Astor called her as soon as she discovered that someone had replaced her priceless jewels with clever fakes.
>
> "The insurance men said they'll pay, but I don't care about money," Mrs. Astor said. "You must help me get my jewels back."
>
> "I'll do my best, dear," Miss Watson replied, and she hopped on a bus to Mrs. Astor's place. . . .

D.
> It was Friday night, and Ana was home again. Ana wondered why she was always stuck at home every weekend. She didn't really feel like reading or watching TV. She wished that her phone would ring and someone would ask her out. Ana thought about that new boy, Kurt.
>
> "But he'll figure out who the popular kids are," Ana thought. "And he'll hang out with them."
>
> Just then, the phone rang. . . .

 See the *Grammar Links* Website for a complete model story.

Adverb Clauses; Connecting Ideas

TOPIC FOCUS
Advertising and Consumer Behavior

UNIT OBJECTIVES

subordinating conjunctions
(*Before* I buy a computer, I'm going to get some advice.)

adverb clauses
(*Before I buy a computer*, I'm going to get some advice.)

coordinating conjunctions
(Some commercials are entertaining, *but* this one is annoying.)

transitions
(The company wanted to know people's opinions. *Therefore*, it conducted a survey.)

This car will change your life.

Grammar in Action

Read and listen to these advertisements.

A

Ruben Valas is an artist. He has never followed the crowd. He never will.

Ruben chose the Individualist **because** it expresses his unique personal style.

Ruben's passion for creating new art forms never leaves him. **After** he spends the day painting in his studio, he moves on to composing experimental music.

Although Ruben's life is complex, his watch is simple.

The Individualist is simply the most innovative and stylish timepiece in the world.

B

Joyce Bailey explores the deepest oceans, **and** she climbs the highest mountains.

Joyce needs a durable, accurate watch, **so** she wears the Adventurer.

Joyce's days are filled with the most extreme physical and mental challenges. In the evening, she writes books about her explorations and figures out new worlds to explore.

Joyce's life is complex, **but** her watch is simple.

The Adventurer is simply the toughest and most accurate timepiece in the world.

C

Edgar Ross is an investment banker. **Furthermore**, he is a director of one of the largest companies in the world.

Edgar wants a watch that reflects the importance of his position. **Therefore**, he wears the Prestige.

Edgar's typical day is a whirlwind of meetings and decision making. **Afterward**, in the evening, he usually attends a charity event.

Edgar's life is complex. His watch, **however**, is simple.

The Prestige is simply the most elegant and precise timepiece in the world.

---

passion = strong enthusiasm. *experimental* = having a new or unusual form.
innovative = newly introduced and different. *timepiece* = watch. *durable* = strong
and long-lasting. *whirlwind* = busy rush. *charity event* = party given to raise money
to help people.

Think About Grammar

A. Connectors connect ideas. Types of connectors include **subordinating conjunctions** (as in advertisement A), **coordinating conjunctions** (as in B), and **transitions** (as in C).

Look at these sentences from the advertisements. Write the ideas that each boldfaced connector connects. Answer the question that follows.

Ruben chose the Individualist **because** it expresses his unique personal style. (subordinating connector)

Ruben chose the Individualist.   It expresses his unique personal style.

Joyce needs a durable, accurate watch, **so** she wears the Adventurer. (coordinating connector)

_____

_____

Edgar wants a watch that reflects the importance of his position. **Therefore**, he wears the Prestige. (transition)

_____

_____

Which kind of connector is connecting ideas that are expressed in separate sentences: the coordinating connector, the subordinating connector, or the transition?

_____

B. Connectors express different types of relationships between ideas—for example, of addition, reason, contrast, and time. Each type of relationship can be expressed by connectors of different types: subordinating connectors, coordinating connectors, and transitions.

Look at the boldfaced connectors in the advertisements. Use them to complete the sentences.

1. **Addition connectors** show that an idea adds more, similar information. Examples

   of addition connectors are _and_____ and _____.

2. **Reason connectors** and **result connectors** show that one idea gives the reason for or the result of another idea. Examples of reason and result connectors are

   _____ , _____ , and _____.

3. **Contrast or opposition connectors** show that two ideas are different or opposites in some way. Examples of contrast or opposition connectors are

   _____ , _____ , and _____.

4. **Time connectors** show the time relationship between two ideas or events.

   Examples of time connectors are _____ and _____.

Chapter 22

Adverb Clauses

Introductory Task: A Questionnaire on Advertising and Your Buying Behavior

A. Mark the box that indicates your level of agreement with each of the following statements.

1. Since I see and hear so many advertisements, I don't pay much attention to them.

   ❑ Strongly agree   ❑ Somewhat agree   ❑ Disagree

2. I often decide to buy a product because I've seen an advertisement for it.

   ❑ Strongly agree   ❑ Somewhat agree   ❑ Disagree

3. Although a few television commercials are memorable, I usually forget most of them in a short time.

   ❑ Strongly agree   ❑ Somewhat agree   ❑ Disagree

4. When a celebrity (e.g., a sports or television star) is in a commercial for a product, I am more likely to want to buy that product.

   ❑ Strongly agree   ❑ Somewhat agree   ❑ Disagree

5. When a new product comes out, I usually don't try it right away. I wait until other people have tried it and ask them for advice.

   ❑ Strongly agree   ❑ Somewhat agree   ❑ Disagree

6. I buy some products because they give people prestige.

   ❑ Strongly agree   ❑ Somewhat agree   ❑ Disagree

> *prestige* = qualities that bring admiration or honor.

B. Work in a small group. Compare your responses to the statements in Part A. Did anyone else in the group give responses similar to yours?

C. In your group, discuss your reactions to television commercials. Which ones do you like? Which do you hate? Which ones are entertaining? Which ones are annoying? Which ones are especially informative, persuasive, or memorable? Why? In your discussion, use sentences with *because*.

Example: I like that fast-food commercial with the little dog because the dog is really cute.
  OR I hate car dealers' commercials because the announcers talk so loud and fast.

Adverb Clauses

FORM and FUNCTION

A. Sentences with Adverb Clauses

MAIN CLAUSE	ADVERB CLAUSE			
	SUBORDINATING CONJUCTION	SUBJECT	VERB	
Sara had to leave	**because**	**her class**	**was starting**	**in a few minutes**.

1. An adverb clause must occur in a sentence with a main clause. It cannot stand alone.

   main clause   adverb clause
   He stays late **because he is the manager**.
   NOT: He stays late. ~~Because he is the manager.~~

2. An adverb clause begins with a subordinating conjunction (e.g., *although, because, if, when*).

   Call me **if** you need me.
   He visits us **while** he's in town.

3. Like all clauses, an adverb clause has a subject and a verb.

            subject verb
   They finished before **they went** to lunch.

4. Most adverb clauses can come before or after the main clause. Use a comma between clauses when the adverb clause comes first.

   We will start the meeting **when he comes**.
   When he comes, we will start the meeting.

B. Use of Adverb Clauses

Adverbs clauses function like adverbs. They modify the verb in the main clause, or they modify the entire main clause. They answer questions like *when* and *why*.

They worked on the project **before he arrived.**
 (tells when they worked)

She was late **because the traffic was bad.**
 (tells why she was late)

Adverb Clauses

1 **Identifying Adverb Clauses:** The Research Behind the Advertising

The following passage contains six adverb clauses, including the example. Read the passage. Underline each adverb clause and circle its subordinating conjunction. (Remember: A clause has a subject and a verb.)

(Before) they try to sell a product, advertisers need to know which group of consumers would be most likely to buy it. Advertisers call these consumers the "target market" for the product. The target market for a product may be very large (e.g., the market for snack foods) or relatively small (e.g., the market for luxury cars). Because they want to advertise effectively, advertisers do a great deal of research on the consumers in the target market. They try to find out about the consumers' habits, interests, opinions, and buying behavior.

Advertisers use various techniques to get information from and about consumers. When consumers buy a product, they are often asked to fill out a questionnaire. They are asked to comment on products or advertisements in telephone surveys or in group interviews. Advertisers also interview or observe consumers while they are shopping. Although consumers may not be aware of it, advertisers gather data about their Internet shopping habits, too. After advertisers have collected all this information, they analyze it. Then they make decisions about products and advertising.

> *consumer* = person who buys and uses a product. *data* = pieces of information.

Types of Adverb Clauses I

FORM and FUNCTION

A. Adverb Clauses of Time

1. Adverb clauses of time tell when the action or state in the main clause occurs. (See Chapter 2, Grammar Briefing 3, page 31, and Chapter 5, Grammar Briefing 2, page 86, for tenses in time clauses.)	He moved to California **after he graduated from college**.
2. Subordinating conjunctions used in time clauses include *after*, *before*, *since*, *when*, *until*, *while*, and:	
• *As*, which means "when, while, at the same time."	I looked up **as** he was coming into the room.
• *As long as*, which means "during an entire period of time."	I've known him **as long as** I can remember.
• *As soon as*, which means "right after."	We rushed over **as soon as** we heard the news.
• *Once*, which means "(right) after."	**Once** you explained the problem to me, I understood.
• *Whenever*, which means "at any or all times."	Call me **whenever** you need me.

B. Adverb Clauses of Condition

Adverb clauses of condition give the condition for the result in the main clause. (For sentences with these clauses, see Unit 9.)	**If you advertise your car in the newspaper**, you'll sell it in no time.

C. Adverb Clauses of Reason

1. Adverb clauses of reason express a cause for the action or state in the main clause.	Let's take a taxi **since we're in a hurry**. (Being in a hurry is a cause for taking a taxi.)
2. Subordinating conjunctions used include *because*, *since*, and *as*. All have the same meaning, but *because* and *since* are more common than *as*.	**Because/Since/As** apartments cost a lot to rent, I'll have to find some roommates.

Types of Adverb Clauses I

2 **Adverb Clauses of Time:** New Products and Consumer Behavior

A. Use the subordinating conjunction in parentheses to combine the pairs of sentences in brackets into one sentence containing an adverb clause of time. Use the sentences in the order in which they are given. Use commas where needed.

---

352 Market Research   Chapter 22

```
Innovators (2.5%)          ⎫
     ↓                     ⎬  Opinion leaders
Early adopters (13.5%)     ⎭
     ↓
Other consumers (68%)
     ↓
Laggards (16%)
```

1. [People began doing market research in the 1920s. Advertisers have learned a great deal about how trends spread through a group.] (since)

   Since people began doing market research in the 1920s, advertisers have learned a

   great deal about how trends spread through a group.

2. [A new product is introduced. Only a few people begin using it.] (when)

   _____

   _____

3. Researchers refer to these interested and adventurous people as "innovators." [Innovators try the new product. They hear that it is available.] (as soon as)

   _____

   _____

4. [Innovators adopt a new product. Some other people will try it.] (once)

   _____

   _____

5. Researchers refer to these people as the "early adopters" of the product. [The innovators and early adopters accept the product. They become "opinion leaders" for other people.] (after)

   _____

   _____

6. [Other consumers try the product. They usually ask an opinion leader for information and advice about it.] (before)

   _____

   _____

---

7. Researchers refer to people who remain uninterested in the product as "laggards." [Laggards may never adopt the product. They live.] (as long as)

_____

_____

8. Innovators and early adopters often pay attention to advertising for certain new products. [Advertisers introduce new products. They want these opinion leaders to notice the products.] (whenever)

_____

_____

9. Opinion leaders have more influence on other consumers than advertising does. [Advertisers must think about these opinion leaders. They are planning their advertising strategies.] (as)

_____

_____

10. If opinion leaders do not accept a product, it probably won't be successful. For example, in Norway, opinion leaders had a negative reaction to microwave ovens. [Microwave ovens were introduced. Only a few Norwegians have started using them.] (since)

_____

_____

B. The time that it takes for a consumer to try a new product depends on the type of product—that is, a person might be an early adopter for sports equipment or music CDs but a laggard for electronic equipment or new clothing styles.

1. Use your ideas about your buying behavior to complete the following sentences.

1. Before I _buy clothes_____, I _usually look at what others in my group are wearing_____.

2. I didn't buy _____ until _____.

3. I will buy _____ as soon as _____.

4. Once someone else has _____, I _____.

5. My friends _____ whenever they _____.

6. I've never bought _____ as long as I _____.

7. As I _____, I get ideas about _____.

2. Work in a small group. Compare the sentences you wrote. Did anyone write similar sentences?

 To learn more about market research and consumer behavior, click on the *Grammar Links* Website.

3 **Adverb Clauses of Reason:** The Opinions You Trust

A. Use the subordinating conjunction in parentheses to combine each pair of sentences in two different orders. Use commas where needed.

1. I needed a computer for my school work. I'd been looking at computer ads. (because)

   I'd been looking at computer ads because I needed a computer
   for my school work.

   Because I needed a computer for my school work, I'd been
   looking at computer ads.

2. I was confused. I needed help. (because)

   _____

   _____

3. I asked a friend for advice. Computers are so expensive. (since)

   _____

   _____

4. Lots of her friends trust her opinion. She is an expert. (as)

   _____

   _____

B. Use your own ideas about the opinions you trust to complete the sentences.

1. Because I wanted _____, I _____.

2. I asked _____ since _____.

3. As my friend _____, I _____.

4 **Using Adverb Clauses of Time and Reason:** Enter the Contest!

A. Imagine that you bought one of the watches—the Individualist, the Adventurer, or the Prestige—shown in the advertisements on page 426. Now the advertiser is having a contest. Contestants must write a paragraph about their watch; the best paragraphs will be used in future ads. Write a paragraph about your watch and why you like it. In your paragraph, use at least two adverb clauses of time and two adverb clauses of reason.

Example: Since I wanted a sports watch, I decided to buy the Adventurer. I've been very satisfied with it because it has everything I want in a watch. For one thing, it's accurate. As long as I'm wearing it, I don't need to worry about being late. Also, because it's so stylish, all my friends admire it. As soon as they see it, they want one just like it. . . .

 See the *Grammar Links* Website for a complete model paragraph for this assignment.

 B. Read your paragraph to the class. Which paragraphs do you think the advertiser will want to use in future advertisements? Why? Use adverb clauses of reason in your discussion.

GRAMMAR BRIEFING 3

Types of Adverb Clauses II

FORM and FUNCTION

A. Adverb Clauses of Contrast and Opposition

1. Adverb clauses of contrast and opposition express content that:

   - Contrasts with the content of the main clause.

   - Makes the content of the main clause surprising or unexpected.

While some people like coffee, others like tea. (contrast between two groups of people)
They closed the business **even though it was doing well**. (The fact of doing well makes the closing surprising.)

2. Subordinating conjunctions used in clauses of contrast and opposition include *while* and *although*, *though*, and *even though*.

While I don't agree with you, I'm not going to interfere.
Although/Though/Even though she wasn't prepared, she took the exam.

3. Clauses with *although*, *though*, and *even though* can occur before or after the main clause.

Even though I just ate, I'm hungry.
I'm hungry **even though** I just ate.

   Clauses with *while* can always come before the main clause. They can come after the main clause only when the adverb clause contrasts with the main clause (**not** when it makes the main clause surprising or unexpected).

   Use a comma between the clauses even when a clause with *while* comes after the main clause.

While some hate the movie, others like it. = Some like the movie, **while** others hate it. (adverb clause contrasts with main clause)
While I wasn't very interested in the movie, I decided to see it. NOT: I decided to see the movie, ~~while I wasn't very interested in it~~. (adverb clause makes main clause surprising)

(continued on next page)

B. Adverb Clauses of Purpose

1. Adverb clauses of purpose express the purpose of the action in the main clause.	Let's take a taxi **so we can save time**. (Saving time is the result we want to get by taking a taxi.)
2. *So* (*that*) is used as a subordinating conjunction.	Do your work now **so/so that** we can go to a movie this evening.
3. The main clause comes before the adverb clause of purpose.	He's coming over **so that we can talk**. **NOT:** ~~So that we can talk,~~ he's coming over.
4. Adverb clauses of purpose usually include modals:	
• *Can* or *will*, if the main clause has a present tense verb.	I get up at six o'clock every morning so (that) I **can/will** get to work on time.
• *Could* or *would*, if the main clause has a past tense verb.	I got up at six o'clock this morning so (that) I **could/would** get to work on time.

GRAMMAR **HOT**SPOT!

Some subordinating conjunctions are used in more than one type of adverb clause. These include *as*, *since*, and *while*.	Lots of people shop at that store **since** its prices are so good. (reason) I've been shopping there **since** I moved to the neighborhood. (time)

GRAMMAR PRACTICE 3

Types of Adverb Clauses II

5 **Adverb Clauses of Contrast and Opposition:** Escape to the Mall

Use the subordinating conjunction in parentheses to combine each pair of sentences in two different orders. Use commas where needed.

1. We didn't need to buy anything. We went to the shopping mall. (although)

   We went to the shopping mall although we didn't need to buy anything.

   Although we didn't need to buy anything, we went to the shopping mall.

2. He had a lot of homework to do. He came to the mall with us. (although)

_____

_____

3. We bought snacks at the food court. We had had a big lunch. (even though)

_____

_____

4. The mall was noisy and crowded. We had a good time. (though)

_____

_____

6 **Using *While* to Show Contrast:** Information About Consumers

A. Complete each sentence and then write it in another way.

1. While some people like shopping, others _hate it_ _____.

    Some people like shopping, while others hate it. OR _While some people hate shopping,_

    others like it. OR _Some people hate shopping, while others like it._

2. Some people prefer to eat dinner at home, while others prefer to eat dinner _____

    _____.

    _____

3. Females account for 51.2 percent of the population, while _____ account for
   48.8 percent.

    _____

4. While it takes a short time to decide which brand of toothpaste to buy, it takes

    _____ which brand of car to buy.

    _____

    _____

5. While very few people had home computers in the 1970s, _____
   now.

    _____

    _____

B. Use your own ideas about any topic to complete these sentences.

1. Some _____, while others _____.

2. While many _____, a few _____.

7 **Reason Versus Contrast and Opposition:** Brand Loyalty

A. Complete each sentence with the correct subordinating conjunction.

Mrs. Meyer is loyal to Dentafresh toothpaste ___because___ she likes its flavor. She will

1 (because / even though)

buy Dentafresh _____ it's more expensive than the other brands of

2 (because / even though)

toothpaste. Another shopper, Mrs. Rossi, isn't loyal to any brand of toothpaste. She bought Glisten

yesterday _____ her husband doesn't like it. Mrs. Rossi bought Glisten

3 (since / although)

_____ it cost less than the other brands of toothpaste.

4 (since / although)

Mr. Eaton always buys Roma Roast coffee _____ he's had good

5 (as / while)

experiences with it. Today his supermarket is out of Roma Roast. _____

6 (As / While)

there are many other brands of coffee at his supermarket, Mr. Eaton won't buy any of them.

Mr. Eaton is going to buy Roma Roast _____ he has to drive five miles

7 (because / even though)

to another store to get it. Mr. Eaton is very loyal to Roma Roast.

brand = an identifying name on a product. *brand loyalty* = a consumer's tendency
to keep buying a certain brand of a product.

B. Use your own ideas about different products and brands to complete the sentences.

1. Though _____ is expensive, I _____.

2. Because _____ is expensive, I _____.

3. I usually buy _____ because _____.

4. I usually buy _____ even though _____.

5. I don't like _____ because _____.

6. I don't like _____ although _____.

8 Adverb Clauses of Purpose: The Psychology of Buying

A. Use *so (that)* to combine each pair of sentences into one sentence with an adverb clause of purpose. Use *can* or *could* for ability. Otherwise, use *will* or *would*. Delete words as necessary.

1. We buy products. We want to be able to fulfill our various needs and desires.

   We buy products so (that) we can fulfill our various needs and desires.

2. Consumers buy food. They want to be able to satisfy a basic survival need.

   _____

   _____

3. People buy some products. They want to stay safe and healthy.

   _____

   _____

4. Scott and Martha bought a car seat. They wanted to be able to protect their baby from injury in an accident.

   _____

   _____

5. People buy some things. They want other people to accept or admire them.

   _____

   _____

6. Jay drove a luxury car. He wanted other people to know that he had achieved financial success.

   _____

   _____

7. Dolores always wore an unusual style of clothing. She wanted to be able to express her individuality.

   _____

   _____

> *fulfill* = satisfy. *individuality* = the qualities that make someone different from others.

B. 1. Use your own ideas to complete the sentences for a market research survey.

1. I wear certain styles of clothing so that _____ .

2. I _____ so that I will be healthy.

3. I _____ so that I could

   _____ .

4. I _____ so that other

   people wouldn't _____ .

5. Recently, I bought _____ so that

   _____ .

6. People need _____ so that

   _____ .

---

2. Work in a small group. Compare your sentences. Are your ideas similar to or different from those of others in your group?

Check out the *Grammar Links* Website to learn more about consumer psychology and influences on buying behavior.

9 Using Adverb Clauses: The Influences on Your Buying Behavior

A. Work in small groups.

1. Choose four of the following kinds of products: toothpaste, shampoo, cola or other soft drinks, coffee or tea, snack chips, fast food, film, jeans, shoes, gasoline, and long-distance telephone service.

2. For each of the four, discuss these questions: Who or what influences your choice of brands? Are you influenced more by advertising or by other factors, such as the opinions of family members or friends, past experience with brands, or price? Why? Use adverb clauses in explaining the influences on your buying behavior. You can use any appropriate subordinating conjunctions, including these:

when	because	although	so (that)	whenever
before	since	even though	while	as

Example: Whenever I shop for new shoes, my friends influence me a lot. I always buy the ones they like because I trust their opinions about styles. OR I don't look for low prices when I buy shoes. Even though I don't have a lot of money, I buy expensive shoes.

B. Write three short paragraphs describing the influences on your buying behavior for three of the kinds of products listed in Part A. Use each of the following types of adverb clauses at least twice: time, reason, contrast or opposition, and purpose.

Example:  Price is the main influence on my choice of gasoline. Although I buy a lot of gasoline for my car, I don't pay attention to ads for it. I buy HiPro as it's cheaper than the other brands. Since all the brands are similar, it doesn't make any difference. OR Advertising is the main influence on my choice of film. I've used QPV film since I saw an ad for it a couple of years ago. Because the ad gave information about the improved quality of the color, I was interested in trying it. OR My family is the main influence on my choice of fast food. While I like chicken, my sister likes hamburgers. I go to Lottaburger so that my sister will be happy.

 See the *Grammar Links* Website for additional model paragraphs for this assignment.

Check your progress! Go to the Self-Test for Chapter 22 on the *Grammar Links* Website.

Chapter 23

Connecting Ideas

Introductory Task: Is It Fair?

Pixie Puffs are an exciting and magical part of a good breakfast!

🎧 **A.** Two people are participating in a panel discussion about issues in advertising. Listen once for the main ideas. Then listen again and fill in the missing connectors. You will use some connectors more than once.

and	besides	but	first	furthermore	however
nevertheless	nonetheless	or	so	then	

A: That commercial for Pixie Puffs cereal fascinates children, __but__ _____ it makes me
                                                                    1

angry. Pixie Puffs are mostly sugar! They cause tooth decay, _____ they make
                                                                 2

children fat. _____, that's not the image the ad presents. _____, it
              3   4

shows healthy, active children eating Pixie Puffs. _____ it uses animated
                                                     5

"magical" characters, _____ children associate the cereal with a fantasy world.
                       6

Advertising to young children really shouldn't be allowed.

B: I agree that advertisers are real experts at tempting _____ persuading children.
7

_____ , I think that advertisers have the right to promote their products to
8

children. _____ , television networks can't provide programs for children without
9

the money they get from selling advertising.

A: That may be true, _____ advertising to young children isn't really fair. They
10

don't have the experience _____ the knowledge to make informed decisions
11

about products. _____ , they can't always distinguish the commercials
12

from the programs _____ fantasy from reality.
13

B: I realize that commercials can cause problems. _____ , I think children need
14

to watch them so that they can learn to resist the persuasive techniques used in advertising.

> *image* = a picture; a symbol that represents an idea. *associate* = bring together in
> one's mind or imagination. *distinguish* = recognize something as different.

B. As a class, talk about the discussion. Do you agree with speaker A or speaker B?
Can you think of other points for or against advertising to children?

GRAMMAR BRIEFING 1

Coordinating Conjunctions

FORM

A. Using Coordinating Conjunctions to Connect Main Clauses

MAIN CLAUSE	COORDINATING CONJUNCTION	MAIN CLAUSE
I cook the meals,	**and**	my roommate does the dishes.

1. The coordinating conjunctions include *and, but, or, so,* and *yet.** All can be used to connect main clauses.

    **For*, which means "because," and *nor*, which means "and not," are also coordinating conjunctions.

    > My job is fun, **but** it doesn't pay well.
    > We could go to a movie, **or** we could just stay home.

2. Put a comma before the coordinating conjunction.

    > I needed some new clothes, **so** I went shopping.

(continued on next page)

B. Using Coordinating Conjunctions to Connect Words or Phrases

1. *And, but, or,* and *yet* can connect words.

   They can also connect phrases.

   Do not use a comma when connecting two words or phrases.

   He is <u>tall</u> **and** <u>good-looking</u>. (adjectives)

   Do you want <u>juice</u> **or** <u>water</u>? (nouns)

   We need <u>a carton of eggs</u> **and** <u>a loaf of bread</u>. (noun phrases)

   Our football team <u>won its first game</u> **but** <u>lost the next five games</u>. (verb phrases)

   My parents are thinking of <u>going skiing</u> **or** <u>taking a cruise</u>. (gerund phrases)

2. *And* and *or* can connect more than two words or phrases. Put a comma between each of the words or phrases.

   <u>Tiffany</u>, <u>Suzanne</u>, **and** <u>Andrew</u> will be at the meeting.

   She's probably <u>doing her homework</u>, <u>talking to a friend</u>, **or** <u>watching TV</u>.

3. The content connected must be parallel. That is, it must belong to the same grammatical category (i.e., adjective, adverb, noun phrase, verb phrase, infinitive phrase, gerund phrase, etc.).

   I like **studying hard during the week** and **having a good time on the weekend**. (gerund phrase + gerund phrase)

   NOT: I like ~~to study hard during the week~~ and ~~having a good time on the weekend~~. (infinitive phrase + gerund phrase)

FUNCTION

A. Signaling Addition

1. *And* shows that information is being added.

   You must write two papers, **and** <u>you must take a final exam</u>.

   Buy juice **and** <u>milk</u>.

2. *Or* shows that information is being added as an alternative.

   You can write two papers, **or** <u>you can take a final exam</u>.

   He is walking the dog **or** <u>playing soccer</u>.

B. Signaling Result

So signals that the content in the second clause is a result of the content in the first clause.

We started working early, **so** <u>we got a lot done</u>.

(continued on next page)

C. Signaling Contrast and Opposition

But and *yet* signal that the information that follows:

- Contrasts with previous information in the sentence.

  > Most students are having difficulty with the material, **but/yet** <u>some</u> find it really easy.
  >
  > He likes English **but/yet** <u>doesn't like math</u>.

- Makes previous information surprising or unexpected.

  > The students find the class difficult, **but/yet** <u>they really enjoy it</u>.
  >
  > English is hard **but/yet** <u>fun</u>.

But is more common than *yet*.

GRAMMAR **HOT** SPOT!

1. Do not connect two main clauses with a comma unless you include a coordinating conjunction. Connecting two main clauses with only a comma is an error called a *comma splice*.

   > My friends went with me, and we had a great time.
   > **NOT:** My friends went with ~~me, we~~ had a great time.

2. Subjects joined by *and* have plural verbs.

   If subjects are joined by *or*, the verb agrees with the subject nearest to it.

   > Alison **and** Latisha **are** home now.
   >
   > My sister **or** <u>my parents</u> **are** home now.
   >
   > My parents **or** <u>my sister</u> **is** home now.

GRAMMAR PRACTICE 1

Coordinating Conjunctions

1 **Coordinating Conjunctions—Meaning:** Children's Wants and Needs

Circle the correct choice to complete each sentence.

1. You can have a Krunchy Kake (or) / and a Twisper bar. You can't have both.

2. First, eat your spinach <u>or / and</u> your carrots. You need to eat both of them.

3. I'll pour you some milk, <u>and / or</u> I'll pour you some orange juice. Which one do you prefer?

4. Krunchy Kakes are mostly sugar, <u>so / but</u> I don't want my children to eat them.

5. Twisper candy isn't good for children, <u>so / but</u> they like it.

6. The ads for Twisper bars are very appealing, <u>so / but</u> my children beg me for them.

7. I want my children to eat healthy food, <u>so / yet</u> I sometimes let them have Krunchy Kakes or Twisper bars.

2 Combining Ideas with Coordinating Conjunctions; Subjects Joined with *And, Or*: Cartoons and Superheroes Sell Toys

Use the conjunction in parentheses to combine the sentences. Use the subjects in the order given.

1. The cartoons are on TV now. Another children's show is on TV now.

   a. (or) _The cartoons or another children's show is on TV now._

   b. (and) _____

2. Robby has seen the ads for those toys. Jenna has seen the ads for those toys.

   a. (and) _____

   b. (or) _____

3. A cartoon character was in the commercial. A superhero was in the commercial.

   a. (or) _____

   b. (and) _____

4. Their grandparents are going to buy those toys for them. Their aunt is going to buy those toys for them.

   a. (and) _____

   b. (or) _____

3 Punctuating Sentences with or Without Coordinating Conjunctions: Image Advertising

Use commas and periods where necessary to punctuate the following sentences. Make letters capital where necessary, but do not add words. If no changes are needed, write *NC*.

1. We buy some products to fulfill our basic needs for food, clothing, and shelter. Other products fulfill our need for safety and security.

2. A consumer's decision to buy a product may be based on logic or on emotions. NC

3. Advertisers know this so they often use images or music to appeal to consumers' emotions.

4. Sometimes commercials don't show the product at all they show positive images that advertisers want consumers to associate with the product.

5. Images of freedom youthfulness and friendship are common in American commercials.

6. Consumers want to protect their family members and to show their love for them.

7. The car seems to be traveling through a terrible storm but the family inside it is safe.

8. The woman in the ad is wearing a diamond necklace but no other jewelry.

9. Hector loves his wife very much and he would like to give her a diamond necklace.

10. Car commercials often show wild driving scenes advertisers know that consumers want fun adventure and excitement in their lives.

11. Naomi isn't really an adventurous person yet she bought a fast sports car.

> *image advertising* = advertising that is designed to make a product seem unique and to give consumers a good feeling about the product and the people who use it. *security* = freedom from risk or danger. *logic* = clear reasoning. *positive* = good, desirable. *youthfulness* = quality of being young.

4 Parallel Structures: The Messages the Images Send

Correct the errors in parallel structure in the following sentences. If a sentence contains no errors, write *NC*. Some errors can be corrected in more than one way.

1. You can be popular, glamorous, and ~~success~~.
    successful

2. Attractive and intelligent people choose this bank and use its services.

3. When you serve these snacks at your parties, your life will be full of pleasure, happy, and friendship.

4. With these tapes, anyone can learn to speak Spanish quickly, correctly, and fluently.

5. As soon as a man buys this car, he begins having exciting adventures and to attract beautiful women.

6. They will know that his car is elegant, powerful, and it costs a lot.

 For links to information about advertising, go to the *Grammar Links* Website.

Connecting Main Clauses That Have the Same Verb Phrase

FORM

A. Using . . . *Too* or *So* . . . with Affirmative Main Clauses

MAIN CLAUSE	AND	SUBJECT	VERB	*TOO*
I'm going away this weekend,	**and**	my roommate	**is,**	**too.**

MAIN CLAUSE	AND	SO	VERB	SUBJECT
I'm going away this weekend,	**and**	**so**	**is**	my roommate.

1. If affirmative main clauses connected by *and* have the same verb phrase, the second verb phrase can be shortened with . . . *too* or *so* . . . :

    - Subject + verb + *too*.

      > I **can come to the party**, and Jessie **can come to the party**. → I can come to the party, and **Jessie can, too**.

    - *So* + verb + subject.

      > I **can come to the party**, and Jessie **can come to the party**. → I can come to the party, and **so can Jessie**.

2. For the verb, use:

    - The (first) auxiliary verb (modal, *have*, *be*).

      > Your daughter **has** been calling you, and your husband **has**, too. OR Your daughter **has** been calling you, and so **has** your husband.

    - Main verb *be*, if there is no auxiliary verb.

      > I **was** at the party, and Jessie **was**, too. OR I **was** at the party, and so **was** Jessie.

    - *Do* in all other cases.

      > Mark **brought** a dessert, and Ashley **did**, too. OR Mark **brought** a dessert, and so **did** Ashley.

(continued on next page)

B. Using . . . *Not Either* or *Neither* . . . with Negative Main Clauses

MAIN CLAUSE	*AND*	SUBJECT	VERB	*NOT EITHER*
I will not be here this weekend,	**and**	my roommate	**will**	**not, either.**

MAIN CLAUSE	*AND*	*NEITHER*	VERB	SUBJECT
I will not be here this weekend,	**and**	**neither**	**will**	my roommate.

1. If negative main clauses connected by *and* have the same verb phrase, the second verb phrase can be shortened with . . . *not either* or *neither* . . . :

   • Subject + verb + *not* + *either*.

   The bus **doesn't go there**, and the train **doesn't go there**. → The bus doesn't go there, and **the train doesn't, either.**

   • *Neither* + verb + subject.

   The bus **doesn't go there**, and the train **doesn't go there**. → The bus doesn't go there, and **neither does the train.**

2. The rules for the verb in the second clause are the same as for sentences with *too* or *so*.

   I **haven't** seen the movie, and Ben **hasn't**, either/neither **has** Ben. (auxiliary)

   They**'re not** ready to leave yet, and we **aren't**, either/neither **are** we. (main verb *be*)

   I **didn't see** anything happen, and they **didn't**, either/neither **did** they. (*do*)

GRAMMAR PRACTICE 2

Connecting Main Clauses That Have the Same Verb Phrase

5 **Connecting Main Clauses: What Are Your Reactions? I**

A. Underline the two verb phrases in each sentence. If the verb phrases are different, mark the sentence *NC* for *no change*. If the verb phrases are the same, shorten the second main clause in two ways.

1. The Space-Lex ads <u>are creative</u>, and they<u>'ve made me aware of a useful product</u>. NC

2. Their TV commercial <u>is informative</u>, and their print ad <u>is informative</u>.

   Their TV commercial is informative, and their print ad is, too.
   Their TV commercial is informative, and so is their print ad.

3. I've seen the Burger Heaven commercial, and my children have seen the

   Burger Heaven commercial.

4. My children see a lot of fast-food commercials, and I'm not happy about that.

5. French fries aren't good for them, and sodas aren't good for them.

6. Barry likes the sports car ad, and Diego likes the sports car ad.

7. The fast driving looks exciting, and the scenery is amazing.

8. Laura can't remember that ad, and Wendell can't remember that ad.

9. I saw the new sneaker ads, and Heather saw the new sneaker ads.

10. The music didn't impress us, and the basketball players didn't impress us.

11. Alvin thinks the commercials on TV are better than the programs, and I think Alvin has watched every one of them.

 B. 1. Work with a partner. Discuss specific ads or kinds of ads that both of you have either seen or heard about. Which ones do you both have the same reactions to? Make a list of six ads or kinds of ads that you both react to in the same way.

2. Join another pair. Each pair tells their shared reactions to the other pair using shortened verb phrases.

Example: I enjoyed the Super Bowl commercials, and Lin did, too.
I don't like pop-up ads on the Internet, and neither does Greg.

6 Using Coordinating Conjunctions: What Are Your Reactions? II

 Think of an advertisement—for example, a TV commercial, a print ad, an outdoor ad, or an ad on the Internet—that you like or dislike very much. Write a paragraph about it. Describe the ad and tell what you think is good or bad about it. Use several different coordinating conjunctions and at least one sentence with connected main clauses that have the same verb phrase.

Example: There are several commercials that I like, but the one I like most is for jeans. The people in the ad are all wearing white shirts and jeans, and they're dancing. The music is from the 1950s, and the style of dancing is, too. . . . This commercial is entertaining, so it's fun to watch.

 See the *Grammar Links* Website for a complete model paragraph for this assignment.

Transitions I

FORM

MAIN CLAUSE	TRANSITION	MAIN CLAUSE
We can finish the work sooner;	**however,**	we will have to charge you more.
We can finish the work sooner.	**However,**	we will have to charge you more.

1. There are many transitions, including *also, for example, however, in addition,* and *therefore.* They can be used to connect main clauses in a single sentence or in separate sentences.

   The apartment is too small; **in addition**, it's too expensive.

   The apartment is too small. **In addition**, it's too expensive.

2. If the transition connects main clauses in a single sentence, use a semicolon before it and a comma after it.

   It's fun to have a roommate; **also,** you can save money if you have a roommate.

3. If the transition connects main clauses in separate sentences, use a comma after it.

   We wanted to advertise on TV. **However,** TV advertising costs too much.

4. Many transitions can also occur in the middle or at the end of a clause. However, the beginning is the most common position. Transitions in any position are separated from the rest of the clause by a comma or commas.

   Different words are sometimes used in different parts of the United States. **For example,** carbonated drinks may be called *soda* or *pop*. OR . . . Carbonated drinks may be called *soda* or *pop*, **for example**.

GRAMMAR **HOT** SPOT!

Main clauses in a single sentence must be separated by a semicolon unless a coordinating conjunction is used:

- If you connect main clauses in a sentence with a transition, use a semicolon before the transition.

  I liked the school; **however**, I decided not to go there.
  NOT: I liked the school, however, I decided not to go there.

- Use a comma only when main clauses are connected with coordinating conjunctions.

  I liked the school, **but** I decided not to go there.

Transitions I

7 **Punctuating Sentences Connected by Transitions:** All Image and No Product?

Punctuate the following items. Each one can be punctuated in two ways. Use a semicolon in three items and a period in three items. Add capital letters where necessary.

1. Advertisers say that image advertising may not "sell" a product however it does influence consumers' emotional response to the product.

   Advertisers say that image advertising may not "sell" a product. However, it does influence consumers' emotional response to the product. OR Advertisers say that image advertising may not "sell" a product; however, it does influence consumers' emotional response to the product.

2. The manufacturer of Infiniti automobiles hoped to create excitement and curiosity about them the advertising agency decided therefore to follow an unusual approach in introducing the cars to consumers.

3. They wanted consumers to associate Infinitis with nature also they wanted consumers to equate the cars with peace of mind and serenity.

4. The commercials consisted of lovely natural scenes in addition they featured an announcer quietly discussing the harmony that exists between nature and man.

5. The commercials showed rocks and trees and rain falling on ponds they didn't show the cars at all however.

6. The announcer talked about the simplicity of nature many people consequently were confused about what was being advertised.

7. The advertisers were convinced that the "no product" commercials were a great success because millions of people were curious about their meaning however the manufacturer decided to hire a new agency.

---

advertising agency = a company that plans and designs advertising. *equate* = consider to be the same. *peace of mind* = freedom from worry. *serenity* = quality of being calm and peaceful. *harmony* = pleasing, agreeable relationship.

Transitions II

FUNCTION

A. Signaling Addition

Transitions including *also*, *besides*, *in addition*, and *furthermore* show that information is being added.	The food in the cafeteria is good; **also/besides/in addition/furthermore**, it's cheap.

B. Expressing Time Relationships

Many transitions express how events are related in time, including:

- *Before* (*that*), *after that*, and *afterward*.

  The students went on a trip; **after that/afterward**, they wrote a report about the trip.

- *Meanwhile*, meaning "at the same time" or "in the time between two events."

  I was doing a search on the Internet; **meanwhile**, Jack was making calls.

  We came back after being away for four years; **meanwhile**, everything had changed.

- *First*, *second*, and so on, for the events in a sequence. *Next* and *then* can also be used. *Finally* can be used for the last event in a sequence.

  First, we're going to study adverb clauses. **Then/Next**, we'll study coordinating conjunctions. **Finally**, we'll look at transitions.

C. Signaling Result

Various transitions are used to signal that the content in the clause that follows the transition is the result of the content in the previous clause. These transitions include *therefore*, *consequently*, and *as a result*.	People are working longer hours; **therefore/consequently/as a result**, they have less time for leisure activities.

D. Signaling Contrast and Opposition

However, *nevertheless*, and *nonetheless* are among the transitions used to signal that the content in the following clause:

- Contrasts with the previous content.

  Some stores in the mall are doing well; **however/nevertheless**, others are in trouble.

- Makes the previous content surprising or unexpected.

  This store is doing well; **however/nonetheless**, the owner has decided to close it.

(continued on next page)

E. Signaling an Example

For example and the less common *for instance* signal that the content in a clause is an example of something stated in the previous clause.

> More students are studying languages. **For example**, enrollments in Chinese and Japanese are growing.

GRAMMAR **HOT**SPOT!

Be careful! Do not use two words that express the same idea to connect clauses.

> **Although** it's cold, I didn't wear a coat. OR It's cold. **However,** I didn't wear a coat. OR It's cold, **but** I didn't wear a coat.
> NOT: Although it's cold, ~~but~~ I didn't wear a coat. OR It's cold, but I didn't wear a coat, ~~however~~.

GRAMMAR PRACTICE 4

Transitions II

8 **Addition Transitions:** Valuable Information?

A. Connect the ideas in the following paragraph by inserting addition transitions at the beginning of the two sentences where they are appropriate. You can use any two addition transitions (*also, furthermore, in addition, besides*).

Many people have criticisms of advertising. They say that it causes dissatisfaction among people who can't afford the products that it promotes. They say that advertising leads to materialism in our culture. It does this by encouraging people to want and buy more things. However, other people point out the benefits of advertising. It informs consumers about services such as health care and educational programs. Advertising gives consumers information about prices and about new products that they might need or want. These kinds of information can be valuable for consumers. Although I can understand both points of view, I believe that advertising has the potential to do more good than harm.

> *materialism* = the tendency to be too interested in money and possessions.

 B. Work with a partner. Write two sentences in response to each of the following instructions. Connect the second sentence to the first with an addition connector. Use each of the following at least once: *also, besides, furthermore,* and *in addition.*

1. Tell two things that people should do to be prepared for a natural disaster.

   Before a severe storm strikes, you should make sure that you have plenty of canned food. Also, it's a good idea to check the batteries in your flashlight and radio.

2. Tell two things that are excellent about the community where you live.

3. Give two reasons why reading fiction is a better form of entertainment than watching television.

4. Give two reasons why teenagers should not drop out of high school.

5. Tell two advantages of being able to speak more than one language.

6. Give two reasons why people should exercise regularly.

9 Time Transitions: At Work at an Ad Agency

A. Use the time connectors given to connect the ideas. Use each connector once. More than one answer is possible.

> First   Finally   Next   Then

This is the agenda for our meeting today. Jack is going to describe the process he used to carry out the market research for a new client. The client is happy with the results, so we can all benefit from Jack's information. Helene is going to give us a progress report on her project. We'll look at and discuss the artwork for the new Space-Lex ads. Those are the ads that Nora and Perry have been working on. We're going to brainstorm ideas for the next Burger Heaven commercials.

B. Write a paragraph about what happened at the ad agency. The first sentence has been written for you. Use the rest of the events in the order they are given in the schedule. Use each transition once. Various answers are possible.

> ### Schedule of Events
>
> 10:00—Ms. Ryan, a new client, arrives from Chicago. (Before 10:00, Jack prepares a report for Ms. Ryan.)
> 11:00—Yuri does research; Nora works on the art for Space-Lex ads.
> 1:30—Perry writes the text for a print ad.
> 3:00—Helene designs questionnaires for a consumer survey.
> 5:00—Everyone gathers for a meeting.

> after that   afterward   before that   finally   meanwhile   next

Ms. Ryan, a new client, arrived from Chicago. . . .

C. Think of a several-step process that you often follow—for example, getting ready to go to school or cooking dinner. Write a paragraph about it. Use at least four time connectors to show the order of the steps.

Example: *This is the process that I go through when it's my turn to cook dinner. First, I look at cookbooks and choose a recipe. After that, I . . .*

10 Result Transitions; Contrast and Opposition Transitions: The Images Versus Reality

Rewrite each sentence using the transition given. Punctuate carefully.

A. 1. This soft drink contains special ingredients, so it gives you energy.

(therefore) *This soft drink contains special ingredients. Therefore, it gives you energy.*

OR This soft drink contains special ingredients; therefore, it gives you energy.

2. One of the "special ingredients" is sugar, so the soft drink causes tooth decay.

(consequently) _____

_____

3. People who use this product have lost weight, so it can make you lose weight.

(therefore) _____

_____

4. Those people ate less and exercised more, so they lost weight.

(as a result) _____

_____

5. Michael Jordan wears these shoes, so you can succeed in sports by wearing these shoes.

(therefore) _____

_____

6. Michael Jordan worked very hard, so he succeeded in sports.

(consequently) _____

_____

B. 1. Dr. Miller is a real doctor, but that man is an actor.

(however) *Dr. Miller is a real doctor. However, that man is an actor. OR*

Dr. Miller is a real doctor; however, that man is an actor.

2. He isn't a doctor, but he plays the part of one in advertisements.

(however) _____

_____

3. The actress has never used that product, but she recommends using it in the ad.

(nonetheless) _____

_____

4. The men in those ads weren't really dentists, but many people believed that they were.

   (however) _____

   _____

5. Using actors to play the parts of "real" people can be misleading, but advertisers continue to do it.

   (nevertheless) _____

   _____

11 Result Versus Contrast and Opposition Transitions: Telling the Difference

Complete the sentences with content that is appropriate to the previous sentence + transition.

1. a. Ed didn't have enough money to pay his bills. Nevertheless, _he bought another car_ .

    b. Ed didn't have enough money to pay his bills. Consequently, _he got a second job_ .

2. a. Howard had more money than he needed. Therefore, _____

    _____ .

    b. Howard had more money than he needed. Nonetheless, _____

    _____ .

3. a. Amanda is a kind and generous person. As a result, _____

    _____ .

    b. Amanda is a kind and generous person. However, _____

    _____ .

4. a. Melissa doesn't have many friends. Consequently, _____

    _____ .

    b. Melissa doesn't have many friends. Nevertheless, _____

    _____ .

5. a. Travis would like for people to admire him. However, _____

    _____ .

    b. Travis would like for people to admire him. Therefore, _____

    _____ .

12 Example Transitions: Can You Support These Ideas?

Follow each of the ideas with an idea of your own that gives an example.
Use *for example* and *for instance*.

1. Advertisers show commercials during the programs that members of their target markets are likely to be watching.

    For example, fast-food restaurants are often advertised during children's programs.

2. Sometimes it seems as though advertising is everywhere. _____

_____

3. If I could control television advertising, I would make some changes. _____

_____

4. I have positive feelings about some advertisements. _____

_____

5. However, my reaction to some advertisements is negative. _____

_____

13 Transitions—Function: Issues in Advertising

Listen to the lecture once for the main ideas. Then listen again and circle the letter of the choice that expresses the meaning that you hear.

1. The lecturer says that advertising has negative aspects. This is

    a. in contrast to the fact that advertising has some benefits for consumers.

    b. a result of the fact that advertising is controversial.

2. After the lecturer talks about defenses of advertising, he will

    a. talk about criticisms of advertising.

    b. answer questions.

3. The lecturer says that a major criticism of advertising is that there is simply too much of it. This is

    a. a reason why advertising is everywhere.

    b. a result of the fact that advertising is everywhere.

4. The lecturer says that advertising can deceive or mislead people. This is

    a. a result of the nature of advertising.

    b. an example of specific criticisms of advertising.

5. The lecturer says that false claims are rare in advertisements today. This is

    a. in contrast to the fact that many years ago it was common for advertisements to make false claims.

    b. additional information about the kinds of claims that advertisements make.

6. The lecturer says that advertisers often use actors to play the parts of "real" people in television commercials. This is

    a. in contrast to the ways in which advertisers continue to deceive or mislead consumers.

    b. an example of the ways in which advertisers continue to deceive or mislead consumers.

7. The lecturer says that advertisers respond to the criticism that advertising leads to materialism by asserting that children learn materialism from their parents and friends. This is

    a. in contrast to arguments with which advertisers defend their industry.

    b. an example of an argument with which advertisers defend their industry.

8. The lecturer says that advertisers point to studies showing that advertising stimulates price competition and lowers the prices that consumers pay for products. This is

   a. additional information about the value of advertising to consumers.

   b. in contrast to the value of advertising to consumers.

9. The lecturer gives information about opticians and prices for eyeglasses. This information is

   a. in contrast to studies that have shown that advertising can lower prices for consumers.

   b. an example of how advertising can lower prices for consumers.

10. The lecturer says that most people probably would prefer to have less advertising in their lives. This is

    a. in contrast to the fact that both critics and defenders of advertising have important arguments to make.

    b. a result of the arguments about advertising.

 For more information about issues in advertising, go to the *Grammar Links* Website.

14 Using Connectors: Your Turn Now

 The two kinds of products that are most frequently advertised to children are toys and "junk food," including highly sweetened breakfast cereal, fast food, soft drinks, candy, and other snacks. Do you think that the advertising of one or both of these kinds of products to children should be restricted in some way or prohibited? Why or why not? (The discussion *Is It Fair?* in the Introductory Task on page 442 can help you with ideas on this topic.)

Write a paragraph that explains your opinion on this topic. Use a variety of connectors to show the relationship of your ideas. Use at least three of the following types of transitions: addition, time, result, contrast and opposition, and example. Also, use at least two coordinating conjunctions to connect main clauses.

Example: There are many commercials for junk food products on children's television programs. These products may be harmful to children's health, so some people believe that commercials for them should not be allowed. However, I believe that there are good reasons for allowing these commercials to be shown to children. First, . . .

 See the *Grammar Links* Website for a complete model paragraph for this assignment.

 Check your progress! Go to the Self-Test for Chapter 23 on the *Grammar Links* Website.

Wrap-up Activities

1 New Coke: EDITING

Correct the 12 errors in the following passage. There are errors in connectors and in parallel structures and punctuation with connectors. Some errors can be corrected in more than one way. The first error is corrected for you.

---

184   Marketing—Case Study

The story of New Coke began in the early 1980s. When Pepsi began using the rock star Michael Jackson in commercials, sales of Pepsi rose rapidly. Young people were turning away from Coke; therefore, the president of Coca-Cola Company decided that Coke needed a new image. He instructed the chemists at Coca-Cola to develop a new recipe for Coke, they produced New Coke. It had a sweeter, less fizzy taste than old Coke. After they developed the new product the company spent $4 million and two years on consumer research. In taste tests, consumers preferred the new taste over the original by 61 to 39 percent. The company was sure that New Coke would be successful. Because its flavor was so popular in the tests.

In 1985, Coca-Cola announced that old Coke would soon be replaced by New Coke. Trouble began, as soon as this announcement was made. Consumers wanted to buy old Coke while they still could. However, they began to buy all the old Coke that they could find. Coca-Cola spent over $10 million on advertisements to introduce New Coke. Nonetheless people remained loyal to old Coke. They hated the flavor of New Coke, furthermore many of them were emotionally upset about the change. Thousands of people wrote letters to the company. One letter said, "My wife doesn't like New Coke, and neither don't I. It's too sweet and flat. We liked drinking old Coke and to feel its tingle in our throats. If you don't bring back old Coke, we'll sue you in court for taking away a beloved symbol of America." Another man wrote and performed a protest song to express his strong feelings. Although the company had spent millions on research and advertising, but they hadn't taken into account people's emotional attachment to old Coke. Millions of consumers were very angry so the company announced that it would bring back old Coke as Coke Classic. No one was disappointed. Today you won't find New Coke anywhere, and Coca-Cola has no plans to change "the real thing" again.

---

2 A Print Advertisement: WRITING

Work with a partner.

Step 1 Choose a product—either a real one or one that you "invent." Discuss the following: Which consumers are in the target market for the product? What are their wants and needs? What will persuade them to buy the product? What kind of magazine should you advertise the product in?

Step 2 Write a one- or two-paragraph ad for the product for a magazine. Make the product sound desirable, and make the ad informative and persuasive. Illustrate your ad with a drawing if you'd like. Use a variety of connectors to link the ideas in the advertisement, including at least four of the following:

> a subordinating conjunction for expressing contrast or opposition (*although, while,* etc.)
>
> a subordinating conjunction for expressing time (*after, once,* etc.)
>
> a subordinating conjunction for expressing reason (*because* or *since*)
>
> a coordinating conjunction (*and, but, so,* etc.)
>
> a transition (*in addition, for instance,* etc.)

Example: Because you've worked hard all year, you deserve a long vacation at the Oasis Resort. At the Oasis you will relax on sunny beaches and eat delicious seafood. In addition, you'll enjoy dancing to live music under the stars every night. The fun starts as soon as you arrive. . . .

3 A Television Commercial: SPEAKING

Work in a small group.

Step 1 Choose a real or an imaginary product. Discuss the following: Which consumers are in the target market for the product? What are their wants and needs? What will persuade them to buy the product? What kind of television program should a commercial for the product be shown on?

Step 2 Write the script for a one- to two-minute commercial for the product. Use your imagination. If you want, make the commercial humorous. There should be a part for each person in the group in it. Use at least one of each of the following in the script:

> an adverb clause of time (e.g., *Allegri softens your hands as it cleans your pots and pans.*)
>
> an adverb clause of purpose (e.g., *Let's take Mom to Burger Heaven so that she can have a rest from cooking.*)
>
> a coordinating conjunction (e.g., *Bambi tissues are soft but strong.*)
>
> a transition (e.g., *The Steamatic cooks rice perfectly. In addition, it can be used to prepare delicious puddings.*)

Step 3 Perform your commercial for the class.

4 An Essay: WRITING

Step 1 Work in a small group. Brainstorm for ideas on the following topic:

The Benefits and Problems of Advertising

First, think of as many benefits of advertising as you can. Then think of as many problems it causes as you can. (The lecture, *Issues in Advertising*, for Exercise 13 on page 468 can help you with ideas on this topic.)

Step 2 On your own, write a list of the benefits and of the problems. Decide whether, in your opinion, the benefits or the problems of advertising are greater.

Step 3 Write a four-paragraph essay on the topic. The first paragraph should introduce the topic.

Example: Advertising has benefits for consumers. However, it causes certain problems. Which are greater—the benefits or the problems?

The second paragraph should discuss benefits of advertising. The third paragraph should discuss problems. The concluding paragraph should tell whether you think advertising has more benefits or more problems and why. Use a variety of connectors to link your ideas, including at least five transitions.

 See the *Grammar Links* Website for a model essay for this assignment.

Exercise Pages

UNIT 2 ■ Chapter 3

Introductory Task: Quiz: What Is Your Time Type?

Scoring for Quiz

16–18 points = a very "fast" person (tends to be extremely aware of time and speed)

12–15 points = a "fast" person (tends to be somewhat concerned about time and speed)

9–11 points = a "slow" person (tends not to be concerned about time or speed)

6–8 points = a very "slow" person (tends to be extremely relaxed about time and speed)

6 Using Present Perfect Progressive: What Have People Been Doing? II

For Student B.

College Campus

10 **Future Time with Simple Present:** An Outdoor Vacation—
Yellowstone National Park

Information for Student B.

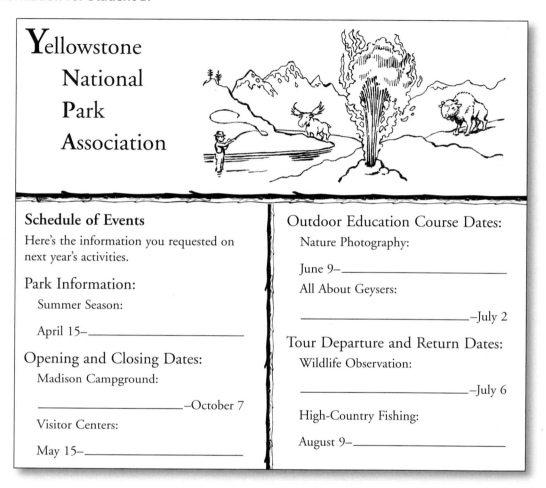

Yellowstone
National
Park
Association

Schedule of Events

Here's the information you requested on
next year's activities.

Park Information:

Summer Season:

April 15–_____

Opening and Closing Dates:

Madison Campground:

_____–October 7

Visitor Centers:

May 15–_____

Outdoor Education Course Dates:

Nature Photography:

June 9–_____

All About Geysers:

_____–July 2

Tour Departure and Return Dates:

Wildlife Observation:

_____–July 6

High-Country Fishing:

August 9–_____

12 **Listening to Tag Questions:** Christopher Columbus

Part B: Information About Columbus

Columbus set out on his first voyage in 1492. He and his crew were not the first
Europeans to arrive in North America. The Vikings had landed on the northern coast of
the continent around the year 1000. Columbus made a contract, or agreement, with the
king and queen of Spain to pay for his expedition, but he was an Italian, not a Spaniard.
Before he arrived in America, no one in Europe knew that North and South America
existed. Columbus believed that he could sail west from Europe directly to Asia.
Columbus made a total of four voyages to America. He landed on several islands off the
coast of North America, and he reached the coasts of Central and South America on two
of his voyages. But he never landed on the coast of North America. Columbus believed
that Cuba was Japan, and he never realized that he hadn't reached Asia. For this reason,
he didn't give the land a new name. A German mapmaker named it America after

Amerigo Vespucci, who explored the coast of South America. Columbus's contract made him viceroy and governor of all the lands he discovered and gave him 10 percent of the profits from his discoveries. At first he became rich, but later he had troubles and lost his titles and all his money.

viceroy = person who represents the king.

UNIT 3 ■ Wrap-up

4 Ask the Oracle

Instructions for the oracle: Copy each answer in the following list on a small slip of paper. Put the slips into an empty container, such as a box or jar. After each question is asked, draw out an answer (without peeking) and read it aloud. After each answer, return the slip of paper to the container and mix it in with the rest.

The oracle's answers:

1. Yes, definitely.
2. No, definitely not.
3. It's certain.
4. It isn't certain.
5. It's possible.
6. It's probable.
7. The answer isn't clear yet.
8. It will happen.
9. It won't happen.
10. The chances are good.

5 Acting Out the Verbs

Lists of Phrasal Verbs for Skits

Telephoning the travel agent:
    call back, call up, hang up, look up, take down, talk over
At the hotel desk:
    add up, check in, check out, hand over, settle in, show up
In a restaurant:
    fill up, pass around, run out of, take back, think over, sit down
Dressing for an expedition:
    have on, pick out, put on, take off, try on, wear out
On a tour:
    find out, finish up, look over, point out, speak up, start off

UNIT 5 ■ Chapter 10

Introductory Task: The Birth-Order Theory of Personality Development—A Test

According to the birth-order theory, firstborns tend to be practical and follow rules, while laterborns are more likely to be creative and willing to bend or break rules. If you circled **a** four or more times, you show the personality characteristics of a firstborn child; if you circled **b** four or more times, you show the characteristics of a laterborn child. (An only child usually has characteristics similar to those of a firstborn.)

Now turn back to page 192 and go on to Part B of the task.

Introductory Task: Sports Trivia

1. b   5. h
2. a   6. g
3. d   7. f
4. e   8. c

4 Passive Sentences with Verbs in Different Tenses— Questions and Answers: Stadiums

Invesco Field at Mile High

1. 2001
2. football and soccer
3. yes
4. to monitor the water needed for the grass and heat the field in winter
5. by selling seats from the old Mile High Stadium

The Skydome

1. 1989
2. football, baseball, basketball, other events
3. no; on artificial grass called "Astroturf"
4. with three panels that take 20 minutes to open or close
5. eight miles of zippers

Introductory Task: The Things Fans Do

Answers: All the statements are true!

4–9

Professor Wendell's solution: The police inspector was about to arrest John Small for the murder of Mrs. Pierson. He said that Small had poisoned her to obtain money that he otherwise might not have gotten for many years. Professor Wendell stepped in and told the inspector that he was making a serious mistake. He said that the real murderers had been Mr. and Mrs. Niles Pierson. He explained that Niles Pierson had been in serious financial difficulty: Hard times meant that people were spending less on luxuries like art. Pierson had tried to raise money by gambling and had wound up deeply in debt. Several months before the murder, Pierson had begun to slowly poison his aunt. He thought that it would look like she had died of an illness and that he would inherit her money. Suddenly, however, she had written a new will, leaving her money to John Small. Feeling desperate after Mr. Torrance had told him that there was nothing he could do about the new will, Pierson had come up with another plan. He would poison his aunt in a more obvious way and make it look as if Small had been the murderer. If Small were found guilty and sent to jail, Pierson would inherit the money after all, and his troubles would be at an end. He got his wife to help him, and on Sunday night, he pretended to be an intruder in the garden, and when everyone left the house, his wife was able to slip the poison in a new bottle of Mrs. Pierson's special Swiss organic grape juice. On Monday, when Niles Pierson and his wife were miles away, old Mrs. Pierson drank the poisoned juice and died.

Appendixes

Spelling Rules for the Third Person Singular Form of the Simple Present Tense

1. Most verbs: Add -s.

   work → works   play → plays

2. Verbs that end in *ch, sh, s, x,* or *z:* Add -es.

   tea**ch** → teach**es**   miss → miss**es**

3. Verbs that end in a consonant + *y:* Drop *y.* Add -*ies.*

   try → tr**ies**

4. The third person singular forms of *do, go,* and *have* are irregular.

   does, goes, has

Pronunciation Rules for the Third Person Singular Form of the Simple Present Tense

The -*s* ending is pronounced as:

- /s/ after the voiceless sounds /p/, /t/, /k/, and /f/.

stops	gets	takes	laughs

- /z/ after the voiced sounds /b/, /d/, /g/, /v/, /*th*/, /m/, /n/, /ng/, /l/, /r/, and all vowel sounds.

robs	gives	remains	hears
adds	bathes	sings	agrees
begs	seems	tells	knows

- /ĭz/ after the sounds /s/, /z/, /sh/, /zh/, /ch/, /j/, and /ks/.

passes	catches
freezes	judges (ge = /j/)
rushes	relaxes (x = /ks/)
massages (ge = /zh/)	

Spelling Rules for the *-ing* Form of the Verb

1. Most verbs: Base form of verb + *-ing*.	work → work**ing** play → play**ing**
2. Verbs that end in *e*: Drop *e*. Add *-ing*.	write → writ**ing** live → liv**ing**
3. Verbs that end in *ie*: Change *ie* to *y*. Add *-ing*.	**tie → tying** **lie → lying**
4. Verbs that end in consonant + vowel + consonant: Double the final consonant. Add *-ing*.	**run** → run**ning** be**gin** → begin**ning**

BUT: Do not double the final consonant when:

- The last syllable is not stressed.   lí**s**ten → listen**ing**   há**p**pen → happen**ing**
- The final consonant is *w* or *x*.   allow → allow**ing**   fix → fix**ing**

Adverbs of Frequency

1. Adverbs of frequency tell how often something happens—from all of the time to none of the time:

AFFIRMATIVE	
always, constantly, continually	We **always** eat breakfast.
almost always	
usually, generally, normally	
frequently, often	
sometimes	
occasionally	
NEGATIVE*	
seldom, rarely, hardly ever	
almost never	I **almost never** go to bed before midnight.
never	

100%

0%

*Negative adverbs of frequency are not used in sentences with *not*.

(continued on next page)

Adverbs of Frequency (continued)

2. Adverbs of frequency usually occur:

• Before main verbs (except *be*).	We **often go** on vacation in the summer.
• After *be*.*	They **are rarely** home in the evenings.
• After the first auxiliary.*	I **will never** forget how nice they were.
	We **weren't usually** allowed to leave.
• After the subject in questions.	Does **he ever** take the bus?
	Are **your parents always** so nice?
• Before negatives (except *always* and *ever*, which usually come after the negative).	He **often didn't** get home until late at night.
	Our friends **usually aren't** late.
	They **won't ever** call here again!

*Adverbs can also precede *be* and a first auxiliary, especially for emphasis (e.g., We **usually weren't** allowed to leave*).

3. Some adverbs of frequency can often occur at the beginning and/or end of the sentence. These include *frequently, generally, normally, occasionally, often, sometimes,* and *usually*.

Sometimes we need to take a break.
We need to take a break **sometimes**.
Often he works late.
He works late **often**.

APPENDIX 5

Spelling Rules for the *-ed* Form of the Verb

1. Most verbs: Add *-ed*.	work → work**ed**	play → play**ed**
2. Verbs that end in *e*: Add *-d*.	live → live**d**	decide → decide**d**
3. Verbs that end in a consonant + *y*: Change *y* to *i*. Add *-ed*.	try → tr**ied**	
4. Verbs that end in consonant + vowel + consonant: Double the final consonant. Add *-ed*.	stop → stop**ped**	permit → permit**ted**

BUT: Do not double the final consonant when:

• The last syllable is not stressed.	lísten → listen**ed**	háppen → happen**ed**
• The last consonant is *w* or *x*.	allow → allow**ed**	box → box**ed**

Pronunciation Rules for the -ed Form of the Verb

The -ed ending is pronounced as:

- /t/ after the voiceless sounds /p/, /k/, /f/, /s/, /sh/, /ch/, and /ks/.

clapped	wished
talked	watched
laughed	waxed
passed	

- /d/ after the voiced sounds /b/, /g/, /v/, /th/, /z/, /zh/, /j/, /m/, /n/, /ng/, /l/, /r/, and all vowel sounds.

robbed	remained
begged	banged
waved	called
bathed	ordered
surprised	played
massaged (ge = /zh/)	enjoyed
judged (ge = /j/)	cried
seemed	

- /ĭd/ after the sounds /t/ and /d/.

started	needed

Irregular Verbs

BASE FORM	PAST	PAST PARTICIPLE	BASE FORM	PAST	PAST PARTICIPLE
be	was, were	been	broadcast	broadcast	broadcast
beat	beat	beaten	build	built	built
become	became	become	burn	burned/burnt	burned/burnt
begin	began	begun	burst	burst	burst
bend	bent	bent	buy	bought	bought
bet	bet	bet	catch	caught	caught
bind	bound	bound	choose	chose	chosen
bite	bit	bitten	come	came	come
bleed	bled	bled	cost	cost	cost
blow	blew	blown	creep	crept	crept
break	broke	broken	cut	cut	cut
bring	brought	brought	deal	dealt	dealt

(continued on next page)

Irregular Verbs (continued)

BASE FORM	PAST	PAST PARTICIPLE	BASE FORM	PAST	PAST PARTICIPLE
dig	dug	dug	know	knew	known
dive	dived/dove	dived	lay	laid	laid
do	did	done	lead	led	led
draw	drew	drawn	leap	leaped/leapt	leaped/leapt
dream	dreamed/dreamt	dreamed/dreamt	learn	learned/learnt	learned/learnt
drink	drank	drunk	leave	left	left
drive	drove	driven	lend	lent	lent
eat	ate	eaten	let	let	let
fall	fell	fallen	lie	lay	lain
feed	fed	fed	light	lit/lighted	lit/lighted
feel	felt	felt	lose	lost	lost
fight	fought	fought	make	made	made
find	found	found	mean	meant	meant
fit	fit	fit	meet	met	met
flee	fled	fled	mistake	mistook	mistaken
fly	flew	flown	pay	paid	paid
forbid	forbade	forbidden	prove	proved	proved/proven
forecast	forecast/forecasted	forecast/forecasted	put	put	put
forget	forgot	forgotten	quit	quit	quit
forgive	forgave	forgiven	read	read	read
freeze	froze	frozen	rid	rid	rid
get	got	gotten	ride	rode	ridden
give	gave	given	ring	rang	rung
go	went	gone	rise	rose	risen
grind	ground	ground	run	ran	run
grow	grew	grown	say	said	said
hang	hung	hung	see	saw	seen
have	had	had	seek	sought	sought
hear	heard	heard	sell	sold	sold
hide	hid	hidden	send	sent	sent
hit	hit	hit	set	set	set
hold	held	held	sew	sewed	sewed/sewn
hurt	hurt	hurt	shake	shook	shaken
keep	kept	kept	shave	shaved	shaved/shaven

(continued on next page)

Irregular Verbs (continued)

BASE FORM	PAST	PAST PARTICIPLE	BASE FORM	PAST	PAST PARTICIPLE
shine	shined/shone	shined/shone	sweep	swept	swept
shoot	shot	shot	swell	swelled	swelled/swollen
show	showed	showed/shown	swim	swam	swum
shut	shut	shut	swing	swung	swung
sing	sang	sung	take	took	taken
sink	sank	sunk	teach	taught	taught
sit	sat	sat	tear	tore	torn
sleep	slept	slept	tell	told	told
slide	slid	slid	think	thought	thought
speak	spoke	spoken	throw	threw	thrown
speed	sped	sped	understand	understood	understood
spend	spent	spent	upset	upset	upset
spin	spun	spun	wake	woke	woken
split	split	split	wear	wore	worn
spread	spread	spread	weave	wove	woven
spring	sprang	sprung	weep	wept	wept
stand	stood	stood	wet	wet	wet
steal	stole	stolen	win	won	won
stick	stuck	stuck	wind	wound	wound
sting	stung	stung	withdraw	withdrew	withdrawn
strike	struck	struck	write	wrote	written
swear	swore	sworn			

APPENDIX 8

Common Phrasal Verbs and Their Meanings

Phrasal Verbs Without Objects

blow up	1. come into being or happen suddenly (as in weather) 2. express anger suddenly and forcefully	catch up	reach the same place as others who are ahead
		check in	1. register 2. see or talk to somebody briefly
break down	fail to function	check out	leave (as a hotel)
break up	1. come apart 2. come to an end	come along	progress
		come back	return
		come out	result, end up, turn out

(continued on next page)

Phrasal Verbs Without Objects (continued)

come over	visit	set off	start on a journey
come up	appear or arise	settle in	move comfortably into
drop out	leave an activity or group	show up	appear
get along	1. have a friendly relationship 2. manage with reasonable success	sit down	be seated
		slow down	become slower
		speak up	speak more loudly
go back	return	stand out	1. be better or the best 2. be different
go on	continue		
grow up	become adult	start off	begin a journey
head back	start to return	start out	begin
head out	leave a place	take off	start (to fly or move); leave
keep up	continue at the same level or pace	turn in	go to bed
		turn out	end or result
let out	end (for classes)	turn up	be found; arrive or appear, often unexpectedly
let up	slow down or stop		
pay off	be successful	watch out	be careful
push on	continue despite difficulty	work out	1. exercise 2. succeed
set in	begin to happen (for weather)		

Phrasal Verbs with Objects

add up	total (a bill)	build up	make stronger
blow up	1. explode 2. fill with air 3. make (a photograph) larger	burn down	destroy by fire
		call back	return a telephone call
		call off	cancel (a plan or an event)
break up	separate into smaller pieces	call up	telephone
bring back	return with	carry out	do as planned
bring down	cause somebody or something to lose power	check in	1. register someone (at a hotel, etc.) 2. return (as a book or equipment)
bring in	earn profits or income	check out	1. find information about 2. take something and record what is being taken (as a book or equipment)
bring off	accomplish		
bring on	cause something to appear or happen	drive back	force to return
		figure out	discover by thinking
bring out	produce or publish something	fill up	make or become completely full
bring up	take care of and educate (a child)	find out	discover (an answer)

(continued on next page)

Phrasal Verbs with Objects (continued)

finish up	end (something)		put up	1. provide (money); invest or pay in advance 2. assemble or build
get through	finish successfully		run off	print or copy
give up	stop doing (an activity)		run up	make an expense larger
hand over	give (something) to someone else		set back	slow down progress
hang up	end a telephone conversation		set off	1. make different from others 2. cause to explode 3. make angry
have on	wear		set up	1. assemble or build 2. create or establish
hold up	stop or delay		show off	display proudly
keep back	1. discourage 2. keep from advancing		sign up	register someone for an activity; add (a name) to a list
keep up	continue something at the same level		stick out	continue to the end of something difficult
leave behind	abandon		take back	return something
let down	disappoint		take down	write (pieces of) information
look over	examine quickly		take off	1. remove 2. make (time) free
look up	search in a dictionary or other reference		take on	accept responsibility for (e.g., a project)
make up	1. invent 2. replace; compensate		take over	get control or ownership of
pass around	give to others in order to share		take up	begin an activity
pass over	disregard		talk over	discuss
pick out	choose or select		think over	consider carefully
pick up	get; collect		think up	create
play down	make something seem unimportant		tire out	cause to be exhausted
play up	make something seem more important		try on	put on (clothing) to test its fit
point out	tell		try out	test
pull along	drag something		turn down	1. make quieter 2. say no to (an invitation)
put down	insult		turn in	1. give to an authority 2. inform an authority about
put off	delay; postpone		turn off	stop from working
put on	1. host 2. dress (a part of) the body in something		turn up	make louder
			wear out	make unusable through long or heavy use
put together	assemble		work out	solve (a problem)

Common Verb–Preposition Combinations

agree with	confide in	know about	pay for	rely on	wait for
believe in	depend on	learn from	plan for	search for	write about
belong to	dream of	listen to	play with	succeed in	worry about
care about	forget about	live on	prepare for	suffer from	
care for	happen to	look after	prevent from	talk about	
check in	hear about	look for	protect from	talk to	
come from	hear of	look over	read about	think about	
concentrate on	hope for	pass over	recover from	think of	

Common Phrasal Verb–Preposition Combinations and Their Meanings

catch up with	come up from behind and reach the same level	keep up with	go at the same speed as
close in on	surround	look forward to	think of (a future event) with pleasure
come out against	1. oppose 2. end with a bad result	meet up with	meet unexpectedly
come up with	discover (an idea)	miss out on	lose a chance for something
cut down on	use or have less	put up with	tolerate
drop in on	visit unexpectedly	run out of	use all the supply of
face up to	confront, meet bravely	run up against	meet and have to deal with
get along with	enjoy the company of	stand up to	1. confront somebody or something 2. tolerate or endure harsh conditions
get back from	return from		
get down to	begin (work)		
get through with	finish	start out for	begin a journey toward a particular place
give up on	admit defeat and stop trying	watch out for	be careful of
keep on at	continue		

Some Proper Nouns with *The*

1. Names of countries and islands:

the Bahamas	the Falkland Islands	the Philippines/the Philippine Islands
the British Isles	the Hawaiian Islands	the United Arab Emirates
the Czech Republic	the Netherlands	the United Kingdom
the Dominican Republic	the People's Republic of China	the United States of America

2. Regions:

the East/West/North/South	the East/West Coast	the Midwest	the Near/Middle/Far East

3. Geographical features:

- Map features:

the Eastern/Western/Northern/Southern Hemisphere	the Occident/the Orient
the North/South Pole	the Tropic of Cancer/Capricorn

- Canals, channels, gulfs:

the Suez Canal	the English Channel	the Arabian Gulf	the Gulf of Mexico

- Deserts:

the Gobi (Desert)	the Mojave (Desert)	the Sahara (Desert)	the Sinai (Desert)

- Mountain ranges:

the Alps	the Caucasus (Mountains)
the Andes (Mountains)	the Himalaya Mountains (the Himalayas)
the Atlas Mountains	the Rocky Mountains (the Rockies)

- Oceans and seas:

the Arctic Ocean	the Indian Ocean	the Sea of Japan
the Atlantic (Ocean)	the Mediterranean (Sea)	the South China Sea
the Black Sea	the Pacific (Ocean)	
the Caribbean (Sea)	the Red Sea	

- Peninsulas:

the Iberian Peninsula	the Yucatan Peninsula

(continued on next page)

3. Geographical features: (continued)

- Rivers:

the Amazon (River)	the Mississippi (River)	the Rio Grande	the Thames (River)
the Congo (River)	the Nile (River)	the Seine (River)	the Tigris (River)

- Names with *of*:

the Bay of Naples	the Cape of Good Hope	the Strait of Gibraltar	the Strait of Magellan

4. Buildings and other structures:

the Brooklyn Bridge	the Museum of Modern Art	the Statue of Liberty
the Eiffel Tower	the Ritz-Carlton Hotel	the White House

5. Ships, trains, and airplanes:

the *Mayflower*	the *Titanic*	the *Orient Express*	the *Spirit of St. Louis*

6. Newspapers and periodicals:

the *New York Times*	the *Washington Post*	the *Atlantic Monthly*	the *Economist*

Spelling Rules for Regular Plural Count Nouns

1. Most verbs: Add -s.

room → rooms	studio → studios

2. Nouns that end in *ch*, *sh*, *s*, *x*, or *z*: Add -es.

lun**ch** → lun**ches**	bo**x** → bo**xes**
bru**sh** → bru**shes**	bu**zz** → bu**zzes**
ki**ss** → ki**sses**	

   If a noun ending in one *s* or *z* has one syllable or stress on the last syllable, double the *s* or *z*.

bus → bu**sses**	**quiz** → qui**zzes**

3. Nouns ending in a consonant + *y*: Change *y* to *i*. Add -es.

stor**y** → stor**ies**	universi**ty** → universi**ties**

4. Nouns ending in *f* or *fe*: Change *f* to *v*. Add -es or -s.

lea**f** → lea**ves**	kni**fe** → kni**ves**

   Exceptions: belief → beliefs, chief → chiefs, roof → roofs

5. A few nouns ending in a consonant + *o*: Add -es.

her**o** → her**oes**	potat**o** → potat**oes**
mosquit**o** → mosquit**oes**	tomat**o** → tomat**oes**

Pronunciation Rules for Regular Plural Count Nouns

The -s ending is pronounced as:

- /s/ after the voiceless sounds /p/, /t/, /k/, /f/, and /th/.

cups	cuffs
hats	paths
books	

- /z/ after the voiced sounds /b/, /d/, /g/, /v/, /th/, /m/, /n/, /ng/, /l/, /r/, and all vowel sounds.

jobs	bones
kids	things
legs	bells
knives	bears
lathes	days
dreams	potatoes

- /ĭz/ after the sounds /s/, /z/, /sh/, /zh/, /ch/, /j/, and /ks/.

classes	churches
breezes	judges (ge = /j/)
dishes	taxes (x = /ks/)
massages (ge = /zh/)	

Irregular Plural Count Nouns

1. Nouns that have different forms in the singular and plural:

SINGULAR	PLURAL	SINGULAR	PLURAL	SINGULAR	PLURAL	SINGULAR	PLURAL
child	children	goose	geese	mouse	mice	tooth	teeth
foot	feet	man	men	person	people	woman	women

2. Nouns that have the same form in the singular and plural:

SINGULAR	PLURAL	SINGULAR	PLURAL	SINGULAR	PLURAL
fish	fish	moose	moose	sheep	sheep
means	means	series	series	species	species

3. Nouns from Latin and Greek that have kept their original plural forms:

SINGULAR	PLURAL	SINGULAR	PLURAL
alumnus (alumna)	alumni (alumnae)	medium	media
analysis	analyses	memorandum	memoranda (memorandums)
basis	bases	parenthesis	parentheses
crisis	crises	phenomenon	phenomena
curriculum	curricula (curriculums)	stimulus	stimuli
datum	data	syllabus	syllabi (syllabuses)
hypothesis	hypotheses	thesis	theses

4. Nouns with no singular form:

cattle	police

5. Nouns with only a plural form:

belongings	clothes	congratulations	goods	groceries	tropics

6. Nouns for things in pairs with only a plural form:

jeans	pajamas	pants	scissors	shorts	(sun)glasses	tongs	trousers

Common Noncount Nouns

1. Names of groups of similar items:

cash	equipment	furniture	jewelry	mail	stuff
change (i.e., money)	food	garbage	luggage	money	trash
clothing	fruit	homework	machinery	scenery	traffic

(These groups often have individual parts that can be counted, e.g., clothing is made up of dresses, shirts, coats, etc.)

2. Liquids:

coffee	gasoline	honey	juice	lotion	milk	oil	sauce	soup	tea	water

(continued on next page)

Common Noncount Nouns (continued)

3. Foods:

bacon	cabbage	chicken	food	lettuce	pie	seafood	vitamin
beef	cake	chocolate	garlic	meat	pizza	spaghetti	wheat
bread	candy	corn	hamburger	pasta	pork	spice	
broccoli	celery	fish	ice cream	pastry	rice	spinach	
butter	cheese	flour	jelly	pepper	salt	sugar	

4. Other solids:

aspirin	detergent	glass	hair	paper	silk	toothpaste
chalk	dirt	gold	ice	rope	silver	wood
cotton	film	grass	nylon	sand	soap	wool

5. Gases:

air	carbon dioxide	hydrogen	nitrogen	oxygen	smoke	steam

6. Natural phenomena:

cold	fire	hail	light	smog	sunshine	warmth
darkness	fog	heat	lightning	snow	temperature	weather
electricity	gravity	humidity	rain	space	thunder	wind

7. Abstract ideas:

advice	education	help	law	permission	tradition
art	energy	history	life	practice	travel
beauty	entertainment	honesty	love	pride	trouble
behavior	freedom	importance	luck	progress	truth
business	friendship	information	music	quiet	variety
competition	fun	insurance	news*	responsibility	violence
confidence	grammar	intelligence	noise	slang	vocabulary
courage	hatred	interest	opportunity	sleep	wealth
crime	happiness	knowledge	patience	space	work
democracy	health	laughter	peace	time	

8. Fields of study:

accounting	business	engineering	journalism	music	psychology	writing
art	chemistry	geography	literature	nutrition	science	
biology	economics	history	mathematics*	physics*	sociology	

*Some noncount nouns, such as *news*, *mathematics*, and *physics*, end in *s*. These nouns look plural, but they are not; they always take a singular verb.

Common Noncount Nouns (continued)

9. Activities

baseball	cards	dancing	running	skating	studying	traveling
basketball	conversation	golf	sailing	skiing	surfing	
bowling	cooking	hiking	shopping	snowboarding	swimming	
camping	cycling	reading	singing	soccer	tennis	

10. Languages:

Arabic	English	German	Japanese	Portuguese	Spanish	Turkish
Chinese	French	Indonesian	Korean	Russian	Thai	Urdu

APPENDIX 16

Pronouns

SINGULAR	SUBJECT	OBJECT	REFLEXIVE	POSSESSIVE DETERMINER	POSSESSIVE PRONOUN
First person	I	me	myself	my	mine
Second person	you	you	yourself	your	yours
Third person	he	him	himself	his	his
	she	her	herself	her	hers
	it	it	itself	its	its
PLURAL					
First person	we	us	ourselves	our	ours
Second person	you	you	yourselves	your	yours
Third person	they	them	themselves	their	theirs

APPENDIX 17

Common Adjective + Preposition Combinations That Are Followed by Gerunds

accustomed to	critical of	good at	responsible for	used to
afraid of	discouraged about	happy about	sad about	useful for
angry at/about	enthusiastic about	interested in	sorry about	worried about
ashamed of	familiar with	known for	successful in	
(in)capable of	famous for	nervous about	tired of	
certain of/about	fond of	perfect for	tolerant of	
concerned about	glad about	proud of	upset about	

Some Verbs That Can Be Followed by Gerunds

acknowledge	complete	encourage*	forgive	mind	recollect	start*
admit	consider	endure	hate	miss	recommend	stop**
advise*	continue*	enjoy	imagine	permit*	regret*	suggest
allow*	defend	escape	include	postpone	remember**	support
anticipate	defer	excuse	involve	practice	report	tolerate
appreciate	delay	explain	justify	prefer*	require*	try**
avoid	deny	feel like	keep	prevent	resent	understand
begin*	detest	finish	like*	prohibit	resist	urge*
can't help	discuss	forbid*	love*	quit	resume	
celebrate	dislike	forget**	mention	recall	risk	

*Verbs that can take either a gerund or an infinitive.
**Verbs that can take either a gerund or an infinitive but with a difference in meaning.

Some Verbs That Can Be Followed by Infinitives

1. Verb + infinitive:

agree	claim	don't/didn't care	manage	refuse	try**
aim	consent	fail	mean	remember**	wait
appear	continue*	forget**	offer	seem	
attempt	decide	hesitate	plan	start*	
begin*	decline	hope	pledge	stop**	
can't/couldn't afford	demand	intend	pretend	struggle	
can't/couldn't wait	deserve	learn	promise	tend	

2. Verb + noun phrase + infinitive:

advise*	command	forbid*	invite	persuade	teach	urge*
allow*	convince	force	order	remind	tell	warn
cause	encourage*	hire	permit*	require*	trust	

3. Verb + (noun phrase) + infinitive:

ask	choose	expect	hate*	love*	need	prefer	want	would like
beg	dare	get	like*	know	pay	prepare	wish	

*Verbs that can take either a gerund or an infinitive.
**Verbs that can take either a gerund or an infinitive but with a difference in meaning.

Grammar Glossary

active sentence A sentence that is not in passive form; often, the subject is the performer of the action of the verb.

> **Millions of people watch the World Cup.**

adjective A type of noun modifier; often describes a noun.

> He drinks **strong, black** coffee.

adjective clause (also called *relative clause*) A clause that modifies a noun.

> A scientist **who studies personality** has developed a new theory.

adverb A word that describes or otherwise modifies a verb, an adjective, another adverb, or a sentence.

> They worked **quickly** and **carefully** on the project.

adverb clause A clause that functions like an adverb, modifying the main clause verb or the main clause.

> **Because they want their product to sell,** companies do market research.

adverb of frequency An adverb that tells how often an action occurs.

> "Night owls" **usually** do their best work at night.

agent The performer of the action of the verb. In a passive sentence, the agent, if included, is in a *by* phrase.

> **The goalie** stopped the ball.
> The ball was stopped by **the goalie.**

article The words *a/an* and *the*, which are used to introduce or identify a noun.

> **a** cook   **an** orange
> **the** menu   **the** recipes

auxiliary verb A verb that is used with a main verb to make questions and negative sentences and to help make tenses and express meaning (*do, be, have,* and modals).

> **Are** you working?
> We **did**n't finish the exam.
>
> She **has** traveled a lot.
> They **should** get out more.

base form of a verb (also called *the simple form of a verb*) A verb without *to* in front of it or any endings.

> **play**   **work**   **be**   **do**

causative verb A verb (e.g., *have, let, make*) used to mean to cause or allow someone to do something.

> John **had** us buy the concert tickets.

clause A group of related words that has a subject and a verb.

> **Before he leaves, . . .**
> **We're back!**
> **. . . because it sells well.**

collective noun A noun that refers to a group.

> **committee**   **family**
> **audience**   **team**

common noun A noun that does not name a particular person, place, or thing.

> **cat**   **coffee**   **students**
> **buildings**   **loyalty**

conditional sentence A sentence that contains a condition clause and a result clause and expresses a relationship between the condition and result.

> **If a storm comes up, you should go inside.**

connector A word that shows how ideas are related.

> **because**   **but**
> **also**   **nevertheless**

■ **coordinating conjunction** A word—*and, but, or, nor, so, for, yet*—that connects clauses and, in some cases, also phrases or words.

> We wrote the proposal, **and** they accepted it.
> I tried **but** didn't succeed.

■ **count noun** A noun that can be counted.

> a **restaurant**   two **restaurants**
> an **apple**   three **apples**

■ **definite article** *The*; used to identify nouns that refer to something specific and are known to both the speaker and listener.

> **The** chef in this restaurant wrote a best-selling cookbook.

■ **demonstrative** *This, that, these, those*; demonstratives can be pronouns or determiners.

> **That** is really good.
> **These** days, dining out is popular.

■ **determiner** A word that comes before a common noun; determiners can be articles, quantifiers, demonstratives, and possessives.

> **the** salad   **many** desserts
> **this** table   **your** order

■ **future** *Will/be going to* + base form of the verb; used to talk about future events; sometimes also expressed with simple present, present progressive, *be about to*, and modals such as *can* and *may*.

> The weather **will be** nice tomorrow.
> They**'re going to see** a movie tonight.

■ **future perfect** *Will/be going to* + *have* + past participle; tense used to talk about an action or state that will occur before a future action, state, or time.

> I **will have finished** my work by then.

■ **future perfect progressive** (also called *future perfect continuous*) *Will/be going to* + *have* + *been* + verb + *-ing*; tense used to talk about an action that will continue to a future action, state, or time.

> They **will have been traveling** for many days when they get there.

■ **future progressive** (also called *future continuous*) *Will/be going to* + *be* + verb + *-ing*; tense used to talk about actions that will be in progress in the future.

> He **is going to be flying** to Hawaii next week.

■ **gerund** Formed from verb + *-ing*; often functions as a noun.

> We enjoy **dancing** and **singing**.

■ **indefinite article** *A/an*; used to introduce a noun that doesn't refer to something specific or that the speaker and listener don't both know.

> **a** banana   **an** author

■ **indefinite pronoun** A pronoun that is used to talk about unspecified people or things or about people or things in general.

> Is **anybody** out there?

■ **infinitive** Formed from *to* + base form of the verb; often functions as a noun.

> We wanted **to go** to the circus.
> **To climb** Mount Everest is our dream.

■ **intensifier** A word that is used before an adjective or adverb to strengthen the meaning of the adjective or adverb.

> That restaurant is **very** expensive.
> We got our food **quite** quickly.

■ **intransitive verb** A verb that does not take an object.

> We **stood** in line for football tickets.

■ **main clause** (also called *independent clause*) A clause that is, or could be, a complete sentence.

> **We arrived late.**
> When we got there, **he had to leave.**

■ **main verb** The verb in a sentence in the simple present or simple past and, in sentences in other tenses, the verb that carries the primary verbal meaning (i.e., not an auxiliary verb).

> We **traveled** to Japan.
> We had **gone** there once before.

modal An auxiliary verb that expresses ideas related to degrees of certainty, social functions, and/or ability.

> She **might** be at home.
> They **must** leave soon.
> We **can** sing well.

modifier A word, phrase, or clause that describes and gives more information about another word, phrase, or clause.

> You look **happy**.
> The man **in white** is the chef.

noncount noun A noun that cannot be counted.

> **rain   sand   happiness**
> **physics   swimming**

noun A word that names a person, place, or thing.

> **Albert Einstein   ocean   table**

noun clause A clause that functions like a noun.

> We think **that they will get married and live happily ever after.**

noun phrase A noun and its determiners and modifiers, if any.

> We ate at **that very charming new restaurant.**

object A noun, pronoun, or noun phrase that receives the action of the verb.

> Paul called **us**.
> The chef prepared **a delicious meal**.

object of a preposition A noun, pronoun, or noun phrase that comes after a preposition.

> for **Mary**   to **them**
> with **my best friend's mother**

particle An adverb that is part of a phrasal verb.

> They set **out** late.

passive causative A structure, with *get/have* + object + past participle, that expresses the idea that someone "causes" someone else to perform a service.

> The players **had** their uniforms **cleaned**.

passive sentence A sentence that has *be* followed by the past participle of the main verb; the subject of the sentence is the receiver of the action of the verb.

> **The World Cup is watched by millions of people.**

past perfect *Had* + past participle; tense used to talk about past actions or states that occurred before another past action, state, or time.

> I **had read** the book before I saw the movie.

past perfect progressive (also called *past perfect continuous*) *Had* + *been* + present participle; tense used to talk about an action that began before and continued to another past action, state, or time.

> They **had been working** for hours when he arrived.

past progressive (also called *past continuous*) *Was/Were* + present participle; tense used to talk about an action in progress in the past.

> He **was sleeping** when the phone rang.

phrasal verb A verb + adverb (particle); its meaning is different from the meaning of the verb + the meaning of the particle.

> They **kept on** despite the difficulties.
> She **called** him **up**.

phrasal verb with preposition (also called a *three-word verb*) The combination of a phrasal verb + a preposition.

> We **ran out of** time.

phrase A group of related words that does not contain both a subject and a verb.

> **on the street   the people upstairs**
> **had already gone**

possessive A word or structure that shows ownership; may be a determiner, noun, pronoun, or phrase.

> **our** homework   **David's** house
> It's **theirs**.   the corner **of the table**

preposition A function word such as *at, from, in,* or *to* that takes a noun, pronoun, or noun phrase as an object to form a prepositional phrase; often helps express meanings related to time, location, or direction.

> **in** the classroom   **around** the same time
> **with** my friends

prepositional phrase A preposition plus a noun, pronoun, or noun phrase.

> **in the classroom**   **around the same time**
> **with my friends**

present perfect *Have* + past participle; tense used to talk about actions or states that occurred at an unspecified time in the past or, with a time expression of duration, to talk about actions or states that began in the past and continue to the present.

> They **have written** a book.
> They **have lived** there for many years.

present perfect progressive (also called *present perfect continuous*) *Have* + *been* + present participle; tense used to talk about actions that began in the past and continue to the present; it often emphasizes that the action is ongoing.

> They **have been cleaning** all morning.

present progressive (also called *present continuous*) *Am/Is/Are* + present participle; tense used to talk about actions in progress at this moment or through a period of time including the present.

> Look! It**'s snowing**.
> He **is studying** in the United States this year.

pronoun A word that replaces a noun or noun phrase that has already been mentioned or that is clear from context.

> **I** need to talk to **you**.
> Al is looking at **himself** in the mirror.

proper noun A noun that names a particular person, place, or thing.

> **Molly Brown**   **Denver, Colorado**
> **the** *Titanic*

quantifier A word or phrase that indicates the quantity of a noun.

> **some** potatoes   **a few** choices
> **not much** oil

quoted speech A way of reporting speech that uses the exact words of the speaker.

> **"I'll love you forever!"** he promised.

reciprocal pronoun A pronoun (*each other* or *one another*) that is used when two or more people or things give and receive the same feelings or actions.

> They stared at **each other** from across the restaurant.

reflexive pronoun A pronoun that is used instead of an object pronoun when the object refers to the same person or thing as the subject of the sentence.

> They bought **themselves** a new car.

relative pronoun A pronoun that begins an adjective clause.

> The author **who** wrote the book gave a speech.
> I like the book **that** we saw in the store.

reported speech A way of reporting speech that does not use the speaker's exact words.

> He told her **that he would love her forever**.

simple past Verb + *-ed*; tense used to talk about actions and states that began and ended in the past.

> We **walked** to school.
> He **looked** healthy.

simple present Verb (+ *-s*); tense used to talk about habitual or repeated actions in the present and about things that are generally accepted as true.

> I **work** in a restaurant.
> Water **freezes** at 32°F.

■ **stative passive** *-ed* adjective following *be* or *get*; unlike true passives, expresses states rather than actions.

> The door **is closed**.
> We **got excited** about the team.

■ **subject** The noun, pronoun, or noun phrase that comes before the verb in a statement and that generally is what the statement is about.

> **Kate** went to the restaurant.
> **The woman in the white hat** ordered coffee.

■ **subject complement** A noun, pronoun, noun phrase, or adjective that renames, identifies, or describes the subject of a sentence.

> He is **a superb chef**.
> They looked like **professionals**.

■ **subordinate clause** (also called *dependent clause*) A clause that cannot stand alone but must be used with a main clause.

> **When we met**, we discussed the ad campaign.

■ **subordinating conjunction** A word (*when, where, because, although, if*, etc.) that begins an adverb clause.

> **Although** they advertised the product, it didn't sell well.

■ **tag question** A statement with a short question ("tag") added at the end.

> You haven't been to London, **have you?**
> He lives here, **doesn't he?**

■ **time clause** A clause that begins with a time word like *when, while, before*, or *after*.

> **After this class ends**, I'm going home.
> They came **while she was working**.

■ **transition** A word (*also, however, in addition, therefore*, etc.) that connects main clauses, sentences, or larger units, such as paragraphs.

> The clients were pleased. **Therefore**, they accepted our design.

■ **transitive verb** A verb that takes an object in an active sentence.

> The golfer **hit** the ball.

■ **verb** A word that shows an action or state.

> **do**   **come**   **be**   **have**

■ **verb–preposition combination** A combination formed by certain verbs and certain prepositions.

> We **looked for** the cat.
> They **heard from** him.

■ **verb with stative meaning** A verb that refers to a state, not an action.

> She **has known** him for years.
> He **is** a good lawyer.

■ ***wh-* question** (also called *information question*) A question that begins with a *wh-* word (*who, what, where, when, why, how*, etc.) and asks for information.

> **Who will win the game?**
> **How far did you travel last night?**

■ ***yes/no* question** A question that can be answered with *yes* or *no*.

> **Do you like chocolate?**
> **Was he at the game?**

■ **[0] article** (called the "zero" article) used instead of *a/an* with indefinite plural count nouns and noncount nouns.

> I bought **[0]** bananas at the store.
> I put **[0]** fruit in the pie.

Index